Also by Eveline Cruickshanks

THE GLORIOUS REVOLUTION 1678–1714

THE STUART COURTS (*editor*)

THE STUART COURT IN EXILE AND THE JACOBITES (*with Edward Corp*)

BY FORCE OR BY DEFAULT? The Revolution of 1688–89

THE JACOBITE CHALLENGE (*with Jeremy Black*)

IDEOLOGY AND CONSPIRACY: Aspects of Jacobitism 1689–1759 (*editor*)

POLITICAL UNTOUCHABLE: The Tories and the '45

Also by Howard Erskine-Hill

THE SOCIAL MILIEU OF ALEXANDER POPE: Lives, Example and the Poetic Response

THE AUSGUSTAN IDEA IN ENGLISH LITERATURE

POETRY AND THE REALM OF POLITICS: Shakespeare to Dryden

POETRY OF OPPOSITION AND REVOLUTION: Dryden to Wordsworth

ALEXANDER POPE: Selected Letters (*editor*)

Studies in Modern History

General Editor: **J. C. D. Clark**, Joyce and Elizabeth Hall Distinguished Professor of British History, University of Kansas

Titles include:

James B. Bell
THE IMPERIAL ORIGINS OF THE KING'S CHURCH IN EARLY AMERICA
1607–1783

Jonathan Clark and Howard Erskine-Hill (*editors*)
SAMUEL JOHNSON IN HISTORICAL CONTEXT

Eveline Cruickshanks and Howard Erskine-Hill
THE ATTERBURY PLOT

Richard R. Follett
EVANGELICALISM, PENAL THEORY AND THE POLITICS OF CRIMINAL LAW
REFORM IN ENGLAND, 1808–30

William Anthony Hay
THE WHIG REVIVAL
1808–1830

Karin J. MacHardy
WAR, RELIGION AND COURT PATRONAGE IN HABSBURG AUSTRIA
The Social and Cultural Dimensions of Political Interaction, 1521–1622

Robert J. Mayhew
LANDSCAPE, LITERATURE AND ENGLISH RELIGIOUS CULTURE, 1660–1800
Samuel Johnson and Languages of Natural Description

Julia Rudolph
WHIG POLITICAL THOUGHT AND THE GLORIOUS REVOLUTION
James Tyrrell and the Theory of Resistance

Anthony Waterman
POLITICAL ECONOMY AND CHRISTIAN THEOLOGY SINCE THE
ENLIGHTENMENT
Essays in Intellectual History

Doron Zimmerman
THE JACOBITE MOVEMENT IN SCOTLAND AND IN EXILE, 1746–1759

Studies in Modern History
Series Standing Order ISBN 0–333–79328–5
(*outside North America only*)

You can receive future titles in this series as they are published by placing a standing order. Please contact your bookseller or, in case of difficulty, write to us at the address below with your name and address, the title of the series and the ISBN quoted above.

Customer Services Department, Macmillan Distribution Ltd, Houndmills, Basingstoke, Hampshire RG21 6XS, England

---

The Atterbury Plot

Eveline Cruickshanks

and

Howard Erskine-Hill

First published 2004 by
PALGRAVE MACMILLAN
Houndmills, Basingstoke, Hampshire RG21 6XS and
175 Fifth Avenue, New York, N.Y. 10010
Companies and representatives throughout the world

PALGRAVE MACMILLAN is the global academic imprint of the Palgrave Macmillan division of St. Martin's Press, LLC and of Palgrave Macmillan Ltd. Macmillan® is a registered trademark in the United States, United Kingdom and other countries. Palgrave is a registered trademark in the European Union and other countries.

ISBN 0–333–58668–9

This book is printed on paper suitable for recycling and made from fully managed and sustained forest sources.

A catalogue record for this book is available from the British Library.

Library of Congress Cataloging-in-Publication Data
Cruickshanks, Eveline.
  The Atterbury plot / by Eveline Cruickshanks & Howard Erskine-Hill.
    p. cm. – (Studies in modern history)
  Includes bibliographical references and index.
  ISBN 0–333–58668–9
    1. Atterbury, Francis, 1662–1732. 2. Conspiracies–Great
Britain–History–18th century. 3. Church and state–England–History–
18th century. 4. Great Britain–History–George I, 1714–1727. 5. Tories,
English–History–18th century. 6. Church of England–Bishops–Biography.
7. Politicians–Great Britain–Biography. 8. Exiles–Great Britain–Biography.
9. Stuart, House of. 10. Jacobites. I. Erskine-Hill, Howard II. Title. III. Studies
in modern history (Palgrave Macmillan (Firm))
DA501.A8C78 2004
941.07´1–dc22   2004041507

10   9   8   7   6   5   4   3   2   1
13 12 11 10 09 08 07 06 05 04

Printed and bound in Great Britain by
Antony Rowe Ltd, Chippenham and Eastbourne

Contents

List of Illustrations

Acknowledgments

We acknowledge the gracious permission of Her Majesty the Queen to draw upon the enormous archive of the Stuart Papers at Windsor Castle, the presence of which in England marks the eventual drawing together, in the early nineteenth century, of the House of Stuart and the House of Brunswick. We acknowledge the kind permission of Lord Harrowby for our use of the Ryder diaries.

We thank Richard Sharp, author of *The Engraved Record of the Jacobite Movement* (Scholar Press 1996), for assistance in regard to our illustrations which, in kindness and interest, has gone far beyond the usual scholarly courtesies.

We acknowledge with gratitude and pleasure the assistance of friends and fellow scholars in our project. They include Professor Jeremy Black, Professor Jonathan Clark, Professor Patrick O'Brien, Dr. Niall MacKenzie, Professor Larry Neal, Professor Murray Pittock, Dr Lawrence Smith, Professor Daniel Szechi, Roger Turner.

The staff of many libraries and manuscripts repositories have been helpful, particularly the British Library, Cambridge University Library, the Ashmolean Museum at Oxford, the Institute of Historical Research in the University of London, the Royal Archives in Windsor Castle and the archives of the Ministère des affaires étrangères at the Quai d'Orsay in Paris.

We acknowledge with particular gratitude the photographic services of the Ashmolean Museum at Oxford and the University Library at Cambridge, in the latter of which L. R. Goodey has, as usual, been of brilliant assistance.

EVELINE CRUICKSHANKS
HOWARD ERSKINE-HILL

Preface

The Atterbury Plot is less well known than the three other major Jacobites attempts, the Irish campaign of 1689–91, the Fifteen and the Forty-five, if only because it did not, like them, eventuate in battles and civil war. It is, however, just as historically and intellectually interesting, and in its own way just as dramatic, revealing a shifting kaleidoscope of human figures: the warily neutral, the opportunistic supporter and the subtle traitor; the impetuous leader, the cautious advocate, the resolute opponent, and the people of all conditions who were steadily loyal to the Jacobite cause. The actors of this rapidly changing drama were kings and first ministers, great aristocrats, generals, officers, common soldiers, Thames watermen, confidence-men and double-dealers, informers and keepers of brothels. Amidst all these, the heart of the matter was the constant, detailed, reconfiguration by the plotters of their plans, the precariousness of the Hanoverian state in the early 1720s, and the absolute resolution of Robert Walpole to act on the disputable Whig interpretation of 1688 and to support the Hanover succession against what he saw as the real danger of a second Stuart restoration, supported by High Anglicans, Tories out of place and a discontented capital city: London.

Eveline Cruickshanks has been primarily responsible for the sequence of Chapters 1–9, which present this central material. Howard Erskine-Hill has been primarily responsible for the Introduction, the final Chapter on the aftermath, and the Conclusion. Each has, however, contributed to all parts of the book.

EVELINE CRUICKSHANKS
HOWARD ERSKINE-HILL

Frontspiece. *Francis Atterbury, Bishop of Rochester, holding a portrait of Archbishop Laud.* Anonymous engraving, c. 1722. (Ashmolean Museum)

1

Introduction:
Continuous Conspiracy

Models of revolution

Apart from the 'English Civil War', now better described as the 'Wars of the Three Kingdoms',[1] the seventeenth century had supplied two other models for fundamental political change. The first of these was a peaceful revolution (in the neutral sense of that term): the restoration of the Stuart monarchy in 1660. The second, armed invasion from abroad, was the achievement of the Prince of Orange in 1688–89: what used to be called 'the Glorious Revolution'. While those who later conspired to overthrow the Williamite or Hanoverian hegemonies would develop or combine many different strategies, 1660 and 1688 remained, well into the eighteenth century, the potent historical examples.

For this reason anyone who wants to understand the Atterbury Plot, conducted on behalf of the exiled Stuart dynasty in 1720–22, should look with care at the revolutions of 1660[2] and 1688. While each was acclaimed by its supporters as peaceful, qualifications must be made. By 1660 Cromwellian rule, which might have founded a new dynasty, had collapsed. The remains of the Long Parliament had reinstated themselves and begun to call for new elections to a Convention Parliament. At the same time two parliamentary commanders, Lambert and Monck, led significant military forces; especially Monck, who moved steadily south from Scotland and kept his own counsel. There seem to have been three reasons for the Restoration in 1660: the collapse of the Cromwellian project, the difficulties experienced by the Rump of the Long Parliament in imposing its authority, *and* the quiet resolution of a military strong man, Monck, to go over to the Stuart cause. The military factor had thus been crucial in bringing about this peaceful change.

The military factor was still more important in 1688. Here the Prince of Orange, as stadtholder of Holland and thus the effective leader of the United Provinces, sailed with a formidable armada and, having had once to put back owing to contrary winds, managed to land in the West Country with an army twice the size of James's.[3] Nevertheless, a battle on Salisbury Plain seemed probable until some of James's officers began to desert, the defection of Colonel John Churchill, in due course to become Duke of Marlborough, being particularly damaging. James finally resolved upon flight to France, making it clear by the drawing up of a draft declaration, and by other symbolic gestures such as the throwing of the Great Seal of the Kingdom into the Thames as he departed, that he withdrew only to fight again.[4] This was not abdication in his own eyes. Further, while William's revolution was achieved with a few skirmishes in England, civil war broke out in James's other two kingdoms, James himself landing in Ireland with French support and triggering the most serious Irish civil wars since Cromwellian times. These were not terminated by the Battle of the Boyne, but continued until the Battle of Aughrim and the subsequent Treaty of Limerick. Military force, merely threatened in 1660, was exerted on a large scale in 1688, and determined the success of William's revolution.

The question of treason

In the eyes of the returning king and the great majority of those who supported his restoration, what happened in 1660 was the termination of treason. The question had been even more vexed at the outbreak of the seventeenth-century civil wars, and so it was in 1688 and after. Yet rebellion and conspiracy to rebel were profoundly ambiguous undertakings. Because they were, at least at first, divisive and usually violent projects, both aggressors and defenders required justification which, whether by the antiquity or the comprehensiveness of their claim, sought to transcend conflict and show that it was more than a naked fight for self-interest. The promptings of self-interest were, nevertheless, salient in significant political decisions, including military commitments; so, no doubt more rarely, was the open-eyed hazarding of total self-sacrifice. Depending on success in the public realm, and usually on the field of battle, arguments of justification could be turned rapidly around. Those who held the state in their grip for the moment could hold any move against them by native subjects, albeit sometimes by native subjects in exile, to be treason. However, as Sir

John Harington, the godson of Queen Elizabeth I and one who knew a good deal about plots against that queen, wrote:

> Treason doth never prosper, what's the reason?
> For if it prosper, none dare call it Treason.[5]

Motives and oaths

1688 was a dynastic revolution, dynasticism being one of the chief ways to secure fundamental change in that time. To change society one might seek an alternative prince. As is now well recognised, a powerful mix of motives lay behind the changing of the king on the throne. It was by no means chiefly a response to James's policies during his short reign. William was deeply engaged in a grand coalition against the power of France and wished to secure James's kingdoms and naval forces for his alliance. So long as James's heir was the Protestant Princess Mary, William's wife, William could expect James's kingdoms to come into his sphere of influence on the death of James. The birth of a male heir to James II in 1688, an heir who was furthermore a prince who would obviously be brought up a Catholic, threw all William's expectations into question. Then James's slow Catholicising policies, beginning to grant toleration to Protestant dissenters and to Catholics, profoundly disturbed the established Anglican Church. Its ideology (long familiar within the ancient constitution) was to show passive obedience to the king or queen identified by legitimate male or (failing that) female primogeniture. This seemed to parallel the way in which property generally descended in society at large. Under the Catholic James, Anglicans could perhaps preserve their loyalty so long as his heir were a Protestant and indeed a Church of England princess. A Catholic male heir suggested that the King of England might be Catholic for ever. In this crisis seven political lords – no very wide sample of the political public – secretly invited William to do what he may well have contemplated before the birth of James's Catholic male heir: invade the kingdoms of his father-in-law by force.[6]

Here one sees a clash of interests which was not primarily a clash of material interests. James, anxious to do something for the Catholics and counting too much on the loyalty of Anglicans, began to open the offices of state to Catholics and Dissenters, relying on the royal prerogative in doing so. The outrage of the Church of England was not just in reaction to the threat to its material interests, as the Trial of the Seven Bishops and subsequent record of many of these bishops as nonjurors against William make clear. William, for his part, was not an Anglican like his wife, but a northern European Protestant and a Calvinist, a sympathiser with the Dutch Reformed Church. All these were people of faith. We are not contemplating the Hobbist nightmare of a naked struggle for advantage.

The taking of, abiding by, evasion or refusal of oaths was not, of course, a matter for the Church of England alone. Oaths were the means by which any government in this period sought to bind its sub-jects and identify its opponents. After 1688, new oaths were devised to attempt to flush out people who were radically disaffected yet cautious. Oaths were a conscientious religious matter, and if they had not been taken seriously by the generality of the people there would have been little point in governments devising or imposing them. Two cases are interesting here. The Earl of Ailesbury, who remained loyal to James II after the accession of William and Mary, roundly acknowledged in confidence that he took the oaths to the new monarchs in order to dispel suspicion and be thus better able to serve his old and rightful king. There is here quite a paradox of bad faith and good faith, and it is worth noting the extremity of Ailesbury's political and ethical posi-tion.[7] The case of Lord North and Grey (1678–1734), who would be one of the most important conspirators in the Atterbury Plot, deserves more detailed attention.

North and Grey's short and little known MS treatise, 'Considerations on the Nature of Oaths at present' was seized by the government in 1722, and it is not known when it was written. It argues that, as averred by 'The ingenious and Pious Dr. Sanderson' (1597–1663), chaplain to King Charles I and Bishop of Lincoln after 1662, an oath is 'A religious Act by which God is called to witness to confirm a doubtful Matter', that is a commitment (otherwise uncertain) by the oath-taker and, secondly, again from Sanderson, that 'no oaths take away a Prior Obligation'.[8] This means that any oath taken to William and Mary, Anne or George I, could not absolve the oath-taker from the force of any previous oaths taken to James II or his predecessors. It is easy to see in this advice Sanderson's own situation: while surviving into the Civil War period, he must have taken his first oaths under the earlier Stuarts. Sanderson's view, and it was the view of a divine who was known to have published important works on cases of conscience, would in prin-ciple have justified Ailesbury's attitude to the oaths, though Ailesbury, as quoted above, justified himself more pragmatically. North and Grey, however, was too young to have taken an oath to James II.[9] It is inter-esting that the polite difference acknowledged by North and Grey between himself and Sanderson concerned the question whether, if any original oath could be subsequently shown to have been unlawful, 'the Breach of such an oath were Perjury', albeit it may certainly have been a 'sin'. North and Grey denied perjury in such a case.[10] This may suggest that North and Grey, in his paper, sought to extenuate his record in having taken oaths to William, Anne and George I and, perhaps, his having subsequently broken them. To have done so, North and Grey argues, was certainly a sin, but to have acted contrary to them was not 'Perjury'. North and Grey's treatise may seem – in the absence of stronger evidence – to have been written after 1714.

Such a complex argument, with its roots in the writings of an Anglican divine accounted an authority on oaths and cases of conscience, shows that a Jacobite activist in the earlier eighteenth century had, on the one hand, no superstitious attitude towards oaths, nor on the other a purely cynical or secular one. This has important implications as to the nature of the society in which the Atterbury Conspiracy was planned.

Situations and aims

After the Treaty of Limerick the exiled House of Stuart kept up its claim, supported by France. In 1692, when the English Jacobites were able to raise 7000–8000 men,[11] a formidable naval invasion attempt from France, in support of James II, was abandoned owing to contrary winds and Anglo-Dutch naval opposition. Mary II died in 1694, leaving the Princess Anne as the next heir to William III. William, Duke of Gloucester, Anne's son by Prince George of Denmark, died as a boy early in 1700. Meanwhile the young Stuart Prince of Wales thrived with his exiled family in France in the Palace of Saint-Germain-en-Laye. This prompted a decisive new move on the succession to William III. By the Act of Settlement of 1701, the succession to the three kingdoms, now ruled by William, was limited to Protestants of the family. This diverted the succession from the senior line (and from many other claimants) to the Dowager Electress Sophia of Hanover, a distant descendant of Charles I, and her Protestant children. William III died in a riding accident in 1702, leaving the Princess Anne as the heir to his *de facto* crown and his continental wars, soon renewed in the War of the Spanish Succession. In 1708 another French-backed naval expedition was aimed at Scotland. The exiled Stuart heir, now King James III, was aboard, and in some danger, but the plan miscarried and the expedition returned safely to France.

Like William III in his earlier years, Queen Anne was in principle ready to turn to the Whigs or to mixed administrations; in her later years she accepted a Tory government led by the moderate Tory, Robert Harley, later Earl of Oxford. This administration had, as its chief end, the termination of the War of the Spanish Succession and what had been virtually 21 years of continental war. This step by Britain horrified the more resolute members of the continental anti-French coalition, such as the Dutch Netherlands and the Electorate of Hanover. It was beginning to become clear that the Bourbon rather than the Imperial candidate for the throne of Spain might actually become the next Spanish king, and eventually so it proved.

Those who were ideologically committed to the Stuart king in exile, or who were dissatisfied with the rule of Queen Anne, or who feared the consequences of the succession of the Elector of Hanover (the Electress Sophia being now dead) could console themselves with the continuing possibility of a second restoration. This could have come about, on the death of Anne, had James III decided to abandon Catholicism and thus qualify himself for the royal succession under the Act of Settlement. This James continued to refuse to do. Alternatively, it was speculated, Anne was not without sympathy for her young half-brother, and might conceivably lend her support to a Tory repeal of the Act of Settlement. This was anticipated by many Whigs. But Anne died suddenly, having given the White Staff to Lord Shrewsbury, 'the wise and great'.[12] Many Tories tried to make themselves acceptable to the new king, George I.

The Elector of Hanover's becoming King George of Great Britain stresses again the great importance of dynastic change for religious, civil and foreign policy in his new kingdoms. George could hardly be blamed, given his own point of view, for distrusting the survivors of the Tory peace-party, but it soon became clear that his inability to rise above his initial prejudices (compare the counter-example of the restored Charles II) was going to make a heavy impact on the political and social life of Britain. To a modern historian of these times, it is almost incredible to see, under George I, Robert Harley, Earl of Oxford, the first prime minister of Great Britain (surely in that role before Walpole?) imprisoned in the Tower, along with George Granville, Lord Lansdowne, a potent minister under Harley, civilised though now impecunious. Equally astonishing was the escape to the Continent of the popular Captain-General of the British forces, the Duke of Ormonde, who had, under the Tories, replaced the Duke of Marlborough. Another great statesman who fled into exile was Henry

St John, Viscount Bolingbroke, deeply and honourably involved in the settlement of peace in the Treaty of Utrecht but the most active of Harley's antagonistic high Tory colleagues. George I, as any early eighteenth-century potentate might have done, made his mind up about British political parties. He did not want to attempt to achieve some kind of reconciliation of parties under the new House of Brunswick. He wanted to identify his friends and support them. The four men just mentioned might have been drawn in to serve the new king but were not.

The Jacobite rebellion of 1715

A man who reacted to the new situation differently from Bolingbroke and Ormonde was John Erskine, Earl of Mar. He had been a supporter of Harley and Secretary of State for Scotland.[13] Appreciating, no doubt, that what was now happening 'was not a change to an all-Whig ministry' but 'a whole social revolution',[14] Mar took ship for Scotland where, in well-disposed north-eastern regions which he knew well, he raised the standard of King James III. Of course at this time the exiled Court had, as at most other times, a strategy in hand for a combined expedition and rising to bring King James home. Mar's action was so precipitate that the Jacobites abroad were taken by surprise. One consequence was that while there was some co-ordination between Mar and the Northumberland Jacobites, who rose with the idea of securing the important port of Newcastle-on-Tyne, a larger co-ordination which should have included a previously planned naval landing by the Duke of Ormonde in south-west Britain entirely failed. As soon as the news broke, James III made haste to travel to Scotland (no easy feat when he risked arrest at almost every stage), but he arrived too late to be much help to Mar. Mar himself, while a highly intelligent politician, had proved a fairly poor military leader. The 1715 Rebellion had great energies on its side, but was an opportunity which was, if not thrown away, at least a historical crisis which the Jacobites could have exploited better.[15]

Nevertheless, bearing in mind the history of Jacobite plots before and after 1715, some credit should be accorded to the Earl of Mar. The typical situation envisaged in these plots was that the Jacobites at home would rise in the event of a credible landing of troops from abroad. On the other hand, continental troops would not usually be committed to a naval landing without secure assurances that the Jacobites in Britain were already committed to a rising. Mar at least broke this hopeless circle, and brought about a most significant military rising in the British kingdoms, if mainly in Scotland, without up-to-the minute promises of continental help. He showed what could be done within Britain. To many half-sympathetic to the Stuart cause, no doubt, the failure of the Fifteen and the execution of many of its leaders was a warning to lie low and be circumspect. To the more committed, on the other hand, it must have suggested what could be done.

Continuous conspiracy

In the period of more or less continuous conspiracy which succeeded the failure of the 1715 Jacobite Rebellion, composed of the 1716–17 Swedish Plot, the Hispano-Scottish landing at Glenshiel of 1719, and the early phases of the Atterbury Conspiracy, one may see a clear reaction to the Fifteen and the ways in which it went wrong. In each case a serious effort was made to secure backing from a major continental power. In 1717 this was the Sweden ruled by the famous Charles XII. He was, if he could be interested, ideal for Jacobite purposes since, apart from his reputation for military brilliance and dauntless recovery from defeat, Charles was both a Protestant and a north European rival of George I as Elector of Hanover. (Jacobitism was a largely Protestant movement, although widely accused by its enemies of being Roman Catholic, for obvious reasons.) Large sums were raised from Jacobites at home and abroad to fund a naval descent upon Britain by Charles XII. Soon, however, the London government got wind of the conspiracy; the diplomatic immunity of the Swedish ambassador was violated and some evidence of the design was disclosed. The plot was aborted. Soon after Charles XII died, apparently from a random bullet while besieging the important naval fortress of Frederichstadt, a base from which a seaborne expedition against Hanoverian Britain might have been launched.[16]

After Sweden, the exiled Stuart court, surveying the condition of Europe, perceived that something was to be hoped for from Bourbon Spain, now ruled by Philip V. Philip V, like Charles XII of Sweden, had strong reasons for opposing George I, and was persuaded to invite the Duke of Ormonde to Spain to take command of a naval expedition against Britain. The main part, to be led by Ormonde, was aimed at England, with a subsidiary expedition to Scotland. It was to comprise 29 ships, 5000 soldiers (about the size of Prince Charles Edward's army on his invasion of England), and arms for 30,000 more. A small diversionary expedition to Scotland under the Earl Marischal was the second part of the design. Finally, James III was to embark with Ormonde from Corunna with the larger part of the invasion fleet. In the event, as is well known, the larger part of the fleet was fatally damaged by a terrible storm on its voyage from Cadiz to Corunna where King James, after a journey of great difficulty, had managed to join Ormonde. It seems they had no alternative but to abandon the enterprise. The small Scottish expedition got through, landing on the Isle of Lewis, but at the mountainous Battle of Glenshiel was defeated by Hanoverian troops from Inverness.[17]

Clearly the design of 1719 got a lot further than that of 1717. Difficult as it inevitably was to mount a significant and properly co-ordinated naval expedition from so far away as Spain (as sixteenth-century history testifies), the plan seems to have been well conceived in the light of recent experience. The 1715 Rebellion had been confined to Scotland and the north of England. The 1719 plan aimed at the English heartland. The Fifteen had lacked support from a sponsoring European power to kick-start the rising in the right way and afford some protection for the earliest native volunteers. 1715 had taught the Jacobite planners that many native British would rise, and the arms for thirty thousand men which the main fleet would have landed show this was expected again. Finally Mar's precipitate action in 1715 meant that King James had arrived in Britain too late. This time it was planned that he would be present at the main landing, as the Prince of Orange had been in 1688. Mention of the Prince of Orange prompts a final comparison. His invasion fleet too had initially been driven back by storm and had to be fitted out for what was, strictly, a second expedition. This was a mark of William's iron resolution. Whether the Catholic wind which originally drove William's fleet back was less violent than the Protestant wind which assailed Philip V's fleet in 1719, or whether James and Ormonde were less resolute than William had been, or had a more precarious purchase on Bourbon Spain than William had on the Dutch Netherlands (surely this must have been so) need not concern us here. The balance of the design, defeated only by Nature, is of more relevance.

Kinds of plot

In the earlier eighteenth century, one way of alluding to affairs of state and issues of war was through the narrative metaphor of the card game.[18] An example is the game of *ombre* in Canto III of Pope's *Rape of the Lock* (1714). It is possible to ask of each side in a civil conflict: what cards did they *wish* to play? – and what cards *could* they play? The most transcendent and providential card of all to play – if such a thing ever *can* be played – was of course the completely peaceful restoration of Charles II in 1660. The idealised and in the end legendary and providential nature of this event would be a continual snare and delusion to exiled Jacobites. Despite the eventual absence of military combat, the knowledge that there had been a military ace to support the king was crucial in 1660. And if then, how much more so in 1688 with William's armed landing and the outbreak of civil war in Scotland and Ireland? The most obvious thing in the political experience surveyed in this chapter is that the ability to wield military force, and the wielding of it, was the strongest available card that could be played. That card related to another, hardly played perhaps in 1660 or 1715: the sponsorship of a militarily significant foreign power, as in 1688, 1692, 1708, the 1717 design, and 1719. Almost always, however, that depended on a significant native rising as soon as foreign assistance arrived. Native sympathisers, however, had frequently been disarmed. This in turn connects with another factor: serious disaffection in the land to be invaded and in which dynastic change is sought. In yet another connection this sometimes linked up with elections. The Rump Parliament agreed to a new parliamentary convention in which it was credibly supposed Royalists would have a majority. James II, at bay before the threat of William, agreed to call a new Parliament. As we shall see, in the Atterbury Plot, the timing of an invasion and a rising with a general election was a fine card to play. There was a further card: one likely to be overlooked or discounted in modern secular discussion. This, in Jacobite and much other history, was the presence of the *de jure* monarch: the presence of the sacred king himself on the soil over which God had made him shepherd of his flock.[19] The restoration of Charles II was coterminous with his landing in England. It was no accident that James III moved heaven and earth to join Mar in Scotland in the 1715 Rebellion, or underwent so many dangers to join Ormonde in Corunna in 1719. This was no eagerness for the rewards of real kingship. As the medallic record of the Jacobite movement bears out,[20] it was an attempt to bring the face of the king into the presence of his people. The presence of the *de jure* king, and equally no doubt the absence of the *de facto* king who saw himself as *de jure*, were significant matters. Finally, there was a card, apparently never played, though sometimes feared: that of assassination.

It should not be thought that the history of the three kingdoms from 1660 to 1722 simply consisted of a pack of cards or a book of plots out of which Jacobite plotters could be allocated a hand or choose a design. They surely desired to learn from history but, on the one hand, circumstances did not always deal them the hand they desired, and on the other, there were also totally new and unpredicted possibilities. One such, as we shall see in the next chapter, was the rise to power in France of the Scottish economist, John Law. In the meantime it is necessary to close with a brief account of the three chief *dramatis personae* of the Atterbury Plot: George I, James III, and Atterbury himself.

Dramatis personae

The great point to grasp about King George I, however strange and unsympathetic he may originally have found his new realm of British politics, is that he was no irresolute or incompetent monarch who, by gratefully ceding his royal power to his ministers, inadvertently advanced constitutional monarchy. On the contrary, he was a strong ruler on the seventeenth-century model who always knew his own mind, rewarded only those he felt he could trust, appointed the ministers he wanted provided they could command a majority in Parliament, and kept out those whom he suspected or feared. Above all, he laid the foundation of the system which kept the Tories out of office until 1760, and he resolved to ostracise rather than come to terms with potentially penitent Jacobite statesmen. He (naturally) feared his Jacobite rival overseas, and did all he could to persuade the emperor to prevent James's marriage with Clementina Sobieska.[21] A strong supporter, like William III before him, of the Imperial-led coalition against France, he took the first step, supported by his ministers, to ally with France because France was no longer the France of Louis XIV, but of the infant Louis XV and the Regent d'Orléans, under whose authority the young James III had been expelled from France to Bar-le-Duc, Avignon, and eventually to Italy.

For a king with a very contestable right to the throne, it was quite important that George should have appeared charming, conciliatory and clement, and a man with an edifying life. This was not the impression he gave. His personal life seemed full of scandal after his wife, the Electress Sophia Dorothea, was unfaithful with Count Königsmark and spent the rest of her days imprisoned in one of George's German fortresses. This liaison was probably not quite early enough to call in question the legitimacy of George's son George, now the Hanoverian Prince of Wales. The fact that George I and his son appeared at daggers drawn only increased the plausible scandal; and to many it must have

King George I. Engraving with etching by Jacob Houbraken after Sir Godfrey Kneller, 1752. (Private Collection)

seemed that there was poetic justice between the two dynasts since, according to the politically launched 'warming pan' plot, the son of James II was not legitimate, an allegation abandoned at length as a result of sheer evidence to the contrary. Now the swirling scandal around George I and Sophia Dorothea seemed to suggest that neither might George's male heir be legitimate. Each dynast thus suffered from politically inspired derogation. On top of all this, George's mistresses did not find favour in the eyes of the British public. At the time of the rise of the stocks of the South Sea Company it does appear – and after the collapse of the stocks, was certainly alleged – that the king and his mistresses had received stock for which they did not pay.[22] At the same time, the hostile relations between George I and the Prince of Wales, though there were some staged moments of reconciliation, led the king's ministers to assume that on the death of George I most of his ministers would certainly be thrown out of office. While on the quite late death of George I in 1727 this did not become the case, it was a factor in the conduct of some chief ministers during the period of the Atterbury Plot.[23]

James III, 'the new King' as Defoe's *Colonel Jack* calls him while a professional soldier in Italy early in the eighteenth century,[24] was a far different figure. He was the legitimate son of the last legitimate king of the three kingdoms according – not indeed to contractual theory – but to the ancient constitution. He had never been on bad terms with his parents. He was good-looking, conciliatory and, as his campaigning with the French forces during the War of the Spanish Succession showed, personally brave. On a visit during these campaigns to Fénelon, the famous Archbishop of Cambrai, he won the approbation of the Catholic prelate most highly esteemed by English Protestants.[25] As noted later by the historian Thomas Innes, James risked his 'sacred person' in his journey to join and sustain Mar's Scottish rising in the 1715 Rebellion.[26] James was, however, as firm a Catholic as George was a Lutheran. Had he converted to the Church of England on the principle that 'a Mass was worth London' he would have been likely to succeed Anne. As it was he was a fluent English speaker, a student of English history and of the statutes of George I, interested in the most recent English literature, including Pope's *Homer*, and, like George, interested in opera. Indeed, several operas produced in Rome were dedicated to James.[27]

James had, in general, excellent relations with his queen, Clementina Sobieska, but they fell out over one thing, the education of their son, the young Prince of Wales. James insisted that he must be instructed in

King James III. Engraving by Marie-Nicole Horthemels after Alexis-Simon Belle,. 1712. (Private Collection)

the Protestant as well as the Catholic faith. This proved intolerable to Clementina, a fervent Catholic. The dispute widened to the question of James having Protestant as well as Catholic advisers. This damaging rift caused a temporary separation between the two, but the quarrel was eventually compromised and a reconciliation took place.

To any who could see through the anti-Catholic prejudices of the time, James was a far more edifying figure than George. It is said that he was weak and gullible; his letters show that he was circumspect and aware of his need for expert advice. If he was too trusting, George was too suspicious. If George's salient characteristic was tenacity, that of James was patience.

Between these two contrasting dynasts, we must see Francis Atterbury, by the time of the conspiracy which bears his name Bishop of Rochester and Dean of Westminster. By comparison with the patient James and the tenacious George, the character of Atterbury was one of exceptional energy and ambition. The paradox of Atterbury's career was that he was entirely devoted to the Church of England as it stood in the reign of Charles II but that also, within the precarious structures of the church, he was a formidable political figure, recognised as such by friend and foe alike, seen by the latter as a man it was essential to challenge and oppose, and by some of the former (such as Robert Harley) as a clever, eloquent and independent figure whom it was necessary to 'manage' and appease. In his middle years, Whig politicians, especially perhaps the intelligent and energetic young Robert Walpole, may have sensed that the church was not the limit of his aims but only the means to his ends. This, we believe, was a misconstruction, but in so far as it existed it marked Atterbury as a dangerous man.

The son of a sometime Cromwellian clergyman, Atterbury was educated at Westminster School and Christ Church, Oxford, where in due course he became a Student, that is to say a Fellow. From Atterbury's incredibly energetic early and middle career five interesting points emerge. The first is that, at the time when the church and the universities seemed in danger from the Catholicising policies of James II, Atterbury with others resisted the king's measures, and Atterbury himself challenged the Catholic Master of University College, Obadiah Walker, over his views on Lutheranism and the Church of England. In his *Answer to some Considerations on the Spirit of Martin Luther and the Original of the Reformation* (1687) Atterbury denied that the English Church was identical with that which Luther had founded, though he also defended Luther against Walker. Atterbury did not, like the famous

Anglican John Kettlewell, preach Passive Obedience to the Roman Catholic king. There is no evidence that Atterbury became a nonjuror after the expulsion of James II, as did William Sancroft, the saintly Archbishop of Canterbury. Atterbury showed not the least sympathy, either by principle or by sentiment, for the Stuart king or for those who were close to him.

The second point is that while Atterbury will be chiefly remembered as a churchman and politician, he would, had he not been so prominent in the public sphere, have been remembered still as a man of letters. He was of a complex sensibility; literary interests and high political concerns ran together in his mind. In 1681–82 Atterbury translated, with a younger colleague, Francis Hickman, Dryden's loyal and highly topical rhyming poem *Absalom and Achitopel* (1681) into Latin hexameters. The project was well managed and Atterbury, who was later to follow Milton in preferring unrhyming to rhyming poetry, at least in ambitious works, may have had a particular pleasure in giving a greater classical dignity to an English poem he admired. Two years later he showed his love of neo-Latin poetry by editing an anthology, *Poemata Italorum qui Latine scripserunt* (1684). He gives his highest praise to Giacomo Sannazaro (1458–1530), and the terms in which Atterbury commends him, in the judgement of a modern scholar of the neo-Latin, suggest 'a Catullan view of poetry'. This anthology was inherited by Atterbury's future friend, Alexander Pope, who revised, expanded and republished it in 1740.[28] Atterbury's literary attachment to the reign of Charles II found expression in his 'Preface to the Second Part of Waller's *Poems*' (published anonymously in 1690), a milestone in the history of English literary criticism. When he questions 'whether in Charles the Second's reign English did not come to its full perfection; and whether it has not had its Augustan age, as well as the Latin', he may have been the first to apply this well-known term to English culture. Whatever his general opinion about rhyme, he writes here with the sharpest of eyes on the management of rhyme before and after the Civil Wars, and is unusual in citing the example of John Donne.[29] In general Atterbury was devoted to Virgil and Horace, to Sannazaro and other neo-Latin poets, and to Milton, Dryden and Waller. Shakespeare too captured his imagination, though he may not always have remembered him accurately. When in the final dangerous days of the Atterbury Plot it was Atterbury's duty, as Dean of Westminster Abbey, to officiate at the state funeral of the Duke of Marlborough, one of his enemies, a half-recalled promise from *Hamlet* floated into his mind: 'Poor Ghost, thou shalt be satisfy'd – or some thing like it', he wrote to Pope. What he recalled, possibly from a theatrical performance, is now found at I. v. 4: 'Alas poor ghost', and v. 190: 'Rest, rest, perturbed spirit!' What one takes away from this reminiscence is a hint of Atterbury's sense of the danger and corruption of the world of political greatness, and of his ability to feel compassion for a dead foe.[30]

Both as an undergraduate and as a Student of Christ Church, Atterbury must count as one of the leading Christ Church Wits, and so too when he became Head of the House. Here he was familiar with and helped to promote Anthony Alsop (1669–1726), 'the English Horace', the greatest neo-Latin poet in England in that age, and no doubt one of the greatest poets in any language in these islands in the later seventeenth and eighteenth centuries. Alsop moved within a circle of Jacobite sympathisers (some shared with Atterbury) and his poems express unmistakable Jacobite sympathies. Each was, however, in his earlier years, more noted for his part in the celebrated *querelle* about the Hellenic authenticity of the *Epistles of Phalaris*. Involved here were the Hon. Charles Boyle, later the 4th Earl of Orrery and a participant in the Atterbury Plot, Sir William Temple, whose 'Essay on Ancient and Modern Learning' sparked the whole debate off, Alsop whose edition of Aesop (1698) was a part of the controversy, and Richard Bentley, the great classical and linguistic scholar, who demonstrated at least to the judgement of posterity, the inauthenticity of the *Epistles* as a classical Greek text. Atterbury's defence of his old protégé Boyle, *Dr. Bentley's Dissertations on the Epistles of Phalaris Examined* (1698), has been described by his modern biographer as 'academically unscrupulous, personally malicious, eminently readable, and very funny.'[31] In other words, it was a satire. Jonathan Swift's *The Battle of the Books* (first published with *A Tale of a Tub* in 1704) took the satirical project further. In the ludic world of the work the dispute between the 'Ancients' and the 'Moderns' comes to the fore. By the standards of scholarship, as has long been recognised, Bentley was wholly in the right. But there were positive human values at stake on the other side of the *querelle* which concerned literature as a source of pleasure and imaginative instruction. Alsop, in his Preface to his edition of *Aesop*, was circumspect about these issues. He explained that if all the fables he included were not the work of the historical Aesop they were written in his spirit, *Aesopicarum* not *Aesopi*, and were just as useful to the reader. Aesop is of course a central figure in *The Battle of the Books*.

It is not certain when Atterbury first became acquainted with Swift and Pope. Swift's first letter to Atterbury, to congratulate him on his promotion to be Dean of Christ Church was on 1 September 1711. His second letter, to congratulate Atterbury on becoming Bishop of Rochester, dated 3 August 1713, bespeaks a good deal more familiarity, and hints that Swift hopes to see further promotions for Atterbury, to London, and to Canterbury. On 18 April 1716 Swift writes to Atterbury to say, *inter alia*, that 'I congratulate with England for joining with us here in the fellowship of slavery'. Atterbury's first letter to Pope appears to have been in December 1716, when he advises the poet on the Preface to his forthcoming *Poems*, 1717.[32] These early exchanges of letters presuppose long earlier acquaintance. Pope's correspondence with Atterbury chiefly concerns literary matters, though sometimes one becomes aware of an intimated political sub-text. They discuss Virgil, Horace, Milton, the question of rhyme and, often, the art of the epitaph, the last topic being one Pope certainly remembered when, in 1732, he came to compose an epitaph on Atterbury himself.

Atterbury could write searing satire, translate Horatian odes with grace and appreciate, perhaps write, love poetry in the Cavalier mode, and in rhyme. Whether the occasion were love, religion, civil contest, exile, sickness or death, Atterbury was a man of strong and various emotion; he had both a hot temper and a delicate aesthetic sensibility. Literature, pagan and Christian, accompanied him in his mind in a public career of ambition, anger, defiance, grief and, occasionally, hope, because head and heart, if they did not invariably act together, remained always in touch.

The third point concerns the well-known Convocation Controversy of the 1690s. Convocation, the 'parliament of the Church', had been under the earlier Stuarts an institution of some, if minor, significance. Atterbury, though not the first to seize upon the new significance of Convocation in the 1690s, correctly saw that if there were any institution outside Parliament which might mount a challenge to Williamite and latitudinarian trends in the church it was Convocation. It may be that Atterbury was standing in support of the special character of the Church of England, somewhat as Jonathan Swift was to see the situation in his *Tale of a Tub* (1704). Atterbury was now aware of the vulnerability of the Church of England to attack from two opposite sides. Atterbury's *Letter to a Convocation Man* (1696), based itself on the well-known doctrine of 'the Two Societies', coterminous yet distinct spheres, dealing with body and soul. In theory, Convocation was no more under the royal prerogative as to its meetings than Parliament was. As Mark Goldie has put it, 'Atterbury's rhetorical achievement was the linkage of the Church's claims to conventional claims for English liberties in Parliament.'[33] Atterbury thus found a forum in which an ordinary clergyman – he was then Vicar of St Bride's, Fleet Street – could challenge the ecclesiastical policies and promotions of the crown. It was by no means easy. Atterbury had some triumphs and many setbacks. The long-running Convocation cause did show, however, two things: first, that Atterbury was as hostile to William III as he had been to James II when it came to defending the Church of England; secondly, that, though a member of neither the Lords nor the Commons, he was a significant political figure who had, almost, shaped his own parliament in order to drive home his own views.

The fourth relevant point from Atterbury's earlier career concerns the trial of Henry Sacheverell in 1709–10. Sacheverell was a charismatic and popular High Church preacher in whose sermons the Whig government of the time thought (correctly) that it detected in the sub-text some most unwelcome political tendencies. In particular his sermon on 2 Corinthians, xi. 26, *In Perils among False Brethren* seemed to revive the traditional Church of England doctrine of '*Absolute* and *Unconditional Obedience* to the *Supreme Power*, in *all* things *lawful*, and the utter *Illegality* of *Resistance* upon any *Pretence* whatsoever'. Its sense of urgency, indeed desperation, is conveyed by the text itself:

> In journeying often, in perils of waters, in perils of robbers, in perils by mine own countrymen, in perils by the heathen, in perils in the city, in perils in the wilderness, in perils in the sea, in perils among false brethren.

This suggested to the Marlborough–Godolphin administration that the church, through the mouth of Sacheverell, was rowing back on the 'happy Revolution' of 1688 and preparing the ground for a restoration of the young James III on the death of Anne. Like the Convocation Controversy, the Sacheverell Trial has been the subject of excellent modern studies.[34] Our concern here is with the specific question of how far Atterbury's involvement in the Sacheverell Trial marked a development in his thought. Sacheverell was summoned for trial before the House of Lords for '*High Crimes and Misdemeanours*; Upon an Impeachment by ... Parliament Assembled ...'. This must have seemed to many a most disproportionate reaction to a preacher who was only repeating a part of traditional Church of England teaching, and was, in his rather slippery mode, far from calling people to arms. On the announcement of the extraordinary trial, it may have seemed a contest between an over-mighty Whig government and the Church of England, in which the able, eloquent and political Atterbury would have obviously thrown his weight on the side of the Church. If by 'False Brethren' Sacheverell had merely been complaining about Dissenters who were Occasional Conformists, that again would have been par for the course. It seems likely, however, that Atterbury and his supporter Sir Simon Harcourt must have been aware that the government designed a prominent show-trial, as a result of which several widely accepted traditional religious and political doctrines would henceforth stand condemned. Even more challenging, a particular, minority justification of 1688 was to be propounded by the government speakers as the new orthodoxy: namely the argument that government rested upon an original contract between people and ruler, and that James II had violated this contract. In the Convention debates this argument had been relatively insignificant. What had persuaded a majority to recognise William and Mary as the new sovereigns was a combination of the obviously fallacious argument that James II had abdicated, and the more subtle argument for a distinction between a king *de jure* and a king *de facto*, James remaining king *de jure*, William and Mary joint sovereigns *de facto*.

Early in Sacheverell's trial, however, Nicholas Lechmere (speaking after the opening speech of the Attorney-General) described the Constitution as resting on 'an Original Contract between the Crown and the People' and declared that this was 'an eternal Truth, essential to the Government in itself, and not to be defaced, or destroy'd, by any Force or Device'. Following this line, though not in the same precise terms, Robert Walpole spoke 'in Defence of the Necessary and Commendable Resistance used at the Revolution...'.[35] We do not wish to suggest that all the speeches against Sacheverell were stage-managed by the government, but just that their determination to crush publicly the Passive Obedience argument had the effect of rewriting the real history of the Convention of 1689. Sacheverell was convicted, but when it came to consideration of the penalties to be imposed on him so few votes favoured severity that the verdict seemed almost like an acquittal. The quiet advice of Atterbury and the public defence of Sacheverell by Sir Simon Harcourt turned him into a hero, and he was fêted round the land.

What did Atterbury think he was doing in helping to defend Sacheverell? Did he just want to give the Whig government a bloody nose in the name of the church? This certainly was the immediate effect and had its impact on the next general election. It is, however, hard to read through the published transactions of the *Trial* without being persuaded that the preacher, in his devious and defensive mode, *was* attempting to prepare the ground for a Stuart restoration. Atterbury must have seen this; at least he must have seen that the sermon could be so construed. It may be therefore that Atterbury's careful involvement in the defence of Sacheverell is a mark of a change of position on his part. Previously he had supported Convocation as a way by which the traditional Church of England could speak for itself in the public sphere. Now, one may think, he was beginning to consider who, in the longer term, might be the patron, Governor and perhaps unlikely saviour of the church.

A fifth significant episode concerns Atterbury's conduct immediately after the death of Queen Anne. Now Bishop of Rochester and Dean of Westminster, Atterbury seems at this time to have been closest to Harcourt and Ormonde. It should be noted that Ormonde, like Atterbury, had not been of King James's party at the time of the Revolution. Yet *The English Advice to the Freeholders of England*, drafted mainly by Dr Charlton, under the general guidance of Bolingbroke, Ormonde and Atterbury, was a ferocious attack on the Whigs and the Hanoverian succession. Proceedings for the impeachment of Oxford and Bolingbroke now went forward with the result, as we have seen, that the former was imprisoned in the Tower and the latter fled to France. At this juncture Atterbury appears to have advised Ormonde to follow Bolingbroke's example.[36] There were probably two reasons for this. The first is obvious: Ormonde too was going to be impeached. Flight would save him from the consequences. The second is more speculative, given the uncertainties of the times. Ormonde was a great military figure and a popular one into the bargain. If Atterbury's thoughts were turning towards the possibility of a Stuart restoration to save the church, the availability of so popular and formidable a British commander to lead a loyal invasion attempt would certainly have been a powerful consideration. Ormonde was, as we have seen, a powerful card to have been played, both in 1715 and 1719.

We have written here of the political pack of cards, and the book of political plots. These will be found enduringly potent factors at almost all stages of the Atterbury Plot. But, in the meantime, a quite new opportunity arose.

1
John Law and the First Phase of the Atterbury Plot

The Tories and the Hanoverian succession

France, the friend and protector of the Stuarts in exile, had made repeated attempts to restore James II from 1689 to 1696.[1] The Peace of Ryswick of 1697 proved but a temporary truce. Before James II's death, in September 1701, Louis XIV recognised his son, James Francis Edward Stuart, heir to the throne, henceforth known as James III.[2] This was followed by the War of the Spanish Succession (1702–13), which left Britain and France militarily and financially exhausted. It took all the skill of Robert Harley, made Lord Treasurer by Queen Anne, to restore financial stability. The Tories won the 1710 and 1713 elections by landslides, although Harley used little of the government patronage and influence at these elections. He made peace with France and Spain the first priority, and persuaded James III to issue instructions to his friends in England to support peace before raising the issue of the royal succession.[3] According to Oxford's former ally but now rival, Henry St John, Viscount Bolingbroke, the Tories were divided into those who would not accept James III unless he conformed to the Church of England, the Jacobites who would accept James III on the throne even though a Catholic, and a group of about fifty Hanoverian Tories who would not have accepted James even if he conformed to the Church of England.[4] In January 1714 Oxford and Bolingbroke made separate efforts to get James to conform, but he refused either to do so or to dissemble his religion, as Charles II was believed to have done.[5] The last months of Queen Anne's reign saw Oxford harassed in Parliament on two fronts: on the one hand by the Jacobites who wanted him to repeal the Act of Settlement of 1701, which had settled the succession on George, Elector of Hanover, fifty-eighth in the royal line but the nearest Protestant heir, and, on the other, by the Hanoverian Tories. Those two groups voted together, for different reasons, on several occasions and defeated the commercial treaty with France in 1713 for tactical reasons. From 1712 onwards, the Duke of Marlborough, who had governed jointly with Lord Chancellor Godolphin until 1710 and had been dismissed as Captain-General of British armies, headed a group of Whig army officers, led by General Cadogan, who had grown rich out of the war, and who were determined to stage a *coup d'état* if the Tories attempted to alter the Hanoverian succession.[6] Queen Anne had obtained a secret agreement with her half-brother, James III, not to press his claim while she was alive.[7] The Duke of Ormonde, the Tory idol, and Marlborough's successor as Captain-General, was in charge of James III's affairs in England. Ormonde hoped 'to settle the army' in the spring of 1714 so as to secure a restoration. He spoke to Queen Anne at last at this time, when they 'both agreed to bestir themselves' on behalf of James.[8]

The Duke of Ormonde and Atterbury: Proscription of the Tories

Ormonde had travelled a long way since he had joined the Prince of Orange in 1688 out of opposition to James II's policy of religious toleration for Protestant Dissenters and Roman Catholics. He had been, presumably, relying on William of Orange's declaration in 1688 that he had no designs on the crown, as he voted in the Lords against making William and his wife Mary king and queen. Subsequently, he held royal Household office and served with the Allied armies in William III's as well as Queen Anne's reign. The Dukes of Ormonde were quasi-hereditary Viceroys of Ireland, the only Irish dukes, with vast Irish, Scottish and English estates. Ormonde was a notable patron of the arts and dispensed magnificent hospitality. His fortune, however, was impaired by his father's debts, incurred in the service of the Stuart monarchy, expenses on Irish elections, and his own lavish style of life. He was vilified by the Elector of Hanover and the Whigs for obeying the queen's orders to cease military operations in 1712. Promoting the peace, however, increased his already great popularity among the Tories. In 1714 Ormonde was Chancellor of the universities of Oxford and Dublin, High Steward of Westminster, Bristol, and Exeter, Lord Lieutenant of Somerset and Norfolk, Constable of Dover Castle and Lord Warden of the Cinque Ports, Knight of the Garter, Colonel of the 1st Foot Guards, and Captain-General, more English honours than were bestowed on Marlborough.[9] Oxford had not favoured purging the Whigs from the army or from places under the government, still cling-ing to the notion of mixed ministries which had prevailed since 1689. There was not time for Ormonde to remodel the army before the death of Queen Anne on 1 August 1714. In retrospect, Ormonde should have prevented the Hanoverian succession while he commanded the army as Captain-General, but Ormonde was not the type of man who would carry out a *coup*. He was a conciliator by nature, who had made repeated attempts to heal the breach between Oxford and Bolingbroke. Oxford, Bolingbroke, and many Tories for their part, appear to have expected to be employed after the Hanoverian succession. George I, however, was one of the most authoritarian rulers in Europe, with no knowledge of the English language and little understanding of British institutions or constitutional practice. He threw himself entirely into the hands of the Whigs, proscribed the Tory ruling classes, and having proscribed the Tory party, proceeded to rule over a one-party state. The Whigs proved as ruthless and vindictive as Oxford had been conciliatory and dilatory. Before the election of January 1715, Tories had been dismissed from office, national and local, and the army had been purged of Tory officers with the exception of a handful of Hanoverian Tories. The Whigs impeached Tory ministers, resulting in the flight of Bolingbroke, who then became James III's secretary of state in France. Ormonde was persuaded by Atterbury to flee rather than submit to the new regime by signing a declaration that he would live as a dutiful subject of King George, as Stanhope, the Whig secretary of state, demanded.[10] Oxford remained in England and was imprisoned in the Tower of London until 1717, which led him to write from the Tower to offer his services to James III.[11]

The 1715 rebellion

Once more the Tories appealed to Louis XIV for help. He agreed to provide arms but no troops, and his death in September 1715 deprived the Jacobites even of that limited help. Louis had remained well disposed to the Jacobites, as is shown by his last letter to his nephew Philip V of Spain, recommending him to look after James III's interests.[12] In England Tory discontent erupted in 1715 into wide-spread riots all over the country. These led to the passing of the Riot Act. Ormonde's secretary, however, was bribed by Lord Townshend, the senior secretary of state, into revealing the names of the leaders of the rising, including that of Lord Lansdowne (see below) and of his

James, 2nd Duke of Ormonde. Mezzotint by John Simon after Michael Dahl, 1714.
(Private Collection)

brothers, who were arrested in September 1715.[13] In Scotland, however, Lord Mar (see below), the secretary of state for Scotland in Oxford's administration, began the Fifteen rising without consulting the English Jacobites and raised a large army. James arrived late. Mar's army, was defeated at Sheriffmuir, through his inept military leadership, while a northern English rising was defeated at the Battle of Preston in 1715.

Atterbury appointed James III's representative in England: The Whigs and the Anglo-French alliance

The failure of the Fifteen did nothing to reconcile the proscribed Tories to the Hanoverian regime or to prevent their rallying to the Jacobite cause. In September 1716 Atterbury was given a patent from James III constituting him:

> his Resident in England to and by whom he will from time to time transmit his pleasure, commands, and directions to all his subjects of that kingdom, whom he thereby wills and requires to have entire trust and confidence in him, as one entirely trusted by him, and that they give credit to none other, unless they shall see it under the King's own hand.

Atterbury was given full powers to raise money in James III's name and to act in everything as he should judge proper. Only specific orders from James himself could override him. John Menzies, the Jacobite agent in London since the days of Queen Anne, carried the patent over and placed this document into the Bishop of Rochester's hands.[14] This meant that all moves in Britain to secure a Stuart restoration had to be approved by Atterbury. Oxford had recommended Atterbury's appointment, no doubt seconded by Ormonde, who was with James at Avignon at that time. Lord Mar, who remained attached to Oxford, became James's secretary of state after the dismissal of Bolingbroke, who had failed to send money or arms to Britain during the Fifteen. Many Tories regarded Oxford as the man responsible for the disaster which engulfed their party at the accession of George I. The divisions within the party were no longer between the supporters of Oxford and Bolingbroke, but within the friends of Oxford and the supporters of Atterbury and Ormonde, though these differences did not come to a head until the later stages of the Atterbury Plot. There were differences too on national interests between the English, Scottish and Irish

Jacobites. These national divisions existed among Whigs in Hanoverian Britain, too. George Camocke, who had a distinguished career in the Royal Navy before being dismissed as a Jacobite in 1715 and who had become an admiral in the Spanish navy, was an Irishman, but he was well aware of the harm these national differences could do. He wrote to James III:

> The Duke of Ormonde is your man, for in England which is your Majesty's sheet anchor, nothing can be done without him. Scotland and Ireland signify not the fifth wheel of a coach of your Majesty's affairs. Old England is to pay the piper, and for God's sake, Sir, dance to the Bishop of Rochester's tune.[15]

The Jacobites still looked to their traditional ally, France. Philippe, Duke of Orléans, the Regent, was well disposed to the Jacobites and to James III at first. This so alarmed George I that he made the first overture to the Regent for an Anglo-French alliance.[16] Good natured but indolent, the Regent behaved like a perpetual schoolboy towards his former tutor, Guillaume Dubois. Dubois was a man of learning, which he transmitted to the Duke of Orléans. But hard work and discipline were no part of the curriculum and Dubois accustomed his pupil to a life of debauchery.

For the Jacobites, Dubois was the great fly in the ointment, the architect with his 'illustrious friend' Stanhope of the Anglo-French alliance of 1716. Small, thin and weasel-faced with a leaden complexion, Dubois always wore a blonde wig. His unprepossessing appearance was relieved by his eyes which showed his intelligence and cunning.[17] Madame, the young Louis XV's aunt, wrote that Dubois reminded her of a fox lying low ready to spring on a hen. He lacked, she thought, any kind of truthfulness, faithfulness or honesty.[18] Of obscure origins (his father was an apothecary), he had known poverty, and love of money was his chief passion. He owed his influence to sheer determination and a prodigious capacity for work, which well suited the Regent's indecision and indolence. He accustomed his pupil to vice from an early age and delighted in organising sexual orgies on Good Friday or other great feasts of the church, to the scandal of Christians. Stanhope spent some time in Paris in 1697. Dubois introduced him to the Duke of Orléans at one of these parties.[19] The links between Orléans, Stanhope and Dubois remained. Dubois was 60 and with no official status when George I, infuriated by the Duke of Orléans's readiness to marry his daughter to James III, and anxious to safeguard

Hanover from possible attacks by Russia and Sweden, made the first approach to the Regent for an alliance with France. This gave Dubois his opportunity.[20] Without any official post, Dubois negotiated the Anglo-French alliance of 1716 with Stanhope. This alliance guaranteed the Treaty of Utrecht, a very bold step in view of the vilification of the peace by the Whigs in the reign of Queen Anne, and it bound Britain in closer links to France than had existed between Charles II and Louis XIV. The treaty guaranteed the Hanoverian succession and promised to end French support for James and his adherents. Dubois had even supported Stanhope's request that James should be handed over to the English government, a proposal the Regent had rejected with indignation.[21] It obliged France to work for the expulsion of James III from Avignon, the papal enclave in France where James and his followers had taken refuge after the Fifteen, and to drive him beyond the Alps. As an inducement, the Regent promised James a pension of 750,000 *livres* a year if he went to Rome.[22] With surprising frankness, the treaty acknowledged that it was designed to enable the new English ministers to withstand popular demand in England for a reduction of the standing army, which they needed in order to maintain themselves in power, as well as to 'oppress' the party opposed to them, i.e. the Tories.[23] What did France get out of it? France needed peace after the years of war, but had that already. Dubois worked on the fears of the Regent that the friends of the Old Court (Louis XIV's) would reassert Philip V of Spain's right to the French crown and to protect himself from popular resentment at the Regent's having torn up the will of Louis XIV in order to assume power for himself. The treaty supported Orléans's claim to the throne of France against Philip V's in the event of the early death of the infant Louis XV, who was regarded as a sickly child.[24]

Dubois was ambassador to London between 1716 and 1718, entered the Council of Foreign Affairs in 1717 and became secretary of state for foreign affairs in 1718. The lengths to which Dubois was prepared to go to please George I may be judged by his agreeing that since George I called himself King of France, the young Louis XV should be referred to as His Most Christian Majesty but not as King of France in course of the negotiations![25]

Was Dubois in the pay of England?

Dubois's attitude to England was servile, more that of an informer than a French minister. There are many contemporary allusions to a 'Secret' or 'Great Secret' involving Dubois, implying (perhaps) that he had a secret pension from England received through Stanhope. In France, the duc de St Simon, the marquis de Dangeau, well informed contemporaries, as well as the marquis d'Argenson, a future French foreign minister, all state that Dubois was an English pensioner.[26] General Dillon was of opinion that the Anglo-French alliance, deeply unpopular in France, was brought about by the 'industrious management' of Dubois 'for a particular view of recompense' as he preferred 'his private interest to the good of this kingdom'. It was not only well-informed Frenchmen who said Dubois was in the pay of England: Lord Orrery thought Dubois was a pensioner of Hanover, as did Charles Caesar.[27] Evidence has proved elusive, as Dubois's papers were destroyed at his death on his orders, and English service accounts, which would have given details of such a pension, have not survived for this period. These accusations are likely because bribery was the chief instrument used by Whig ministers in the Hanoverian period. Alberoni, the chief minister of Spain, spurned the offer of a pension of £40,000 if he would give up his scheme for a restoration of the Stuarts in 1719. After his fall from power, he nevertheless accepted an English pension in exchange for intelligence about Jacobite plans.[28] Another example was François de Bussy, a French diplomat, who became envoy to London and acted as a paid English agent for many years, unbeknown to Louis XV or the French government.[29]

Abandoned by France, the Jacobites turn to Sweden and Spain

France, the chief friend and protector of the Stuarts, had now become the chief obstacle to a restoration. This led the Jacobites to look for other support, first to Sweden and then to Spain. In the Swedish Plot (1716–17), money was raised by the Jacobites in Britain to pay the army of Charles XII of Sweden, in return for his sending over Swedish troops to restore James. This plan was approved by Atterbury, but was mainly directed by Charles Caesar, a prominent Tory acting under the direction of Oxford from the Tower. With Atterbury in charge of the fund-raising, the Jacobites undertook to raise £60,000 and sent £20,000 in advance to Sweden. Caesar had several important Swedish contacts, notably his relation by marriage to Count Gyllenborg, the Swedish envoy in London. The British government discovered the plot and against all laws of diplomacy, seized Gyllenborg's papers and secured the arrest in the Dutch Netherlands of Count Göertz, Charles XII's minister.[30] Undeterred, the Jacobites turned to Spain, where Ormonde's party took the lead. Cardinal Alberoni, who had been nominated for a cardinal's hat by James III, was the chief minister of Spain. Ormonde was summoned to Spain by Alberoni and was appointed Captain-General of all the Spanish armies, including the Irish regiments in Spanish service. The Spanish court was full of Jacobites and the personal guard of Philip V, commanded by Sir Patrick Lawless (see below), consisted of Irish troops. Alberoni's grandiose plan was an invasion of England led by Ormonde and an invasion of Scotland led by the Earl Marischal and his brother James Keith. There was widespread discontent in France against the English alliance, especially in Britanny. A Breton rising was to coincide with the Spanish expedition. When it miscarried, many Bretons went to Spain to serve in the army under Ormonde.[31] Ormonde retained his contacts in Britanny and a base round Morlaix, where he had a house, which played a significant part in later stages of the Atterbury Plot. The 1719 attempt had a broad European dimension, for it planned a landing in Scotland by Charles XII of Sweden to coincide with the Earl Marischal's expedition and a Breton rising in France.[32] The suspicious circumstances of the death from a 'stray' bullet of Charles XII, the great Jacobite hero, has given rise to much speculation, with George I as a possible culprit. Assassination was, after all, a favourite device of George I's, who was one of the chief beneficiaries from Charles's death.[33] The ever-helpful Dubois had already alerted the British government to Alberoni's plans.[34] In the end, it was the weather off Cape Finisterre which shattered Ormonde's fleet, while the smaller expedition of the Earl Marischal reached Scotland, but was defeated at Glenshiel.[35]

John Law's genius

After the failure of the Swedish and Spanish attempts, a new opportunity arose in France for the Stuarts through the rise to supreme power of a Jacobite Scotsman, John Law. As chief minister in France he could be expected to bring the whole power of the French state to exert itself in favour of a restoration. This would end the stranglehold of the Anglo-French alliance, the greatest obstacle to the Stuarts' return. Law has been the subject of much study by economic historians, who knew little or nothing of his Jacobite links. The object here is not to re-examine Law's economic theories, but to do what has not been done before, to look at Law as a Jacobite and to try and explain how a Scot managed to attain supreme office in France. It is, therefore, worth studying both aspects in some detail.

Law has been described as 'one of the greatest economic and financial minds' Britain has produced.[36] He was the very opposite of the backward-looking stereotype of a Celt. His aim was to bring the 'financial revolution' to France. He could be regarded as the inventor of state capitalism, as he came to control the central bank, the tax system, foreign trade, the Mint and France's overseas colonies. Thus, he was the first to develop capital markets for financing an all-encompassing state monopoly.[37]

Origins of John Law

John Law was said to be descended from James Law, Archbishop of Glasgow 1615–32. He was baptised in St Giles's Cathedral on 21 April 1671, the son of an Edinburgh goldsmith by Jean Campbell, a distant relation of the Duke of Argyll, with whom Law had links throughout his career. Educated in Edinburgh, he showed himself to be a mathematical genius and was much addicted to games of chance. In 1684 he inherited Lauriston in the parish of Cramond, which he sold to pay for debts of £25,000 Scots left by his father, but which was preserved in his family by his mother buying it back. His father had contacts in France and the Scottish community there, for he went to Paris for medical treatment, died there and was buried in the Scots College.[38] Tall and handsome, a beau and a dandy, Law made his way to London, where he had an instant success with women besides having great success at cards. His outstanding mathematical abilities enabled him to calculate the odds so as to make large wins at gambling tables.[39] He was not a cheat and made large profits by keeping the bank, the only way, he thought, of winning consistently. Law found his rise in London society cut short in 1694 when he fought a duel with, and killed, one Edward Wilson, a professional gambler who lived in great style without visible means of support. There are conflicting versions of the cause of the quarrel. Duellists were usually able to absent themselves abroad for a time and then return. Exceptionally, either because he was Scottish or because Wilson's family had powerful friends among the Whigs, Law was convicted at the Old Bailey of murder and sentenced to death. The sentence was commuted to manslaughter, but Wilson's family appealed. Before the appeal was heard, Law made his escape to Scotland. This meant he was effectively barred from returning to England.[40]

Law now went to Amsterdam, where he studied Dutch financial institutions and took an interest in the foundation of the Bank of

John Law. Engraving with etching by L. Schenk, 1720. (Private Collection)

England. It has previously been thought that Law stayed in Holland for some years, but in 1695 he was at the Stuart Court in Saint-Germain-en-Laye. He chose to reside near that court 'having always had a warm inclination to that party'.[41] He took over with him Katherine Knollys, daughter of the titular 3rd Earl of Banbury, eloping with her, as she was already married to a Mr Seignor. There, he would have met the Prince of Wales, the future James III, as well as General Dillon, who commanded the Mountcashel brigade, the most illustrious Irish regiment in France. It was there too that he became acquainted with the Oglethorpe sisters, particularly with Eleanor Oglethorpe, later marquise de Mezières, who was to wield influence at the Court of Versailles and who made a vast fortune out of Law's Mississippi scheme.[42]

By 1700 Law was back in Scotland, where he promoted unsuccessfully a Scottish council of trade to rescue the country from financial collapse after the Darien Company disaster. In 1705 he made proposals to the Scottish Parliament for a Bank of Scotland to issue paper money on landed security as a more convenient form of trade. According to George Lockhart of Carnwarth, a prominent Scottish Jacobite, Law's scheme was supported by the Duke of Argyll and other Scottish nobles but was rejected on political rather than economic grounds.[43] In 1708, probably after the death of her husband, Mr Seignor, he was said to have married Katherine Knollys in Scotland. Scotland had its own legal system, which did not necessarily involve a written record of marriage, unlike the English or French systems. Either because there were none of the written legal records so dear to the French, or because the couple had lived together in France while unmarried in the 1690s, the validity of Law's marriage was questioned in France.[44] At this time he returned to St Germain, but whether his return had anything to do with the 1708 Jacobite attempt in Scotland has not been ascertained. In the following years, he appears to have roamed through Western Europe, but lived mainly in Brussels, with frequent visits to Paris, where he became well acquainted with Philippe, Duke of Orléans. He made great gains at the gaming table, in the Dutch lottery, and by remittances to the army of Victor Amadeus of Savoy. In 1713, when he went to live permanently in France, his personal fortune was valued at 1.5 million *livres tournois*, that is £110,000.[45]

Law's System

The death of Louis XIV and the coming to power as regent of the Duke of Orléans, uncle to the young Louis XV, was followed by great changes in French society. The devout tone and moral restraint of the later years of the Court of Louis XIV was followed by unbridled sexual licence and thirst for experiments of all kinds. Law was never one of the rakes in the Regent's circle, but the new regime provided him with his opportunity. Rich, respectable and middle-aged (he was 44 in 1715), he had settled down to happy family life and had acquired a reputation for financial probity. Madame, the dowager Duchess of Orléans, the Regent's mother, said Law spoke French well 'for a foreigner' though he sometimes used what would now be called franglais.[46] He believed that a radical change in handling money was the key to releasing the world's resources in the service of man, that metallic money was not the same thing as wealth and that it was not even a convenient medium of exchange, whereas paper money was easier to handle and could be given, he thought, a stable value. In fact, he was the first person to appreciate that the banking system need not be anchored by gold and silver. Law realised that the amount of money in circulation was not the same as inherent wealth, but that it must correspond to accessible wealth. He had a unique talent for explaining complicated financial matters with great clarity and contemporaries noticed that he was having longer and longer meetings alone with the Regent.[47] The War of the Spanish Succession (1702–13) had left France with huge debts and Law's proposals for restoring credit and generating wealth proved attractive. This explains how a foreigner was able, in a society as hierarchical and opposed to change as the France of the *ancien régime*, to overcome opposition from the Paris Parlement, the clan of the Noailles, the most powerful at Versailles, the farmers-general and receivers general, and other strong vested interests.[48] The Noailles were pro-Jacobite and great friends of Mary of Modena, James II's queen, but the duc de Noailles had supported the downfall of the secretaries of state and advocated instead government by various councils, a step meant to restore power to the great nobles, and he resented the demotion, at Law's request, of the council of finances of which he was the effective head. In 1716 Law, who had now become a naturalised Frenchman, was allowed to set up a Banque Générale, the first of its kind in France, which was an immediate success and became within a year the strongest financial institution in Europe. Its patron was the Duke of Orléans himself. In 1717 the Bank purchased through Lord Londonderry (see below) the great diamond of Governor Thomas Pitt, the finest known in Europe, and offered it to Orléans.[49] It was henceforth known as the Regent. The farmers-general had been fighting back and trying to copy Law's methods (the Anti-System), but

Law pulled the carpet from under them when a decree in April 1717 made all taxcollectors give remittances to the Treasury in notes from Law's bank, which notes effectively became the national currency.[50]

In December 1718 the Banque Royale was formed, with branches in the chief provincial towns, then a novelty. It made a large issue of banknotes redeemable in current and thus devalued coin and made payments in gold and silver for sums over 600 *livres* illegal.[51] This was but the beginning of the famous and extraordinarily ambitious scheme of Law, called the System. The bulk of the national debt, the debt of the clergy, the collection of the revenue, the Mint, the tobacco farm and postal services were all taken over. Law was also the head of the Company of the West, popularly called the Mississippi Company, later known as the Compagnie des Indes, formed to develop the Mississippi basin, including a huge area now comprising Arkansas, Iowa, Louisiana, Minnesota, Missouri and Wisconsin. Law's company took over the French East India, Africa, China and South Sea companies. The System in its first form was complete by the end of August 1719.[52] The dividends on the shares of the Compagnie des Indes were backed by the interest received on the National Debt, but also on the profits to be made by the monopoly on all the overseas trade of France. To help to launch his scheme, Law gave large allocations of unpaid-for shares to the duc de Bourbon and the prince de Conti, princes of the blood. Dubois's jealousy of Law was assuaged by a large gift of free shares. Law's confidence in the System was such that in 1719 he entered into a wager with Lord Londonderry on the price a year hence of £100,000 worth of English East India Company stock, in the belief that investors would divert their shares into Mississippi stock, whereas, in the event, in 1720 East India shares rose as part of the South Sea Bubble. This wager was to cost Law dearly. The Banque Royale combined both the rights of the Bank of England in handling government finances and the Bank of Amsterdam in monopolising large-scale commercial transactions. Later, in February 1720, as the South Sea scheme was taking off in England, Law merged the Compagnie des Indes and the Banque Royale in order to perfect the System. The wisdom of this has been a matter of debate among economic historians. Nevertheless, the potential of Law's System was immense. Law brought in workers from other parts of Europe to till uncultivated lands in France and to provide skilled labour where French industries required it. Similarly, European workers from Switzerland, Italy and Germany were encouraged to settle in Louisiana. About 6000 Frenchmen a year left for Louisiana.[53] To try to attract more, alluring prints were circulated showing Frenchmen in Louisiana reclining on piles of precious stones while a noble savage offered them a selection of exotic fruits! French peasants and their families, however, refused to emigrate. Tribunals were encouraged to commute sentences to transportation and people began to be forcibly sent to Louisiana, prisoners, vagrants, prostitutes, orphans, those on the margins of society, amidst scenes which inspired the Abbé Prevost to write his masterpiece, *Manon Lescaut*. Unlike the English and the Scots, the French were not used to transportation as a means of getting rid of criminals and marginals and it did not prove popular.[54]

Law reaches supreme power in France

As an Episcopalian Protestant, Law could not take office in France unless he became a Roman Catholic and in December 1719 he was received into the Roman Catholic Church by the Abbé de Tencin, a life-long friend of James III. His son William and his daughter, Mary Katherine (who later married her first cousin William Knollys, Viscount Wallingford, MP for Banbury 1733–40) also became converts, though not his wife. In January 1720 Law, now a naturalized Frenchman, was appointed Controller General of the Finances. He was now chief minister. Fellow Scots rejoiced, as Edinburgh sent him the freedom of the city in a gold box.[55] Even Lady Mary Wortley Montagu was gratified, writing from Paris: 'I must say I saw nothing in France that delighted me so much as to see an Englishman, at least a Briton, absolute in Paris, I mean Mr. Law, who treats their dukes and peers extremely *de haut en bas*.'[56] At first Lord Stair, the British ambassador at Paris, had praised Law as 'the cleverest man that is'. Law could not have had much liking for the son of the chief perpetrator of the massacre of Glencoe and the instigator in 1716 of the attempt to murder James III, or for a man who directed a network of spying on Jacobites in France.[57] Law's Jacobite sympathies were strong, but he was sufficiently a realist to know how to hide his game until he could help the cause from a position of power. Stanhope was led to believe by Lord Stair that Law regarded the union between Britain and France as the basis of all his projects. Very soon, however, the fundamental rift between Law and Stair became public and Stair sought the overthrow of a minister 'whose daily discourse is that he will raise France to a greater height than ever she was, upon the ruin of England and Holland'.[58] In the end, Law turned the tables on Stair (see below), thus threatening the Anglo-French alliance.

At this time Law had reached the pinnacle of his fortune. He invested in France only. In Paris he purchased the palais Mazarin (built for the cardinal) in the ruc Vivienne, which he made the headquarters of the bank and which later became the Bourse Commerciale. He had a house, the hôtel de Langlée, in the rue Neuve-des-Petits-Champs round the corner, which contained some of the finest furniture in France and a library of 50,000 books for himself and his family. He purchased the hôtel de Nevers nearby, which became the headquarters of the company (and the King's Library in 1721) for 1 million *livres*. In addition, he acquired the domaines de Roissy and du Bourget (he seems to have had a liking for the sites of future airports), Tancarville, the marquisat d'Essiat in the Auvergne and Guermande in the Brie, near Paris. His estates were said to be worth 120,000 *livres* a year.[59]

Law as the friend of James III and the protector of Jacobites

Law's titanic labours did not prevent him, together with his brother William Law, from pursuing a Jacobite agenda. In January 1718 an old friend of Law's, General George Hamilton, a former MP who was out in the Fifteen and then entered James's service, met Law who offered to advance Queen Mary of Modena 100,000 *livres* if he could get a verbal order from the Regent approving the transaction. Law succeeded and James III wrote to thank him for his 'great zeal and attachment' and for the service he had done the queen. Law appreciated the honour of a royal letter, writing to James on 23 March:

> I did not hope that the small occasion I had to show my zeal for the Queen's service should have procured me the honour of a line from Your Majesty. I shall embrace with pleasure every opportunity of showing my attachment and profound respect.[60]

Corresponding with James amounted to high treason in Britain, as Law well knew. General Dillon thought Law 'a top favourite' who could do 'great service', provided he did not 'follow the maxim of courtiers in playing fast and loose and going with the times'.[61] Despite all his commitments, however, in 1719 Law took time to arrange the transfer of the payment of Maria Clementina Sobieska's dowry from Poland to James III in Rome. He was invariably generous to Jacobites in need in Saint-Germain-en-Laye. This led Lord Stair to complain of the welcome John Law gave to Jacobites in France and of the frequent conferences he had with them.[62] After James left

France, the Duke of Berwick, his half brother, arranged for the stoppage of pensions to members of his Household at St Germain who had not followed him to Rome, and many were in distress. Law restored their pensions in full at his own expense. This amounted to a huge sum, no less than 124,050 *livres*.[63] Moreover, he had 100,000 *écus* distributed to indigent Scots in Paris, most of them Jacobite exiles recently returned from Italy and Spain: this drew an official protest from Lord Stair that France was giving support for rebellious Scots, who were even now working for the Pretender.[64] James III fully recognised that many of his friends had become dependent on 'Mr. Law's charity'. William Law, Law's brother, who had come over to France and had become a director of the bank and the Mississippi Company, donated 50,000 *livres* to the Scots College in Paris, a gift the Regent later honoured.[65]

Law's System reaches its zenith

Meanwhile speculation went on in France on an unprecedented scale. Shares in the Compagnie des Indes, still popularly known as Mississippi shares, were bought with only a quarter of the total subscribed in cash and the rest of each 500-*livres* share taken in state bonds (then at a discount of nearly 80 per cent in the exchange in the rue Quincampoix, but taken at face value to make up the purchase value of the shares). Further shares were offered to existing shareholders as 'mothers', 'daughters' and 'granddaughters'.[66] The value of Mississippi stock had risen twenty-fold. The rue Quincampoix in the old Lombard quarter, where Jewish money lenders operated, was narrow and inconvenient for the crowds of speculators of all social ranks and nationalities who flooded into it, and had to be closed by guards at night to prevent all-night dealings. The buying and selling of shares was later transferred to the place Vendôme (William Law's house) and at the last to the hôtel de Soissons belonging to the prince de Carignan, with 160 kiosks neatly arranged in the gardens for this purpose.[67] Successful speculation did wonders for social mobility: great nobles and domestics who had made a fortune on speculation intermarried. The word millionaire was coined at this time. St Simon describes how people tried to force the door of Law's house, came in through the windows or slid down his chimney to see him.[68] Amidst all the turmoil, Law remained calm, planning a reform of French taxation and the provision of free education for students in the University of Paris.

Law's friends

Law did not forget his own friends and relations. Special treatment in the allocation of shares was given to his kinsmen, the Duke of Argyll and the Earl of Islay. Lord Londonderry, who was involved in the later stage of the Atterbury Plot and knew Law well, was allocated shares. Archibald Hutcheson, a prominent Tory MP and political economist (see below) had shares reserved for him.[69] The largest plantations in Louisiana (known as duchies) were allocated to the Oglethorpe sisters, Eleanor, marquise de Mezières, and Fanny Oglethorpe, later marquise des Marches, who were well known at Versailles for their beauty and intelligence. They formed a consortium to send settlers to Louisiana. Eleanor and Fanny were so spectacularly successful in speculating in Mississippi shares that they became two of the wealthiest women in France. Eleanor was extremely active in promoting the Stuart cause, and acted in Paris as secretary to Lord Mar, who could not write in French. Like Law, she spent large sums of money in relieving Jacobite exiles in want and none was turned away from her door. She provided money too for educating the daughters of English gentlemen, Catholics or Anglicans, in France, declaring that English gentlemen would not pay for their daughters' education.[70] This led Bolingbroke, alluding directly to the Oglethorpes, to condemn James III for being so weak as to allow women to intervene in his affairs![71]

While Britain and Holland were alarmed at the prodigious growth in the wealth and trade of France, others rejoiced: Alan Ramsay wrote a poem in praise of the 'Darling of Scots', John Law, who had brought the riches of the world to Paris and made 'Lutecia vie with ancient Rome'. A poem by 'A Lady' on 'The Truly Great Mr. Law' rejoiced

> To see FRANCE and French subjects rul'd by Law,
> To see young LEWIS in his Infant Reign,
> By LAW already make his Glories shine
> Resplendant more by far, than ever he
> Could raise his own by Force or Policie ...
> LET SCOTLAND then be proud, she brought him forth;
> For she alone can glory in his Birth,
> Tho' Law left her when e're she left her K[ing]
> And look'd on her as a mean worthless Thing . . .

The author thought there was 'no place for Law in an usurper's reign' and that the ills of Scotland would not be remedied 'until by Law our monarch be restor'd'.[72]

Atterbury looks to the Regent and John Law for assistance

The position of the Tories in Parliament, where they comprised the majority of the opposition, had been strong during the Whig split of 1717–20 and the open breach between George I and George, Prince of Wales. In 1720, however, any hopes faded of a restoration by parliamentary means through acting with the Whigs in opposition, after the Whigs reunited and King George and the prince were outwardly reconciled. Only the Regent, Atterbury believed, could now secure a restoration. Law's influence on the Regent was essential for success. The bishop wrote to James on 6 May that the Tories had lost 'their balancing power in [the] House of Commons' adding that 'the bulk of the nation will be still in the true interest and on the side of justice and the present settlement will perhaps be detested every day more than it is already and yet no effectual step can be taken to shake it' unless 'the Regent will think it his interest at this juncture to assert your right cause'.[73]

Law, who had now come to regard James's interests as his own, devised a scheme to bring about a reconciliation between the Regent and Philip V and to secure the use of the Irish troops in Spanish service commanded by Ormonde to restore James. James, who very much approved, wrote to Ormonde that everything possible must be done to bring 'Law's idea to perfection'.[74] Law corresponded directly with Ormonde to arrange for the necessary preparations. His friendship with the duke was of long standing for he wrote subsequently that 'le duc d'O[rmonde]' had saved his life.[75] It was presumably Ormonde who secured his escape from prison in 1695, when he was under sentence of death in London. General Dillon, who corresponded directly with Atterbury, reported to him on Law's dealings with Ormonde.[76]

Law gained a great advantage in May 1720 by securing the appointment of Sir Patrick Lawless as Spanish ambassador in France. Lawless, who was a close friend of Ormonde, commanded the Irish troops which formed Philip V's personal guard. It was the same Lawless whose conduct as Spanish ambassador in London in the last two years of Queen Anne's reign had outraged the Whigs, as he went on recruiting Irish troops for the Spanish service, or recruiting for the Pretender, as the Whigs put it.[77] As ambassador in France, Lawless was resolved to act as King James's 'zealous subject'.[78] In addition, Law succeeded in securing the recall of Lord Stair as British ambassador in Paris[79] and may have influenced the choice of the pro-Jacobite Sir Robert Sutton (see below) as Stair's successor. As James's 'chief friend in France' Law appreciated the necessity of neutralising Dubois's influence and found a way of doing so. It was James III's turn to nominate a cardinal at this time and Law suggested he should choose Dubois. Law knew that a cardinal's hat was Dubois's dearest wish, as it would make him the peer of Richelieu and Mazarin and would confer on him the social status he had always lacked. Dubois accepted the offer with alacrity and indicated there was nothing James might not expect from him. Ormonde approved Law's scheme, writing to James to say he hoped that 'Abbé Dubois may get by your means what he desires and that he may not prove ungrateful'.[80] In Rome at any rate, Dubois, as a member of the College of Cardinals, would have to recognise James III as King of England.[81]

Two Jacobite Lords go to Paris

Two emissaries went separately to see the Regent on behalf of the Tories to ask for a Stuart restoration: the Earl of Strafford and the Earl of Orrery. As they played a leading part in the various stages of the Atterbury Plot, some account of their careers and background should be given here. Both were leaders of the Tories in the House of Lords, though they were very different in character and outlook.

The Earl of Strafford

Thomas Wentworth, 3rd Earl of Strafford (1672–1739), an intimate friend of Bishop Atterbury, came to Paris at the particular invitation of Law.[82] His grandfather, Sir William Wentworth, who was slain fighting for Charles I at Marston Moor in 1644, was the younger brother of the Ist Earl of Strafford, Charles's minister, who was executed in 1641. His father, Sir William Wentworth, MP for Thirsk, married a daughter of Sir Allen Apsley, treasurer of the household of James, Duke of York. At the age of 14 in 1687, Thomas, whose mother was a Woman of the Bedchamber to Queen Mary of Modena, became a page in the queen's Household. One of his sisters married Lord Bellew, an Irish Roman Catholic, who fought for James II in the Irish war. Like Ormonde, Wentworth came to terms with the Revolution of 1689. He entered the army as a cornet in Lord Colchester's Horse, and fought in Scotland against Dundee. He took part in the Battle of Steinkirk in 1692 and, as aide-de-camp to William III, was at the disastrous battle of Landen in 1693. He took part in the siege of Namur in 1695, William's first success, by which time he was major in the Life Guards and Groom of the Bedchamber to the king. On the death of his cousin, the 2nd Earl of Strafford, on 15 October 1695 he succeeded to the peerage as Baron

Thomas, 3rd Earl of Strafford. Mezzotint by John Simon after Jacques D'Agar, c. 1710. (Ashmolean Museum)

Raby, but not to the Wentworth Woodhouse estates in Yorkshire which were devised to Thomas Watson, a nephew of the second earl, who changed his name to Wentworth. A long enmity between the two men ensued. In 1697 Raby was given command of the Royal Regiment of Dragoons, which he retained until 1715. In 1698, after the Peace of Ryswick, he accompanied Lord Portland on his embassy to Paris. He served under Marlborough in the 1702 campaign. The next year he was appointed envoy to Berlin, was highly esteemed at the Prussian court and was appointed ambassador there in 1705–11. From 1711 to 1714 he was ambassador extraordinary and plenipotentiary at The Hague to arrange the terms of peace. Swift obtained the post of secretary to the embassy from Raby for a protégé of his, William Harrison. In June 1711, Raby was created Earl of Strafford and he married (with a fortune of £60,000), Anne, daughter and heir of Sir Henry Johnson, MP for and patron of Aldeburgh, a wealthy shipbuilder and a lifelong Jacobite. The marriage was happy as well as fortunate. Strafford was said to be worth £4000 a year, with a house in Twickenham, from which he later corresponded with Alexander Pope, a castle at Stainborough in Yorkshire and a personal fortune worth £46,000, not counting pictures and furniture. Matthew Prior was proposed as a plenipotentiary to negotiate the Treaty of Utrecht when Swift commented 'Lord Strafford is as proud as hell, and how he will bear one of Prior's mean birth on an equal character, I know not', but it appears it was Queen Anne, not Strafford, who objected to Prior, a man of 'mean extraction', being placed in such high position. In fact Strafford liked Prior who, he wrote, 'has an excellent knack of writing pleasant things and tells a story in verse the most agreeable that I ever knew'. Swift thought that Strafford was a man of spirit, but that he could not spell. It is true that Strafford, who had had no formal education, was no scholar, but the niceties of spelling in those days were left to writers and to clerks rather than to gentlemen. Appointed First Lord of the Admiralty and given the Garter in 1712, Strafford was in high favour in the last years of Queen Anne's reign.

On the accession of George I, Strafford was deprived of all his offices and complained repeatedly about difficulties in obtaining repayment for the expenses of his embassy. He was impeached for high treason by Parliament in 1715 for his part in the negotiations for the Treaty of Utrecht. Robert Walpole made a point of reading out from Strafford's papers criticisms of the Allies, particularly the Dutch, with severe reflections on Bothmer, the Hanoverian minister, and the Elector of Hanover. Strafford defended himself ably in the Lords in 1716. The impeachment petered out and he was not excluded from the Act of Indemnity in 1717.

The Earl of Orrery

Lord Orrery, the second emissary, was a different sort of man and much more of a politician. Charles Boyle, 4th Earl of Orrery (1674–1731), was a member of a family where genius was quasi-hereditary. Boyle was the grandson of Roger Boyle, 1st Baron Broghill and 1st Earl of Orrery in the Irish peerage, of Ballymallow, Co. Cork and Marston Bagot, Somerset. The first earl was a Royalist and an Anglican at heart, but he was prepared to serve as one of Cromwell's inner council before taking a prominent part in bringing about the Restoration of 1660.[83] Roger Boyle, the famous scientist, was a brother of the 1st Earl of Orrery. He and his cousin Richard Boyle, 3rd Earl of Burlington, shared a common ancestor in Richard Boyle, 1st Earl of Cork, the 'Great Earl'. Charles was the younger of two sons of Roger Boyle, 2nd Earl of Orrery by Lady Mary Sackville, a sister of the 6th Earl of Dorset, the restoration rake. His parents had a stormy marriage and had separated, so that he was reared by his mother at Knole, the Sackville seat in Kent. Educated at St Paul's' School, Boyle matriculated at Christ Church, Oxford, in 1690 and was tutored by Dr Henry Aldrich, one of the leaders of the High Church party in Oxford. His notion of his high social position was as great as Strafford's, and he was treated with deference by the College. Dr G. V. Bennett described him as 'a priggish and superior youth who took himself and "reputation" very seriously indeed'.[84]

Orrery's undoubted literary and intellectual abilities, however, won the esteem of his Oxford contemporaries. While at Oxford he began collecting a personal library, which was described as one of the finest in Europe, and is preserved in Christ Church today. He shared his family's interest in science and became a Fellow of the Royal Society. Atterbury did his best to encourage him and Aldrich, the Dean of Christ Church, proposed that he should prepare an edition of the *Epistles of Phalaris*. This led him to cross swords with Dr Richard Bentley, head of the King's Library and prompted the celebrated Phalaris controversy, in which Atterbury helped Boyle to reply to Bentley's attack. He sat as an MP in the Irish Parliament for Charleville from 1695–9, and succeeded his brother as Earl of Orrery in 1703. As an Irish peer he could sit in the House of Commons and was a Tory MP for Huntington, with the support of its patron, Lady Sandwich (see below). Becoming a colonel in the army in 1704 and brigadier-general in 1709, he fought under

Charles Boyle, 4th Earl of Orrery. Engraving with etching by Bernard Baron, 1732. (Private Collection)

Marlborough in Flanders and was at Malplaquet in 1709. In March 1706, he married Elizabeth Cecil, a younger daughter of the 5th Earl of Exeter, who died in 1708. An enemy of Marlborough, he became Colonel of the 21st Foot in December 1710, after the fall of the Marlborough–Godolphin administration. In London he was a member of the October Club.

He was critical of Oxford and was disappointed with Bolingbroke's conduct in the last years of Queen Anne's reign. On 5 September 1711 he was created Baron Boyle of Marston, Somerset, which gave him a seat in the House of Lords. From January 1711 until 1713 he was envoy extraordinary and plenipotentiary (and thus Strafford's colleague), to negotiate the Treaty of Utrecht. Unlike Strafford, Orrery was not prosecuted for his part in the Treaty of Utrecht. On the accession of George I, he kept his regiment and he became a Lord of the King's Bedchamber and lord-lieutenant of Somerset, which suggests he was then regarded as a Hanoverian Tory. Turned out as lord-lieutenant of Somerset and deprived of his regiment in 1716, he resigned his Household place. Someone of Orrery's temperament could not have relished being a member of a royal Household in which the English Lords and Gentlemen of the Bedchamber were barred from entering the King's Bedroom, as was the case in George I's.

He may perhaps have been shocked at the brutal treatment of the Jacobite prisoners after the Fifteen, which led to the resignation of Lord Nottingham and the Finches, Hanoverian Tories, in 1716. He voted for the Septennial Act by proxy and did not attend Parliament in 1716. On the Whig split in 1717 he acted with Argyll in opposition and he became one of the circle of George, Prince of Wales. Orrery's links with the Jacobites date from the spring of 1717 when Lord Mar, the Jacobite secretary of state, proposed that Orrery should act as liaison between the English Jacobites and Argyll and his brother Islay. From the middle of 1717 Orrery's name began to figure in the Jacobite correspondence. Cautious and circumspect, he wrote in December 1717 that only 'a considerable force from abroad' could secure a restoration and that it would require strong guarantees to allay people's 'terrible apprehensions about [James's] Religion'. As a military man he could appreciate the strength of the standing army in England, of the additional forces hidden away in Ireland, of the Dutch troops available to the Whigs under the terms of the Barrier Treaties and of George's foreign mercenaries. His Anglican principles did not lead him to any wish to persecute Roman Catholics and, like Lord Burlington, he employed Catholics in his own household. Very soon he became one of James III's most influential advisers and he relayed to James the information he gathered on what went on at the court of George, Prince of Wales (the 'Prince of Hanover' as Orrery called him). The Jacobite Tories were now divided into the followers of Robert Harley, Earl of Oxford, and those of Atterbury, also referred to as Ormonde's party because of the close links between the bishop and Ormonde. Although Atterbury had been Orrery's mentor in Oxford, Orrery was closer to Oxford than to Atterbury. Orrery worked with Anne Oglethorpe, Eleanor's sister, who was Oxford's reputed mistress. She ran great personal risks by carrying James's letters to Oxford, Orrery and Charles Caesar and their replies to him by way of Rotterdam. Cautious and slow to act, Orrery seems to have resented Atterbury's fiery temper and domineering attitude. However, both believed a restoration of the Stuarts was desirable and were prepared to work for it in their different ways. Argyll's reconciliation with George I in 1718 caused something of a breach with Orrery. Argyll was given a British dukedom, enabling him to sit in the House of Lords in his own right (not as a representative peer of Scotland) and was appointed Lord Steward, which reinforced the government's majority in the Upper House. Orrery resented the ministry's domination over the Lords, objected to the creation of 'men of indifferent characters' as peers and to the growing wealth of 'many upstart obscure people' at the expense of the nobility and gentry, so that 'nothing but a total Subversion of the pernicious Scheems of our present managers' could preserve the government and the constitution.[85]

Strafford, Law and the Regent

Strafford was the first to arrive in Paris. General Dillon, James III's representative at the court of Versailles and a friend of Law, wrote to James on 1 April 1720 (n.s.):

> E[arl] of Strafford, who is deeply concerned in the Mississippi company arrived here two days ago, he is very much in the King's interest and perhaps much more than several who make open profession of being so, he and Bishop of Rochester are in perfect good understanding and intimate friends, but I do believe his inclinations to serve K[ing] is not known to many others.[86]

Strafford had shown his zeal in 1719 by sending a letter of credit for £1000 to Atterbury towards the cost of Ormonde's 1719 expedition, a sum later returned to him.[87] Dillon urged James to write to Strafford to thank him for his zeal, especially as Strafford and Law were 'fast friends' and spoke freely of the King's concerns together.[88] Strafford's movements during his two-months' stay in Paris were closely watched by Dillon, who thought Strafford's task was to enlighten the Regent about the real situation in Britain and to try and persuade him to act in union with Spain.[89] Dillon commended Strafford's 'integrity and capacity, his secrecy and caution' and James hoped that Strafford and Lord Orrery who intended going over to Paris later on 'should act in concert'.[90] Matters took a more hopeful turn when James received 'the most favourable general assurances tho not directly from the Regent, with a small supply of money to prove the sincerity of them'. This was the beginning of the payment of the pension, which the Regent had promised but never completely paid.[91]

A bonus was that Law had reserved £20,000-worth of Mississippi stock for Strafford. Law was in Utrecht in 1712, which is presumably when he met Strafford, who now expressed his admiration for his 'old friend Mr. Law, the greatest subject in Europe'.[92] While Lord Stair was still in Paris, however, there were dangers for Jacobites. Earl Poulett, a Tory who gave shelter to John Carnegie of Boysack, a Jacobite out in the Fifteen, felt unable to wait on General Dillon at this juncture and, instead, sent a message through the prince de Vaudemont, an old friend, to apologise. Poulett said that Lord Stair had placed spies on him in his lodgings and that a public meeting with Dillon would 'putt it out of his power to be useful hereafter to paul [the King] whose interest he has much at heart, and will allways be ready to give proofs when occasion offers'.[93]

When Strafford arrived in Paris at the end of April 1720, James had written to him to encourage him in his task. Unfortunately the earl fell ill, 'spitting blood' and 'very apprehensive of some corruption in his lungs'. Strafford, Dillon reported, was 'in no danger, though much out of humour with the French doctors in whose skill he has no sort of confidence'.[94]

While Strafford was incapacitated by his illness, dramatic financial developments took place in Paris. Law had been concerned that too much paper money was in circulation and that it was out of line with the real economy. The Edict of 21 May, as Murphy has shown, was the work of Law himself. It was designed to reduce the price of banknotes and shares to equilibrate them with the reduced prices for gold and silver in order to dampen down speculation.[95] It had serious consequences, however, as it gave an opportunity for Law's enemies, Dubois, the Parlement, the financiers and the *rentiers* (holders of state annuities), who had so much benefited from the corruption of the old financial system, to force through the Edict of 28 May revoking that of 21 May with disastrous consequences. On 29 May Law was dismissed as Controller General and placed under temporary house arrest. Law remained calm and his accounts, when inspected, proved to be in good order. The Regent made a show of refusing to see Law, but gave him an apartment in the Palais Royal, his residence in Paris, and had long meetings with him. Law kept most of his influence with the Regent, who appointed him 'Intendant Général du Commerce'. He kept control of the Compagnie des Indes and the bank. The Regent said publicly that Law had more uprightness and honesty than his critics ever had. Law was no longer in disgrace. Calm returned and the value of shares went up again.[96]

In early June, Law went to see Strafford, who was now recovered, saying he (Law) would always be regarded in France as a foreigner and that 'he could not hope for a solid establishment but by restoring the king and delivering his country from oppression'. Scenting that something was in the air, Stanhope arrived in Paris and went to see Strafford and then the Regent. When Strafford returned Stanhope's visit, as courtesy required, Stanhope told him he had obtained more from the Regent than he had expected. Undeterred, after consulting Law Strafford had an audience with the Regent on 13 June (n.s.). After an exchange of civilities and apologising for his French which 'was not of the best', Strafford said he had come to receive 'the advice of a disinterested friend whom he esteem'd of a long time'. Then, Dillon reported:

E[arl] Strafford touched with applause on the happy beginning of the regency, and the singular penetration in finding out the only man capable to redress decay affairs were in at the late king's death, that the envy of neighbours was the ground form'd to overthrow the prosperous course of his regency in the downfall of Mr. Law. [The] Regent agreed that he knew full well E[arl] of Sunderland had a great share in the matter but shew'd to have a more favorable opinion of Ld. Stanhope which E[arl] Strafford refuted by strong instances and added that the intrigue must have been concerted with some of the ministry here. Regent reply'd that he knew who he meant and named abbé du Bois. E[arl] Strafford infer'd these must be reputed his most dangerous enemys and urged that it was the same people who engaged in the war of Spain unnecessary for the security of the succession ... Regent confessed was sorry for having entered into that war.

E[arl] Strafford came insensibly to the main article of proving to him that the present government of evans [England] could not be of great use to his interest, because ten to one of the nation would act in opposition to it. Regent acknowledged that Stanhope had declared so much to him, then E[arl] Strafford demonstrated that the said government had not even the intention of being usefull to him further than what would secure their own turn.

They and their adherents, Strafford continued, 'form'd a province of the empire from whose interest they would not recede upon his account' and assured the Regent that 'he had but to raise a finger to secure England entirely'. 'I comprehend you said Regent that is by means of the chevalier [James] the other answer'd I need not explain the matter farther to a prince of your penetration.' The Regent observed that he feared war with the emperor but did not fear Holland. This long conference ended with 'many assurances of esteem and friendship' from the Regent for Strafford.[97] On 15 June Strafford went to take leave of the Regent who thanked him for his friendship and frankness. Strafford did not pursue the 'main affair' further and he told the Regent he 'left it to another who spoke better French and would explain matters to him more fully'. The Regent asked who the person was, but Strafford would not name him. The Regent gave his word that Dubois would not be told, but agreed that Law should be fully apprised.

The next day Strafford told Law all that had passed, that the Regent seemed inclined to seek an accommodation with Spain and that Lawless should be given a hint of this. Law thought Dubois was still kept in place 'to bamboozle English ministry'. It was agreed that Strafford would urge Orrery to come to France quickly.

Dillon thought that Strafford had acted his part with 'firmness of spirit' and boldness of temper'. He had broken the ice and taken considerable risks to prepare the ground for Lord Orrery, with whom he had conferred before leaving England.[98] James thought that Strafford had 'acted a wise and generous part', while Law had acted his part 'in an efficacious and solid manner'.[99] To reward Strafford, James sent him a 'letter without any superscription' [i.e. in his own hand] to thank him 'most heartily' for his 'singular attachment and affection'. On his return to England, Strafford acquainted Atterbury and Orrery only with his negotiations in France.[100]

Orrery and the Regent

On his side, Orrery postponed his departure for Paris several times. He wanted to wait until Parliament was prorogued and London emptied.[101] He was involved in speculation in South Sea stock and this may have been another reason for delay.[102] His main priority was to arrive after Lord Stair had left Paris and Sir Robert Sutton, the new ambassador, with Jacobite connections, was in place. Sutton was the nephew and heir of Lord Lexington, a good friend of James, who wrote to Sutton after his appointment, expressing his appreciation of the new ambassador, praising his family's 'merits' and adding that Sutton was now in 'a situation to render him service'.[103] Sutton obliged by not informing the English government of Orrery's mission to Paris. Jacobite counter-intelligence at this time may have been better than the British government's, as Sutton sent his dispatches from Paris through the Jacobite Colonel William Cecil, who succeeded Orrery in 1731 as James's representative in London.[104] In addition, Orrery wanted to confer with John Menzies after his return from Paris, because of Menzies's 'intimacy with Law'.[105] Above all, he sought to give the impression he was travelling merely for diversion and pleasure. On the eve of Orrery's departure, another overture was made to Argyll and Islay by a woman (probably Anne Oglethorpe). James did not approve because, as he wrote to Orrery, 'I am always shy of imploying any body particularly women, who often out of too great a desire of medling in business, love to intrude themselves into nice matters which they have not skill enough to manage.'[106] Given the contribution made by Jacobite women to the cause, this was unfair. Orrery's mission to Paris was very much his own initiative and he insisted that his instructions from or his own letters to Rome might be seen only by James himself.[107] 'Lord Orrery', James wrote, 'has given me very good reasons for his not entering into partnership with the rest.'[108] His aim seems to have been to shake off Atterbury's tutelage. He had refused to attend a meeting of James's friends in England before he left, lest it attracted the government's attention. James was sympathetic to this stance, writing to Dillon that Orrery 'declined entering into society with my other friends, but is not less sincere and may be more useful. I do not believe he will decline seeing you and speaking freely to you in Paris' and thought he would 'behave with the same zeal and prudence he has ever shown in my affairs'.[109]

Orrery arrived in Paris towards the end of July, at about the same time as Lord Lansdowne, Sir William Wyndham and William Shippen, whose presence in Paris was unconnected with Orrery's mission. Bolingbroke, Dillon reported, was doing James 'all the ill offices' he could but although Sir William Wyndham was his 'old companion in diversion', Lord Lansdowne was sure Wyndham was true to his principles and reported that Wyndham himself made a 'strong protestation of his steadfast attachment to the King and readiness to serve him when occasion offers'.[110] In fact Wyndham wrote to James from Paris to assure him of 'his constant duty and zeal to your service'; and hopes for the 'greatest blessing' of his restoration.[111]

From the standpoint of events in Paris, Orrery had tarried too long. He arrived as the price of shares collapsed, there was a run on the bank, and Law was beset by popular tumults. Presumably so as not to attract attention, Orrery refused while in Paris to see Henry Campion, a prominent former Tory MP connected with Ormonde and Arran (Ormonde's brother), who was bringing back from Rome a memorial from James for his friends in England.[112] Despite his fluency in French, Orrery's long awaited private audience with the Regent was a disaster. Reporting to James on 29 July, Orrery wrote:

I made all the haste hither I could upon your earnest desire that I should do so and upon some representations that there was a good disposition in the Regent to serve you, but I arrived here in a very unlucky season, when affairs are in great confusion and they seem to have so much business of their own upon their hands that they cannot think of other people's. I have seen the Regent in private and endeavoured to give him occasion of entering into some necessary particulars, because it would by no means be proper for me to open myself unless he leads the way, which whatever his inclinations may be, I am apt to think he will hardly do in this unfortunate conjuncture of affairs.

For Orrery to expect the Regent to help him out by broaching the subject of a restoration first, was a vain hope, for Orléans had a well deserved reputation for being the most inscrutable man in France. Orrery thought some people might have been too sanguine in their expectations of the Regent or that the situation in France had got much worse. Orléans still retained the Abbé Dubois in place with whom, Orrery wrote, 'I have not courage enough to negotiate', though it was said that Dubois's attitude had changed of late. 'He is much suspected and his general character is so disadvantageous that most people are afraid of him.' Law was 'hearty and sincere' though much taken up with his own affairs and was being accused of being responsible 'for the ills the country groans under at present'.[113] Orrery, Dillon thought, was

> a very judicious, sedate, intelligent man and truly zealous for the King. He is of a nice wary disposition and excessively cautious in his way of acting, by which I fear he is not so proper to treat with the Regent whose uncertain temper requires to have matters facilitated and explained to him in a clear manner and even with a certain convincing resolution.

Unless Orrery took the initiative, his mission would be useless.[114] James, trying to be encouraging, wrote to Orrery in August 1720:

> It was very unlucky you found matters in such confusion, for that cannot but obstruct and delay what was the chief interest of your journey, however I am in hopes that you may be able to find some opportunity of having some free discourse with the Regent and I believe you cannot take better advice in all that relates to him than Mr. Law who is a sincere friend to me. As to Abbé Dubois, Dillon will have sufficiently informed you of my present thoughts as to him and on the whole you will certainly do well to stay some time in Paris in hopes of carrying back some encouragement to our friends in England.[115]

Ignoring James's advice, Orrery went back to England almost immediately. In the end, Orrery's trip did more harm than good. James thought that Dillon could manage the Regent better and that these negotiations had best be left to Dillon, Law and to Lord Lansdowne (of whom more later).

The fall of Law

After Orrery's departure from Paris, Law did all he could to persuade the Regent to support the Stuart cause.[116] His power and influence were waning, however, and public discontent was mounting. As the summer proceeded, Law's System was gradually dismantled.[117] Law, who never sought to enrich himself personally, remained calm. The Regent himself thought Law had more probity and honesty than his enemies. Many people, however, were keener on short-term profit than long-term investment and began to change their paper money back into gold and silver. In the vanguard, was the duc de Bourbon, who sent out his servants in carts loaded with paper money to the bank and changed 25 million *livres* (the rate of exchange was about 14 LIVRES TOURNOIS to the pound sterling) into specie, while the prince de Conti withdrew 14 million.[118] Law was removed as director of the Compagnie des Indes in August, while in mid September banknotes of high denomination and shares were devalued. On 17 November 1720 the bank closed down for the last time.[119] Law was driven into exile and all his properties in France were confiscated. With him went one of the best chances of a restoration of the Stuarts in the eighteenth century. On the other hand, France missed out on the financial revolution and a good system of state borrowing. The return to the old, corrupt and inefficient financial system led to the bankruptcy of the state, a chief cause of the Revolution of 1789.

2

A Jacobite Opportunity: The South Sea Crisis and the Possibility of a Constitutional Restoration

As the eclipse of John Law deprived the Tories of the hope of a restoration with the help of France and Spain, another opportunity presented itself with the bursting of the South Sea Bubble, which rocked the Whig ministry and threatened the very survival of the Hanoverian dynasty. Scandal on such a large scale was made possible by the boldness of the venture itself, insider dealing, ministerial corruption, and the dangers of a too rapid expansion of the money supply, hardly then understood. The crisis hit also the many joint-stock companies which had sprung up at this time and helped to ruin those who had been playing the market.[1] As early as 1719 Daniel Defoe had predicted a 'degenerated Government' involved in corrupt stockjobbing who would 'make a transfer of King George and his Crown for a half per Cent'. Writing to Francis Atterbury on 21 September 1720, Alexander Pope, who had himself speculated in the stocks, spoke of 'universal poverty' and 'universal deluge',[2] while Atterbury himself, in the debate in the House of Lords on 9 January 1721, compared the consequence of the collapse of public credit to a plague or 'pestilence'. In his *Essay towards Preventing the Ruin of Great Britain* (1721) the philosopher George Berkeley held out a picture of the decay of the British: 'they degenerated, grew servile flatterers of men in power, adopted Epicurean notions, became venal, corrupt, injurious, which drew upon them the hatred of God and man, and occasioned their final ruin'.[3] James Hamilton, the Jacobite agent in London, commented 'the humour of stockjobbing was such and the impatient thirst for immense riches was so general in all ranks and persuasions that few who dealt in Change Alley but looked on our

Chimeras as so many philosophers stone, that neither religion nor morality could resist'.[4]

The South Sea Company

The South Sea Company originated in the great appetite of South America for slaves and the Asiento contract, which gave Britain the right to export slaves from Africa to South America, as part of the peace of 1713, was proposed by the new Tory ministry of Robert Harley, Earl of Oxford. Underlying it all, was the age-old dream, going back to Drake and Raleigh, of getting access to South American markets and be paid in Spanish bullion. From the start, the scope of the South Sea Company was hampered by the concession made by Townshend and the Whigs in 1709 (to keep the Dutch on board in the war against France) which gave the Dutch an equal share with Britain in the trade to South America. In the South Sea scheme, the whole £9 million of the National Debt was to be incorporated into the company to carry on the South Sea trade from 1 August 1711. Under the terms of the Asiento Treaty signed on 26 March 1713, the South Sea Company was allowed to supply negroes to the Spanish South American colonies for 30 years at the rate of 4800 negroes a year and to be allowed to have establishments in the ports of Buenos Aires, Havana and Vera Cruz. The company ticked over at first, trading on expectations. In actual fact only one fleet a year was allowed to go to South America and sometimes none, so that this anticipated rich trade proved elusive.[5] Contemporaries were unaware, however, of the real situation.

A Whig takeover of the South Sea Company

At the Hanoverian succession, the Tory directors of the South Sea Company were replaced by Whigs and its first governor, Oxford, was succeeded by George, Prince of Wales.[6] In 1718 George I himself became governor, with the Prince of Wales as deputy governor. In December 1719 subscriptions for South Sea stock were opened, with the notion that the government would be relieved of the burden of the National Debt, which was to be liquidated in 25 years. The basic idea was that holders of annuities for a term of years, which the government could not buy out or reduce to a lower rate unless they consented, should voluntarily exchange them, at a price to be agreed, for a capital sum in the form of a new South Sea stock. The Bank of England, the company's competitor, tried but failed to outbid the South Sea scheme. The managers of the South Sea scheme were Sir John Blunt, scrivener and a Baptist, who had acquired extensive real estate in London. More far-seeing than some other promoters, Blunt had wished for the South Sea Company to get the trade of Africa, Nova Scotia and the formerly French part of St Kitts, which would have made the company more viable, but he failed in this objective.[7] George Caswall, another Baptist manager, MP for Leominster, was a partner in the firm of Turner, Sawbridge and Caswall (described by Defoe as the 'three capital sharpers of Britain'). They were bankers in Lombard Street and operated under the name and charter of the Sword Blade Company. This company had started with making fashionable grooved swords, failed and later became bankers to the South Sea Company, of which Caswall (a Whig supporter of the Prime Minister, Sunderland) was one of the directors. Robert Knight, the cashier of the South Sea Company, who plays an important part in our story, grew so rich during the Bubble that he acquired £67,000 worth of property in 24 counties and became an MP and the patron of the venal borough of Great Grimsby.[8] The Chancellor of the Exchequer, John Aislabie, believed in the viability of the scheme and purchased £22,000 worth of South Sea stock, for which he paid in cash. Emulating the tactics if not the strategy of John Law, however, to help the launch of the scheme and to facilitate the passing of the South Sea Bill in Parliament, the managers turned to gratification and the acquisition of 'friends'.

The 'friends' of the South Sea Bill

After the bursting of the Bubble, the parliamentary report of inquiry looked at the cases of the Lords and MPs who were said to have received stock without paying for it, with the right to sell it back to the company at a profit whenever they chose. Knight acted as the registrar, transferring the shares in his own name, either directly or through intermediaries, so that the real recipients were not known. He entered these transactions in a ledger, with green covers, known as the 'Green Book', which showed the real and bogus recipients. The Green Book was not available to the Secret Committee, who had to rely on information given by some South Sea directors. It was believed that in February to March 1720 £50,000 of unpaid-for South Sea stock was given to George I (which was not published in the Report), and £30,000 to James Craggs, the Postmaster General, who was said by Arthur Onslow (Speaker Onslow) to have been 'the principal agent for the Administration in the whole of the South Sea project and bore the chief blame in the whole iniquity of it'.[9] Sunderland was accused by the Committee of making a profit of £50,000, while the Secretary to the Treasury, Charles Stanhope (Stansgate in Knight's accounts), received £10,000. James Craggs (son of the Postmaster General), who managed the House of Commons for Sunderland and introduced the South Sea Bill in the Commons, suggested the distribution of £10,000 worth of stock each to the Duchess of Kendal, George I's German mistress and his secret morganatic wife, and her two 'nieces', George I's daughters by her. Another German mistress, the Countess von Platen, had £10,000 too. George, Prince of Wales, had his own share of free stock. The distribution of free shares helped to launch the stock, to neutralise the opposition of the Bank of England and to secure the passing of the South Sea Bill through Parliament.[10]

The report of the Secret Committee of Inquiry into the South Sea scheme listed the members of the House of Lords and the House of Commons who were accused of taking free shares before 2 April 1720, the date when the South Sea Bill passed through Parliament. Seven peers were said to have received unpaid-for stock, five Whigs and two Tories. The Tory Lords named were Lord Gower, who had £20,000, and Lord Lansdowne, who had £10,000 in two lots of £5000. As Knight's Green Book was missing at the time of the inquiry, this could not be proved. Edward Gibbon (grandfather of the historian), a South Sea director and a strong supporter of James III, testified, however, that he had a note from Lord Lansdowne accepting responsibility for payment of this stock. Lord Gower, however, had paid for his shares as he purchased South Sea stock from Gibbon's holdings.[11] Twenty-six MPs were said to have received free stock, eight of whom were Tories: Sir Coplestone Warwick Bamfylde, John Bamfylde, Sir John Bland, Sir William Carew, Colonel James Grahme, Charles Longueville, John Roberts and Sir Thomas Sebright. John Chester, a South Sea director and a wealthy West Indian merchant, testified that Sir Coplestone Warwick Bamfylde, Sir John Bland, Sir Thomas Sebright, Charles Longueville and Sir William Carew had bought their stock from him after the passing of the South Sea Bill.[12]

The South Sea scheme accepted by Parliament

Sunderland, the Prime Minister, and Stanhope steered the passage of the South Sea Bill through the Lords. It met with strong opposition at the committee stage on 5 April from Lord North and Grey, and influential Tory peer, who did not speculate in South Sea shares. He declared:

> that in his judgment it was unjust in its nature, and might prove fatal in its consequence since it seemed calculated for the enriching of a few, and the impoverishing of a great many, and not only made way but countenanced the pernicious practice of stock-jobbing, which produced an irreparable mischief, by diverting the genius of the people from trade and industry.

He was seconded by the Duke of Wharton (see below), who forecast accurately what did happen:

> that the South Sea project might prove of infinite disadvantage to the nation; first it gave foreigners an opportunity to double and treble the vast sums they had in our public funds, which could not but tempt them to withdraw their capital stock, with their immense gains to other countries, which may drain Britain of a considerable part of its gold and silver. Secondly, that the artificial and prodigious rise of the South Sea Stock was a dangerous bait, which might decoy many unwary people to their ruin and allure them by a false prospect of gain, to part with what they had got by their labour and industry, to purchase imaginary riches.

Lord Cowper, a Whig who played a leading role in the opposition, and the Duke of Buckingham, who had married a natural daughter of James II, also spoke against the bill.[13] Nevertheless, the South Sea Bill passed easily and it was given Royal Assent on 7 April 1720.

The South Sea Bubble

Party differences were set aside, as people sought to get rich quick. The City of London was set for a boom and the buying spree began in May. Spurred by a determination to make fast capital gains, the price of stock rocketed after the first and second subscriptions. Prices paid for the third and fourth subscriptions were extravagant and bore no relation to the value of the assets and the profitability of the South Sea Company. The market was flooded with South Sea subscriptions which changed hands at ever increasing prices as the price of South Sea stock soared. As the English tried to follow the example of Parisian millionaires, a frenzy of speculation began in Exchange Alley, at the corner of

Lombard Street, London's equivalent of the rue Quincampoix in Paris, and in South Sea House, near Threadneedle Street. The books for the third subscription which opened in June and July 1720 saw the highest price paid for South Sea stock. George I and his German entourage left in June for a six-month stay in Hanover, after selling their South Sea stock and transferring the money to Hanover through Sels, an Amsterdam banker.[14] Shrewd investors, such as the Duchess of Marlborough, John Barber (see below), Thomas Guy, the Dutch and the Swiss sold at the peak. It took time for others to realise that to pay the dividends promised, the company would need to earn £15 million a year. The reality was that South Sea profits proved elusive, as South Americans were hostile to British traders and their ships were kept out by the *guarda costas*, whereas the Dutch were more successful in evading Spanish controls by pretending to sail to the Dutch East Indies.[15]

In September 1720, the prices of South Sea shares began to fall. The bursting of the South Sea Bubble ruined a multitude of people and caused universal anger against the Whig ministry and the Hanoverian royal family. Thomas Brodrick, an independent Whig MP who headed the Secret Committee of Inquiry into the South Sea affair, wrote: 'the consternation is inexpressible, the rage beyond expression, and the case desperate'.[16] Arthur Onslow noted:

> the rage against the Government was such for having as they thought drawn them into this ruin, that I am almost persuaded, the King being at this time abroad, that could the Pretender [James] have then landed at the Tower, he might have rode to St. James's with very few hands held up against him'.[17]

Robert Molesworth, a prominent Whig MP who had embraced 'Country' principles, agreed: 'our whole multitude will turn Jacobite in a very few months more'.[18]

The Jacobite response

The Jacobite tactics were now twofold. First, to do everything in their power, in alliance with Whigs in opposition, to harass the Hanoverian regime and to win hearts and minds in an appeal to the country against parliamentary corruption and the standing army. The persistent demand for a free Parliament, elected without government pressure on elections, looked back to 1660 when a free Parliament restored

Charles II. The inclusion of independent Whig allies was essential to make it a 'constitutional' restoration. The second plan was for an internal Jacobite rising assisted by Irish troops in French and Spanish service (see Chapter 3). Both routes were pursued simultaneously. The Declaration of James III, dated at Rome 10 October 1720, which was written by Lord Lansdowne from Paris and approved by Atterbury, was well designed to appeal to hearts and minds.

> Whilst our countrey [James declared] remained in any tolerable condition of prosperity, We were the less sensible of our own misfortunes, but now that so great a calamity is brought upon it by the avarice of a few miscreants, our tenderness for its re-establishment in plenty and peace encreaseth our impatience to return to our dominions, not so much out of a desire to find Justice ourself, as to do it to others, and to have an opportunity to show Ourself the Father of our People.
>
> We wish for no other method for this our mutual Deliverance, but by the Repentance and Unanimity of our own Subjects; that all past errors may be effaced by their future behaviour, that such a Restoration may be effected as was that of our Royal Uncle King Charles the 2nd, without the least bloodshed, domestick disturbance, or obligations to foreign assistance, that the King and his People may meet and embrace with Hearts overflowing with affection; that trade may again flourish, credit and publik faith restored, and honest Industry encouraged. We call God to witness who inspects and directs the Hearts of Kings, that our ambition is not so much to wear the Crown of our ancestors, as to show that we deserve it.

The Declaration spoke of the recent providential birth of Charles Edward, Prince of Wales. It went on to proclaim that Britain would never be happy under a foreign yoke:

> As our birth was English, so is our heart entirely English, and altho' driven from our cradle to wander in exile, in foreign countries, Our education hath been truely English: We have made the Constitution of Our Countrey our first study, and in that search have been delighted to find that our ancient Laws have provided everything that a just or reasonable King can desire, either for his felicity or grandeur: it is that ancient constitution We wish to be restored and being restored, resolve to maintain ... We promise upon the word of

a King that upon our first accession to the Crown. We will refer the state of the Nation under all its heads of grievance to a free Parliament, that you shall have nobody to blame, if the least article should be wanting to your future security and happiness.[19]

The Declaration was widely distributed and 'hundreds of copies were sent to 'every county in England with good effect'.[20]

The prevailing climate was highly favourable, but Atterbury, giving this as his opinion only, thought action could not be taken at once as:

the losers in this game are under expectation of having their losses made up to them in the approaching session and will not plunge hastily into any new hazardous scheme at this juncture, nor perhaps till they begin to despair. Relief cannot possibly come till some time after the Parliament has met, and then when the hopes of the disaffected will be kept for some time in suspense and while they have such hopes they will not run any such risks, and an unsuccessful attempt ruins the same for many years.[21]

Lord Carteret appointed secretary of state

Stanhope, who had based British foreign policy on close collaboration with France through his friend Dubois, died before the report of the Secret Committee of Inquiry into the South Sea affair. He was not one of the ministers chiefly implicated, though he had accepted some unpaid-for South Sea stock. His sudden death of an apoplectic fit on 5 February 1721 was attributed either to a violent clash in the Lords with the Duke of Wharton, who led the attack on the government on the South Sea affair,[22] or to a thirteen-hour potation at the Duke of Newcastle's house the night before.[23] Stanhope was replaced as one of the secretaries of state first by Walpole's brother-in-law, Lord Townshend, who was shortly afterwards succeeded by Sunderland's choice, Lord Carteret. Carteret had been brought up as a Tory before going over to the Whigs and had family links with Jacobite exiles.[24] Carteret had Jacobite contacts in England, too, for in the summer of 1721 he was said to have paid daily visits to Atterbury.[25]

Destouches and Chammorel, two well-informed diplomats

At this time we have exceptionally good information about English politics, some of it acquired directly from Carteret, by two French diplomats in London. The first was Philippe Néricault Destouches (1680–1754), a minor French playwright, who had been secretary to Dubois as ambassador to London in 1717. The London embassy was usually given to a great French nobleman but Destouches was probably chosen by Dubois, now French foreign minister, to prevent the nature of the links with the British government from being exposed. Destouches was an intelligent observer, who was married to an Englishwoman and understood English. In addition, the close alliance between France and Britain gave him privileged access to English ministers. The second French diplomat was Chammorel, who had been secretary to d'Iberville's embassy in the last months of Queen Anne's reign and was secretary to Destouches's embassy. Chammorel, like d'Iberville, was favourable to the Tories and had many contacts among them.[26]

The Secret Committee of Inquiry into the South Sea Bubble

The Secret Committee on the South Sea affair consisted of thirteen MPs chosen by ballot on 21 december 1720. It included five Tories: Archibald Hutcheson, a lawyer who managed Ormonde's financial affairs but took an independent line, Edward Jeffreys, a prominent lawyer, Colonel Thomas Strangways, who figures in the 1721 list (taken to Rome by Layer), and two active Jacobites, General Charles Ross and the Hon. Dixie Windsor.[27] James Craggs junior, the Secretary of State, died of smallpox on 16 February 1721, the day Thomas Brodrick reported from the Secret Committee. The committee found 'many false and fictitious entries' in the books to conceal 'a Scene of Iniquity and Corruption' and the supposed sale of stock to persons 'whose names were designed to be concealed', in order to facilitate the acceptance of the South Sea proposals. Robert Knight, the chief cashier of the South Sea Company, was reported to have disposed of £800,000 'to Persons of Distinction'. But Knight had fled the country at the end of January, taking with him the Green Book, which revealed the identity of those who had taken bribes in South Sea stock. He went to Antwerp, from which extradition was virtually impossible. The universal cry was to get Knight back to give evidence, but Sunderland and George I, acting through the Duchess of Kendal, secretly blocked moves to secure his return. For instance, Destouches wrote urgently to Dubois and the Duke of Orléans: 'in Heaven's name' disregard the letter from King George to have Knight arrested, hide him, or send him to a country out of reach of England. The Duchess of Kendal particularly asked that this be done.[28] George I was believed to have gone as far as to give orders that Knight should be assassinated.[29] The Secret Committee, however, had the evidence of Sir John Blunt, who thought his best safeguard was to co-operate with the committee. It turned out that £10,000 of the free stock given to Sunderland was not for him, but was given as further gratifications to George I's German favourites, though this was not revealed to Parliament.[30] The names of Charles Stanhope and of James Craggs the elder, the Postmaster General, were revealed. The Duchess of Kendal, her two 'nieces' and the Countess von Platen were named, but not George I, who had received £50,000.[31] Charles Stanhope was saved by three votes, with the help of Walpole and after Sir Joseph Jekyll and Viscount Molesworth had received messages from George I asking them not to vote against Stanhope, whereupon they abstained. Philip Dormer Stanhope, Lord Stanhope, the future Earl of Chesterfield, helped to save his kinsman by making a very good speech, invoking the memory and achievements of James Stanhope.[32] All Scottish members voted with the Court, except General Ross and Alexander Urquhart, two Jacobites.[33]

Sunderland seeks an alliance with the Tories

Sunderland's position had now become precarious, though he retained the favour of George I. He had been forced to take into his administration Walpole and Townshend, but had little prospect of acting in harmony with them. To save himself, Sunderland made overtures to the Tories. He held out the prospect of an early dissolution of the 1715 Parliament, which had been continued for seven years by the Septennial Act of 1716, and of a new Parliament with free elections, that is without the use of government influence and money: a free Parliament as in 1660. This is what had been demanded in James III's Declaration. In the prevailing political climate, it was thought that there would be a Tory landslide at such an election. Sir Robert Walpole later told Sir Dudley Ryder, the Attorney-General, that 'Sunderland had entered into a scheme to bring over the Pretender. After his death a letter to thank him was found among his papers'. Walpole was of opinion that a free Parliament would be a Tory Parliament and that it would lead 'inevitably' to a Stuart restoration.[34] This would lead to a constitutional restoration and Sunderland was not involved in the insurrectional part of the Atterbury Plot. The length to which Sunderland was prepared to go to preserve himself from the hostility of George, Prince of Wales, was shown by a document in the hands of Charles Stanhope, found by the prince after his accession to the throne: Sunderland had contemplated the seizure of the prince and his deportation to any part of the world chosen by George I and had agreed with Charles Stanhope's view that this could be justified, since (Stanhope' had added extraragantly) the Son of God himself had been sacrificed for the salvation of mankind.[35]

Who did Sunderland deal with in his negotiations with the Tories? Atterbury had his own lines of communication with Sunderland at private meetings on the plans to build a new dormitory for Westminster School, which Sunderland supported.[36] Moreover, Atterbury was said to be in secret correspondence with Sunderland.[37] Any discussions he had with Sunderland on the new Parliament, however, were not reported to James III, or else his letters on this subject are missing. From the available evidence, the Tories principally involved in the dealings with Sunderland were Lord Arran (Ormonde's brother), Lord Orrery, Charles Caesar, Lord Aberdeen and Alexander Urquhart, all of whom, apart from Arran, were connected with Oxford rather than with Atterbury. Lord Oxford, who was then 'at death's door',[38] took no direct part in the negotiations. Archibald Hutcheson, who conducted a separate correspondence with Sunderland, argued that free elections were the only solution to solve the country's ills.[39]

Meanwhile popular protests reached an unprecedented scale. Destouches reported that 50,000–60,000 copies of the London Address expressing public anger at the failure to punish the guilty in the South Sea scandal had been printed, that towns and counties followed London's lead, and that the scale of discontent was compared to that at the end of James II's reign. The whole nation was calling for a new Parliament. On the one hand a republican party was growing, on the other there was talk of an invitation to King James. There was a 'horrible hatred' for the royal family, especially for Caroline, Princess of Wales, who had offended nearly all the English ladies of her Household in public, and people complained that the crown was in the hands of foreigners. Instead of Whigs and Tories, there was now the court party, the republican party and the Jacobites, the last two were equally dangerous to King George.[40] Public credit as well as the nation was ruined. The Civil List was used up and the government bankrupt. It turned out that many receivers of the land tax had gambled their receipts on South Sea stock, so that taxes had not come in. Sunderland seemed disconcerted and indeed frightened. Destouches reported that Sunderland had tried to persuade the King there was no resort left but to throw himself into the hands of the Tories, and he was certain that Sunderland had canvassed many persons in that party. Speaker Onslow subsequently wrote that Sunderland's 'desperation drove him into negotiations with the Pretender'.[41]

Charles Caesar, writing to James, confirmed the picture given by Destouches and concluded:

> the ferment is so high and without any prospect of being lay'd but by your restoration. I am in great hopes it will be brought about without foreign assistance. Lord Orrery having given you a full account of what Lord Sunderland has judged to do for your service, it is unnecessary for me to enlarge upon that affair ... He [Sunderland] has it in his power to remove all difficulties that lie in the way of your restoration. I am induced to believe he will act sincerely because I cannot see he has any other way to secure his head but by throwing himself at your feet.

At this time, Lord Orrery persuaded Lady Sandwich, a keen Jacobite, to attend Court so as to gather any information useful to James.[42]

Charles Caesar reported to James that Sunderland 'offered the Tories *carte blanche* if they would heartily come in to support the present government, but they will not hearken to any offers but what shall be for your restoration'. Lord Oxford, who thought Sunderland was the ablest politician in England, seems to have approved the negotiations with him.[43] Orrery confirmed this, writing that Sunderland had made 'great offers' to Lord Arran, Ormonde's brother, and that the Tories would not come in unless he entered into measures for a restoration by 'putting the Army and the Parliament into their hands'. Sunderland had two or three meetings with Orrery without coming 'plain to the high point'.[44] We do not know the *eventual* outcome, as the letter from Orrery to James reporting on these meetings appears to be missing from the Stuart papers. Orrery again sought to keep his negotiations with Sunderland independent from Atterbury's because the bishop's behaviour was not 'liked by many here'.[45] Sunderland's chosen intermediary was Alexander Urquhart, a Scottish MP and a close friend of Colonel James Grahme, James II's former Privy Purse. Urquhart's brother, a naval officer, had refused to accept Hanoverian rule and gone into exile to join the Russian navy under Thomas Gordon, its Jacobite admiral.[46] Sunderland, James Hamilton, the Jacobite agent in London, reported,

> contrived a meeting with Mr. Urquhart and told him freely that he was sick of the Whigs who were ungovernable enthusiasticks and as

he knew Mr. Urquhart to be a man of honour and principle he gave him full power to assure the Tories if they would be his friends in keeping off the impeachment his enemies designed against him, he would order things to their desire and put life his and fortune in their power for a security. Mr. Urquhart immediately communicated this to some of his friends and managed the business so well as to bring Sunderland and them to talk the matter together and even brought about a meeting between Sunderland and Ld. Orrery but the mistrust and shyness of both kept them off the main point. Sir there this matter stands and tis Urquhart's opinion that nothing more can be expected from Sunderland than hints considering his present situation. But Sunderland will give his friends his honour that the Parliament shall be sent a packing ... also that the H[ouse] of Commons shall be entirely of their own making so that the Tories shall have a way open for England to do the thing themselves and if the Tories do not make the most of the opportunity 'twill be none of E[arl] Sunderland's fault.[47]

The Tories save Sunderland

On 15 March 1721 the adjourned report of the Committee of Secrecy on the South Sea relating to the Earl of Sunderland came before the House of Commons. The motion was that '£50,000 of the capital stock of the South Sea Company was taken in by Robert Knight, late Cashier of the said Company, for the use and upon the Account of Charles Earl of Sunderland, a Lord of Parliament and First Commissioner of the Treasury, without any valuable consideration paid or sufficient security given for Payment for, or Acceptance of the same'.[48] Sunderland, John Menzies, the former Jacobite agent in London, reported 'acted his part with great dexterity' and that many of his Whig friends as well as Tories 'engaged to him' stood by him and voted for the noes. 'The Prince of Wales laying aside all impartiality or dignity, was in the gallery, to animate MPs against him by his presence. Sir Thomas Hanmer [a Hanoverian Tory] the mouth of that interest, made a very elegant but in effect a very violent speech against him and tho in smooth words pleaded no less than that he ought to be hanged.'[49]

The motion was lost by 172 votes to 233, a majority of 61 only, with many Tories voting for Sunderland. However, two prominent Jacobite MPs, George Lockhart and William Shippen, voted against Sunderland. Shippen exclaimed afterwards that he would be 'against them all in their turns. Overcome, overcome all Whigs'.[50] Walpole, nicknamed 'the Screen', saved Sunderland, not out of goodwill but to protect King George.[51] Had Knight been in England still, Menzies thought, the outcome would have been very different.[52]

James III had been sceptical about Sunderland's sincerity, but had left it to his friends in England to pursue negotiations with that minister, provided they did not impair plans for a rising in England and Scotland. He was pleased that Lord Oxford had recovered and that he was ready to serve him once more.[53] He was grateful for Captain Urquhart's endeavours to serve him, and left it to his friends in England to take the measures they thought best to bring about his restoration.[54] Speaking about Lord Orrery's negotiations with Sunderland, James thought it was in his interest 'to rebuke nobody and to gain as many I can provided the Tories are not imposed upon, or to detach some of the party and make it less able to serve me'. A new Parliament was not enough and he 'must have assurances about the army to pave the great work'. To Orrery himself James wrote on 22 April 'I am extream glad to find you think the affair in so favourable a disposition and the measures you propose to be pursued by friends with you cannot fail having sooner or later the desired effect.'[55]

Cowper's Cabal

At this time two important organisations dominated the political scene on the opposition side: Cowper's Cabal and Orrery's Club, known as 'the Burford Club' in the Secret Committee's report into the plot, from one of Orrery's code names.

Cowper's Cabal began operating in January 1721 and was at its most effective from the autumn of 1721 until 1723. It is generally agreed that most of its members were Jacobites, but it has been argued that its head, Lord Cowper, was always an orthodox Whig and that the Duke of Wharton, one of its most influential members, was not a committed Jacobite until some years later.[56] There is much evidence to contradict these assertions. Sir Robert Walpole would tell Sir Dudley Ryder in 1743: 'Lord Cowper himself had been reconciled to the Pretender'.[57] Lord Chancellor Cowper, a highly respected Whig politician, joined the Whig split in 1718 when he became associated with George, Prince of Wales. He did not rejoin the main body of the Whigs in 1720 and refused offers of office from Walpole and Townshend in 1722. Mary Caesar, the wife of Charles Caesar, confirmed Cowper's change of heart in her journal. Cowper and Caesar had in the past been bitter opponents in Hertfordshire elections, but by the 1720s Cowper was a frequent visitor at Benington, Caesar's seat in Hertfordshire. Mrs Caesar trusted Cowper so far as to show him 'the Restoration hangings', which commemorated Charles II's Restoration, when Cowper remarked 'They that once thought they served their country by Endeavouring to keep Him out, Found they had no way to save it, but by Bringing Him Home.' She then guided Cowper to the picture in the closet, which seems to have been that of James III sent to her in 1717. This was treason itself. She recorded that Cowper looked at it through a glass earnestly for some time, then commented that the sitter had 'Not only a Sweet but a Sensible Countenance, and a Likeness to both Parents More than Usual'. Lord Cowper went further by asking James III through the Duke of Hamilton for a picture of his queen, Maria Clementina. Subsequently, Philip Neynoe, a minor conspirator, told Walpole that Cowper had been working for a restoration.[58]

Destouches, who first described 'La Caballe' of Lord Cowper, wrote that he had placed himself at the head of the opposition in the Lords 'despite his reputation for wisdom'. His technique in debates was to unleash his two greatest firebrands: Lord Coningsby, a Whig, the elder and the madder, followed by the Duke of Wharton, the younger and the more clever. Then he would rise like Cato and take up the same arguments in a more restrained and statesmanlike way. The French envoy, who had obtained these details from Lord Carteret, went on to say that these tactics could not succeed as the Court had a majority of between fifty and sixty in the Lords. This did not deter Cowper, who remarked that, if he could not take the fortress, he could at least bombard it.[59] Lord Coningsby, an eccentric Whig peer, was well known for hostility to Tories, yet at this time he was urging Sunderland to dissolve Parliament and to refrain from using secret service money at the new election in order to produce a moderate Tory majority in the Commons.[60]

The Duke of Wharton

Philip Wharton, the son of Thomas, Marquess of Wharton, the great Whig Junto leader, succeeded in 1715 to the title and to vast estates encumbered by his father's debts. He went over to France in 1716 when he espoused the Jacobite cause and declared that he 'would sacrifice his life and fortune in the effort to secure the restoration of the rightful monarch'.[61] He then proceeded to Avignon, where he had a secret meeting with James III, writing afterwards: 'I do solemnly protest and declare, and take God Almighty to witness, that I will always to my last breath serve nor know no other King of England than James III and his lawful heirs.'[62] He was then created Duke of Northumberland in the Jacobite peerage. After returning to England, to the astonishment of his contemporaries, he was created Duke of Wharton by George I, who acted as godfather to his son. He had been expected to join the government Whigs but did not and was constantly in the company of Lord Cowper, either at the Court of George, Prince of Wales or at Cowper's house in London. At the Prince of Wales's Court, which Orrery attended to find out what was going on, a close relationship developed between Wharton and Lord Orrery, which lasted for the rest of their lives. He did not adhere to Walpole and Townshend at the end of the Whig split, but was then described as an 'errant Tory'.[63] In Cowper's Cabal, Wharton drew ever closer to Atterbury. When in December 1721 Wharton rejoined the court party, he continued to go and see Atterbury in the mornings. His purpose, it seems, was to find out the plans of the Whig government and communicate these to Atterbury. He secretly assured Sir Henry Goring (see below) that his real sympathies and loyalty to James were unchanged. Further, he gave a pledge to Sir John Bland, a leading Tory MP and his neighbour in Yorkshire, with 'oaths and imprecations' of his 'inviolable fidelity' to King James and that he would 'pull off the mask' and appear against the government whenever required to do so.[64] Wharton proved as good as his word when Atterbury was in the greatest danger.

The campaign of Protests in the House of Lords

Cowper's Cabal met every morning to plan their tactics before attending the House of Lords. The central feature was the drawing up of signed Protests against the votes won by the government. These reached their peak from January to March 1722. The Protests were published in newspapers, notably in *The Freeholder*, a journal edited by Thomas Carte, one of Atterbury's associates. They were circulated in newsletters too. This campaign caused considerable embarrassment to the government. We do not know all the members of Cowper's Cabal, but the fullest list is the canvassing list drawn up by Atterbury. The group consisted of about thirty-one Lords and three Tory MPs: William Shippen, Sir John Packington and William Bromley. Atterbury, who was a leading member, drew up the canvassing list in his own hand.

It was said that some of the Protests drawn up by Atterbury were toned down by Cowper. Other leading Lords were Bathurst, Orrery, Strafford, North and Grey, Guildford, Scarsdale, Compton, Foley,

Bingley and Dawes, Archbishop of York. All were Jacobites except Compton, and the Archbishop of York who was regarded as a Hanoverian Tory. The main speakers were Cowper, North and Grey, Atterbury, Bathurst and Strafford.[65] Particularly embarrassing Protests were against the Lords of the Treasury being able to appoint directors of the South Sea Company to manage the execution of the South Sea Act. The Protests demanded that the papers relating to British foreign policy towards Sweden and Spain be submitted to Parliament, as well as the instructions that had been given to the navy in the Baltic, which amounted to an indictment of the use of the Royal Navy to acquire Bremen and Verden for Hanover and which was regarded as the cause of the increase in the navy debt (all matters of particular concern to Jacobites). There was a Protest against the Mutiny Bill, which imposed the death penalty on deserters from the army. Atterbury's popularity among the lower clergy was reflected in his nomination as President of the Corporation of Clergymen. He was defeated by only one vote after strenuous efforts of the government on behalf of the court candidate.

The successful campaign of Protests increased Atterbury's prestige in England. He opposed the bill to enable Quakers to affirm rather than take the oaths as an indulgence for 'a set of people, who were hardly Christians'. A petition of the London clergy against the Quaker bill was supported by Atterbury, the Archbishop of York, North and Grey, Strafford and Cowper. Atterbury was greatly concerned that the Convocation, which he had used to such great effect over the Occasional Conformity controversy in the previous reigns, was no longer allowed to sit. This was unfair as clergymen were unable to stand for the House of Commons on the grounds that they were represented in Convocation. There was a strong Protest against rejecting the London clergy petition, when the government argued 'that the Protest seemed to establish a Right of Convocation to Petition the Parliament, whereas they ought to do it to the King as in a Legislative capacity'.

Archibald Hutcheson was foremost in promoting the bill for the freedom of elections when he denounced the abuse of election procedures, admitting unqualified voters and the bribery of returning officers. He condemned MPs so chosen who received 'ample recompense and rewards for the secret service they have covenanted to perform here'. Several Protests were drawn up against the rejection of the bill for securing the freedom of elections. The Protests had been based on the standing order of the House of Lords of 5 March 1641/2, which was rescinded. There was a curb on Protests in the House of Lords, motions that they should be expunged from the *Lords Journals*, as well as new regulations in March 1722 which made it more difficult to draw up such Protests. The heavy-handed tactics of the government showed how much they feared the effectiveness of the Lords Protests.[66]

Lord Orrery's Club

Lord Orrery's Club, the 'Burford Club' (from Orrery's name in one of the Jacobite ciphers, as the government discovered subsequently) was said to have met monthly at the London house of its chairman in Glasshouse Street, Piccadilly. We know less about the Burford Club than about Cowper's Cabal. It was probably concerned with raising funds to buy arms for the rising, and with parliamentary tactics in the Commons as well as in the Lords. Subsequently, Christopher Layer testified that John Plunkett (who had contacts in Orrery's Club) had said to him that 'Lord Cowper had told him that two hundred Tories and ninety Grumbletonian [dissatisfied] Whigs, who are in the House of Commons' would try to effect a restoration. The club included Lord Strafford, Lord North and Grey, Lord Cowper, Lord Scarsdale, Bishop Atterbury, Lord Bingley, Lord Gower, Lord Bathurst, Lord Craven, Archibald Hutcheson, Sir Henry Goring, William Shippen, Sir Constantine Phipps, General John Richmond Webb and James Dawkins, all of whom (except Phipps) were at some time in the Westminster Parliament. Cowper was the only Whig in this list, all the rest were Jacobites.[67] In a list of the Burford Club in Lord Townshend's papers at Raynham, the Duke of Wharton's name appears, though his name was not on the list printed in the parliamentary papers relating to the Atterbury Plot.[68] Members of Orrery's Club who also belonged to Cowper's Cabal were Orrery, Strafford, North and Grey, Scarsdale, Bishop Atterbury, Bathurst, William Shippen Lord Bingley, Lord Gower, Lord Craven, Archibald Hutcheson, Sir Henry Goring, Sir Constantine Phipps, General Richmond Webb and James Dawkins. According to letters by John Plunkett to General Dillon 'Burford and his Club' thought Joseph (James III) 'was their only refuge' and 'would have a finger in the Pye'. Christopher Layer was active in 'spurring on the Club' and persuading them to take a more active part in the plot than some were inclined to do.[69] Members of the Club were deterred by the equivocal attitude of the Regent, the Duke of Orléans. One of the Regent's agents, however, probably Chammorel rather than Destouches, told Plunkett that had the Club 'a true Concert', the Regent 'would come in with them'.[70] When the names of Orrery's Club were revealed to Parliament, Lord Cowper and Archibald Hutcheson issued a public denial that they were members of such a club or that it ever existed, but so did Lord Strafford and Bishop Atterbury.[71]

Chammorel thought that a new Parliament, in the present dispositions of the nation, would mean a Tory Parliament and that Sunderland was prepared to bring some Tories into the ministry.[72] Destouches reported that Sunderland had agreed with leading Tories that there should be a new election, in which the king would not meddle, and that the people would be able to choose a new Parliament without using bribery. Sunderland thought this would reconcile the Tories towards King George and would restore public support for him (Sunderland). It would permanently exclude Walpole with whom the Tories would never work. Destouches, however, did not believe King George would be safe in the hands of the Tories. In the event, George I distrusted the Tories too much to agree to free elections, fearing a revolution, with the result that Sunderland began to lose favour with his royal master.[73] At this time it was hoped that the Duke of Ormonde, Lord Mar and Lord Bolingbroke would be included in a new bill of indemnity. Atterbury himself had an audience with George I to press for a pardon for Ormonde, while the Duchess of Ormonde and Lord Arran waited on Caroline, Princess of Wales to plead for him.[74] It was usual for friends to try to intercede on behalf of persons whose estates had been forfeited and it was not an attempt to come to terms with the Hanoverian regime. These hopes, however, were disappointed.

The bill of indemnity

The hands of Lord Orrery and the Lords who dealt with Sunderland were weakened, however, by the Bill of Indemnity passed on 28 July. This did not include Ormonde, Mar, or Bolingbroke as had been expected, but Sunderland only and those accused of taking South Sea stock without paying for it. The Tories and opposition MPs had not suspected anything was afoot and were consequently absent. George I attended the House of Lords unexpectedly in a thin House and the bill was approved by the Lords in half an hour. It was immediately sent to the Commons where the Speaker had been briefed and asked if the House approved 'some 20 said yes, a larger number said no and the rest [were] silent'. As no division was demanded, the Speaker ignored the dissentients and said as the House approved the bill it should be sent back to the Lords, whereupon the King gave it his Royal Assent. Sunderland was now safe and began to see less of his Tory allies. A boon for Ormonde, however, was that his forfeited estates in Ireland were vested in his brother, the Earl of Arran.[75] At this time Lord Aberdeen, one of the Tories negotiating with Sunderland (together with Lord Strathmore and Lord Balmerino) was chosen a representative peer of Scotland with Sunderland's help, which was regarded as auspicious. To Orrery, who was still optimistic, James wrote on 3 August 1721:

> As to the negotiations with Ld Sunderland I am entirely at ease on that head being fully persuaded that you will make the best advantage of it without putting it in his power to do hurt if he be not sincere, hitherto it is not possible to make a judgment of him, it having not come in his way to give us any essential proof of his sincerity, but I think he has motives enough to determine him to undertake our affair heartily and to put a speedy conclusion to it for by acting a doubtful part and not making a reasonable despatch, he ventures fairly losing himself with both parties. Since you do not propose to me to send any message to him by your canal either directly or indirectly I conclude it is not yet time for that but whenever you think it proper, I give you ample leave to give him all the encouragement in my name you think proper and if he be a man of honour one would think that his love for his country and the glory he will gain by serving it so effectually should alone sufficiently oblige him to act his part steadily.

James, however, urged caution so that these negotiations did not interfere with nor obstruct any other project undertaken from abroad on his behalf.[76]

Jacobite London

In England the 'universal outcry against the government was as great as ever in all ranks and parties'. The City of London and the county of Middlesex drew up addresses for a dissolution of Parliament. The Whig lord mayor was pressed in vain to summon a court of aldermen, so that the London address could be presented at the Bar of the Commons. This would have given a lead to the counties. But the alderman next in the chair for lord mayor was a Tory, aptly named Stewart, who was attended 'by a prodigious Tory mob' at the lord mayor's show, shouting, 'A Stuart, a Stuart for ever'. Two Tories had been elected sheriffs of London in Common Hall by a large majority, despite strenuous efforts of the Court to keep them out.[77] The Tories dominated the popular part of the City of London, the Common Hall and the Common Council, as the Whigs had done during the Exclusion Crisis, and, with the choice of two Tory sheriffs and a Tory lord mayor, they were in a very strong position indeed.

The early dissolution of Parliament, however, failed to materialise. Charles Caesar reported to James that Parliament would meet on 19 October 1721, at the very time it had been expected a new Parliament would be called after an early dissolution. Sunderland assured Caesar 'that he had opposed the Parliament meeting again as far as prudence was fit for him to do at this juncture and that he at last yielded to it upon the strongest assurances that could be given that no attempt should be made to continue its duration'. James replied

> I find you are still of opinion that Ld. Sunderland intends to serve me effectually. I wish it may prove so, but you are certainly much in the right that any dependence we may have on him should not hinder our helping ourselves any other way.[78]

Under the provisions of the Septennial Act a new election was due in March 1722, probably sooner. Townshend and Walpole had persuaded George I and the Germans that an early meeting of Parliament would grant money for the next year, thus enabling them to leave for Hanover sooner than they expected. James Hamilton, the Jacobite agent in London, went to see Orrery but could not tell whether Sunderland 'will be able to prepare matters for the main object in view agreeably to the desires from friends in England'. He did not know what had induced Sunderland to patch things up with Walpole. Lord Aberdeen tried to go and see Sunderland, but was told he was out and, when he did see him in the House of Lords, Sunderland apologised but 'did not enter into the main affair'.[79] Reporting to James on 21 October, Orrery wrote

> The expectations of your friends to have a new Parliament this winter by the interest of Ld Sunderland were disappointed. About the latter end of the last sessions he gave us to believe he should carry that point which we thought the most material of any that it was proper at that season to ask. He now says as I hear that E[lector]. of Hanover was worked up against it by those belonging to the ministry and by the Germans about him that he did not think fit to push the matter too far.

The most he could achieve was to get the ministers to agree they would not prolong Parliament further by a new law. The Tories, Orrery wrote, were deeply disappointed:

> For my own part I must own that I always had a distrust of E[arl] Sunderland's sincerity not only from the false nature of the man, but because he never could be prevailed upon to come into the necessary measures for securing a good Parliament tho he professed his zeal for a new one. However I was of opinion it was fit to entertain a negotiation with him provided that the Tories were not diverted by that treaty from pursuing their views by all proper methods they could devise and I still think it is not their business to fall upon him singly.

Orrery concluded that the great animosity between Townshend and Walpole on one hand and Sunderland on the other would lead Sunderland 'still to pretend to be our friend'. Orrery thought the Tories should listen to what Sunderland had to say while pursuing the main object and to try to get assistance from a foreign prince. A new Parliament was not enough, as corruption was so widespread and there were so many little venal boroughs that 'a majority will hardly be carried by the inclinations of the people'.[80]

The last session of the 1715 Parliament

George I came back from Hanover at the end of October to open the last session of the Parliament. George, Prince of Wales would not hear of a new Parliament without 'meddling in elections'. Some people thought the Tories would have a great majority in the new Parliament, but others believed that if the Court spent enough money, the Whigs would triumph. Destouches conferred with Lord Peterborough, who said the King should employ Whigs and Tories equally. Destouches thought that would have been wise at the beginning of the reign, but it was now too late. Privately, he disapproved of any ending of the proscription of the Tories, as it would make Britain less dependent on France.[81]

The 1722 election

As the new election approached it was reported that the animosities between Walpole and Sunderland were irreconcilable and that each was doing his utmost to have particular friends chosen in the new Parliament, while the Tories did their best to promote their own friends. The Tories were sure of the counties, but the little boroughs were carried with money and Lord Oxford and Charles Caesar were thought to be the best persons to raise money for the elections. Caesar, who was in close touch with Oxford, was confident a restoration could be achieved without the use of foreign troops and James expressed his satisfaction if he could 'see both the nation and myself owe our satisfaction to ourselves rather than to foreigners'. Urquhart (who was said to have refused a pension offered to him by Sunderland), kept up his pressure on Sunderland about the elections.[82]

As the general election approached, James III expressed further doubts about Sunderland's sincerity, as he had never heard from him directly nor had he had solid proofs of his goodwill.[83] However, he felt that the careful way Lord Orrery had dealt with Sunderland would ensure no harm would come of it. James was diplomatic, however, in writing to Urquhart, who was a principal channel of communication with Sunderland:

> It was with no small satisfaction that I received a few days ago the accounts you transmitted to me in relation to Ld Sunderland, one of his experience good sense and penetration that has the good of his country sincerely at heart cannot fail at last of serving me effectually and tho the measures he may take may happen to be something slow, I doubt not of their being efficacious towards the end he proposes to himself. I put all the value imaginable on his friendship and have all manner of confidence in him and in bringing about my restauration. I hope he will reap the greatest honour and advantage from it and you may assure him from me that he shall ever find me full of gratitude for his endeavours to serve me ... It is in his power now to make himself the greatest man of his age.

James enclosed a note written in his own hand to be delivered by Urquhart to Sunderland, without either subscription or superscription. Dated 31 January 1722 the note reads: 'a correspondence directly with yourself would be most agreeable to me, and if you are inclined to it, you may be assured of an inviolable secret and that betwixt you and I, my own hand shall only appear'.[84]

Sunderland may have been sincere in seeking free elections and offering office to the Tories. The political reality was that Sunderland and Walpole were the bitterest of enemies, that Sunderland was still 'making great advances to the Tories' and had declared publicly he was 'for allowing everybody of any consequence a share in the settlement'.[85] Walpole was against admitting any Tories into the ministry or places of public trust as he believed they would be spies for their own party and betray the Whigs (an opinion Walpole held for the rest of his life). Sunderland, on his side, had gained popularity for having the present Parliament dissolved and calling for new elections. Sunderland, it was reported:

> observes that the Tory party of themselves were now formed into so great a body that nothing but dividing or breaking them could secure the government from their attempts at home or their solicitations for foreign powers abroad to assist them in pursuit of their principles or their revenge. This he maintains cannot be effected but by gaining a few of the chief and more considerable men of that party to join in the measures of the Court by giving them money, places or pensions. They have suffered so much of late in the South Sea project that at present it could be no difficult matter to persuade them.[86]

At the general election in Scotland, Sunderland's people put out there was 'a perfect understanding between Sunderland and James'. Sunderland asked that at least six of the representative peers of Scotland should be Tories. Walpole and Townshend told the Germans how pernicious that would be for King George's affairs and called a Cabinet Council, when:

> the Earl of Sunderland opposed the buying of the ensuing elections, that it was a method very expensive [in] the present situation of affairs... It was impossible for the Treasury to hold out by procuring pliable persons to be elected, who after they were chosen must be maintained with places and pensions etc. In answer to this Walpole, Townshend and Argyll held forth on the inconveniencies it would draw His Majesty into both at home and abroad, if men of other principles than staunch Whigs were let into the Government, and Mr. Walpole asked with some heat if his Lordship was for bringing in the Tories and having a Tory Parliament? To this the Earl replied that the Tories and Whigs were equally entitled to a share in the Administration and that he was not for governing by Brigades. King George stared the Earl of Sunderland in the face at the name of a Tory Parliament, for it seems nothing is so hideous and frightful as a

Tory... The debate went so high that the Earl was near throwing up his employment and retiring from business.[87]

More Tories than ever stood at the elections, including some who had never taken the oaths before. All 'this Bull Baiting' would go on till the end of March when numbers could be computed. Destouches commented that despite all the efforts of the Court, Tories would be elected for the counties and large towns, but the Court would win in little places selling themselves to the highest bidder, but not without spending £200,000–£300,000 at least.[88] Lord Orrery suggested that part of the money raised for the buying of arms should be used to promote Tory candidates at the election.[89] This was ill-advised as the Tories could never match the funds at the disposal of the government.

A brilliant propaganda campaign

Since our political narrative opened with the reaction of the Jacobites to the Mississippi scheme and the South Sea Bubble, it is right to focus first on the brilliant medal of James III struck on this occasion, designed by Ottone or Ermenegildo Hamerani, of the family of Papal medallists. It seems to have been ready by December 1721, when a hundred in silver and two hundred in brass (perhaps copper) were sent off.[90] This medal, the best designed for the Stuarts and one of the best medallic works of art pertaining to Britain in the eighteenth century, displays on the reverse a view of London from the south bank of the Thames, showing St Paul's, the new churches, London's column and London Bridge. This was almost certainly prepared from a recent engraving. In the foreground the White Horse of Brunswick tramples down the lion and the unicorn, while on the left the figure of Britannia looks on and mourns. In the middle distance, but still on the hither side of the Thames, three figures apparently carrying booty hurry towards the east. The legend: 'Quid gravius capta', 'what more grievous captivity', is taken from the lines of Hermione to Orestes in Epistle VIII of Ovid's *Heroides* (1. II), which speak of conquest and beg for the recovery of the right. It is a woman's plea and the words are in effect uttered by Britannia. When the medal is turned, the obverse reveals the bust of a godlike James III, in Roman garb, a figured sun beaming from his breast and, above, the legend 'Unica Salus', 'the only cure', or (remembering the South Sea Bubble) the only security. The words echo the speech of Aeneas to his followers as Troy burns, in Virgil's *Aeneid*, II. 354 (see also II. 329–30: the *horse* full of armed men).

The reverse of the 'Unica Salus' medal, showing a view of London with St. Paul's and the new churches from the south side of the Thames. In the foreground the white horse of Hanover tramples down the British lion, while Britannia mourns. The medal was designed by either Ottone or Ermenegildo Hamerani, and the London scene almost certainly based on a modern engraving.

The date 'MDCCXXI' marks not only the year of issue but the year of the corruption which demanded a cure.[91] The medal was in fact issued in silver, copper and pewter. The last is interesting because it must have been intended to be distributed, among others, to the relatively poor, even perhaps to those who could read its pictures but not its relatively simple Latin words. It catered for the desire to see representations of James III and his queen, shared even among the previously hostile aristocracy. Thus in November 1721 Lord Cowper, Lady Orkney and Lady Fortescue all wanted pictures of Queen Maria Clementina.[92]

The propaganda portrayal of James III, 'Unica Salus' on the 1721 medal, may be compared with the skilful but fictional narrative of the experience of an English Protestant traveller in Rome, supposed to have arrived there on 20 March 1721, and to have written an account to his father in England on 6 May of that year. First, in an accidental encounter, he discovers that he can hear the Anglican service on Easter Day – which as an Anglican in Rome he very much wishes to do – in the Palace of the Pretender. He is informed that the Pretender is 'far from any sort of bigotry' and very much resembles Charles II. Next, again by chance, the traveller meets the Pretender:

> easily distinguished from the rest by his star and garter, as well as by an air of greatness which discovered a majesty superior to the rest. I felt in that instant a strange convulsion of the body and mind, such as I was never sensible of before ... [Following what others did the traveller made him a salute] He returned it with a smile, which changed the sedateness of his first aspect into a very graceful countenance.

The traveller was later invited to a concert by the princess (i.e. Maria Clementina). There the 'Pretender spoke of English families as knowingly as if he had been all his life in England. He told me of some passages of my grandfather, and of his being a constant lover of Charles I and II...' At this, the traditionally minded traveller could not but kiss his hand. But, after the instinctive gesture which recognised the true king, the underlying objections could not but be expressed also:

> it's true, Sir, that affairs in England lye at present under many hardships [he says] by the South Sea mismanagement: but 'tis a constant maxim with us Protestants to undergo a great deal for the security of our religion, which we could not depend on with a Romish government. I know, replied he, this is the argument some who have a

very slight share of Religion do make, in order to delude the honest well-meaning people. I assure you these latter and I would agree very well and be happy together.

His object, James is made to say, is to be a good king of all his people, and to keep the promises of his Declaration. This brilliant piece of Jacobite propaganda – which concludes with the polite Protestant kissing the hand of the infant Charles Edward – has been well recognised by Daniel Szechi as a paradigm of how, at this historical moment, James wished to be seen by the Protestant Jacobites of England, and indeed the other Protestants desperate for national salvation after the South Sea crash.[93]

On 8 May 1721 Chammorel reported the London petition on the South Sea collapse: the disaster for trade and credit, the English nation dragged in the mire. Chammorel was surprised that the petition for redress was *not*, as usually the case, addressed to the king (i.e. George I). He also reported that the *London Journal*, not usually a Tory organ, had published strong criticisms of the Court in fictionalised Roman form, for example a letter from Brutus to Cicero during the rise of Octavius:

L'on reconnait facilement, [he explains,] le personage du Roy Jacques Second sous le nom de Jules Caesar et celuy du Roy Georges sous la figure d'Octavius, le Parlement sur celle de Cicéron. Il n'est plus question que de trouver la personne que l'on désigne sous le caractère de Brutus, que l'on aime assez dans ce pays cy.[94]

This letter was, of course, one of the most notable of the famous collection of *Cato's Letters* by Trenchard and Gordon (1 April 1721, No. 23 in the series of papers published periodically). It was also thought by some that Lord Molesworth and Lord Cowper wrote certain of these papers under the name of Cato.[95] To read this letter, and then the interpretation of Chammorel, is not to be *entirely* convinced by the identifications that he proposes. His interpretation is nevertheless highly significant in its indication of how intelligent political commentators read *Cato's Letters*. If the reader were indeed dealing entirely with person-to-person equivalence, Julius Caesar might indeed allude to James II, George I to Octavius, and in this line of interpretation Brutus could be Ormonde (originally against James II, but beloved in England, and now in exile). Cicero, however, in Chammorel's view, means parliament *tout court*, rather than any one great parliamentarian, and thus 'la personne' who is loved in this country is perhaps more likely to be the personification of liberty than any individual exile, however well esteemed.

The Roman idiom of *Cato's Letters*, certainly not Jacobite in itself, and not as hostile to George I as James II, was soon picked up by Jacobite propaganda. The fiery, anti-Hanoverian letter published by Nathaniel Mist is really a pointed celebration of the Restoration of Charles II. It came out on 27 May 1721 in *The Weekly Journal or Saturday's Post,* Mist's newspaper, which had the largest circulation of any newspaper at the time. The letter begins with an appeal to 'Friends, Britons, Countrymen' and sliding from Commonwealth and Cromwellian tyranny to Hanoverian, inveighs against a tyrant who behaves like a miser rather than the father of his people, and against Hanoverian ladies (initials given), old ugly whores who would not find custom in the most infamous brothels, who ruin the nation. A usurper, having got hold of a land that does not belong to him, takes no notice of the damage it suffers. Then, resuming its 1660 theme, the paper declares:

> when we least expected it the monarchy was restored in the royal house of Stuart in the person of a prince with a thousand outstanding qualities. Then the Ormondes, the Clarendons, the Southamptons ... were at the head of affairs.[96]

On 22 December 1721 Lansdowne, purporting to write to Lord Molesworth from Rome, takes up the matter of the mysterious presence of Robert Knight in that city. Expatiating on the 'Unica Salus' theme, Lansdowne hints at an honourable contact between Knight and James III ('the Pretender has publicly declared he will receive no application from him, in case he makes any, but upon the terms of giving satisfaction to the nation') and remarks:

> It would be a strange event if after so many fruitless endeavours on our part, we should at last be beholden to the Pretender for coming to the bottom of this mystery of iniquity.

Defending James III, he concludes:

> There are very few who merit to be well-spoken of. Let us not retrench the number by scandalising those who do, whatever country, religion or party they may be of. Such sentiments would be unworthy of the sentiments of the great Cato, and such I profess myself to be, with the spirit of an old Roman, in true Rome.[97]

This paper, whether or not actually intended to be published in *Cato's Letters*, adopts the fictionally distanced mode of the *Letter from an English Traveller*. Thus James III is 'the Pretender' and thus the writer, a real Jacobite in Paris, adopts the *persona* of an interested observer in Rome, well able to distinguish between the Catholic Rome of the early eighteenth century, and the 'true Rome' of the ancient world, whose *virtú* is the meeting ground between *Cato's Letters* and Lansdowne.

Chammorel, who had a good eye for propaganda, whether in journals or on the stage, reported on 26 January 1722 an opera recently performed in London in which there was a scene where the legitimate heir, who was kept in prison by a usurper, was restored to the throne and the usurper in his turn put in chains. At this point, with no regard for the presence of the King (i.e. George I) there was loud clapping and all present, including the courtiers, says Chammorel, drew their own conclusions.[98] This opera was almost certainly Handel's *Floridante*, libretto by Paolo Rolli, adapted from Silvani's *La Constanza in trionfo* as revised in Livorno in 1706. It may be noted that Rolli, an acquaintance of Alexander Pope and a Catholic, was under the patronage of the 3rd Earl of Burlington. It is interesting to speculate how far the plot was chosen for the times. It is also worth noting that apparently there was some minor collaboration between Handel and Chammorel's senior diplomatic colleague, Destouches, so one would expect the two diplomats to have been well informed on matters such as these. *Floridante* was often performed that winter and had last been performed on 5 January 1722.[99]

Before turning to those pamphlets explicitly addressed to the Jacobite interest at the general election of 1722, it is worth noticing a work of an entirely different kind from anything else discussed in this chapter. This was Alexander Michael Ramsay's *Life of Fénelon*, the famous Archbishop of Cambrai, translated by Nathaniel Hooke from the original French, and republished in 1723. Much in the Stuart Papers bears upon the production of this work. In brief, the Abbé Southcott, head of the English Benedictines and a fervent Jacobite in France after the Fifteen, conceived that the way to draw the Catholic and Anglican churches together (or rather the latter to the former) was not through Jansenism, nor yet Gallicanism, but through the teaching and example of the famous and widely revered Fénelon. Ramsay, Southcott had written to James III, was perhaps an even greater man than Fénelon, though both Ramsay and his translator Hooke were disciples of the archbishop. The *Life*, which Southcott warmly praised to James on several occasions, was short, dramatic and highly readable.

Further, in its French version it gave an account not only of James's visit to Fénelon when the young king was campaigning in the War of the Spanish Succession, but of Fénelon's shrewd, steady and uneulogistic character of the Stuart king. Both Ramsay and Southcott wanted the book to be dedicated to James, but James himself, while writing in appreciative tone, was for several reasons wary, not least, perhaps, because Fénelon was a far from uncontroversial figure in France and in the Catholic Church. It was then suggested that the book might be dedicated to the Earl of Oxford whom the continental Jacobites wished to draw into the central counsels of the Plot and perhaps even to assume authority over Atterbury. In the event the English version of the *Life* bore no dedication, and did not explicitly include the character of James. Ramsay's *Life of Fénelon* is perhaps demeaned by being regarded as propaganda, but there is no doubt that the Abbé Southcott and Ramsay himself saw the work as serving their common cause as well as doing justice to a very great churchman and author.

As the general election approached, a ferocious Jacobite pamphlet appeared from the British press: *The Second and last Advice to the Freeholders of England* (London 1722). It must have been intended to recall the *Advice to the Freeholders of England* (1715), a pamphlet published anonymously under the guidance of Atterbury, Ormonde and Bolingbroke. It seems to suggest that it was composed by a member of the House of Lords ('I was present in the House of Lords when he [Oxford] was ordered to the Tower', p. 15) though possibly this might mean only that the writer was present as an observer or that he was assuming the *persona* of a peer or a bishop. It is just possible that this is the work of Atterbury himself, not merely one who wanted to invoke Atterbury's 1715 tract; or it may be (since this was the way Atterbury often worked) that the 1722 tract was written under the general guidance of the bishop. At any event it abandons Atterbury's earlier art of smooth persuasion and adroit ironic strategy and goes over, as many a public critic before Atterbury and later, to a mode of rough, contemptuous, Junevalian attack.

The Second and last Advice accuses the Lords of giving up the Magna Charta (p. 3), King George of making peers 'among the lees and dregs of the people', the House of Commons of not being the choice of the people (that is, elections are bought or rigged), and yet, it concedes, the actual government has indeed changed:

> At one time it was Mademoiselle Schullenberg and the Duke of Marlborough, with Walpole, Townshend and Stanhope; At another

it was the Duchess of Munster, Walpole and Townshend; at another it was the Duchess of Kendal, Lord Sunderland with Craggs and Stanhope, then the Duchess with Lord Sunderland, Walpole and Townshend (p. 5).

With such wonderful variation, who could deny the English enjoyed political freedom? A scornful assault on George I's ministers is mounted, followed by a defence of Ormonde and Strafford (pp 13–14). The king, when he goes about in public, is greeted in silence: this should make him think (p. 16). The Jacobite gentlemen who surrendered at Preston (in 1715) on a promise of mercy were treated with indignity and great cruelty (p. 21). A long survey of Hanoverian foreign policy implicates both George's German advisers and the Abbé Dubois in making alliances against the interest of England. King George, who spent seven months out of the year in Hanover, 'sold out a vast deal of fictitious' South Sea stock (p. 27), while England was engaged in war to seize Bremen and Verden, which belonged to the King of Sweden, in the interests of Hanover (p. 28). The German ministers, unlike their English counterparts were 'at least acting in the interest of their own country' (p. 30). As for the South Sea, it is true both Whigs and Tories speculated in the stocks, but not all were guilty of 'the foulness of it' (p. 36).

This tract must surely have damaged the Hanoverian cause in the eyes of any who read it. The final Jacobite tract published at this time which claims our attention is also a bitter criticism of the Hanoverian scene, but it takes a broader view and is a more studied literary effort. This is *A Letter from a Nobleman Abroad to his Friend in England*, published in 1722 though probably not from London as claimed. It was written by the eloquent Lansdowne and consciously adopts the mode of *Cato's Letters*, especially the letters published almost a year earlier from Brutus. It is the figure of Brutus, assassin of Julius Caesar but opponent of Antony and Octavius, who is in focus in Lansdowne's peroration:

Let then no other Denominations be heard among us, no other distinction but that of good *Englishmen*; let all who would merit that Name unite, embrace, and take a *Roman* Resolution to save their Country, or perish with it.

Brutus was a sworn enemy to *Pompey*, the Murderer of his Father; but when it happened that Rome must perish, or *Pompey* be supported, *Brutus* became *Pompey's Friend*.

Brutus took an Oath to *Caesar*, but *Brutus* never swore to be an Enemy to his Country.

Brutus owed much to *Caesar*, but *Brutus thought* private Benefits as well as private Injuries, were to be sacrificed to the Publick Safety. And Brutus was an honourable Man.

The Interest of the State is the first Object of Men of Honour; Piety and Loyalty are included in it; to be false to one's Country is to be false to God and the King.[100]

Plainly Brutus is here used as a noble Roman example to bring together in a patriotic cause many of those whom the last three decades of political history had divided. There is too, perhaps, a low key attempt ('no other Denomination') to override the question of James III's Catholicism, as there had been in Lansdowne's 'Friends, Britons and Countrymen' Letter. Perhaps, however, what most readers would remember from this tract was its stirring opening:

At this critical juncture when the Rumour of a new Parliament sounds like the last Trumpet, to awaken the Genius of Old *England*, and raise departed Liberty to Life, it would be a Crime to be silent. (ibid. p. 144)

We can well appreciate in Lansdowne's correspondence with James III[101] how the sounding of the trumpet to achieve a Stuart restoration reminded him of the last trumpet which would sound at the Day of Judgement. In his *Letter* it is again 'like the last Trumpet...'; Lansdowne has in mind the First Letter to the Corinthians in the King James Bible:

Behold, I shew you a mystery; we shall not all sleep, but we shall be changed.

In a moment, in the twinkling of an eye, at the last trump, for the trumpet shall sound, and the dead shall be raised incorruptible, and we shall be changed.

(1 Corinthians 15, 51–2)

In Lansdowne's High Anglican, albeit Romanised, vision, a restoration of the Stuart king would be a providential redemption, as miraculous no doubt as 1660 had seemed at the time; it would require human resolution and would rest on divine providence, and would be, after the recent corruptions of the public realm, truly transformative.

Inflamed by these writings and discontents at the burst of the South Sea Bubble, elections in the large constituencies were the most tumultuous of the time. Destouches, who had been asked by Dubois to tell the whole truth, reported that the fury of the people against the Court had to be seen to be believed, that libels were going round in which the royal family were treated 'with the greatest insolence' and that King George needed his friends abroad to preserve him from public fury. The election for Westminster surprised contemporaries, as it was a constituency where many people were dependent on the Court and government for their livelihood. The Tory candidates were Archibald Hutcheson and John Cotton. Cotton had been appointed by Ormonde deputy steward of Westminster and was financial adviser to Atterbury. Their opponents were William Lowndes, secretary to the Treasury and Sir Thomas Crosse, a government supporter. Atterbury had secured the appoinment of his son-in-law, William Morice, as high bailiff, or returning officer. The election was conducted like a military operation by Hutcheson, who led 7000–8000 supporters on foot and horseback' with drums beating and colours displayed' accompanied by 'many seditious outcries'. This angered King George as these events took place in his own parish of St James. Hutcheson and Cotton won on a poll in which Hutcheson had twice the number of votes obtained by Lowndes. Atterbury boasted of his defeating the Court, which angered Walpole. In Coventry, two Jacobites, Fulwar Craven and Sir Fulwar Skipwith, were returned after a tumultuous election in which Thomas Carte and his brother the Rev. John Carte (see below) were particularly active. Lord Craven marched at the head of 2000 men, horse and foot 'with green twigs and leaves in their hats' (the symbol of the Restoration of 1660), 'drums beating and trumpets sounding' shouting 'No Hanoverians! No seven years Parliament!' In London, George I personally appealed to the Dissenters his 'hearty friends' for support, but all four government candidates were defeated and three Tories and an independent Whig were returned. In Middlesex a Tory shared the representation with a Whig, but in Yorkshire, the largest constituency in England, two Jacobites, Henry Dawnay, Lord Downe and Sir Arthur Kaye, were returned unopposed. Traditionally, London, Westminster and Yorkshire were regarded as representing the sense of the people and it may be concluded that the Jacobites had won hearts and minds. Destouches was greatly alarmed, but as Hoffman, the senior diplomat in London told him, in England he should never be surprised at the noise of elections or the loss of elections by the government, as the Court would win elections in small boroughs and Parliament would invalidate the elections of opponents. The Court had over 100 places to give to MPs, as well as pensions. This proved correct as 379 Whigs were elected and 178 Tories (as against 217 in 1715). Tory numbers were reduced to 169 after petitions and double returns were heard along party lines. The Westminster election was declared void. Two other Whigs were returned at a new election held when Atterbury was a prisoner in the Tower of London.[102]

3
A Call to Arms

The bursting of the South Sea Bubble led the Jacobites to prepare for a general rising, while taking measures in Parliament to try and secure a constitutional restoration. Lord Strafford thought the great discontents over the South Sea affair would motivate a popular rising.[1] The Jacobites could not count on the kind of massive foreign invasion which had made the 1688 attempt succeed. They assumed, however, that France and Spain would allow them to use the Irish regiments in their service to land in England and Scotland to make a spearhead to protect them from preventative arrests. The size of the standing army and the availability of Dutch mercenary troops to defend the Hanoverian regime, however unpopular it was, made an unsupported internal rising in England very difficult. In Scotland, the situation was more favourable to the Jacobites because the clans had not been effectively disarmed after the Fifteen and private armies could be trained in the parts of Scotland where heritable jurisdictions remained and the Whig government's authority did not run. This was the crux of the second phase of the Atterbury Plot.

The birth of the Prince of Wales

A powerful incentive and a happy omen for the Jacobites was the birth of Charles Edward Stuart, son of James III and Queen Maria Clementina Sobieska on 31 December 1720. He was born in the presence of about a hundred persons, including foreign ambassadors, leading lights in the Roman nobility, members of the royal Household and selected cardinals from the College of Cardinals. The birth was celebrated in a carnival atmosphere in Rome, and Peter the Great, Philip V and the emperor sent congratulations. The pope was generous in gifts on the birth of the prince and the King of Spain was lavish in his promises of sending more money. James declared:

> Our son, who is a brave lusty boy ... is looked after ... in the English way, for though I cannot help his being born in Italy, yet as much as in me lies he shall be English for the rest all over.[2]

Dr Freind chose and sent to Rome Mrs Hughes, the wife of a nonjuring clergyman, as nurse to the prince as well as an English maid for the queen. Freind, an eminent physician who was a pioneer in the technique of inoculation against smallpox, was the brother of the headmaster of Westminster School, a leading Jacobite MP and a close associate of Atterbury's.[3] He had been ready to sacrifice his own career by going to Rome to act as the prince's physician, but he was dissuaded from doing so in his own interest by James.[4] Warm congratulations poured in from British Jacobites, headed by Charles Caesar, Orrery, Oxford and Strafford.[5] Lord Ailesbury wrote from Brussels, where he was in exile, sending warm congratulations and assurances of his continued devotion to James.[6] The birth was seen as 'a presage of a happy turn of your affairs for the future'.[7] Their joy was celebrated in a poem sent to Rome by Lancelot Ord:

> Long may they live the Royal Pair
> James with his Clementina Fair
> Their matchless issue still secure
> To reign while sun and moon endure
> Lett Germin Mungrills now give place
> To Sobyesky's Royal Race
> And never more disturb our peace
> O Happy Island could you see
> The blessing now bestowed on thee
> O gift next to eternity
> For King, Queen, Prince then lett us pray
> And Solemnise this glorious day
> With bells and drumm and trumpetts sound
> Lett Charles the Prince his health go round.[8]

The quest for troops

Bishop Atterbury, however, thought nothing could be done without troops and that most of James's friends in England were of the same opinion.[9] Orrery felt that:

our present governors and all their agents grow every day more and more both into aversion and contempt and the body of the people seem much better disposed than ever to welcome any assistance that will come to their deliverance.

He added that foreign help was still required but on a lesser scale than before, as the Tories were 'pretty well disposed'.[10] A month later Orrery reported that the Government was held in general contempt by Whigs as well as Tories and that

the officers of the Army as far as I can learn express almost as much discontent as any other set of people and what I look upon to be almost as favourable a part of the present disposition as any is that several of the Tories considerable friends that appeared very reserved till lately have conversed with their friends with more freedom than usual and pretty openly expressed their good inclinations towards bringing about the main affair [i.e. a restoration].[11]

Encouraged by violent discontents in England, the unpopularity of the Hanoverians, and on the occasion of the birth of a Stuart heir, the Jacobites in Britain made a new plan to restore the Stuarts. This became known as the Atterbury Plot and something should be said, at this stage, about the careers of the leading players in the Atterbury Plot, at home and abroad.

We have already met Lord Strafford and Lord Orrery, who continued to be centrally involved. The other two leaders in England were Lord North and Grey and the Earl of Arran, both of whom, like Strafford and Orrery, had military experience.

Lord North and Grey

William, 6th Baron North of Kirtling in Cambridgeshire and 2nd Viscount Grey of Rolleston (1678–1734) travelled in Italy, Spain and Flanders where he acquired a good knowledge of languages. Returning to England, he took his seat in the House of Lords in 1699 and was a frequent and influential speaker. At first, however, his career was primarily a military one, acting as lieutenant colonel of the 1st Foot Guards in 1702, then colonel of the 10th Foot, a regiment full of Granvilles and Jacobites. North distinguished himself at the Battle of Blenheim, where he had his right hand shot off, and served at Ramillies and Malplaquet. In the years after 1709 Lord North

William, 6th Baron North and 2nd Viscount Grey of Rolleston. Mezzotint by John Simon after Sir Godfrey Kneller, c. 1710. (Ashmolean Museum)

remained in England, taking part in the debates on the impeachment of Sacheverell in the spring of 1710 where he said 'our reputation abroad very good for everything but our fidelity and obedience'. He defended the peace preliminaries in December 1710, when he advocated the retention of Dunkirk as 'a terror of the Dutch'. In 1711 he became lord lieutenant of Cambridgeshire, where his main estates lay, and the following year was appointed governor of Portsmouth, when he purged the corporation of Whigs. A Privy Councillor, he belonged to the Honourable Brotherhood, a club of committed Jacobites. In 1713 he opposed the motion to expel James from Lorraine and spoke strongly against putting a price on his head. Dismissed from all his offices on the purge of the Tories at the accession of George I, he also lost his regiment. A leading speaker in the House of Lords, on 1 June 1715 he spoke in favour of hearing a petition from the persons accused in the Assassination Plot against William III in 1696, who had been imprisoned without trial ever since (contrary to English law), but failed to have it heard. Described by the Duke of Berwick in 1715 as 'a brave honest man by principle', he was said in 1717 to 'wait but a call anywhere' in support of a Stuart restoration.[12] His 'Considerations on the nature of oaths', arguing that newly imposed oaths could not supersede obligations previously entered into and that the breaking of oaths falsely imposed should not be accounted perjury (see Appendix A), is a fascinating and a very rare document. As we have seen, he was a leading member of Cowper's Cabal, as well as the 'Burford Club', Orrery's Club.

The Earl of Arran

Charles Butler, 2nd Earl of Arran in the Irish peerage (1671–1758), was the brother of James Butler, 2nd Duke of Ormonde. He was Lord of the Bedchamber to William III 1699–1702, colonel of the 5th Dragoon Guards 1697–1703, colonel of the 3rd Troop of Horse Guards 1703–15, fighting at the Battle of Blenheim, and Master of the Ordnance in Ireland 1712–14. Losing his offices on the proscription of the Tories by George I, after the flight to France and the attainder of his brother Ormonde, Arran was by a large majority chosen chancellor of the University of Oxford in 1715 in succession to Ormonde, whom he also succeeded as high steward of Westminster, presumably with the support of Atterbury as Dean. Arran appointed the high bailiff, who was the returning officer of Westminster, one of the most populous and influential constituencies in England, and helped Atterbury to run its parliamentary elections. He was regarded as a genial man, 'modest and good natured'[13] though not highly talented.

Plans for the rising were coordinated with the Triumvirate in Paris, consisting of Lansdowne, Dillon, who directed James's affairs in France, and Mar.

Lord Lansdowne

The most eminent and most influential of these was George Granville, Baron Lansdowne (1666–1735), the grandson of Sir Bevill Granville of Stowe, the legendary Royalist commander in Cornwall during the Civil War. His uncle John Granville, 1st Earl of Bath, a cousin of General Monck, was the most powerful magnate in the West. Granville was ever conscious of his family's loyalty to the Stuarts and these notions were reinforced by his tutor, William (later Sir William) Ellis (subsequently treasurer to the Stuart Court at St Germain and in Rome), who had taught him the 'precepts of loyalty.[14] His cousin, Sir Thomas Higgons, had been James III's secretary of state. He had a lifelong admiration for Mary of Modena, and wanted to fight for James II in 1688 when his father restrained him. In 1690 he appears to have visited St Germain, where his uncle Denis Granville, whom he idolised, was Anglican chaplain. Living in retirement in the reign of William III he made a reputation as a poet and playwright with *The She Gallants, Heroick Love: a Tragedy* and *The Jew of Venice*, a very popular modern adaptation of Shakespeare. Granville was one of the first to recognise the talent of Alexander Pope, who promised 'miracles' at the age of 17 or 18 and Pope subsequently paid tribute to 'Granville the Polite'.[15]

With an established literary fame, Granville became a major Tory politician in the reign of Queen Anne, with a pension of £3000 a year secured on the Duchy of Cornwall and a seat for Fowey procured by Lord Bath as manager for the Cornish boroughs, on the recommendation of his friend Henry St John. Like St John, he attached himself to Robert Harley in Parliament. During the minority of the 3rd Earl of Bath, he led the Granville interest on behalf of the Tories at the 1708 general election. He advocated the reconstruction of the Tory party on a High Church basis, often acted as an intermediary between Harley and St John, and naturally opposed the impeachment of Dr Sacheverell in 1710. He was appointed secretary-at-war in the new Tory administration headed by Harley, and had spectacular successes in Cornish elections, when he had the advantage of being related by blood to nearly every county family in Cornwall. He spent nearly £5000 of his own money on the elections, a sum never repaid him by Harley. On the death of the 3rd Earl of Bath without male heirs in 1711, he took possession of Stowe, the Cornish family seat and of estates worth £6000–£8000 a year, in the belief that the title and estates would devolve to him as the male heir. The same year, he married Lady Mary Villiers, daughter of the 1st Earl of Jersey and widow of Thomas Thynne MP, with a jointure of £12,000 a year. He had four daughters but no son by his wife, who was young, handsome, had extravagant tastes and a love of entertainments. Granville became Baron Lansdowne as one of the twelve Tory peers created in 1712 to secure the passing of the Peace with France in the Lords. Removed as secretary-at-war, before long he was given places in Queen Anne's Household instead. He obtained great victories in Cornish elections in 1713, but spent large sums of his own money doing so, again without repayment from Harley, now Earl of Oxford, the Lord Treasurer. In March 1714, his hopes were dashed when the 1st Earl of Bath's daughters, who contested the inheritance to Stowe and the Granville estates won their lawsuit.

Lansdowne lost all his offices on the accession of George I and retired to Longleat, the magnificent seat of his young stepson, Viscount Weymouth. He was regarded as totally devoted to James III and corresponded with his kinsman Sir Thomas Higgons. In September 1715 he was arrested on a charge of high treason, was kept in the Tower but was never brought to trial and was released in 1717. Thereafter, he was a leading speaker in the House of Lords, opposing the repeal of the Occasional Conformity and Schism Acts, when he attacked Gibson, the Bishop of Lincoln, as the successor of Bradshaw (the regicide) rather than Laud. He suffered further financial losses in the South Sea Bubble and went over to Paris with Lady Lansdowne in the summer of 1720. His financial difficulties increased, rather than lessened, as he was defrauded by his English landlord in Paris and was lent 15,000 *livres* by James III to bail him out. His polished manner and fluent French made him an instant success in French society, as well as a useful intermediary between James III and the Regent and he was sent by James powers of plenipotentiary with the Regent.[16] He excelled at yet another function as he directed much of the most powerful Jacobite propaganda from France. Leading English Jacobites were anxious to have Lansdowne as the secretary of state to James III in Rome, partly to lessen the influence of the Scots there, but this did not happen for reasons to be subsequently explained.[17]

General Dillon

Arthur, Viscount Dillon (1670–1733), had fought for James II in the Irish War, refused to submit to William of Orange after the capitulation of Limerick in 1692 and, as a result, forfeited some of the largest estates in Ireland: 2800 acres in Mayo, 815 in Roscommon and 1042 in Westmeath. He was one of the leaders of the Wild Geese, who fled Ireland over the years and went to serve in James II's army in France and in Louis XIV's Irish regiments in French service. He distinguished himself at the victory of Cremona in 1703. The stand of the Irish, fighting to the last at Cremona, was much celebrated in Ireland as well as in France, and he was made a brigadier in the French army. Becoming lieutenant general in 1706, he served with distinction in the 1714 campaign under the Duke of Berwick, James III's half brother. He kept close links with the Stuart Court, having married Catherine Sheldon, maid of honour to Mary of Modena, and, along with much of the Jacobite exiled community, continued to live in St Germain after Mary's death in 1718. Dillon was at the centre of the cult of the Irish brigades, which restored the self-esteem of Catholic Ireland, embodying the yearnings for a restoration of the Stuarts and the recovery of Irish forfeited estates. General Dillon was regarded as 'the only properest person to command an expedition to Britain' from France. In 1716 while James was in Avignon, he was sent on a mission on behalf of the Regent. He obviously produced a favourable impression on James, who employed him afterwards as his envoy to the court of Versailles. All the while, Dillon remained in command of the Mountcashel Brigade, the most distinguished Irish regiment in French service.[18]

The Earl of Mar

John Erskine, Earl of Mar (1675–1732), the third member of the Triumvirate, inherited an estate encumbered with debts, which he managed to clear by good financial management. Colonel of the 9th Foot from 1702–9, he allied with Queensberry and the Squadrone and was one of the chief promoters of and commissioner for the union with Scotland in 1707. Mar was a representative peer of Scotland in 1708, 1710 and 1713. He appears to have been a politic Presbyterian before 1712 and a moderate Episcopalian thereafter, building a chapel at Alloa for an Anglican service 'betwixt the bare unbecoming nakedness of the Presbiterian service in Scotland, and the gadie, affected and ostensive way of the Church of Rome'.[19] His political career followed a similar pattern and by 1711 he was Robert Harley's key man of business in Scotland, becoming secretary of state for Scotland in 1713 with a pension of £3000 a year from Queen Anne. Mar's links with Harley were sealed by a marriage alliance, when Harley's eldest daughter, Abigail, married Mar's brother-in-law, George Hay, Lord Dupplin, the son of the Earl of Kinnoul. Mar sided completely with Harley, now Earl of Oxford, in the struggle against St John, now Viscount Bolingbroke, in the last days of Queen Anne's reign. As a Scottish nationalist, Mar had become very disillusioned with the Union and, allied to Argyll, strongly supported its repeal in September 1713 in the belief that a dissolution of the Union was 'absolutely necessary'. His financial position greatly improved in June 1714, when he took as his second wife Lady Frances Pierrepont, daughter of the Whig Duke of Kingston, 'a buxom, vigorous young woman' with a portion of £6000, a jointure of £1500, and £12,000 for the children of the marriage. Known as 'Bobbing John' because of his changing politics, Mar was a clever and effective politician, with a great sense of his own importance and what the Master of Sinclair described as 'a malicious, meddling spirit'. George Lockhart, a Scottish Jacobite of absolute integrity, wrote of Mar:

> his great talent lay in the cunning management of his designs and projects, in which it was hard to find him out when he desired to be *incognito*; and thus he showed himself to be a man of good sense but bad morals.

To his credit, he had artistic tastes and was a patron of architecture.

On the accession of George I, Mar first tried to come to terms with the new régime, stressing his devotion to the Protestant succession, but he was snubbed by the new king and dismissed from all his offices. He then turned to the Jacobite option in earnest but, wholly Scotocentric, did not concert his plans with English Jacobites or with James III, raising the standard at Braemar on 6 September 1715 at a time when James had countermanded his orders for a rising after the arrest of the English Jacobites in the West, where the English rising was to begin. Mar would identify wholly with James's pledge to restore Scotland to its 'free and independent state' and 'a free and independent Scots Parliament'. Such was the strength of opposition in Scotland to the Union, allied to loyalty to Scotland's Stuart kings, that nearly 20,000 men joined Mar, including the most influential nobles in the Highlands, as well as half of Argyll's clansmen and Lowland nobles and gentlemen. Unfortunately, Mar was a mediocre general without a clear plan of campaign or tactics to have been concerted with Brigadier Mackintosh and the Northumbrian Jacobites. Mar was defeated at Sheriffmuir on 13 November 1715, while the northern English Jacobites and a portion of the Scottish Jacobite army under Mackintosh was beaten at the Battle of Preston on 14 November. Illness and obstacles from the Whig government had prevented James III from coming to Scotland until he landed at Peterhead on 22 December 1715, by which time the rising had been defeated, so that he and Mar had to seek refuge in France in February 1716. Mar's estate was forfeited and his pension of £3000 was stopped, nor were the arrears of £6500 owed to him repaid by the Whig government.

The Fifteen had formed a bond between James III and Mar, the older man, who was the first to have taken up arms for the Stuart cause, and Lord Dupplin's younger brother, Colonel John Hay (Mar's brother-in-law), who fought in the campaign. These links were to be important for the future. James created Mar a duke in the Jacobite peerage as a reward. Mar attempted to throw all the responsibility of the failure of the Fifteen on Bolingbroke, who had become James's secretary of state after his flight to France in 1715, for his failure to send arms or money to Scotland during the rising. George Keith, hereditary Earl Marischal of Scotland, who had himself taken part in the Fifteen and forfeited his estates as a result, laid the blame on Mar's military incompetence. Mar persuaded James to dismiss Bolingbroke in March 1716 and to choose him as secretary of state instead.

Mar followed James and the Stuart Court to Avignon in 1716 and to Urbino and Rome the following year. From Rome he was active in working for a restoration with help of troops from Charles XII of Sweden in 1716–17, a scheme masterminded by Lord Oxford and Charles Caesar. Mar sought to engineer an alliance between Sweden and Russia to help James III. He was the head of a powerful Erskine Clan in Russia, where his cousin Dr Robert Erskine, physician to Peter the Great, was able to influence Russian foreign policy. Dr Erskine wrote 'any Erskine must support the restoration ... if they do not, they are unworthy to come of that family' and he wrote explicit letters to Mar describing Peter the Great's hatred for George I and support for the Jacobites. Dr Erskine was ably supported by Admiral Thomas Gordon who, as a Jacobite, had to leave the Royal Navy after 1715 and went on to found Peter the Great's Navy, for which he recruited many Scottish Jacobites. Mar and Ormonde left Italy in 1717 to work for bringing about a peace and an alliance between Sweden and Russia. While in Paris Mar met his old acquaintance Lord Stair, the British ambassador, and asked for permission from the Whig government to go to Bourbon to drink the waters there, promising to 'live quietly and give no manner of trouble', a meeting Stair did not report to the British government. The same year Mar wrote to Sunderland and to Cadogan, the British envoy at The Hague, proposing that George I should relinquish the British crown to James III in exchange for expanding Hanoverian territories on the Continent. The offer might have been tempting to George I, but not to his ministers, who depended on King George to maintain the Whig hegemony. Mar, who had returned to Rome, resigned his secretaryship of state, probably because he did not want to go to Spain to take part in expeditions sponsored by Alberoni.

In 1719 Mar left Italy, not by the most obvious route via Genoa, but through the Milanese, a territory belonging to George I's ally, the emperor. He was thus arrested and imprisoned in Milan. Mar then renewed his contacts with Lord Stair, who wrote to Stanhope that Mar would not sever his links with the Pretender unless he received a pension or a pardon in exchange. Mar now told Stair he wished to live quietly in France, but not to do anything to damage his reputation and he kept James informed of his dealings with Stair, without going into details. But neither Craggs nor Sunderland would promise Mar anything unless he deserted the Jacobite cause and agreed to be 'a spy' for them. Released from imprisonment, he proceeded to Bourbon, then returned to Paris in October 1720. In January 1721 he was offered and accepted a pension of £2000 a year by Sir Robert Sutton, the new ambassador at Paris, who was then secretly acting with the Jacobites. Mar obtained James's subsequent approval of this pension, of which he received only £400. There is no evidence that Mar gave the Whig government any information at this time. Nor did Eleanor Oglethorpe, marquise de Mezières, who acted as his secretary, Dillon or Lansdowne question his loyalty.[20]

The Atterbury Plot was now managed in France by Lansdowne, who was highly regarded by English Tories, by Lord Mar, who had powerful contacts in Scotland and Russia, and General Dillon, who had good contacts in Ireland. It was a good team except, fatally, for Mar who was cornered by Walpole and Townshend after Sunderland's death.

The Duke of Ormonde

In Spain, the situation was promising for the Jacobites because the Duke of Ormonde commanded all the armies of Spain, and because the Spanish court was full of Jacobites. Ormonde's privileged position in Spain was described by the duc de St Simon, whose *Memoirs* immortalised so many of his contemporaries, and who was French ambassador to Spain at the time of the Atterbury Plot. St Simon, who took an instant liking to Ormonde, wrote:

> I found in the Duke of Ormonde a greatness of spirit that no reverse of fortune could alter, the nobility and courage of a *grand seigneur*, faithfulness in all trials and complete loyalty to King James and his party, despite the setbacks he had experienced and which he was ready to face anew as soon as he could hope for any slight success in the affairs of so unfortunate a prince ... The Duke of Ormonde enjoyed in Madrid the greatest consideration from everyone, including the ministers. He was much sought after and kept an abundant and excellent table for noblemen and officers. He had ample funds from the King of Spain. He went nearly every day to the Palace, where he was warmly welcomed and I have never seen him near the King or Queen without their talking to him and often staying some time with him with every sign of regard and goodwill. He wore the Garter in public [from which he had been ostensibly stripped by King George] and was addressed as the Duke of Ormonde [his forfeited title]. He did not attend functions when heads were covered, but otherwise he was treated in every particular as a grandee. He was rather short, stout and short-necked but bore himself very gracefully, with the air of a *grand seigneur* and great politeness and nobility of manner. He was deeply attached to the Anglican religion and invariably refused great offices offered him in Spain which would have meant abandoning it.

St Simon, who spoke freely to Ormonde of the 'chains' that bound France (alluding to Dubois), had been instructed to maintain civil but distant relations with Ormonde, but to befriend Colonel Stanhope, the British ambassador. Instead, St Simon and Ormonde met in secret and became fast friends, so that they could hardly keep a straight face when they pretended to be aloof with one another at the Spanish court. Prince Eugene's picture of Ormonde was equally eulogistic: 'the finest Cavalier and most complete gentleman that England bred, being the glory of that nation, of so noble spirit that he would sacrifice all to his Church and sovereign'. This explains the veneration of the Tories and of Atterbury particularly for Ormonde. As Captain-General, Ormonde wielded wide powers of patronage in Spain and was able to obtain pensions and or army commissions for Jacobites, notably for the Earl Marischal, one of the leaders of the Fifteen in Scotland and for his brother James Keith, both of whom were to take part in the planned rising in 1722.[21]

Christopher Layer and John Plunkett

The first step taken in England was to send to James in Rome an estimate of support of a rising in the English and Welsh counties, annotated to mark 'doubtfuls' or 'Whigs' from whom opposition could be anticipated. This was carried, with great secrecy by Christopher Layer and John Plunkett, not themselves authors of this survey. They planned their departure in November 1720 and left in the company of two other persons, making for Antwerp, whence Plunkett wrote to James on 21 March 1721:

> The Gentleman I mentioned to you formerly, is come out of the Country with Instructions to wait on you, and tender their service, he offers to bear my Expenses if I go with him; as I take it that my going will be more useful than my staying now, I believe I shall accept his offer ... I believe you will have Messages from all Parts to tender their Services, one comes with me and sets out in few Days to let you see what they intend to do and comply with their desire forthwith.

Christopher Layer (1683–1723), who took Plunkett with him to Rome, was descended from the Layers of Booton Hall, a substantial Norfolk family, members of which had served as aldermen, mayors and MPs for Norwich since the sixteenth century. He was brought up by and was heir to his uncle Christopher Layer of Booton, who had been arrested as a Jacobite suspect in 1695, and was educated in the nonjuring principles of his uncle and of their friend and neighbour Sir Nicholas L'Estrange. He entered the practice of Henry Rippinghall, a leading attorney in Aylsham, Norfolk and a High Tory, and kept the court leet of Oliver Le Neve, a member of one of the oldest families in Norfolk, a training then regarded as the best possible one for a young lawyer. On Layer's marriage in 1709 to Elizabeth, daughter of Peter Elwin of Aylsham, his uncle settled Booton, worth £800 a year, on the young couple. They later moved to London, Layer being admitted to Gray's Inn in 1715 and called to the bar in 1720. Living in Southampton Buildings, near Chancery Lane, Layer had a thriving

Christopher Layer. Anonymous engraving, 1740. (Private Collection)

legal practice, including among his clients the Earl of Yarmouth, an impoverished but still influential member of the Paston family, Lord North and Grey, Layer's principal client, and Lord Londonderry. As early as August 1720 James regarded Layer as a person of consequence in his affairs. Thus Layer was far from being the penniless adventurer depicted by some historians. Before leaving he made his estate over to a relation to preserve it from forfeiture in case disaster befell him.[22]

Travelling with Layer was John Plunkett (also spelt Plunket), a Roman Catholic who was not in orders. In his testimony before the House of Commons Committee, Plunkett said he was born in Dublin and educated in the Jesuits' College in Vienna, where he studied Civil Law. He had been secretary to Count Gallas, the Imperial Envoy at London, and carried out missions on Lord Oxford's behalf in the reign of Queen Anne. He corresponded with the Duke of Berwick, Sir William Ellis, treasurer to the Stuart Household in Rome, and had visited Mary of Modena at Saint-Germain-en-Laye.

After leaving Antwerp, Layer and Plunkett arrived in Paris in April 1721. They conferred with General Dillon, who reported to James:

> As I am not acquainted with those persons nor informed except in general terms of their message which Plunkett pretends to be of great consequence, I judged it would not have been prudent to stop their journey; and the more that they undertake it at their own cost by which its to be presumed they have material points to tell the King which they were directed not to confide to any other.[23]

Keeping secret the names on the list Layer was carrying (see Appendix B) was an essential precaution.

When Plunkett and Layer arrived in Rome, Plunkett proved useful in arranging a first meeting between Layer and James, as the following letter from James to Plunkett, dated only 'Thursday' shows:

> This only to direct you not to mention any Thing of Business to any Body till I have seen you; I have not much leisure at Night to expect visits, but however, I shall be glad to see you alone, and agree with you the most private Way and Manner for your companion and me to meet; The Bearer F. Kennedy [James's secretary] will bring you very privately to my House to Night about eight a clock. signed James Rex.[24]

It was the usual practice for James to see visitors from England at night to minimise the risk of British spies finding out their identity.

According to Barnaby Fairfax, physician to Layer's family, Layer told him that he was admitted to a private audience with James in Rome and that when 'a Scotch colonel [John Hay] broke in upon them' James took Layer aside into another room, where Layer presented his credentials. Layer did not tell Fairfax what these credentials were.[25] Layer had the honour of being allowed to kiss Queen Maria Clementina's hand and to see the infant Prince of Wales.

The 1721 list

The Secret Committee on the conspiracy grasped the importance of the list of supporters in English and Welsh counties which Layer took to Italy, which was described in Jacobite papers merely as 'the list', but neither the Committee nor the British government ever had a copy of it. Headed 'State of England' [Appendix B] the list divided England by counties or groups of counties, much as Sir George Booth and Edward Nicholas had done for the proposed Royalist rising of 1659. It is the most important list in the Stuart papers. We do not know absolutely who drew up the 1721 list, which was received at Albano, James's country retreat near Rome, in August 1721. It is likely that it was drawn up by Lord North and Grey in collaboration with Lord Strafford and Lord Arran.

Cornwall, the stronghold of the Royalists in the Civil War, has the longest list of supporters for the proposed rising. It gives the fourteen 'chiefs' in several counties and two '2nd chiefs'. Lord Lansdowne was chief in Cornwall, Lord Bruce (brother to Lord Ailesbury) 'first chief' and General Webb '2nd chief' in Wiltshire. Other chiefs were Lord Digby in Dorset, Sir Henry Goring in Hampshire and Sussex, Lord Winchilsea, a nonjuror, for Surrey and Kent. Lord North and Grey, Layer's patron, was chief in Cambridgeshire, Huntingdon and Bedford. Lord Craven was 'first chief' in Warwickshire, with Sir John Packington as '2nd chief', as well as 'chief' in Berkshire. Lord Strafford was 'chief' in Northamptonshire and joint chief with Lord Carmarthen in Yorkshire. Lord Abingdon was chief in Oxfordshire and the Earl of Plymouth in Worcestershire. Lord Gower was chief in Staffordshire and Cheshire. Herefordshire and Radnorshire, counties governed or under the jurisdiction of Lord Oxford, were said to be 'of no great use'. Though Lord Oxford was in regular touch with the Stuart Court at this time and, with Charles Caesar, had masterminded the Swedish Plot of 1716–17, he was distrusted by Atterbury. The list includes Whigs, presumably those from whom opposition was expected, and 'dubious' in various counties.

Layer's list of sympathisers in Norfolk

The most urgent task at this time was to raise money for the purchase of arms for a Jacobite rising and it is likely that this was discussed in the course of the several meetings between Layer and James and with Sir William Ellis, a nonjuror, the treasurer at the Stuart Court, with whom Layer struck up a friendship and later corresponded. Layer himself drew up in Rome for James III a second list of 114 'Persons of fortune' in Norfolk, his own county (Appendix C), who were 'desirous to show their loyalty and affection by joining with any attempt that shall be thought advisable to bring about a speedy and happy restoration'. It gave the yearly value of their estates, presumably with a view to raising money from them. Layer said that Thomas Pitt, Lord Londonderry, colonel of a regiment of horse, 'the little soldier' in Layer's cipher, had entered into an association to lead the Norfolk gentlemen and proclaim the king. Londonderry, who had a mortgage of £50,000 on the estates of the Earl of Yarmouth, which Layer himself had transacted, was promised the reversion to the earldom of Yarmouth after a restoration. Londonderry was a Whig, (though his kinsman Robert Pitt had Jacobite sympathies), who had been ruined by the South Sea Bubble and rich pickings after a restoration would be better than being governor of the Leeward Islands, which is where he ended up.

The christening of Layer's daughter

Before Layer left Rome, he asked for a token and received a signal honour for his services: James and his queen agreed to become godfather and godmother to the child Mrs Layer was expecting. It was a daughter, named Mary Clementina. After his return to England, he asked Lord Orrery to act as proxy-godfather through Simon Swordfeger, Lord Orrery's secretary. Orrery declined, then reconsidered, by which time Lord North had agreed to act as proxy for James, with the Duchess of Ormonde acting as proxy for Maria Clementina Sobieska. Aaron Thompson, the chaplain of the 3rd Earl of Burlington, performed the christening at a house in Chelsea.[26] After his return from Rome, Layer was much in demand in London. He cherished his moment of glory: he had met his king, had been allowed to kiss the hand of his queen and to gaze at the infant Prince of Wales. He described himself an 'old servant' of Lord North,[27] but drew closer to Lord Orrery at this time. Orrery's secretary, Simon Swordfeger, delivered to Layer a message in Orrery's own hand. This note read as follows: 'when Mr. Lear comes to town if he has anything material to say to me, and will take the trouble to come down to Britell [Britwell] for a few Days, we may have a good opportunity there you may tell him to talk together'.[28]

Lord Burlington

Burlington, who, inspired by Palladio and Inigo Jones, introduced the eighteenth-century style of Palladian architecture into England, was a follower of Walpole from 1717 to 1733 and outwardly an orthodox Whig. Burlington was a Renaissance man, who travelled widely on the Continent of Europe, a patron of the arts, a nobleman who was a practising architect, and one chosen by Atterbury to build the Westminster dormitory. Like Orrery, he had Roman Catholic servants, something the anti-Catholic Walpole would never have done. Did he have a secret Jacobite agenda? Swordfeger, Orrery's Flemish secretary, said the first time he met Layer 'was at Lord Burlington's where he drank with him in company with Mr. Thompson, Lord Burlington's chaplain'. Plunkett was also present and they talked of their journey to Rome. How much did Burlington know of the meetings going on between Swordfeger, Layer and Plunkett in the chamber of his chaplain Aaron Thompson at Burlington House? Burlington must have come to know of the christening of Layer's daughter and who her real godparents were when it became public knowledge, yet he did not dismiss Thompson, who was promoted to a good living in 1724. Aaron Thompson was involved in the Jacobite correspondence in France under the cover of George Waters, James III's banker there. Andrew Crotty, Burlington's steward, was a Jacobite agent. Burlington was an intensely secretive man, who had many Jacobite friends and contacts including his brother-in-law Sir Henry Bedingfield, a Catholic and an active Jacobite.[29] The evidence is indeed only circumstantial, but there is a good deal of it.

James III's financial resources

Before any rising could take place, there had to be enough money raised to buy arms. The funds for this came from diverse quarters. At this stage of the plot we know more about what was obtained from abroad than about what was raised at home, though Lord Strafford wrote to James in January 1721 that the king's friends in England would do their 'utmost to raise money ready' and would borrow all they could to lend to him.[30] The assumption was always that James would repay after the restoration. On the other hand James thought that Scotland, as the poorer country, would be able to provide little money.[31] The King of Spain was ready to give James 15,000 crowns plus 3000 more.[32] For his part, the pope gave James 20,000 crowns.[33] In France, the cardinal de Noailles raised once more the question of the repayment of James II's late queen's dowry by Britain, so often promised but never reimbursed. The Regent, however, would not press for the return of her jointure at this time. The Marshal Duke of Noailles, head of one of the most powerful families at Versailles wrote to James that, as a trusted friend of James II and the late queen, he was honoured to be of service by delivering personally James's letter to the Regent, who received it as warmly as their links of kinship and friendship dictated. The maréchal de Villeroy, another influential friend of James, also intervened on his behalf. The upshot was that the Regent promised that, despite France's financial difficulties, 54,000 *livres* would be paid to James regularly every three months. This was James's original pension from France, which had now at last been restored. It coincided with Dubois being created a cardinal on James's nomination in July 1721. Dubois wrote to 'le Roi d'Angleterre', expressing his undying gratitude.[34] Like all other members of the College of Cardinals, Dubois had to recognise James as King of England, in Rome at least. Although James always distrusted Dubois's 'pretended friendship' for him and believed he had no enemy in France except Dubois, the renewal of his pension from France could not have come at a better time.[35] In addition, James raised 30,000 crowns on the security of the Stuart jewels.[36]

Robert Knight in Rome

An unexpected source of funds arrived in Rome in the autumn of 1721: Robert Knight, as we have seen, lately treasurer of the South Sea Company. Knight appears to have been able to take abroad with him a substantial part of his fortune as he carried £40,000–£50,000 in plate and jewels, apparently designed for the Stuart Court. At first, Knight was mistaken for the 2nd Duke of Leeds (son of Danby, Charles II's first minister), who was an active Jacobite at this time and had stopped at Leghorn to collect money to bring to James. Knight apparently knew and had high regard for James Murray (the son of Viscount Stormont in the peerage of Scotland and the brother of William Murray, later Earl of Mansfield). James Murray, who was an influential Tory MP in the last two Parliaments of Queen Anne's reign, had joined the Stuart

Court in Rome and subsequently became Earl of Dunbar in the Jacobite peerage and secretary of state to James. Knight was soon on friendly terms with John Hay, who trusted Knight as far as to show him some of the Jacobite correspondence. However, James was anxious not to be seen to protect Knight because of the adverse effect this would have on public opinion in England and had no meetings with him. Knight, on his side, assured Hay that he was anxious not to cause difficulties for the Stuart Court. It is possible that Knight had taken his Green Book to Rome to offer it to James as proof against George I and his German favourites. This is suggested by Lansdowne's letter to Lord Molesworth, a leading independent Whig, which painted a very favourable picture of James and urged Molesworth to prove himself worthy of 'a disciple of the great Cato', by placing before Parliament evidence provided by Knight on the frauds in the distribution of free South Sea stock, 'so that we should be beholden to the Pretender for coming to the bottom of this mystery of iniquity'. Any such scheme came to an end when Knight was escorted out of Rome on its governor's orders in January 1722.[37]

Thus a substantial amount of money, from various sources, was made available to James in continental Europe.

The search for troops

Atterbury exercised his powers as James's representative in England to the full. He approved and amended any memorial drawn up in England to be sent to James, Ormonde, or the Triumvirate in Paris or any Declaration by James sent for distribution in England. He shared with his associates, Arran, Strafford, North and Grey and Sir Henry Goring the belief that the support of some regular troops was necessary for any successful rising in England.[38] Other leading Jacobites such as Lord Orrery and Charles Caesar, who were closer to Lord Oxford than to Atterbury, had their own channel of communication with James. They wished to take part in the rising and agreed in thinking that the king's friends could not rise 'without some foreign assistance'.[39] At home, Lord Orrery thought that serving officers in George I's army were 'as discontented as any other set of people' and that some of them at least might be gained, while Tory officers purged from the army by the Whigs in 1715, such as Generals Webb, Lumley and Portmore, were regarded by Lord North and Grey as ready to take up James's cause.[40] Discontented half-pay officers too would be very useful for organising the English side of the rising. In search of troops,

Atterbury and his associates looked primarily to the Irish regiments under Ormonde in Spain and under Dillon in France to land troops in Britain to support a general rising.

The Jacobite regiments

The commanders of the Jacobite regiments in France and Spain were Irish but the regiments contained Englishmen and Scotsmen too. They were recruited in James III's name and took the oaths to him as well as to the kings of France or Spain. James was consulted in any appointments or promotions made in these regiments, which were regarded by the Jacobites as 'the King's own subjects'. The Duke of Berwick punctually executed James's orders regarding promotions in these regiments in France.[41] The Jacobite regiments followed the flag of St George, wore the livery of the King of England, and played English marching tunes, including 'The King shall enjoy his own again', the best known royalist and later Jacobite air. Before the rising was expected to take place in 1722, James wrote to the commanders of the Irish regiments in French service, Michael Rothe, Andrew Lee, Christopher Nugent, Andrew Sheldon, Daniel O'Connell, Matthew Cooke, Charles O'Brien, Viscount Clare and Lieutenant General Dillon:

> The particular zeal and forwardness you expressed for my service some years ago assure me that you will not be less desirous now in contributing to its advancement in the manner which will be further explained to you by Mr. Dillon. I heartily wish for my sake that you will be able to give your personal assistance on this great occasion, but at least I hope it will be in your power to render some of your officers and soldiers of your regiment in assisting in this great undertaking.[42]

They would no doubt have wished to take part in a landing in Ireland, but none was considered at this time because, although Catholic Ireland was the most disaffected part of the British Isles, it was heavily quartered with troops, partly to hide the real size of the standing army from Parliament, but mainly to keep down the Irish Catholic majority.

General Dillon told Ormonde 'we have numbers of officers in France extremely willing and very fit' to serve James when called upon. Dillon proposed to send 2000 soldiers from these regiments over to England. Atterbury believed that this number was too small, but Goring, who had not been consulted, disagreed and thought they would 'not want numbers' once that force had landed and that the 'great persons' who were pledged to join would do so 'at one day's' notice'. It was hoped that Ormonde could provide a further 2000 men. There were arms ready in the Dutch Netherlands and a further 6000 arms were available in Spain, while Sweden had promised more. Captain Morgan (see below) had four ships ready to transport troops and arms from Spain to England.[43]

'The time has now come'

By the spring of 1721 Goring and Atterbury agreed that the time was ripe for action. Goring wrote to Ormonde:

> the kingdom begs a reprieve as well Whigs as Tories and if you could come with one thousand soldiers [and] ten thousand arms, it is a safe gain ... I conversed with Earl Strafford, Lord North and Lord Gower are yours, and I don't doubt many more will be so when it is proper to talk to them.[44]

On 22 April 1721 Atterbury was able to send his exiled king one of the most dramatic letters he ever penned:

> Sir, the time has now come when with very little assistance from your friends abroad, your way to your friends at home is become safe and easy. The present juncture is so favourable and will probably continue so for many months to be so, that I cannot think it will pass over without a proper use being made of it.
>
> Your friends are in good earnest interesting themselves for that purpose and under a full expectation that an opportunity may some time this summer be given them to show their zeal for your service. They will never despair but must always think this the most promising juncture that ever offered itself.[45]

Sir Henry Goring's mission to Paris

Atterbury had not entered into particulars in order to preserve secrecy. Instead, he sent 'the worthy Sir Henry Goring' to Paris in May to confer with Lansdowne, Dillon and Mar. As we shall meet Goring again and again in this story, we need to know his background. Sir Henry Goring 4th Bt. of Highden near Steyning in Sussex, had represented Horsham and Steyning as a court Tory in the reign of Queen Anne. He served as captain in Colonel Masham's Horse, rising to the rank of colonel, and sat on the new board set up by Ormonde to take army commissions out of the hands of the Duke of Marlborough. He was forced to sell his colonelcy at the outbreak of the Fifteen rebellion and like Atterbury was close to Ormonde.[46] General Dillon was impressed with Goring who would 'press this matter with much vigour, zeal and spirit' and thought he had the 'general esteem and confidence of friends in England'.[47] From Paris Goring reported to James (16 May 1721) that friends in England were 'more unanimous than ever' and were prepared to sign an association if necessary. Writing to Ormonde, again from Paris, he went on to explain what was expected from Spain:

> I am of opinion the King of Spain cannot refuse our master the troops in his service which are his own subjects, or at least I hope he will connive at their going with you, sure he will furnish you with arms and money and tho he will not suffer them to go with you entire, the least he can do will be to let you take with you what number of them you can bring with you and ships which will be sent to you for that service.[48]

One O'Brien, an Irish merchant in Malaga, 'a very zealous active man' for the Stuart cause, reported that there were three Irish regiments stationed near Malaga, which might be used.[49] Goring had a long meeting with Dillon, as well as with Mar and Lansdowne to settle on arrangements to be taken on both sides. The list of supporters in the counties which Layer was taking to Italy reached James in the summer. Meanwhile, General Dillon sent to Ormonde a copy of a 'Scheme proposed for a private army in England'. This arranged that as soon as the preparations abroad were ready for 'an attempt in England and Scotland' England would be divided into a number of districts and the commanders and commissary general for each district would receive their commissions from James. At that point:

> the persons confided in should on receipt of advice promised make overture of the design to the commanders-in-chief, agree about commissarys general, give them their commissions, divide amongst them as equally as can be the blank commissions for the field, officers of horse and dragoons and regiments of foot and give them instructions. Each to repair immediately to his district, make choice of the field officers for the regiments he is to raise whereof the majors ought to be men skilful in military exercises.

Each troop, assisted by one or two experienced officers, would prepare and bring horses without regard to size and any arms and accoutrements available without attracting attention. The commanders-in-chief in each district should establish a means of communication by means of ciphers or expresses 'to be informed of the debarkation which should point to the time of the general rising'. Money lying in customs houses or in the hands of receivers of the land tax should be taken to provide for the king's forces (as was done in 1688 and 1745). The commissary general in each district would then summon all persons of note in each district 'to join personally the King's standard without any toleration' and those who refused were to be seized. All roads to London were to be blocked by the commissaries. The king and Captain-General (Ormonde) would give instructions as to time and place for a general rising in all parts of the kingdom, which would deter 'foreigners' from giving any opposition.[50]

Lansdowne's trumpet

The proposals sent by Atterbury were received enthusiastically by Lansdowne, who wrote to James a letter as striking as Atterbury's own:

> It would be a miserable circumstance indeed to be surprised when the trumpet sounds as not to be able to follow the call: I can compare it to nothing but the condition of those unhappy souls who shall be found unprepared at the last day.
>
> I had it lately in a letter that a motion will be tried to make it high treason to introduce any foreign troops into the kingdom without the consent of Parliament. If that should be carried, we can desire no surer signal of the nation to deliver itself. There is hardly anyone circumstance of confusion which preceded the last Restauration but what now appears amongst all ranks and opinions to bespeak another.[51]

At this time, the king's friends in England thought that James needed an English secretary of state. James III realised that the Scots were over-represented at his Court and he was ready to agree. Matthew Prior, the writer and the friend of Charles and Mary Caesar, was suggested but turned down. Leading English Jacobites hoped that Lansdowne might be persuaded to go to Rome. This would have meant forfeiture of his estates and the ruin of his family. Somewhat reluctantly, Lansdowne expressed his readiness to serve James III in whatever capacity was required of him. Meanwhile, other circumstances intervened and he did not go to Italy in the end.[52]

Plans in Scotland

As for the arrangements in Scotland, Mar was appointed Lord Lieutenant and High Commissioner for Scotland on 28 June 1721. The Duke of Hamilton, who was young and inexperienced, and Lord Tullibardine were to command in Scotland. At this time James thanked the Duke of Hamilton for his 'zeal and affection' and assured the duke that he would be given 'proper share' in bringing about a restoration. Lord Tullibardine, Mar proposed, should be made Admiral of Scotland. Although Mar thought Goring to be 'a worthy frank fellow', he complained that Scotland was being neglected and he argued that General Dillon and his officers should land in Scotland, not in England. In addition, he regretted the fact that Lord Oxford was not centrally involved in the plans.[53]

The Duke of Orléans asked to intervene

In addition to the 4000 troops from the Jacobite regiments Dillon and Ormonde hoped to muster, the Jacobites applied to the Regent for the use of French forces. Lansdowne in Paris was granted an audience with the Regent, in the course of which he offered the setting up of an association signed by leading English noblemen, with a promise that the crown of England would reimburse France for any expenses incurred in restoring King James. The troops requested from France for England and Scotland were 4000 infantry and 2000 cavalry or dragoons with arms and accoutrements. Horses would be provided for the French cavalry in England. These troops would form a bridgehead before the start of general risings in England and Scotland. The Regent was asked to consult the Marshal Duke of Berwick, who knew more than anyone the state of the army in France and how things stood in England.[54] An English banker 'of great standing' (probably George Waters) went to see the Regent to confirm what Lansdowne had said and to stress that it was 'not a question of military conquest but of helping the greater part of the English nation to help themselves'. A memorandum on the state of England, drawn up by three English Lords not named (presumably Arran, North and Grey and Strafford) written in London on 31 July 1721 (o.s.) and translated into French, was presented to the Regent. It argued that the efforts of Parliament to relieve the South Sea sufferers had been useless and that the Court was about to impose further crippling taxes. Trampled upon by the Court and betrayed by Parliament, the people sought a restoration of King James and an end to usurpation. Foreign help was needed because there were enough regular troops in the kingdom to crush poorly armed people, whereas a landing by 3000 regular troops could protect those who joined the rising and would allow the king (James) to land. Arms and munitions were also required. In addition some troops should be sent to Scotland, where there were a lot of supporters.[55] Not revealing the names of the three Lords or any others involved was a good idea as Dubois, as foreign secretary, had to be sent a copy!

After all this flurry of activity in Paris, James wrote to Lord Arran on 21 July that he would have heard of 'the great affairs now pending' from Sir Henry Goring and General Dillon. Everything possible would be done on this side 'but that you on yours must decide'.[56] All this was based on the assumption that Sunderland would be able to obtain new elections free from Court pressure in the autumn of 1721 (see Chapter 2).

The anti-Jacobite alliance

As the hopes of James III and his supporters rose, there was another setback. In order to try and prevent Spanish help for the Jacobites, George I wrote to Philip V promising to restore Gibraltar to Spain. His English ministers had other ideas, however, so that King George had to write again to tell King Philip that this had proved impossible. Another tack, apparently suggested by Dubois, was tried. Philip V was very uxorious and his second wife, Elizabeth Farnese, was anxious to provide for the future of her son, who as a younger son would not inherit the Spanish throne. To please Elizabeth, Parma and Piacenza in Tuscany were provided as territories for her son. The negotiations to achieve an alliance between Britain, Spain and France did not go without much interference from the numerous Jacobites in Spain and were brought to a standstill as Spain claimed compensation for its fleet destroyed by Admiral Byng at Cape Passaro, while Britain claimed compensation for goods seized by Spain from British merchants before the declaration of war in 1719. In addition, Spain refused to allow more extensive British trade with South America and would not listen to any demands from George I for the removal of Ormonde as commander of the armies of Spain.[57] In the end, the Triple alliance was concluded between Britain, Spain and France in the summer of 1721. In what way it benefited France is problematic, though Dubois may have had his reward from

Britain. For the Jacobites, it meant that France and Spain would not be able to assist them openly. Another blow was the recall of the British ambassador in Paris, Sir Robert Sutton, who had provided Lansdowne with information and a safe passage for Jacobite correspondence.[58] A hopeful sign, however, was the peace concluded between Russia and Sweden. Urquhart undertook to find out from Sunderland what George I was planning to do.[59] King George, on his side, grew very alarmed when the tsar sent troops to Mecklenberg, thus threatening Hanover.

A change of plans

Atterbury and his partners now realised they would obtain no French troops from the Regent. Preparations for the rising, however, went ahead on the basis that the agreed number of officers and men from the Jacobite regiments and a sufficient quantity of arms would be able to land in Britain with the connivance of the Regent and Philip V. The Duke of Ormonde's passage from Spain had been arranged so that he could land in the West Country 'at the proper place and at the proper time' with as many arms and officers as he could muster.[60] Ormonde was to come over on the *Phineas* of Bristol which was commanded by Captain William Arnold. It was chartered by Captain Halstead (see below), who went to see Atterbury before leaving for Spain. Lord North and Grey paid for part or for the whole of the trip. The crew was hired by Roger Nowell of Whalley in Lancashire, a merchant, and the ship, which carried no freight, left Gravesend for Bilbao in the spring of 1722.[61]

All set

After receiving a satisfactory memorial from England, James wrote to his friends on 3 January 1722:

> There remains therefore nothing to be done at present but to hasten on all sides with all speed the necessary preparations for the proposed insurrection with what money our friends in England will be able to provide and with what I shall send from hence, notwith-standing all my disappointments we shall be still in a condition to answer the proposed ends.[62]

Mar and Dillon were to land in Scotland, where 'the first motion' was to be made and the rest would follow soon after.

At the same time as Mar and Dillon left Paris, James would leave Rome. Knowing that everything would be done to try and prevent his journey, he was prepared to leave Rome by sea (despite his suffering from seasickness) to go to Rotterdam where William Dundas (a Jacobite agent) would get a ship ready for him. Dillon thought that the 45,000 Roman crowns available would suffice for Scotland and he hoped the friends in England would be able to raise what was necessary for England, although he was 'very sensible of the risks of applying to many persons for money in England and yet more of doing the like in France'.[63]

At length, James wrote to Atterbury:

It is not easy for me to express the satisfaction I received from those accounts and the deep sense I have of the great share you have had in managing and bringing matters to the length they are arrived ... By the next post I shall send to Mr. Dillon the commissions mentioned in my reply and with them four warrants for your worthy partners. I am truly mortified not to be able to give you a like token of my favour, but I hope the time will yet come in which you may enjoy a rank superior to all the rest after having been so signally instrumental in my restoration. I have an entire confidence in the continuance of your application to bring it about.[64]

The Jacobite establishment

The Council of Regency chosen by James to administer Britain until his arrival consisted of the Duke of Ormonde, Lord Arran, the Earl of Strafford, the Earl of Oxford, Lord Orrery, Atterbury, Lord Gower, Lord North and Grey and Lord Lansdowne, with a quorum of five in all decisions.[65] James wrote to Lord North and Grey thanking him for his 'distinguished zeal and forwardness on this occasion' and sending him a commission as lieutenant general, another as commander-in-chief in and about London, and a warrant creating him an earl.[66] Lord Lansdowne was sent a commission to act as secretary of state with the seals in case of an expedition, with a patent creating him Earl of Bath in which the rights of Lord Gower and Lord Carteret (as members of the Granville family) were safeguarded, together with a commission to command in Cornwall (as in the 1721 list).[67] Lord Strafford, who was to command in the North (as in the 1721 list) was thanked by James for his

singular attachment and zeal for me and my cause, by your late resolution you have given me the greatest proofs of it and by the execution of it you may be well looked upon as the deliverer of our country and the restorer of my family ... I take your presence in the North to be most essential in this juncture.

Strafford would be created a Duke.[68] Lord Arran already had his commission of 'General of all England and Ireland' in his brother's absence and was to be granted a new title. James thanked him for his 'zeal and forwardness in my cause', adding 'I am sure you will not take it ill of me to wish that D[uke] of Ormond's speedy joining you may render the commission you have in your hands to command in his absence of a short lasting'.[69] Sir Henry Goring was appointed governor of Bristol, with a commission as major general and to be created a viscount.[70] General Dillon was sending out blank commissions for colonels, lieutenant colonels and majors. Alexander Urquhart was given a commission of colonel, while his friend and mentor James Grahme had a commission as major general.[71] It was at this time that the Duke of Wharton sent assurances of loyalty to James, who was surprised at first, but concluded that 'when the mask is once off we shall have more friends and fewer enemies than we are aware of'.[72] Finally, James told Ormonde to do all he could to comply 'with the call of friends from England' and to let them know, with due regard to secrecy, when he was leaving and what officers and arms he could bring with him. He hoped that Captain Morgan would still be able to dispose of the ships available to him.[73]

To lull the British government into a false sense of security, a letter dated 12 February was sent from London through the common post, endorsed 'written to be intercepted', which found its way to the secretary of state's office. This suggested no rising was intended and that while the Tories were prepared to take measures against the ministry in Parliament, their zeal went 'no further than talking and drinking healths'. It conveyed the message that there was no danger to Hanover from any intervention from the tsar.[74] Counter-intelligence was not a one-way traffic and several such letters of disinformation from the other side are to be found in the Stuart papers.

Elections and insurrection

The time of the insurrection in England was to be during the general election of 1722, when the army had by law to be withdrawn from constituencies and there was the greatest excitement on each side. This was a good time, and we have seen the ability of the Tories to mobilise

and organise their supporters in a quasi-military force in such constituencies as Westminster and Coventry. James thought that his
friends in England would 'seriously and speedily go about the necessary preparations for action' and he advised Lord Strafford that there
were 'more dangers in delay than can be imagined'.[75] He wrote to
Dubois saying that the disposition of people in England was more
favourable to his restoration than it had ever been and that France
could reap great advantages from it. The English government maintained itself by corruption and armed force, but the people were eager
to shake off the yoke. All he asked Dubois to do was to speak to the
Regent, to turn a blind eye to what went on, and to give James money
in secret.[76]

Scotland left out

Although the amount of material in the Stuart papers concerning the
Atterbury Plot is daunting, there are gaps, and some pieces in the
jigsaw are missing. This is due to Atterbury's reluctance to put anything relating to a rising in England in writing, and because some
material referred to in the collection is missing, either lost when the
Stuart papers were taken to England in the early nineteenth century or
possibly taken by collectors subsequently. The evidence as to what
occurred next is far from complete and has to be pieced together as
best it can. What we do know is that as the Triumvirate in Paris were
waiting to hear from the Jacobites in England. Lansdowne received in
March 1722 a letter from Dr Freind, who with James's approval had
been let into the secret of dispositions made for the English rising
by Atterbury, Strafford, North, Arran and Goring.[77] Unfortunately,
Lansdowne gave the letter to Lord Mar to decipher, whereupon all hell
broke loose. Whereas Mar had insisted that General Dillon should land
in Scotland while Ormonde landed in England, the English Jacobites
now wanted to abandon the plan of an insurrection beginning in
Scotland with the English rising following on, an arrangement always
opposed by Ormonde. Mar was outraged at what he saw as adopting
one half of the project, which, he felt, was bound to make it mis-
carry.[78] This was awkward for James, who tried to soothe Mar by
sending him a letter emphasising his devotion to Scotland. Mar
thought it would 'touch every Scotch heart'. He then suggested that
Lord Oxford and Atterbury should jointly direct the project and that
the money collected in England should be secretly sent to Scotland.[79]
This was the best way of provoking a breach between England and

Scotland. Mar even took the initiative, writing to Lord Oxford directly, complaining of Atterbury's attitude, which had led to 'some people at home concerting only among themselves' without consulting others. He thought, however, that whatever former misunderstandings there may have been between them, there was no doubt of the Bishop of Rochester's 'good intentions' and he felt that the bishop would not refuse to act with Lord Oxford.[80] Tactful as ever, James wrote to Dr Freind to thank him for 'the many marks of friendship' he had received from him, notably in choosing the servants sent over to Rome from England. He was sorry that Mrs Hughes, the prince's nurse, who had been 'devoted to her charge', was leaving Rome to return to her husband and family, though he could understand her motives.[81] In order further to pour oil on troubled waters, James appealed to Orrery, who was to take part in the rising, to encourage unanimity in England by his 'example and advice' and to assure him that Ormonde and he would join them as soon as possible.

The rising postponed

At the last minute the rising scheduled to take place during the elections was postponed 'for want of money'. There was not enough money available to buy arms and ammunition 'for supplying England, Scotland and Ireland' at the time of the elections, so that Ormonde and James were unable to set out. Half the sum asked for by the Triumvirate had been raised, but since they insisted on the whole, the rising had to be put off.[82] Lord Strafford thought Atterbury had been the chief cause of delay as 'he is so full of his own abilities that if he can't have things go his own way, he would rather they did not go on at all'. Sir Henry Goring was said to have complained of Atterbury's dilatoriness, when the bishop shook him by the collar and said 'this is rocking the cradle indeed'.[83] James concluded that the five persons now concerned in managing the rising (Atterbury, North, Strafford, Arran and Sir Henry Goring), however considerable, had been unable to raise sufficient funds. Lord Orrery, Lord Gower and 'that set of friends', James felt, would be pleased if Lord Oxford were included in the management and in raising money. This should be presented as Ormonde's rather than Mar's advice to friends in England. The sum of money agreed should be lodged in Amsterdam or any other secure place to buy arms and to hire ships to transport the officers, with a guarantee from James that it would be used for no other purpose. The Earl of Oxford was to join with Atterbury in sending the money and keeping a concert within the kingdom, while General Dillon would oversee the buying of arms and settling the officers who were to come over. More persons had to be let into the secret if more money were to be raised and James wrote to Lord Orrery asking him to assist in raising the money required.[84]

We do not know the immediate reaction of Atterbury and his associates to the new scheme. Outwardly, however, Atterbury obeyed James's wishes with good grace. As ever, rather than putting anything in writing, Atterbury sent his secretary, George Kelly, to Paris to see Mar 'entirely alone'. Kelly's record of his meeting one to one with Mar states that Atterbury agreed to 'joyn both hearts and hands with E[arl] Oxford' and to treat him with 'all the deference and respect that was due to a person who has so justly filled the stations he has been in'. There was not much good to be expected 'from the present managers' and the bishop thought Lord Oxford and himself were 'the fittest persons' for the task. Kelly remarked, however, that Oxford was away in the country, while the bishop was ill 'of his old Distemper' (the gout) and his wife was 'miserably reduced by a consumption', so that Atterbury and Oxford could not meet for another four to five weeks, but when they did they would be able to give 'the finishing stroke' in the collection of money. Kelly mentioned that Lord Lansdowne would have to be brought round as formerly he had been 'as much disobliged with E[arl] Oxford as any body'. As the Bishop of Rochester was 'averse to writing by post', it was agreed to settle a safe link of communication between Mar and the bishop by special boats to and from Boulogne.[85] This is clear enough. However, several documents alluded to in the Jacobite correspondence at this point are missing. Lord Mar's prose is somewhat opaque as shown in his letter to Ormonde of 16 April 1722. Mar states that a paper given to him by Kelly (missing) 'was written by [the] Bishop of Rochester to his partners, which they approved of'. Lansdowne though this was Atterbury's 'real opinion of things and that he took that pretext only of showing it them as if he intended it to be intercepted, but truely to let his real sentiments be knowen to Mr. Dillon, Lord Lansdowne & D[uke]. of Mar which for his partners he was not otherwise at liberty to do'. Mar thought there was 'a great deal of truth in it; but if it be all so, any undertaking on that foot, against the Government, were almost madness to be attempted'. The paper given by Kelly to Mar was not sent to be intercepted in the common post as the letter of 12 February had been. Mar may have used 'intercepted' here to mean it allowed Kelly to show the letter to Mar, Lansdowne and Dillon.[86]

From Rome James now wrote to Atterbury:

It appears to me that for the present our project is at an end and it has certainly manifestly failed for lack of money and from being pursued on too small a bottom and without the concurrence of a greater number of friends ... tho' I am sensible of the importance of secrecy in such an affair yet I do not see how it will be possible to raise a sufficient sum or to make a reasonable Concert in England without letting some more persons into the project. You on the place are the best judge how these points are to be compassed.[87]

There was optimism, however, that with a wider concert, a rising as soon as George I left for Hanover would be at as good a time for an insurrection as during the elections. A considerable advantage was that:

the King's friends in a great measure know what land officers they may depend upon, what nobility and gentry may be inclinable to join them, what counties are disposed to the King's interests and where the most useful efforts may be made.[88]

While Sunderland lived nothing was done to stop the activities of Atterbury and his partners. His sudden death on 19 April 1722 changed the whole scene.

4

Walpole and the 'Horrid Conspiracy'

Sunderland's death

Sunderland and Walpole had fielded different candidates in many constituencies and Sunderland was annotating the returns as they came in, when a bombshell struck the political stage: Sunderland died suddenly on 19 April 1722.[1] The next day Lord Carteret wrote to Dubois with the news and assured him that the close links with France would continue.[2] Sunderland had been struck with pleurisy two days before, was bled six times, and died at 3 p.m. in the afternoon. Destouches thought there had been only three men in England on whom France could rely completely, Stanhope, Craggs and Sunderland. Now there was none.[3] On the day of Sunderland's death (before he could have received Carteret's letter), Dubois sent advice by an express to Lord Carteret, through Sir Luke Schaub in Paris, that there was a plot against King George and that the Jacobites had asked the Regent for 4000 men. Dubois did not give the names of those involved, which had been withheld from him.[4] While Sunderland was alive nothing whatsoever was done to put a stop to the Atterbury Plot. It is equally certain that Dubois said nothing about there being a plot while Sunderland was in office. Assuming that Dubois had been receiving a pension from Stanhope and Sunderland, as all the signs were, he would have been desperate to avoid exposure at the hands of Townshend and Walpole, who had the accounts of Secret Service money. The 'great secret', it seems, did not die with Stanhope or Sunderland and Dubois went out of his way to be helpful to the new English government. The official line in England was that the revelation had come from the Regent, presumably in order to protect Dubois, the real informer. James III was astonished to find that the English ministers would go as far as to accuse their ally, the Regent, publicly, in order to protect their source. The foreign ministers in London were told that a 'horrid conspiracy' had been discovered, but were given no other information. Most believed, however, that Dubois, not the Regent, had revealed the existence of a plot. Walpole and Townshend tried to make the most of the discovery to discredit Sunderland and to consolidate their own power. It was put out that proof of the plot had been found in Sunderland's papers.[5]

Sunderland's papers searched

On 21 April the Duke of Newcastle sent one of Sunderland's servants to inform the Duke of Marlborough (who was then senile) of Sunderland's death and his papers were sealed with his coat of arms. Newcastle had wanted them to remain sealed until the return of the 4th Earl of Sunderland, who was then in Rome in the company of Lord Ryalton (the Duchess's nephew). Notwithstanding, Carteret and Townshend as secretaries of state, the Duke of Kingston as Lord Privy Seal, and Lord Carleton as President of the Council, broke the seals and removed some papers from Sunderland's desk, in the face of strong protests from the Duchess of Marlborough.

Rumours began to circulate at once, repeated subsequently by Speaker Onslow, that a letter from the Pretender had been found in Sunderland's papers which revealed the existence of a plot. The French envoy reported that though governments had been known to invent plots to get out of political difficulties, on this occasion the ministers seemed seriously alarmed, adding that Sunderland was capable of anything to maintain himself in power.[6] Dr Freind wrote that 'the beginning of the discovery was made from some of Lord Sunderland's papers' and that he knew that before he died Sunderland had said it was well for the Jacobites that Townshend and Walpole 'had not in their hands what he had'.[7] Walpole did find crucial evidence among Sunderland's papers: James wrote to Lansdowne that 'among Lord Sunderland's papers there has been found the two letters of which I sent you copies, together with the private note [the military commissions for the rising] to Captain Urquhart which covered them and which to be sure, never came into Sunderland's hands'.[8] Meeting Urquhart in May 1722, Walpole remarked 'he very well knew the confidence that was between him and Earl Sunderland' and mentioned Mr Vincent (the code name for Urquhart in the Jacobite correspondence) and Mr Stone (the code name for James) 'by which Mr. Urquhart well knew he meant what had been found in Lord Sunderland's scrutore'.[9] Other papers which may have been found were 'a few articles' which had been sent by James in May 1721 'for my Lord Sunderland' and were delivered to him.[10] From Paris Schaub reported that the Regent had told Dubois that Sunderland had entered into 'engagements' with the Pretender six months ago 'the first article of which and the guarantee of the rest, was to procure the election of a Tory Parliament, and that the Jacobites were in despair at his death'.[11] The Duchess of Marlborough was equally suspicious, writing:

> My Lord Sunderland was so fearful lest the King should die before his son, that he made an alliance with several Jacobites and particularly carried on a correspondence with Mr. Hutcheson, making them believe he would work matters so as to bring in the Chevalier. This makes Sunderland's character still worse than Mr. Harley's [Oxford].[12]

Archdeacon Coxe's verdict was that 'the conduct of Sunderland at this period is involved in so much mystery, as to leave his character open to every suspicion'.[13]

At this time, the Duchess of Kendal went to see her friend Destouches, exclaiming; 'Au nom de Dieu à qui se fier dans ce pays ci?' She explained that the new ministers had been telling the king that Sunderland had been in correspondence with the Pretender, and asked Destouches whether this could be true. He replied he thought it unlikely that Sunderland would have wanted to bring in the Pretender during the lifetime of the king, but as he feared the mortal hatred of the Prince of Wales, it was likely he had made a pact with the Tories to bring in the Pretender on the king's death.[14] James III's view of Sunderland's death was that 'the present government has lost an able and useful minister and tho some particular friends of mine may have also lost a personal friend in him yet I see no reason the good cause will suffer by his death'.[15] He very much underestimated the value of the umbrella Sunderland had provided for his friends in England.

The Jacobites keep their heads down

As damage limitation, Jacobites publicly ridiculed the idea of a plot. Several of them who had been involved in the negotiations with Sunderland sought to keep out of the limelight. After the death of 'his Great Patron', Sunderland, James Grahme left London.[16] Lord Orrery and Charles Caesar also retired to the country for the time being.[17] This was the season of bonfires of Jacobite papers. Atterbury destroyed his correspondence from 1712 onwards at this time.[18] Lord Strafford weeded most of his papers in May 1722.[19] Lord Orrery followed suit.[20] Lady Cowper destroyed most of her diary for the years 1720 to 1723 and a substantial part of Lord Cowper's papers were weeded of political matters for those years.[21] An interesting development was that John Machin, an eminent astronomer and secretary of the Royal Society, who had been receiving and transmitting Jacobite correspondence, absconded at this time.[22] As Lord Orrery and Lord North and Grey were Fellows of the Royal Society, there may have been a group of Jacobites inside the Society.

All this left Walpole and Townshend with little hard evidence to go on. Grahme thought that 'Mr. Walpole and Lord Townshend would not draw any blood in the account of the plot but that Mr. Walpole would spin it all the lengths he could to prevent George's going abroad this year'.[23] Charles Caesar reported: 'it is from letters they have got, at least copies of letters, that they pretend to have made the discovery of this plot as they call it', but even the ministers did not 'pretend to have any evidence against any one person whatsoever'.[24] Everyone had heard about the plot, but they could find out no reliable evidence, so that public opinion grew sceptical.

Did Lord Mar give information?

Orders were given to intercept letters sent to and from France and Spain. Historians have claimed that the Jacobites were gullible fools who had sent and continued to send treasonable correspondence through the Post Office, all of which was easily decoded by an omniscient Walpole and his agents.[25] This is not so. It was common knowledge that letters were often opened at the Post Office, so that the correspondence of the leading Jacobites in England went by couriers. Moreover, special precautions were taken at this time to make sure no Jacobite letters should be sent 'the common way', i.e. through the post.[26] Yet at the trials of George Kelly and of Atterbury, the government claimed that they had obtained crucial information from letters sent via Boulogne, which were intercepted by the Post Office. The three letters which secured Atterbury's conviction, in particular, were represented as so intercepted. It will be argued subsequently that these three letters were most probably forgeries. Walpole claimed that the three letters were intercepted on their way to Gordon, the Jacobite banker in

Boulogne. However, George Kelly and Mar had settled a safe way of communicating through Gordon by the use of special vessels, i.e. the 'bye boats' referred to above, not regular packets, precisely to avoid such interception. Walpole would have had to find out some of the code names used in the Jacobite ciphers to make the three letters credible. Did Mar help him? The government put out rumours that Mar had made discoveries. Mar wrote to John Hay:

> It seems that they are hard put to find something to ground the plot upon, when they endeavour to make the world believe that the late [forfeited] Lord Mar has had a great hand in discovering of it to the Government. Had that Lord known any thing of a plot of that kind, it is hard to think in his old days after the part he has acted that he would be the discoverer and scarcely to be believed that he could find his account in it, had he thrown his honour and reputation aside as he might have done in that case ... had Ld Sunderland been alive we had heard nothing of it.[27]

Dr Freind advised Lord Lansdowne that

> a noble friend of yours now at Paris advised one related to him, even four months ago, not to meddle in the Jacobite scheme because of his certain knowledge the ministry were apprised from your side of the water of every step taken towards a rebellion or invasion, but possibly this might have been said to pump or terrify.[28]

This would certainly sow distrust among the Jacobites, one of Walpole's favourite devices. Mar's intimacy with Sir Robert Sutton (like Lansdowne's) did not have the significance previously ascribed to it[29] since Sutton was acting with the Jacobites, as we have seen. Mar had met Colonel Churchill, Marlborough's bastard nephew, sent to Paris to investigate. He had a meeting with Schaub. In the course of these meetings, he probably revealed some of the names used in the Jacobite ciphers. Schaub added that Mar did not want Lady Mar to know what he was doing.[30] It has been argued that Mar was threatened with the loss of his pension or public exposure as a traitor to the Jacobite cause if he did not co-operate with Walpole, Townshend and Carteret by writing an incriminating letter to Atterbury. The letter of 11/22 May 1722 said to be sent through the Post was signed 'Jo. Motfield' (Mar) to 'Mr. Illington' (Atterbury). It expressed sympathy at his plight on the loss of his wife and at his old 'distemper', the gout.[31] The letter, written by Mar or for him, had nothing of business to convey, but it identified Atterbury as 'Illington' in the Jacobite correspondence. Nevertheless, Carteret suspected still that Mar was a Jacobite at heart. Certainly, Mar does not seem to have co-operated with Walpole willingly, as is shown by a letter from Anthony Westcombe, an English diplomat to Walpole's brother Horatio:

> the indulgence my Lord Mar has received from the King deserves a better return than what he makes, but I perceive the character his own countreymen give of him truly confirm'd that he can be no more just to any one than gratefull, & a double part is his master piece.[32]

What Mar wanted was to secure the reversal of his attainder and the recovery of his estates, to preserve his clan and a repeal of the Union of 1707, all of which he would get in the event of a Stuart restoration. He had received little money from his pension from England (which he accepted with James's retrospective consent) and he was given no reward for whatever help he gave Walpole in 1722.

England put on alert

There were well-founded rumours that the Pretender and the Duke of Ormonde were about to land, that the Tower of London, the Bank of England and South Sea House were to be seized and that there was to be a rising all over England.[33] A proclamation was issued to execute the laws against papists and nonjurors, to drive them out of London and for their horses to be seized. On the breaking of the plot, the British government insisted that France and Spain should order Irish troops in their service away from the coasts.[34] Dutch troops were asked for under the terms of the barrier treaties. The Dutch States refused to provide them at once, but agreed to send over 6000 troops if they were required. Six regiments were brought over from Ireland by General Maccartney, and General Carpenter was sent over to command in Scotland.[35] All officers were recalled to their posts and more troops were brought South. London was to be guarded by an encampment in Hyde Park consisting of three regiments of Guards and the Horse Grenadiers. George I reviewed the troops in Hyde Park and he and the Prince of Wales dined in General Cadogan's tent. This was the first time George had eaten with the Prince since he came to the throne.

The impressive show of force in Hyde Park soon deteriorated into more of a fair than a military camp, many in the encampment getting drunk day and night and all kinds of ladies paying extended visits to the officers and soldiers, so that, as Destouches commented, Bacchus and Venus rather than Mars were the presiding deities.[36] The irony was that with everyone going in and out of the camp as they pleased, and the soldiers growing restless at being kept in tents for months, it became, as we shall see, a fertile recruiting ground for James III's supporters.

Kelly's arrest

In search of evidence, Walpole arrested Atterbury's secretary George Kelly. On 21 May 1722 Kelly was seized at his lodgings in Bury Street in London by three messengers. While two of the messengers were searching his rooms, Kelly held the third messenger at sword point while he burnt some papers on a candle with his left hand, after which he calmly surrendered.[37] Walpole and Townshend were infuriated by these proceedings.[38] Kelly was examined by a committee of the Council about the cant name 'Illington' (Atterbury), but he denied any knowledge of that name. At this stage 'Harlequin' a 'very fine spotted dog' brought back from France by Kelly as a present from Lord Mar to Mrs Atterbury came into the story. The little dog had a broken leg and Kelly left him with his landlady, Mrs Barnes, to recover. Kelly told the committee the dog was his present for Mrs Barnes.[39] Mrs Barnes was questioned by the committee of the Council on 21 May but said little. However, at a second examination two days later, probably not realising the significance of what she said, she told the committee that she was looking after Harlequin until he was cured as the dog was meant for the Bishop of Rochester.[40] Without the evidence of the burnt papers, Kelly had to be released.

Jacobite propaganda

Leading Jacobites laying low for a time did not prevent the party from keeping public discontent alive by publishing incendiary libels, depicting the Court in the most odious colours. The great impact made by these publications led to widespread arrests of 'seditious' printers and their apprentices at this time.[41] Destouches sent Dubois two of the most daring and popular of these publications. One was the influential pamphlet entitled *An Historical Account of the Advantages that have accrued to England by the succession in the illustrious House of Hanover*

(1722). It is really in the popular genre of the secret history (the 'Secret History of the House of Hanover' is a phrase used) attempting to challenge the legitimacy of George I and of the Prince of Wales, as for a time the 'warming pan' allegations had sought to challenge the legitimacy of James Francis Edward, Prince of Wales. Giving a detailed account of the adultery of Sophia Dorothea with Count Königsmarck, it alleged that the Prince of Wales was not the son of George I and that George had never owned his children by her until King William had made it a condition of the Act of Settlement. The Hanoverian family was urged to refer the circumstances of the birth of George, Prince of Wales to a free Parliament, as William of Orange had promised but failed to hold an enquiry into the birth of the Prince of Wales in 1688. It gave high praise to Lord Cowper's political conduct. Then it went on to argue that a stress on 'the false fear of Popery here among the great, vulgar and the small' had been used as a ploy to 'establish a foreign family on the throne and ruin English trade'. The British fleet had been sent to the Baltic and the Mediterranean by George to engage in a foreign war against the national interest, contrary to the Act of Settlement. It was no longer a question of Whig and Tory, Church of England or Dissenter but a choice between English liberty and foreign arbitrary dominions. Destouches thought it was exaggerated but that it contained many things that were true. George I gave orders that it must be suppressed at all costs, so that Destouches had to pay dearly to get a copy for Dubois.[42] The publication of such a provocative tract at this time showed that the Jacobites were not to be intimidated or stopped by Walpole.

5

The Military and Naval Resources of the Jacobites

The plot continues

Despite the hullabaloo and the wild rumours flying about, Walpole and Townshend had no evidence to go on that would stand up in a law court. Lord Strafford thought an opportunity as favourable as the present one would not occur for another seven years and that plans for a rising should continue. James felt that 'it would be better not to undertake anything at all' than make an attempt 'without a reasonable probability of success', but on balance he decided that 'this favourable juncture may not be let slip'.[1] The climate had changed, however. While Sunderland was alive, whatever his real intentions towards the Jacobites may have been, no action was taken against the conspirators. Dubois too had remained silent. An additional obstacle for the Jacobites now was that official protests to France and Spain by the new English ministers made it more difficult to use openly the Irish regiments in French and Spanish service. However, probably because of James's opinion recorded above, the plot went ahead despite Sunderland's death and Walpole's attempt to play the Jacobite card against it.

The time appointed for the rising was the early autumn of 1722 when the camp at Hyde Park was expected to have broken up and before George I's return from Hanover for the opening of Parliament. Some hundreds of officers in the Jacobite regiments in France and Spain were to be brought over to discipline those taking part in the rising, together with an appropriate supply of arms and ammunition.[2] In addition, soldiers from George I's army in England as well English sailors were recruited with remarkable success in James III's name, as we shall see. There were three other groups of armed men, who were to take part in the rising. One was the Minters, debtors who sought the privilege of the Mint in Southwark as a refuge. The second was the Waltham Blacks, smugglers turned poachers, made famous by the work of E. P. Thompson, who were recruited into the service of James III by Sir Henry Goring. The third, about whom we know less, were the Thames watermen, led by the Duke of Wharton. Measures were taken to enable Scotland to assist England on this occasion, but James feared it could not 'be so easy to make Ireland as useful', for reasons already explained.[3] This was the third phase of the Atterbury Plot.

Fundraising

All depended on sufficient money to buy an adequate stock of arms to enable James to come to the assistance of his faithful subjects when a general rising took place. Atterbury himself was less active at this time as he suffered the loss of his beloved wife, who died after a long illness. James wrote to him on 8 June:

> My sincere and affectionate friendship for you do not allow me to be silent on this melancholy occasion and I hope you will do me the justice to be persuaded of the particular share I take in the loss you have lately made, time alone can diminish the trouble and grief which such losses produce.

The letter was not written in James's hand to lessen the risks, but forwarded via Dillon, to whom James confided: 'the more I see of him the more I like him'. James hoped that Atterbury would co-operate with Oxford and that Lord Orrery would concert his fundraising campaign with the bishop.[4] Orrery acted with determination and a good deal of ingenuity in this task. The better to maintain secrecy, James's letters to Orrery were delivered to the wife of Orrery's Flemish secretary, Mrs Swordfeger, who was Orrery's mistress and the mother of his illegitimate children.[5] Swordfeger himself seems to have accepted this ménage à trois and did not seek personal revenge against Orrery. As in the case of Orrery's account of his meetings with Sunderland, the account of Lord Orrery's plan is missing in the Stuart papers. The central part of it, according to other evidence, was sending to Orrery blank promissory notes signed by James on which money could be raised. The amount of money given on a note was to be redeemed after a restoration. Spreading his net wider, Lord Orrery was doing better in collecting money for the cause than Atterbury had on his own. It was a joint effort, however, as Orrery's fundraising was conducted with Atterbury's assistance.[6] Orrery, as he wrote to James, had reservations in co-operating with Atterbury

> for whom I have always professed a personal regard, having been bred up under him and lived in constant friendship with him and whenever I have thought it for your service have talked pretty openly with him upon the subject of your affairs and still continue to do so, but 'tis fit I should acquaint you at the same time that many of your friends ... have been shocked with many parts of his behaviour ... I know this is a great prejudice to your affairs and incapacitates the Bishop from being able to do you all the service he might.[7]

This judgement was probably because Atterbury, by keeping plans to himself and co-operating with a small number of associates only, had caused the abandonment of a rising at the time of the 1722 general election because insufficient funds for buying arms had been raised.

With the new leadership, Orrery was able to get Lord Bathurst's agreement to carry out whatever James required of him.[8] Orrery reported he had had 50 letters (i.e. promissory notes from James) and that he was getting a large enough sum and had promises from 'several money'd men' to pay several sums more on the promissory notes. Lord Strafford too co-operated with Orrery in raising money on the promissory notes. Lord Oxford, however, was unable to be of any great assistance owing to his 'ill state of health' at this time, though Charles Caesar, who did nothing without consulting Oxford, was active in the fundraising.[9]

The donations

We know the identity of some donors at this time. Lord Falkland sent £500 through General Dillon. Sir Brian Stapylton of Yorkshire (5th Bt. MP Boroughbridge until 1715 and one included in the 1721 list) was asked for a contribution by Lord Falkland to free the kingdom from 'tyranny and usurpation'. Stapylton obliged and received assurances from James that his money would be applied only for the purposes for which it was raised.[10]

Orrery drew up a plan for the collection of money in London and important persons in the City expressed willingness to contribute. In this task John Barber, a prominent Jacobite alderman, and his friend

Alderman John Barber. Engraving with etching by Gerard van der Gucht after Bartholomew Dandridge, c. 1735. (Private Collection).

Dr Charlton played leading rôles. Charlton was a person who could influence 'the leading men of the common council' of the City of London. Dr Charlton was Lord Arran's secretary and handled correspondence between James's friends in England and Ormonde. He had written the first and second parts of *Advice to the Freeholders of England*, the influential pamphlet distributed at the general election of 1715, and *The Character of the Parliament commonly called the Rump*, a satire on the 1722 Parliament. It was Charlton who introduced to Orrery 'those active in raising money by [the] distribution of promissory notes'.[11] Charlton had an additional advantage of being a friend of Archibald Hutcheson, who had great prestige in the City. James asked Charlton to convey to Hutcheson 'the particular regard and esteem I have for one who has distinguished himself by his public spirit and his love of his country' and expressed the hope that 'he will not separate my interest from that of my country whose true friends will ever be mine'.[12] The necessary funding began to flow as Alderman John Barber passed through Paris in mid-May on the way to Rome to take to James £50,000 already raised. Another £50,000 was said to have been sent to Ormonde in Spain.[13]

The quest for funds in London

The main effort in raising funds was in London. A list survives in the Stuart papers of 'Citizens of the first importance' in London 'to be remembered' in future, presumably of the leading contributors,[14] They were:

Samuel Robinson, a common councilman, MP for Cricklade 1710–13.
Richard Brocas, a Tory alderman.
Humphry Parsons, a wealthy brewer, sheriff of London 1721, 1722–3, MP for London 1727–41, the only alderman in the eighteenth century to have been chosen twice as Lord Mayor of London (1730 and 1740). He distributed Jacobite propaganda in London.
Francis Childs, the head of the great banking house of Francis Childs & Co., Director of the East India Company, sheriff of London 1722–3, Lord Mayor 1731–2, when he was thanked for his services by James III. MP for London 1722–7, for Middlesex 1727–40.
John Crawley, Humphry Parsons's brother-in-law, common councilman, MP for Marlborough 1737–47.
Richard Lockwood, director of the Royal Exchange Assurance, a wealthy Turkey merchant, MP for London 1722–7.

Henry Hoare, an eminent banker, known as 'the magnificent', MP for Salisbury 1734–41.[15]

Wealthy Londoners were approached for donations (see Appendix D).[16] It cannot be assumed, however that those on this list necessarily gave any money.[17]

A 'weighty friend' in the City of London, not named, was expected 'to be of good service in the money affair' and Lord Orrery left instructions and powers to negotiate with a further 'two friends at London'.[18]

Thomas Southcott, the head of the English Benedictines in France, suggested that Richard Cantillon, the wealthy banker and economist, son-in-law of Sir Daniel Arthur, a Jacobite banker in Paris, would give money if approached in the right way. Cantillon obliged by sending to John Plunkett a promissory note for 930 *livres*.[19] By 2 August James was able to write that half of the proceeds from the promissory notes for money had arrived in Rome and that he was expecting the rest soon.[20] Subsequently the Secret Committee of the House of Commons estimated that the Jacobites had raised £200,000, a huge sum in those days.

Layer's lottery

No stone was left unturned. Layer devised a scheme for a lottery for the benefit of the cause, ordering two copper plates to be made, one for the printing of the scheme in English and the other for printing the tickets in Italian, as the prizes were to be drawn on a bank in Rome, presumably Belloni's, bankers to the Stuart Court. Layer's lottery was to raise 100,000 Roman crowns on the security of the bank in Rome, with tickets to be sold at 10 Roman crowns each, and with prizes to be drawn in the manner of Dutch lotteries. As Layer argued, there was nothing illegal in the scheme.[21] Layer's lottery scheme, hidden in a parcel of silk stockings as gifts for James and his queen, was taken to Rome by Andrew Hay, who travelled with John Barber. Hay was a man who grew wealthy by buying pictures and works of art for English collectors like Edward, Lord Harley (Oxford's son) and Sunderland, and made frequent trips to Italy, so that his journey would not attract the attentions of the British government.[22]

Military commissions

In addition to raising money, Orrery believed in the importance of gaining some serving officers as the government 'could not easily pack any army of Englishmen entirely'. Lord Strathmore agreed on the importance of cultivating 'the friendship of the Army' for 'advancing our interest'. Orrery took over the distribution of military commissions 'of all sorts' sent to England by James.[23] Orrery was still hoping they could use a substantial number of Irish troops in the French service, but James could not see how they could be procured without the Regent's permission. He advised Orrery to be guided by Dillon's advice, who knew more about the situation in France than anyone else. The best that could be done was 'to get some officers by stealth and some few men who may leave with them in France as their servants'. James added that he was grateful that General Richmond Webb (a friend of Sir Henry Goring), an eminent MP and a distinguished officer now on half pay, had offered to take part in the rising.[24]

London is the key

As in 1660 and 1688, the first priority was to capture London, where the seat of government and most financial and many military resources lay. Under the command of Lord North and Grey plans were made to seize the Tower of London (where the Ordnance was situated), the Bank of England and the Royal Exchange, before the general rising in the counties could proceed. Christopher Layer was particularly energetic in assisting Lord North in this task.

Jacobites in the corporation of London

A list in Christopher Layer's papers gave the names of the Court of Aldermen (the executive) and the Common Council (the legislative) for the City of London, chosen on 21 December 1721, with most names divided into 'G' (Good, i.e. favourable to the Jacobites) and 'B' (Base) and eleven not so marked.[25] Out of thirty-three members of the Court of Aldermen twelve were marked as 'G' and ten as 'B'. Heading the aldermen as 'G' were Sir William Stewart, the Lord Mayor, followed by Sir Samuel Garrard Bt. (who, as Lord Mayor, had invited Dr Sacheverell to preach his celebrated sermon 'In Perils among False Brethren' on 5 November 1709, sparking off the Sacheverell crisis), Sir Francis Forbes Kt., Richard Brocas, Humphry Parsons, Lancelot Skinner, Francis Childs, John Barber, Sir George Mertins, Sheriff, Edward Beecher, Sheriff, Sir George Ludlam, Chamberlain, John Lingard, Common Sergeant. Having the lord mayor and the two sheriffs, who controlled law and order in the City, on side would be an incalculable advantage in any attempt. Out of 234 members of the

Court of Common Council 139 were marked as 'G'. In the following Wards all common councilmen were marked as 'G': Aldersgate Within, Billingsgate, Bishopsgate Within, Bishopsgate Without, Castlebaynard, Cripplegate Within, Cripplegate Without, Farringdon Within, Lyme Street and Portsoken.

A new Declaration from James was required at this stage and he suggested that Lord Lansdowne should draft it as James would 'not be ashamed to own' what came from that pen.[26] Lansdowne, however, agreed with Orrery that it should be written in England and it was thought Atterbury drafted it.[27]

Enlisting for James III

Alongside the collection of money, went the task of recruiting forces for James III in England. Orrery reported that there was 'considerable support in the army among the inferior officers and common men'.[28] He was ready to take an active part in the rising, as well as in raising funds, for he had received from James III a commission of lieutenant general for himself and a commission of brigadier for a friend of his, probably Colonel William Cecil.[29] It was reported that people generally were very discontented, the Whig ministers were quarrelling among themselves and that soldiers were 'pretty generally' well inclined.[30] In the camp in Hyde Park soldiers and sergeants grew weary of living in tents for months at a time, and many proved ready to enlist for James III. The rising was to be at the break-up of the camp, when recruits were told to leave without their arms, so as not to arouse suspicion and that they would be provided with fresh arms and ammunition after they left. As a result of the purge of Tory officers from the army after the Hanoverian succession, most of the officers recruited were half-pay officers.[31] Because the initial step was to capture London, where Lord North and Grey was commander-in-chief, recruiting went on in the Guards who were stationed in London. Apparently, such was the obsession of George I (a man of short stature) with recruiting only men of prodigious height for the Guards that Irishmen and Jacobites had been employed, who now readily enlisted in James's forces.[32] Among some of those recruited were soldiers who had been 'out' in the 1715 rebellion or had served in Spain. Christopher Layer, who described himself in a letter to James as 'an old servant of Ld. North and Grey', took a leading part in recruiting soldiers and sergeants, as well as in raising money on the ten promissory notes he was entrusted with by Lord Orrery.[33] The Secret Committee later concluded that every step taken by Layer had been approved by Lord North. Lord North recruited the officers. Layer wrote that the soldiers 'will do anything' for Lord North. He spent most of his time among the soldiers 'some of the best in England employed'. 'Burford' (Lord Orrery), with whom Layer was in regular contact, was involved. Ideally, they would have liked the Irish regiments commanded by Dillon and Ormonde, but the King's friends believed they could succeed 'without the assistance of any foreign auxiliary'. Lord North wanted to have King George (if he had returned from Hanover), described by Layer in his letter to James as 'the tenant of your house', and Cadogan, Captain-General of the army, seized at the start of the rising in London, so that 'by the sitting of Parliament in October next James's friends would expect him in England'. Some military men suggested that Cadogan and King George should be killed when captured. James Hamilton recoiled from the plan as 'there is something so shocking in assassinating that no one of principle of Christianity can hear of [it]', adding that 'Lord Orrery and others of the King's friends' wanted no part in this.[34] On a lighter note, Dr Sacheverell was to preach to the recruits to animate their spirit. Just as during the Swedish Plot in 1717 Atterbury had agreed to 'do his part in animating the clergy and warning the City of London from the pulpit the Sunday before the invasion is expected', Dr Sacheverell, 'whose interest with the mob is as great as ever', had 'faithfully promised to obey orders and lift up his voice like a trumpet when the word of command' was given.[35] The soldiers who enlisted for James were encouraged to go and hear Dr Sacheverell preach in St. Andrew's, Holborn.[36] In fact, the Jacobites had such success in recruiting for James in King George's army, that Sir Luke Schaub reported that they no longer applied to foreign powers for troops.[37] The French envoy also commented on Jacobite success in gaining over large sections of George I's guards, concluding that the king could not rely on his own army.[38]

Layer's lists

Layer's lists of the regiments in London, not all of them annotated, are a unique and hitherto unused source for military historians, for these lists name the sergeants and the soldiers. The first move in the London rising was to secure the Tower, where the Ordnance was situated. For this, gaining officers and men on Tower guard, was essential. There are lists of the 1st Troop Grenadier Guards, marked 'W' (Whig) and 'G' (Good).[39] The 3rd Troop of Horse, which had three German officers, had two marked as 'h' (honest), including Brigadier

Edmonds. Lord North had particular success in the Grenadier Guards in which he gained Sir Harbottle Luckyn, 4th Bt. (grandson of Sir Capel Luckyn, MP for Harwich under Charles II) and Captain William Lloyd. In the 1st Foot Guards, Lord North's former regiment, Lieutenant Colonel Thomas Ingolby was a particularly important catch as he was on 1st Tower guard, while in the same regiment Layer brought in his own cousin Ensign Erasmus Earle of Heydon in Norfolk.[40] In the 1st Foot Lieutenant Colonel Richard Ingolsby was recruited, an important gain as he was on 1st Tower Guard.[41] The Colonel of the 1st Foot Guards, General Cadogan, was so unpopular with his own men that they volunteered to kill him. The 3rd Regiment of Guards, the Scots Guards, brought five recruits.[42] The 2nd, 3rd and 4th Troops of Horse Guards are listed but no gains marked in them.[43] There were no marked recruits in the Coldstream Guards.[44] The 1st Regiment of Foot brought in Captain Dunbar and Mr Kemsey.[45] A spectacular success was that sixty of the men on the 2nd Tower Guard were recruited.[46] Twenty-three officers not on half pay joined, who are not identified, probably because Lord North not Layer recruited the officers. Sergeant Matthew Plunkett (see below), who was serving in the Invalids, undertook 'to pick out as many serjeants as he knew in the Guards ... for disciplining of the mob, who were to rise' and to recommend them to Layer. The numbers besides the names of each sergeant on the lists stood for the number of men each could bring in. Layer's role was to engage the sergeants and bring them to Lord North for approval. 'Enquire of Lord North' is a frequent entry in Layer's lists. Such an entry reads: 'Cornet Ed. Reading of the Blue Regt., served in Flanders under Lord Strathnaver, has estates in Suffolk and was j.p. until the King [George] came in, enquire of L. N. and G'. The Secret Committee commented on the accuracy of Layer's lists and concluded that Lord North had approved every part of Layer's scheme.[47]

The plan to capture London

Layer's Scheme, which was found in his papers after his arrest, and which formed an important part of the evidence at his trial and of the Secret Committee's report into the plot, was headed 'Au défaut de la force, il faut employer la ruse'. It gave precise details of the arrangements on the first day of the rising in London, in which George Wilson, a very experienced sergeant, was to play an important part. We learn from it something about the part the Duke of Wharton's Thames watermen were to play. The general in overall command was Lord North. The scheme ran as follows:

1. Let the General, and only one Officer of Note in the Camp, agree upon a day for Execution.

2. Let the Officer that Day put himself on the *Tower-Guard*.

3. And as there is eight Serjeants (viz.) three of the first regiment of Foot-Guards, three of the Second, and two of the Third, all ready at an Hours warning to obey Orders; early that Morne, let the Officer see a single Person, namely *George Wilson*, who manages these Serjeants, and give him Directions to bring them all to some convenient Place at four that Afternoon.

4. Then the Officer must give each Serjeant Money sufficient for the Purpose, and direct 'em, that each Serjeant order twenty-five Men (making together 200, which are ready) to go singly out of the Camp, and meet together at Churchyard, exactly half an Hour past eight in the Evening, when and where another Officer that they know, must meet 'em, and take the Command, give 'em Muskets ready loaded, and March them in a Body to the *Tower-Gate* at 9 that Night exactly.

5. Our Friend, the Officer within, must precisely at that Hour of 9 be on the Guard at the *Tower-Gate*, and seeing this Body of 'em appear, order the Garrison to let 'em in, as a Recruit sent to the *Tower-Guard*.

6. As soon as they have entered to seize the Arms at the *Tower-Gate*, shut the Gate up, and secure every one in the Tower, that the Officer on Guard gives them orders to secure, but not shed any Blood.

7. The *Tower* being thus seized, to leave only a small Guard there under that Officer who lets 'em in and then, with all those that join you, march directly to the *Exchange*, where the great Doors must be ready opened, and the General there in Person.

8. At the exact Hour of 9, that the *Tower* shall be seized, the Persons of some great Men to be arrested *at their Houses*, brought directly into the City, and delivered to the General.

9. That upon our Meeting at the Exchange, the annexed Proclamation to be spread about, the Gates of the City to be shut up, and Pieces of Cannon brought down against 'em, but every Man that desires to enter the Gates, before any regular Force appear, to be admitted to come in, and after the General has appointed a Guard at each Gate, and Inlets of the City, with proper Officers to command there, let him march back to *Tower-Hill*, for a Place of

General Rendezvous under the Cannon of the *Tower* and Order the Lord Mayor a good Guard to watch over the *Bank*, but first take Money from thence to the *Tower*, in order to pay the Men.

10. That on the Morne of this same Day, our General to have an Interview with some other *principal* Officer of the Camp, and order him to engage all Friends to attend at their respective Posts, and expect x* [the significance of x* is not explained] Token to be sent to each of them as that every Night, on receipt of which Token they are to draw their Men out, and march directly to the *Artillery in the Camp*, as a Place of General Rendezvous; and that the Captain of the Artillery may not be alarm'd, let this *Principal Officer* previously send a Message to him, that Orders had come from the General (*Cadogan*) to double the Guard of the Artillery, on a Rumour that is spread of the Mob being up in the City.

11. The Party being come to the Artillery with the said principal Officer at the Head of 'em, let 'em immediately draw the Guns round 'em, and stand upon their Defence, without making any Declaration, until said Principal Officer, who commands in chief there, receives certain Intelligence from our General that the *Tower* is seized upon, and the City all in Arms; and then under a Pretence of securing the King's Person from the Insults of the Mob, let this Officer make a Detachment to take him into Custody, and send him into the City to the General at the *Tower*.

12. To facilitate these Proceedings, let the General the same Day speak to the *Horse Officers* in the Camp, who he knows to be our Friends, and upon the very first Alarm of the City being revolted, let 'em march their Men to either *Ludgate* or *Newgate*, on pretense to suppress the Mob; and when they are at the Gate, as a token of being their Friends, let the Watch-word be *This Morning* and upon giving us the Word there, to open the Gates and let 'em in, and as soon as they entered, to march directly to *Tower-hill* and join themselves with the General there.

13. Let the General also the same Day, order 4 of the Half-pay Captains to take upon 'em the following Commands (*viz*)

14. First Captain to go into *Southwark* [see Minters below], and exactly at the Hour of 9, to make a Bonfire in the Fields there, and give some Money among the Mob, and when you have got a Number together, send an Account to the General, take the Arms that must be lodged there, and distribute out amongst 'em to your Acquaintance in the first Place, and to those which they recommend, and then issue out the Declarations, and after a Receipt of a

Token from the Captain next mentioned, who is to command in *Palace-yard*, to ferry thither in Lighters, with the Watch-word *This Morning*, and join the Captain in *Palace-yard*.

15. Second Captain exactly at the Hour of 9 to be in *Privy-Garden* adjoining to *White-hall*, with a few Gentlemen armed, and seize upon the great Guns there, and then spread the Declaration, and stay there under the Cannon till a greater Body join you from *Southwark*; or otherwise nail up the Cannon and march directly to the next Captain in *St. James's Park* with the Watch-word *This Morning*, and then send the Token, as above to the first Captain in *Southwark*, and let the Messenger you send, conduct him and his Men to you in *St. James's Park*.

16. Third Captain, at the said Hour of 9, to go into *St. James's Park*, with the key that is given you of the private Door out of *Arlington-street*, and appoint only some few Gentlemen to meet you there exactly at that Hour and ready, one to have the Watch-word you give 'em, which must be *This Morning*. Let your first Rendezvous be at the little Grove under the Gate leading to *Hyde-park*; and there you'l meet Fire-Arms ready charged. Then march down to the Parade next the Horse-Guard, and seize upon the Cannon there, and Ammunition in the Storehouse, and the better to secure *St. James's Park* for a Place of general Rendezvous, you shall have an Officer out of the Camp exactly at the Hour of 9 come to your Assistance with some Men, as he and you shall agree in the Morne of this Day, and as soon as you have seized the Cannon here, and Ammunition aforesaid, you are to put your selves in a Posture of Defence, and publish the Declaration, and send forthwith to the General at the *Tower* to let him know of your Situation, and also send to the Captains in *Palace-yard*, *South-wark* and *Tuttle-fields*, that they immediately come and join you.

17. Fourth Captain, exactly at the Hour of 9, the Evening of the same Day to be in *Tuttle-fields*; raise the *Westminster* Mob there, and with the Arms that are there *lodged*, equip 'em as you can; publish the Declarations, and march directly to *St. James's Park* and join with 'em there, who, on giving 'em the Watch-word, are to admit you into the Park.

18. So here being two Bodies of Men thus gotten together the first Night, *viz.* One on *Tower-hill*, and the other in *St. James's Park* (besides our Friends at the Artillery in *Hyde-park*). The next Morning, if not Sooner, let our *General* order a Detachment to *Lincoln's-Inn Fields*, and some Cannon to be placed on the Terras of the Garden there, lest the Enemy come in there between *St. James's Park* and the City.

19. A proper Captain must be appointed to head the Watermen belonging to the *Thames*, and previous to the Day of Execution, he must agree with the Duke's [of Wharton] bargemen, that upon the least Notice to be given 'em, that they alarm all the Watermen, and bring 'em to a Rendezvous the same Hour of 9 that Night of Execution, and this Captain's Rendezvous must be at *Greenwich*, where he must seize the Magazine of Powder, and take out such part of it as each Man will carry, then blow up the rest, march from thence to the *Tower*, and join the Men with the General there, to whom he must first send a Messenger with the Watch-word, and an Account of his Numbers.

20. Some time before Execution, the General to send a Messenger to particular Men in the Country, that they rise in their respective Countries upon the first News of what is done here.

21. An Officer, etc. to go to Richmond, and at the exact Hour of Nine to seize upon Prince *Pritty Man*, [George, Prince of Wales, an allusion to Buckingham's play the *Rehearsal*] and bring him away to Southwark to some particular Place appointed, where an Agent from the General must meet 'em with his further Orders.[48]

Man the barricades

We have details too of the arrangements for a popular uprising in London with Lord North in command:

That the Arms be dug up immediately, and dispersed in small Parcels; begin in *Southwark*, *Whitechapel*, *Wapping*, *Holborn* and *Smithfield*; march into City; possess the Gates. Against the Horses, Barricades in the narrow Streets, especially at both ends of *Fleet-Bridge*, *Shoe Lane*, *Fetter Lane* and *Chancery Lane*; possess *St. Clement's* Church-yard, by a party from *Holborn*; a strong Barricade in the narrow Part of the Street; line be thrown by Women and others unfit to bear Arms. Lighters with Ammunition under Coals lie at *Black-Friers* and *Milford Lane*. No dependance or Assistance from *Westminster* and those Parts, except some few by Water, the Communication being cut off. Message to the Lord Mayor by three Lords [North, Arran and Strafford]. Proclamation made to oblige all who shall not come in, to bring in their Musquets and Militia Arms. Declaration ready printed to be dispersed among the People. Twenty three Officers of the Guards to be depended upon, a great many others well affected, especialy the common Centinels.[49]

We seem to be in Paris in 1789 rather than in London in 1722!

Once London was captured, the general was to send messengers 'to particular Men in the Country, that they rise in their respective Countries' (i.e. counties). The general rising was to start when 'a beacon was put on the hill that every lord and gentry' would bring their people armed.[50] The rising in the counties presumably followed the lines given in the 1721 list, adapted subsequently to divide England into seven districts. Besides these, two groups were to take part in the rising: the Minters, who sought sanctuary near the Mint in Southwark, and the Waltham Blacks, who had been recruited by Sir Henry Goring.

The Minters

The Minters consisted of 'several thousand' people driven to insolvency by the burst of the South Sea Bubble, losses in trade and other misfortunes, who sought refuge in Suffolk Street, Southwark 'commonly called the Mint, a place of great poverty and want, and tho not prisoners in the King's Bench, were deprived of liberty as if confined' and had to live in 'vast numbers, crowding in houses' with 'rents thrice the real value' with the landlords 'daily distraining upon the goods of poor unfortunate gentlemen, merchants and tradesmen'. This was the downside of a polite, commercial society. Before the general election of 1722 the Minters had extended the privilege of the Mint to another four streets round Southwark, half a mile around, decreeing that 'no person should presume to arrest any body there'. They had set up their own jurisdiction: 'one Mark is called their General; Gilding their Recorder, Sanders and Martin Judges; Steed, Townshend and Wright their Beadles and Messengers'. Persons going near the Mint did so at the peril of their lives. The sheriff and under-sheriff of Surrey could not execute any process in the Mint without the *Posse Comitatus* and the help of 'Javelin-men' and dared not go over St George's Fields at all. Minters allowed warrants for felony to be served but no escape warrants. Men called 'Spirits' 'dressed in long black gowns, which go over their heads with holes, made to see out at' acted as lookouts for bailiffs. Persons trying to serve subpoenas were forced by the Spirits to kiss a bat steeped in human excrement and to chant:

> I am a rogue, and a rogue in grain,
> And damn me, if ever I come into the Mint again.

Minters applied the 'law of the Mint' themselves with their own court headed by a man dressed in a red coat, a cap shaped like a laurel crown, and a staff in hand. Like the Waltham Blacks, the Minters had little to hope for from King George's government, who denied them any relief. Lord North and Christopher Layer counted on the Minters to play their part in capturing London for James III. It was no coincidence that, after his escape from the custody of a king's messenger, Layer made for St George's Fields and the sanctuary of the Mint. This is probably the main reason why Walpole abolished the privilege of the Mint in 1723.[51]

The Waltham Blacks

Unable to employ the bulk of James's 'own subjects' abroad (the Jacobite regiments in France and Spain) Sir Henry Goring successfully recruited his own local force: the Waltham Blacks. E. P. Thompson rejected any links between the Blacks and the Jacobites as he did not think the Jacobites would ever have been able 'to organise seriously among the common people', but evidence proves him wrong. Goring's activity presents the additional interest of the involvement in Blacking of Alexander Pope's kinsmen Charles and Michael Rackett as well as James Tooker, something of a poet and an early correspondent of Pope. The gentleman with the hook-hand may have been Lord North and Grey, who lost his right hand at Blenheim (see supra).

The Dutch envoy, l'Hermitage, reported that the Waltham Blacks were a gang operating contraband trade on the southern coast and that Sir Henry Goring, who was burdened with debts, had helped them to organise diversionary tactics against customs officers, thus enabling them to carry off their booty. In return, Sir Henry had been in the habit of receiving agreed sums of money from the Blacks. Goring's military experience no doubt accounts for the success of the quasi-military tactics of these Blacks. This smuggling consisted of running wool from the English coast, destined for Lille and other French textile towns, and bringing back some wine and tea, but mostly brandy. By 1720 this contraband accounted for the bulk of the trade of Calais and a substantial part of that of Dunkirk. The smugglers crossed over from Dungeness, Deal and Margate and dealt with British merchants in France, several of them known Jacobites. The smugglers risked their lives, but the profits were enormous. They were helped by the fact that, then as now, most people did not regard smuggling as a crime. After 1720, according to l'Hermitage, the English government began to use fast sloops against the smugglers, with devastating effect on their trade and this is what made them turn to deer stealing. Goring's link with them, his aide-de-camp as he called him, Philip Caryll was a member of the Shipley branch of the Roman Catholic Caryll family, whose head, until his death in 1711, had been John, 1st Baron Caryll of Durford (a Jacobite title), one of James II's secretaries of state at St Germain. The present head of the family was John, 2nd Lord Caryll, the early friend and patron of Pope. Philip Caryll frequented the Blacksmith's Arms in the parish of Portsea, Portsmouth, kept by Mrs Howard, who had been nurse to the Prince of Wales in 1688, and Caryll and other gentlemen were in the habit of drinking the health of 'Mrs. Howard's nurse child' at her inn. The smugglers operated in Hampshire, Sussex and parts of Kent, and the links between smuggling and the Goring and Caryll families went back to the 1690s and probably earlier. L'Hermitage later reported that Goring, one of the principal persons involved in the conspiracy, had formed a company out of the Waltham Blacks for the Pretender's service and that their numbers had grown a hundredfold. Recruits were said to have been enlisted by a well-dressed man who gave the Blacks five guineas each, the use of a horse and a further fifteen shillings a week for the horse's feed. Walpole's discovery that the Blacks had been enlisted in the Pretender's service led to the bringing in of the Waltham Black Act (1723), one of the most repressive pieces of legislation ever passed by Parliament.

Goring gave a vivid description of the Waltham Blacks in a letter written to James:

> I had settled an affair with five Gentlemen of that Countrey who were each of them to raise a Regiment of Dragoons well mounted and well arm'd which I knew they could easily do, for the men had Horses & Armes of their own, & were, to say the truth, the Persons who some time since rob'd the late Bishop of Winchester's Parke, & have increas'd in their number ever since they now go by the name of the Waltham Blacks tho' few of them live there, which is a most loyal Town your Father call'd it his little Green Town, for as he was passing thro it to Winchester or Portsmouth, they got a great number of green Bowes & dress'd the Town up that there was hardly a house to be seen. I once saw two Hundred and upwards of these Blacks in a Body within half a mile of my own house they had been running of Brandy there was 24 Customs House officers following them who they abus'd heartyly & carried off their Cargo. I am told there is not less than a thousand of them & indeed I believe if, they now have taken Loyalty into their heads, & will I hope prove very useful, this mr Caryll was the Person who I intended to send to give these Gentlemen before mention'd, their orders when to rise & to tell them the place of Randevous.

Goring's words suggest that the Waltham Blacks' allegiance to James III was not of long standing, but their daring and experience would have made them no less valuable in the short term as part of King James's forces in England.[52]

Jacobite ships and seamen

The enterprise needed ships to bring in arms and to transport officers and others to England and Scotland. The Triumvirate in France (Dillon, Lansdowne and Mar) were to leave on ships chartered by Gordon of Boulogne, the Jacobite banker, to carry them to England and Scotland. This was the same Gordon who had arranged to convey correspondence safely to and from Atterbury and others in England on 'bye ships'.[53] Lansdowne was to land in Cornwall to lead the rising in the West. Taking another route in going to Scotland would be Lord Seaforth, Campbell of Glendarule, Clanranald, Strowan, Lochiel and others who made their way to Morlaix in Britanny to a house belonging to Giraldin of St Malo, who had been active in the Fifteen and was getting ships for them.[54] Captain Morgan had three ships already armed cruising in the Bay of Biscay without ever coming to port in Galicia. His base was Morlaix, where Ormonde owned a house.[55] Captain William Morgan had served in the Royal Navy, like Camocke (see below), he went into exile in 1716 and commanded three ships in the Spanish Navy. He had a licence from Charles XII of Sweden to command the Madagascar pirates, with the privileges of Swedish subjects, and to become governor of Madagascar if he could secure control of the island.[56] In 1722, however, Morgan's time was spent on organising James III's fleet. He and other Jacobite naval officers had unlimited leave from the King of Spain to look after James's ships.[57] Morgan was ready to take Ormonde to Bristol (Ormonde had a long connection with Bristol, having been its High Steward). James's ships flew English colours and were manned by English crews, who had readily joined.

Bilbao

The Jacobite officers in Spanish service were to leave from Bilbao, a town with a flourishing trade with Catholic Ireland. There were reported to be 12,000 arms ready and plenty more to be sent to England. Some of the arms were stored at the house of a Mr Brown, a Jacobite merchant who had a house between Bilbao and the sea. When Sir Anthony Westcombe, a British diplomat, went to investigate, he met with a wall of silence from the Spanish as well as the Irish population.

There were over 400 officers from the Jacobite regiments in Bilbao ready to embark, but when questioned, the Spanish governor replied their presence there was sheer coincidence.[58] Ships had come over from London to Biscay with large quantities of muskets and other firearms for the Jacobites in Spain to take to England. One Rose, a mate, came over with two chests of muskets made in London. The muskets were marked J.R. with a crown over it. Half the population of Bilbao had seen them, but Westcombe found no trace. It would be useless, Westcombe reported, to ask the King of Spain to seize these arms because the Privilege of the Province of Galicia would make it impossible.[59] Westcombe wrote of Bilbao:

> there is no town in Spain so convenient for the Jacobites and their Cause as this is; the great Liberty the Country enjoys, their having no publick Person [diplomat] from Britain and the great number of Irish Papists dwelling here are very great encouragements to the Jacobites to lay their Designs this way. This town, tho' not big, is very populous and one half are Irish Papists. The few English merchants that live here are cowed and stand in Awe of them to a Degree that's ridiculous.[60]

Ormonde had made his way to this neighbourhood as Jacobites from all parts of Spain flocked to Bilbao. The two Nicholas Wogans (one the eldest son of Wogan of Rathcoffee and the other his cousin, the brother of Sir Charles Wogan, who had rescued Princess Maria Clementina Sobieska from Innsbruck and brought her safely to Italy as James's bride[61]) arrived, one to command one of Morgan's ships, with the other Nicholas acting as his lieutenant. Ormonde stayed at Ventofilla, the seat of the Duke of Medina Celi, dining with Lady Arthur (of the Spanish branch of the Irish banking dynasty) as he had no knives and forks.[62]

Corunna

At Corunna there were Captain Tyrrol and Captain Salter Talbot, two Irishmen who had been in Spanish service. Their chief was Sir Peter Stafford, who had been knighted by James III 'a sort of merchant without business, trade or pay' from the King of Spain. Yet they had plentiful funds to 'debauch' English sailors as well as to help those who came over from Ireland or those who suffered for the cause.[63] Sherlock, a relation of Sir Peter Stafford, commanded a Jacobite regiment in Spain and was an agent for James in Madrid. Priests in disguise had gone over to Ireland to recruit for Sherlock's regiment. One of them, an English Benedictine monk, who had thrown off his habit to fight in the Fifteen, acted as courier to England. Recruits from Ireland, who went through England, came in aplenty, 450 from Cork in two small boats arrived to join Sherlock's regiment.[64] Several hundred more landed, enough for two entire battalions of Sherlock's regiment with hundreds more to spare. Westcombe was incredulous at the sheer numbers coming over from Ireland. The surplus men were ordered to join regiments in Spanish service but, instead, 'they threw down their Pay and declared they would serve no other Prince than King James, for whom they were listed in Ireland'.[65] Scotland was said to have engaged to provide 20,000 men for the rising. The Earl Marischal, who was to be one of the leaders in Scotland, was in Spanish service under Ormonde. He was to leave Valencia for Biscay ready to embark. His brother James Keith, also in the King of Spain's service, and Brigadier Campbell, who had been in Russian service, were to go to Scotland ahead of the rising via Rouen, where Robert Arbuthnot, a local merchant (who was brother to Dr John Arbuthnot, the friend of Pope and Swift), was to provide a ship for them.[66]

The Swedish ships

Sweden was to provide several of the ships to carry James III and his entourage over to England. The new King of Sweden, who was pressed to repay the loan the Jacobites had made to Charles XII 'the late King of glorious memory' in 1716–17, agreed, after taking the advice of Baron Sparre, to reimburse the loan as soon as possible.[67] The moving spirit in this transaction was Camocke, who suggested that instead of reimbursing the loan in money the King of Sweden might provide 12,000 troops to be sent to England or Scotland.[68] Instead of money or troops, Sweden chose to repay the loan by sending ships for James III, together with arms and munitions. One of the ships sent by the Swedes was no ordinary ship, but one which was powerfully symbolic for the Jacobites. She was the *Revolution*, bought in England for Charles XII to take Swedish troops from Norway to Scotland to assist a restoration in 1719, before he was killed by a 'stray' bullet at Frederichstadt. In the cabin of the *Revolution* were the royal arms of Sweden and the name Carolus. Charles XII was a great Jacobite icon and James III was to be taken to England in his ship.[69] Sweden also sent two frigates and a substantial quantity of arms and cannon powder to Genoa, ostensibly for the Swedish Madagascar Company to trade to the coast of Brazil, but in reality for James III's service, in repayment of the loan made to Charles XII. Peter the Great was reported to have had ships fitted out at Archangel to send to the Jacobites.[70]

Genoa

At the beginning of August, James III left incognito for Bologna, a city where he and his queen had paid several official visits, so that his presence would not attract notice.[71] From there he was to make his way to Genoa, the port from which he was to embark for England. At this time, Captain Morgan and his son left Cadiz for Genoa with two ships flying English colours: the *Revolution* and the *Lady Mary*. They were manned with English sailors 'debauched' from British ships with money, according to English sources. But, judging from the great numbers of English sailors who came over, many more than were required, they probably did so out of a commitment for the Jacobite cause. Indeed, so many English sailors wanted to join, they had to be turned over to serve on Spanish ships. In Genoa, the *Revolution*, which was to carry James III to England, was manned with 40 guns, with 120 officers on board and was commanded by Captain Gardiner, whose real name was Galloway. On board were Sir Francis Forbes, a Scot in Spanish service and a knight of the Order of St Jago, and Morgan's son. The *Lady Mary*, commanded by Captain Patrick Campbell, had 14 guns (could carry 24), was loaded with great quantities of arms and could carry several thousand men.[72] Also in Genoa was the *Fortune* commanded by Captain Butler (a relation of Ormonde's) carrying 1000 muskets, 1000 carbines, 2000 bayonets and 300 barrels of powder, which Morgan had paid for with 12,000 pieces of eight.[73]

The Jacobites in Britain and in continental Europe had made a Herculean effort in collecting money, buying arms and recruiting soldiers and sailors for the cause. By the summer of 1722 everything was ready. Then Walpole struck.

6
The Arrests

Walpole's response

The summer of 1722 saw one of the largest witch hunts in British history. In August 1722, as James Hamilton reported:

> The ministry gave out that there was a conspiracy formed and carried on by two hundred persons to assassinate all the illustrious house and this hopeful ministry. One of the ministers as he was coming down the cockpit stairs from council, said pretty loudly (on purpose to be heard by the crowd) that they had found enough to head and hang above a hundred persons of distinction and that he did not doubt but many of note would be flying out of the kingdom.[1]

Lord Townshend told Destouches he had learnt there was in England an Association in favour of the Chevalier de St Georges (James III), signed by many great nobles, based on the 1688 Association against James II and in favour of William of Orange. As we have seen, a text of this Association had been shown to the Regent when James appealed to him for the use of Dillon's troops, but the Regent was not given the names of those who took the Association nor of its signatories. Cardinal Dubois's relationship with England was no longer one of private friendship with James Stanhope. The new ministers, Walpole and Townshend, were determined to make sure that it was payback time as far as the cardinal was concerned. Townshend warned Destouches that if he attempted to keep his sources secret, Dubois would 'order him to reveal from whom he had information about the Association'. Destouches replied it was from a French Catholic who

Robert Walpole, Earl of Orford. Anonymous etching with stipple engraving, c. 1800. (Private Collection)

gave music lessons to members of English leading families. When the music master was questioned, he testified he had this information from a Jacobite perfume-maker, 'a madman', who 'gave out fantasies as fact', so that the trail led nowhere.[2] At this time Destouches was being bypassed as Townshend and Walpole were dealing with Dubois directly through Sir Luke Schaub in Paris. Describing himself as a zero in cipher, Destouches was further irritated by British ministers whispering in his ear how pleased they were with His Eminence (Dubois). Thomas Crawford, the British envoy in France, who was probably ignorant of the nature of the relationship between Dubois and the Whig ministers, was sidelined too, as Townshend dealt with Sir Luke Schaub only on all important matters.[3]

The ministers had little or no evidence to go on that would stand up in a court of law. A belief in the fairness of English justice and the rule of law was shared by Whigs and Tories alike. This did not deter Lord Townshend, who was a bully by nature, or Walpole. Walpole in 1722 was not the mellower Walpole of later years, but a ruthless Walpole who used any means to get power and to secure Whig hegemony and an effectively one-party state. What they did was to nip the plot in the bud by pre-emptive arrests and holding suspects in prison without bail or trial, contrary to all the rules of common law.

Dennis Kelly

On Saturday 28 July Dennis Kelly, a cousin of George Kelly, was arrested as he was about to go over to France to take an account of the state of affairs in England.[4] Captain Kelly had frequented the Cocoa Tree and Wills Coffee House and was regarded as having close links with General Dillon and Lord Lansdowne.[5] Boyer reported:

> Dennys Kelly Esq. an Irish gentleman, with his spouse and her mother Lady Bellew, sister to the Earl of Strafford, were apprehended by some of the King's Messengers, at Lady Bellew's lodgings at the Cockpit, as they were going to embark for France and came on board.[6]

Lady Bellew had married Lord Bellew, an Irish Catholic who had fought for James II in the Irish War. They were about to take a ship which went fortnightly from London to Rouen and the customs officers took out from the ship an iron trunk containing papers which were examined by the Council. Kelly was said to be carrying £4000 to take over for the Pretender's use.[7] In his papers, it was reported, were found ciphers and a list of the quarters and numbers of all military forces in Britain.[8] Townshend had wanted to send Lady Bellew into the custody of a messenger, but she told him she was from as noble a family as his and that it was 'her privilege by birth' to be sent to the Tower. Fellow Jacobites praised her conduct as it showed 'that Women are as capable of bravery as much as Men, and reputed as such, since they do them the Honour to make them Plotters'.[9] It was through her intervention that on 30 July Dennis Kelly was sent to the Tower rather than to face the horrors of Newgate.[10] Messengers, backed by 30 soldiers, arrested the master, the entire crew and the passengers of the ship on which Captain Kelly was to sail and impounded the ship's cargo. Lord Bathurst, who was related to Lady Bellew, interceded on her behalf so that Lady Bellew, her daughter and granddaughter were not questioned, but ordered to stay in their lodgings, while their servants remained in custody.[11]

The net spreads wider

More and more people were seized. Soldiers among the Guards were reported to have been taken up for disaffection. Random arrests followed. Robert Cotton of Steeple Giddings in Huntingdonhire, a nonjuror who had been out in 1715 and escaped after the Battle of Preston, was arrested on 4 August at his lodgings near Somerset House, together with his landlady and his servant. He had been denounced by Patten, the informer in the Fifteen who had 'taken up his old trade again'.[12] Robert Cotton was tried at Westminster on 16 February 1723 (not for involvement in the Atterbury Plot, but for another offence) before Lord Chief Justice Pratt, who later presided at Layer's trial. The messenger who went to arrest him testified that he asked Cotton whose picture was on his wall, whereupon Cotton replied 'it is the Queen of England, King James's Queen' and the messenger's testimony was confirmed by two other witnesses. Notwithstanding, the jury took only a quarter of an hour to acquit Cotton, much to the displeasure of the Lord Chief Justice.[13] Cotton's son, John, who had also been out in the Fifteen, escaped to France with Thomas Carte.[14] On 6 August Mr Campbell, a Scottish gentleman returning from abroad, was arrested. Two days later, Thomas Cochrane and Peter Smith were brought prisoners from Edinburgh.[15] Cochrane had a letter in Lord Mar's hand on him when he was arrested and was said to have sent £2000 to Dillon's secretary in Paris. He was imprisoned in the Tower on 8 August on a charge of high treason.[16] Peter Smith, who worked for Gordon's of Boulogne, the Jacobite bank, was involved in Jacobite correspondence and had recently been to see the Duke of Hamilton. Cochrane and Smith were sent south because the Lord Justice Clerk would not keep them in prison for more than the eight days allowed in Scotland before being tried or bailed, whereas in England the laws of the land were no longer observed. Lord Townshend went to interrogate Cochrane in the Tower on 13 August.[17]

Thomas Carte

On 13 August there was a proclamation for the arrest of Thomas Carte, the Jacobite historian, who was in charge of *The Freeholder*, the Jacobite newspaper. A reward of £1000 was offered for his capture. Like George Kelly, whom he replaced as Atterbury's secretary, Carte had taken the oaths to Queen Anne but refused to take them to George I. The government sought him as one of Atterbury's secretaries and probably because Carte and his brother, the Rector of Hinckley, had been very active in the Coventry election of 1722 when violent Jacobite riots took place to the cry of 'No Hanoverians, No seven years Parliament!' George Kelly was reported to have said of the Coventry Tory mob he 'never saw Fellows of such mettle, so well train'd, so fit for Business'. The election of the two Tories for Coventry was voided by the Commons on party political grounds for 'riots, tumults and sedition'. Carte had made expeditions in the spring of 1722 to Cornwall, Warwickshire, Nottinghamshire, Derbyshire and Staffordshire, which aroused the government's suspicions. But, after being tipped off by a clerk in Lord Townshend's office, Carte had fled to France.[18] James III wrote to thank Carte for his 'former and present endeavours' and asked him to convey his thanks to Sir John Packington 'whose merits are more particularly known to me'. It was Packington who paid for Carte's upkeep in exile.[19]

Members of Parliament were not immune either, as on 24 August William Shippen's house was searched for papers and Mr Fleetwood (probably Henry Fleetwood MP) was taken prisoner on 16 September.[20]

Philip Neynoe

Another arrest gave Walpole his first breakthrough: that of Philip Neynoe. Neynoe, an Irish nonjuring clergyman who had studied at Trinity College, Dublin with George Kelly, went to see Walpole in

Chelsea with offers of information. George Kelly had introduced him to Thomas Carte and he began to write for *The Freeholder*, making a mark in 1721 with the issue on the restoration, which so much annoyed the government. In this capacity, he was given the use of Lord Orrery's library in London, where he saw people came and go. Being impecunious, he obtained from Walpole sums amounting to £400 for snippets of information: that the plot abroad was directed by General Dillon and Lord Lansdowne, that the Tower was to be seized and that there was to be a rising in the counties. He apparently boasted to Walpole he had drafted memorials for the Regent of France! Each time he saw Walpole, he went to see James Hamilton, the Jacobite agent in London, to tell him what he had said to Walpole, even offering to act as a source of disinformation by telling Walpole whatever Lord Orrery wished. Hamilton, who thought Neynoe was 'an absolute knave' advised him escape to France for his own good. Neynoe attempted to follow Hamilton's advice, but was arrested at Deal in the company of Edward (also called Edmund) Bingley, an Irish Jacobite and a fellow student of Neynoe's at Trinity College, Dublin.[21] In four depositions made from 12 to 27 September Neynoe implicated George Kelly and Thomas Carte and testified 'that the Bishop of Rochester, Lord Orrery, Sir Henry Goring and Lord North were the principal leaders and directors of the whole design and that Lord North was to command the rebels'. It may have been intelligent guesswork, but it was accurate enough.[22] Pressed to put his testimony in writing, Neynoe wrote a paper in his own hand but left it unsigned. Cornered, he tried to escape from the custody of Mr Crawford, a King's Messenger in Manchester Court, near the Thames. He got out of a third floor window by tying blankets and sheets together and climbing along the wall of a neighbouring garden adjoining the river. Not knowing the tide was high, and unable to swim, he leaped into the river and was drowned. This deprived Walpole of his principal witness.[23]

John Sample

John Sample, variously described as page, butler or secretary to Sir Robert Sutton on the Paris embassy, was arrested on 4 August for high treason and placed in the custody of a King's Messenger. He was examined that day at the Cockpit by Walpole, Townshend and Carteret, in the presence of Sir Robert Sutton. A trunk belonging to him had been seized which contained his correspondence with his kinsman Francis Sempill, son of Lord Sempill who lived in Paris. The letters mentioned

Jacobite exiles such as Ormonde, the Earl Marischal and Francis Kennedy but not those in Britain. His first examination merely confirmed what was in the letters.[24] We do not have copies of the other two examinations or of what he confessed under threat, as he alleged later. While in the custody of the messenger, he jumped out of a window two stories high, landed safely and climbed over a wall into a foreign minister's garden. He was allowed passage through the house by the diplomat's family and, during a hue and cry after him, was sheltered by two women who enabled him to get away. He arrived in France, crossing over on Sir Henry Goring's yacht, which suggests his escape had been masterminded rather than opportunistic. In a published statement, he proclaimed his 'zeal towards my Lawful Sovereign James the third' and went on to say that after his arrest he was examined three times by the Lords of the Cabinet Council when

> Sir Robert Sutton my Master and Protector was Charged to screw from me some lights which the Ministry required. I received from everyone of the Lords of the Council much harder usage than should be imagined from persons of their degree. I was threatened with gibbets, racks and fire; an order was given me to read by Lord Townshend whereby I was immediately to be hurried into the dungeon of Newgate, there to be loaded with irons, and to have the greatest severity of that prison inflicted on me, but when I was reputed sufficiently terrified, Lord Townshend made me a proposal of pardon and five hundred pounds a year pension, provided I would swear ... against Lord Strafford, Lord Cowper, Lord Orrery and one Mr. Smith [Peter] ... Then Lord Townshend returned to his furious temper with frightful oaths and execration, he was seconded by Mr. Walpole and Lord Carteret, the latters violence reached to foaming in the mouth, handling me roughly and giving me a blow in the breast; Lord Cadogan acted a counterpart and sought to gain upon me by soothing words, he advised me in a friendly and compassionate manner to comply with the desires of the Council he promised to make my fortune, and besides what had been proferred me by Lord Townshend, he assured me of a commission in the Army.[25]

A reward of £1000 was offered for his capture. There was a warrant for Sir Henry Goring's arrest, but he could not be found since (as we have seen) he had made his escape to France from Sussex on his yacht taking John Sample with him. James agreed to pay for Sample's upkeep as he did for Layer's in the Tower.[26]

Bishop Atterbury

James III was relieved to know that Sir Henry Goring was 'out of harm's way', adding 'would to God the Bishop of Rochester was in as great safety as he, for I own I dread the malice of those he has to do with and his resolute behaviour will I fear exasperate them even more'.[27] He was right to fear the worst. On 25 August, Bishop Atterbury was arrested on a charge of high treason. Before a peer of the realm could be arrested, the House of Lords had to be notified and the charges explained to the Upper House, but this was not done. Moreover, the Treason Trials Act required the testimony of two witnesses before charges of high treason could be brought. There were *no* witnesses against Atterbury. Nevertheless, against the law of the land, he was seized at the Deanery by two officers, an under-secretary and a messenger. He was in his nightgown and, while he was dressing, the messenger brought out a paper which 'he pretended to have found in his close-stool'. Atterbury protested saying that the paper had not been found on him (i.e. that it was planted), but this was ignored. Instead the messenger treated the bishop with great insolence and 'said, if he did not make haste, and put on his shirt, etc. that he would carry him away naked as he was'.[28] The bishop was examined for an hour before the Privy Council, behaving with great firmness, and was sent to the Tower of London, escorted by a captain of the Guards and four messengers. He was kept under strict confinement and no one was allowed to speak to him.[29] Atterbury's gout was made worst by the close confinement he was kept under and he was not allowed to see his children.[30] The severe treatment of Atterbury, according to Chammorel, was because he was regarded as 'l'âme du parti jacobite' and the man who advised Ormonde to go into exile rather than to come to terms with the new régime. He was suspected to be behind everything which was said or written against the Court. He had boasted of having defeated the court party at the Westminster election. Some regarded him as a modern Cicero. The ministers had been waiting for an opportunity to get hold of him and they thought they had got it at last. The difficulty was that there was no witness against Atterbury and because of this all the Council had been against arresting him except for Townshend and Walpole, who were determined to send him to the Tower, and were supported by King George and the Prince of Wales, who each insisted that the bishop should be incarcerated.[31] On the other hand, people remembered the Sacheverell case and thought that a misconceived prosecution of a bishop would have ill consequences.

Another consideration was that the Bishop of Rochester was no fool, was well versed in the law and would have known how to cover his traces.[32] A fortnight after the bishop's arrest Sir Constantine Phipps, a prominent Tory lawyer, presented a petition at a session of the Old Bailey in the name of Mrs Morice, Atterbury's daughter, praying that in view of the bishop's ill state of health, he should be brought to a speedy trial, bailed or discharged. As soon as he learnt of Atterbury's arrest, Lord Orrery had written offering to stand bail for him.[33] The petition was circumvented under the pretext that the judges of the commission to deliver the goal of Newgate could not bail prisoners out of the Tower. The Habeas Corpus Act of 1679 (31 Car. II cap. 2), however, the jewel in the crown of the Whigs during the Exclusion Crisis, specified that in cases of treason those indicted must be tried the next term or bailed. As the Habeas Corpus Act was not suspended until 10 October, after the meeting of Parliament, the prolonged detention of the prisoners was illegal in any case since the Act extended to all places of imprisonment.[34] On 21 September, similar applications for bail or prompt judgment from George Kelly and Cochrane were rejected.[35]

There was widespread public sympathy for Bishop Atterbury. On 16 September public prayers were said for the bishop in most churches and chapels in London and Westminster, much to the government's annoyance. In an attempt to calm down the clergy, Dr Gibson, Bishop of London (later known as Walpole's Pope), issued a pastoral letter saying that the Bishop of Rochester had been treated with indulgence, going on to praise the great respect with which the king regarded the bench of bishops. Ironically enough, Gibson's own secretary was arrested as a suspect.[36] Nevertheless, Atterbury continued being prayed for in most London churches.[37] Atterbury's chaplain, Thomas Moore, vicar of St Botolph's Aldersgate, was dragged from his pulpit in the middle of a sermon and sent to prison, but he was discharged subsequently.[38]

Walpole's 'evidences'

The two principal witnesses against Christopher Layer were Sergeant Matthew Plunkett, who was arrested on 22 September, and Sergeant Stephen Lynch, taken on the 23rd, who both turned king's evidence.[39] As a result, on 24 September, Colonel Daniel O'Carroll was arrested. O'Carroll, a Jacobite icon, was a Knight of St Jago, had been in an Irish regiment in Spanish service in the Canaries, and was later persuaded by Lord Galloway to join the British army in Portugal, becoming Colonel of Horse, before being placed on half pay in George I's army. He was the former commander of Matthew Plunkett, who had served under him in the Canaries and who denounced him. Nothing was found against O'Carroll, who was released immediately.[40]

In September 1722 George I returned from Hanover and went to the camp at Salisbury where he inspected 4000 troops, infantry and cavalry. He was accompanied by the Prince of Wales and it was noticed that they spoke together several times. King George then went to Portsmouth where he received popular cheers. This was the first time he had ventured out of the vicinity of London since his accession.[41] The government made the most of the situation to try and improve the public standing of the Hanoverian royal family.

Christopher Layer

Layer had not been named by Neynoe but Lord North was. On 19 September, Christopher Layer was going to Lord North and Grey's house at Epping when he was arrested. He managed to send a servant to let Lord North know of his arrest 'so that Lord North might provide for his own security'. While in the hands of William Squire, a King's Messenger, in a house bordering the Thames, on 20 September he jumped out of a window two stories high into the river to make his escape and gave a sculler some guineas to carry him over to Southwark.[42] He got as far as St George's Fields and was within sight of the Mint and safety when he was retaken. To recapture him, the messenger had pretended that Layer was a thief who had robbed him and got him seized by three thief-takers who were given three shillings each. He was then imprisoned in the Tower.[43] Chammorel described Layer as a gifted young lawyer and one of most devoted adherents of the Pretender.[44] It was reported that Layer's arrest would enable the ministers to get to the bottom of the conspiracy and to obtain proofs, so far lacking, to justify to Parliament their raising the alarm and to punish the culprits. Layer was immediately assured of a pardon if he would testify against Atterbury, which he refused to do again and again. As a result, Layer was treated with unprecedented severity by being placed and kept in heavy irons in the Tower, the most secure prison in the land.[45] In search of proof, Mr Sawyer of the Temple, an associate of Layer's, and Mr Stewart, his clerk, were arrested too. On 26 September, unaware of her husband's arrest, Mrs. Layer was arrested in Dover, returning from France where she had been to place her elder daughter Nanny to be educated in France under the care of General

Dillon's wife and Lady Lidcott.[46] Walpole had his breakthrough against Layer later, when Mrs Mason, a brothel keeper, at whose house Layer had lodged and where he had hidden treasonable papers the day before he was arrested, was seized in 2 October and turned king's evidence. On 18 October John Plunkett, Layer's companion on the journey to Rome, who (according to Chammorel) had served as amanuensis to Atterbury, was arrested and taken into the custody of a messenger. Plunkett, however, gave no evidence against Layer.[47] Destouches reported that Lord Townshend and Lord Carteret were working night and day to uncover the conspiracy.[48]

Lord North and Grey

As soon as he knew of Layer's arrest, Lord North left Epping Place, heavily disguised, and made his way to Portsmouth, then to Yarmouth on the Isle of Wight, where he stayed with Colonel Henry Holmes, a Tory MP who was governor of the Isle of Wight when Lord North was governor of Portsmouth. Walpole thought Lord North had been warned through the complicity of Lord Carteret (a protégé of Sunderland) and for years afterwards blamed Carteret for this warning. On 26 September Lord North boarded a sloop belonging to a man named Boyse 'a notorious smuggler' and 'a person disaffected to H.M. government'. Unfortunately for him, a local Whig overheard the mate saying the sloop was bound for Cherbourg or Havre de Grace and tipped off the Whig governor of the Isle of Wight, who had Lord North and his servant arrested.[49] Chammorel described Lord North as an ardent Tory, keen and brave. The ministers told the French they had proof North was to be commander-in-chief to the Pretender.[50] On the 28th Lord North was brought to London in the custody of Lieutenant General Maccartney (again a man the Tories abhorred), kept at his London house under guard overnight, questioned by the Council next day and sent to the Tower by water accused of high treason.[51]

Lord Orrery

On the day of Lord North's arrest in Hampshire, his house in Great Queen's Street, London, was searched. The messenger found Simon Swordfeger, Lord Orrery's secretary there, and promptly arrested him. The next day, 27 September, Orrery was arrested at Britwell, his country house in Buckinghamshire 20 miles from London. Guarded by 30 soldiers he was kept at his house in Glasshouse Street in London, examined by a committee of the Council next day and sent to the Tower on a charge of high treason. People were surprised to see him among the accused, reported Chammorel, as he was regarded as an intelligent, learned, and wise man and living a semi-retired life.[52] It was said that Orrery had been in contact with Layer, which was true. However, the Duke of Argyll, a friend of long standing, and Lord Carleton, Orrery's Whig kinsman, appear to have blocked any prosecution of Lord Orrery in the Lords.[53] On 20 October James wrote to Lord Orrery to assure him that 'all money sent from England already spent on the purchase of arms' was safe and would not be misapplied. The letter was somehow conveyed to Orrery in the Tower, but he was obviously unable to reply.[54]

Not all the leaders of the Atterbury Plot were Walpole's targets. Lord Strafford and Lord Arran escaped arrest and prosecution. The proceedings at subsequent trials indicate that the government had decided they should be immune.

Intercepted correspondence

The main Jacobite correspondence, handled by James Hamilton and Anne Oglethorpe, between Atterbury, Orrery, Strafford, Arran, Charles Caesar and others with the Stuart Court, did not go through the Post Office, but by courier to and from Rotterdam. There was a warrant for the arrest of James Hamilton, who escaped to Rotterdam. Similarly, Anne Oglethorpe took refuge in the Dutch Netherlands.[55] Less important letters in cipher and Jacobite propaganda (which could not be pinned down to an individual) had been sent through the Post Office and began to be intercepted within days of the death of Sunderland, but did not result in arrests. For instance, George Clarke, MP for Oxford University (a man hitherto regarded as a non-Jacobite Tory), had 'treasonable correspondence' intercepted, as did Sir William Stewart, the Lord Mayor of London, whom we know as a Jacobite. The government scored a victory in mid October when they secured the election of a Whig Lord Mayor despite all the efforts of the Tories to prevent it.[56] Archibald Hutcheson's correspondence was also being intercepted as suspect.[57] James expressed great concern at the plight of his friends under confinement and urged them to unite against the 'violent measures now taken'. He asked Dr Charlton, Lord Arran's chaplain, to let Archibald Hutcheson know:

> the particular regard and esteem I have for one who has distinguished himself by his public spirit and his love for his country.

Pray let him know that I do not yield to him in the last as I hope he does me the justice to believe. I am persuaded he will not separate my interest from that of my country whose true friends will ever be mine.

Dr Charlton, however, had absconded rather than stay 'at the mercy of Mr. Walpole and Ld. Townshend'.[58]

Proceeding in Parliament

The King's Speech on 11 October at the opening of the new Parliament denounced conspirators working for a popish Pretender, who asked for help from foreign powers and being refused, was determined to use his own strength to carry out his pernicious designs by engaging officers in foreign countries. Walpole said the plotters had asked for 6000 men, then 3000, and later resolved to rely on their own forces and to begin by seizing the Bank and the Exchequer.[59] The re-election of Spencer Compton as Speaker was strongly opposed by Sir John Packington, a prominent Tory and a Jacobite, who spoke with 'warmth and eloquence' against choosing as speaker for another seven years one who had always done the bidding of the Court and could not be impartial as he held several lucrative places, including the paymastership of the army, the most lucrative place of all. This had little effect on the solid phalanx of Court supporters and augured ill for the Tories.[60] The suspension of the Habeas Corpus Act (which would legalise the imprisonment of Atterbury and the others being held) was strongly opposed in the Lords by Lord Anglesey, Lord Bathurst and Lord Cowper, who argued that this Act had never been suspended until King William's reign and again at the beginning of this reign (1715) and felt that these repeated suspensions were fatal to liberty and that the maximum suspension should be for three months only. To people's surprise, Cowper's 'young pupil' the Duke of Wharton left him to rejoin the Court, supporting suspension with vigour and eloquence and taking the chair of the committee on the bill to suspend the Act.[61] As we shall see, Wharton was playing a subtle game.

In the Commons on 16 October there were long and heated debates. Charles Caesar represented the dangerous consequences of suspending an Act essential to 'the rights and liberties of Englishmen' and was seconded by John Hungerford, another Tory. William Bromley, a senior Tory, said that the question whether it should be suspended for six or twelve months should be discussed at the committee stage and moved successfully to go into committee of the whole. Spencer Cowper, an opposition Whig and Lord Cowper's brother, moved it should be suspended for six months only and was supported by Sir Joseph Jekyll, an independent Whig, and Archibald Hutcheson. Lord Oxford had come up to town 'in order to assist the Bishop of Rochester' in Parliament and James sent his thanks to him through Anne Oglethorpe, as he would not risk writing to Oxford directly at this time.[62] When the Tories tried to get the suspension rejected altogether, most of the Whigs reunited and granted suspension for a year, as the Court asked, by 248 votes against 193.[63]

The Court got its own way in everything, including an increase in the army. James Hamilton, observing events from the Netherlands, wrote to James:

> had the King's friends gone into Lord Orrery's proposal in the spring to raise a quantity of money to be laid out in managing elections [they] would not be faced with the present House of Commons.[64]

True enough, but had they been able to raise enough money they could have made an attempt while Sunderland was still alive. King George was pleased with the turn of events, which meant he would be able to return to Hanover earlier than he had anticipated.[65]

The Duke of Norfolk

Much to everyone's surprise, the Lords were notified on 26 October that the Duke of Norfolk, hereditary Earl Marshal of England and a Catholic, had been arrested in Bath and placed under house arrest. The Duke was sent to the Tower on 27 October.[66] Townshend said Norfolk had been engaged in 'a traitorous conspiracy'. The arrest was vigorously opposed by Lords Aylesford, Cowper, Strafford, Bathurst and others and there was a Protest against it.[67] The party against the Court led by Lord Cowper made strong objections, demanding that any accusations against Norfolk be laid before the House, but the Court won by 60 votes to 28. Destouches was shocked that Lord Waldegrave, an Anglican convert from Catholicism, who had great obligations to the Duke of Norfolk, voted against him. Norfolk was examined by the Council on four articles against him. There was a report that an intercepted letter from him sending money to the Pretender had been found and that he had acted as guarantor of a sum for his service. The ministers put it out that Norfolk and other Catholics had been sending money to the Pretender for years. Lansdowne was surprised at the arrest of Norfolk, 'a man upon watch against anything that might expose him to the least hazard'.[68]

The tax on Catholics

Walpole introduced in the autumn of 1722 a tax of £100,000 on Catholics to pay for an increase in the army. The emperor, the King of Spain, the King of Sardinia and other Italian princes all made strong representations against the persecution of Catholics. To everyone's surprise, there was no protest from France. At a dinner given by Count Staremberg, the Austrian ambassador, for the English ministers and the diplomatic community, the subject of France's attitude was raised. Townshend and Carteret said nothing, but the Grand Marshal of Hanover made a coarse and indiscreet comment at Dubois's expense (an allusion, presumably, to his pension). Put in an impossible position, Destouches reminded Dubois that the young Louis XV had been opposed to the Anglo-French alliance of 1716, and that Dubois had brought him round with the argument that a Protestant prince would be better able to protect English Catholics than a prince of their own religion. At length, the Regent ordered Dubois to make a protest. Walpole, at his most cynical, told the envoys that he thought most Catholics were innocent, but the tax was a warning to Catholic powers that, if they tried to help the Pretender, English Catholics would be made to pay.[69] However, there was more opposition in the Commons than Walpole had anticipated and Walpole did not get the £100,000 tax through until 1723.

James III's Declaration

On 16 November, Townshend delivered a message to the House of Lords that 'a scandalous' Declaration, entitled the Declaration of James the Third, King of England, Scotland and Ireland, but one from 'a Popish bigotted Pretender' was being dispersed everywhere. It expressed concern at the plight of his subjects, at the violations of freedom of elections seen of late and the proscription of honest, well-meaning men. Proposing to maintain all treaties, alliances and settlement since the Revolution, it offered 'a general amnesty'. It claimed that his restoration to the throne of his ancestors would serve the interests of the nation and of the whole of Europe. He suggested that if King George would deliver to him the possession of his throne, he would secure for him the title of king of his native dominions and have it confirmed by other states, which would put an end to a 'forever disputed' succession. It ended with expressions of the deepest grief at the sufferings of his people, whose happiness was his first concern.[70]

The Declaration was ordered to be burned by the common hangman, as usual, and Parliament voted a loyal address.[71] The government gave out that the Declaration had been drawn up by Atterbury.[72] The procedure of reading James's Declaration in Parliament (though not printed in the Reports) and then again at the Royal Exchange (before being burnt) ensured the maximum amount of publicity for it. Lord Lansdowne commented: 'The declaration has had a very thorough operation, it has made both Houses break a great deal of wind which will stink all over Europe'.[73]

More arrests

In November 1722, Layer's friend Richard Berney, MP for Norwich until 1715, and other Jacobites in the corporation of Norwich were arrested on suspicion of high treason.[74] Lady Petre was taken into custody also.[75]

A very late arrest in February 1723 was that of Philip Caryll, Sir Henry Goring's henchman in recruiting the Waltham Blacks into James III's service. It happened because the government sent John Hutchins, a messenger, to Horn Dean, near Petersfield, looking for Thomas Carte at the inn kept by William Basing. The messenger did not find Carte but reported that Sir Henry Goring had frequented Basing's inn and that Caryll 'a Papist, who lived at Clanfield', a little village two miles from Horn Dean, had been seen at Basing's inn with Goring.[76] Philip Caryll, that 'wolf in sheeps' clothing' as Goring called him, turned king's evidence, probably, Goring thought, under torture, and revealed his and Goring's dealings with the Waltham Blacks.[77] Another late arrest was that on 15 March 1723, of Dr John Freind MP, an eminent physician and an intimate friend of Atterbury's with whom he was related by marriage.[78] He corresponded with James III under the cant name of 'Clinton', but the government decipherers had been unable to identify him. It was the evidence given to the Secret Committee of the House of Commons that Dr Freind had chosen Mrs Hughes as the nurse to the Stuart Prince of Wales that led to his being seized.[79]

Arrests abroad

There were arbitrary arrests overseas, too. In December 1722 Captain Scott, on board the *Dragon*, made his way to Genoa. He demanded to seize the *Revolution* and its crew of 'traitors and rebels to the King'. The Doge refused. The Republic of Genoa too denied him, saying in reply that Genoa was a *Porto Franco* and that it was their custom

> to afford refuge to People that fly into their Arms; that it was very well known, that the rebels to the Crown of England were harboured in France, and Rebels against France harboured in England, and Rebels to both protected in Spain.[80]

Arbitrary measures, however, were not confined to Britain. Scott proceeded to force his way into the harbour of Genoa to seize the *Revolution* and to try to arrest its captain Andrew Gardiner (whose real name was Galloway) and its crew. Walpole knew how much this ship meant to the Jacobites and the blow its seizure would be for them. Galloway had left Genoa, having burnt his papers, so that Scott found nothing. The crew too were prepared. The first mate William Haynes and the second mate Robert Franklin said they thought they were bound for the South Seas and produced notes under the hand of Captain Gardiner stating they had been forced into the service, as had the rest of the crew.[81] Other British officers, who were in Spanish service were immune from arrest in any case. Gardiner wrote to Lord Carteret complaining that the seizure of his ship had no legal basis as it was trading on behalf of Sweden (for the Swedish Madagascar Company) and as he had sold the *Revolution* to Mr Fordyce, a major general in the King of Spain's army, to go to the Spanish West Indies. He was sorry if Lord Carteret thought Captain Morgan was 'an incendiary or an enemy to the Government'. If Morgan was, Gardiner continued, 'he ever concealed it from me whom he knew to be otherwise inclined'.[82]

The English prisoners

In the end, the only person arrested who was tried before a common law court, as there were two witnesses against him, was Christopher Layer. There was no evidence that would stand up in a law court against John Plunkett, George Kelly or Bishop Atterbury. They were tried before Parliament, not by a Bill of Attainder which carried the death penalty (as Sir John Fenwick had been in 1696), but by bills of

pains and penalties before Parliament, in which charges were decided
by parliamentary votes along party lines.

The rest of those who had been arrested were eventually bailed. Lord
Orrery, who was in poor health, was bailed on 12 March 1723 for £20,000
with his kinsmen Lord Carleton and Lord Burlington acting as sureties for
£10,000 each. On 28 May the Duke of Norfolk and Lord North and Grey
were bailed for £20,000 each, and four sureties of £1000 each, while
Dennis Kelly and Thomas Cochrane were bailed for £4000 each and four
sureties of £1000 each. Dr Freind was released on 21 June on a bail of
£4000 with four fellow physicians acting as sureties for £2000 each. These
were exorbitant bails, designed to breach the fortunes of the prisoners.
Williamson, deputy governor of the Tower and a great persecutor of the
Jacobite prisoners, noted in his diary when they left the Tower:

> I had not the least present from 'em nor did I indeed expect such
> thorough enemys of the Illustrious house of hanover should give
> money to one they knew was so warmly affected to King George
> and his family as I was.[83]

Other prisoners were also bailed. Among them was Captain Halstead
who was bailed for £4000. The Earl of Lichfield, President of the
Honourable Brotherhood, the Tory Club which met at the Cocoa Tree
in Pall Mall, who had probably been under house arrest rather than in
a prison, was bailed for £2000. Edward Harvey of Combe MP was bailed
for £2000 at the same time.[84] An ardent supporter of the Stuarts,
Harvey had been arrested because a letter of 20 July 1722 from him to
a Jacobite agent was intercepted by the government. Showing the
depth of his anger against the Hanoverian regime, it ran as follows:

> a cargo of new German ladies of the largest size are coming, and
> Mahomet Ulrick [the King's Turkish servant] is to be chief over them
> ... In short, only villany, beggary and Mahomitism is countenanced
> by those in power.[85]

Walpole had stopped the Atterbury Plot, which was well planned and
enjoyed widespread popular support, by arresting its leaders and
holding them in prison illegally for some time. Those who were released
eventually had to pay extortionate sums for bail, which damaged their
fortunes. The great state trials which followed were designed to subdue
the Tory party, underwrite Walpole's monopoly of political power and
to drive Bishop Atterbury, Walpole's great enemy, into exile.

7

The Case of Christopher Layer*

The examinations of Christopher Layer

After his arrest, Layer had asked to speak to Lord Carteret in private. This was granted but, unknown to him, two clerks had taken notes behind the arras and these were produced at his trial.

In all proceedings relating to the trials, as well as in the documents published by the Secret Committees of the House of Commons and of the House of Lords, all references to King James or James III were changed to the 'Pretender' and references to 'the Elector' changed to 'the King', with often comical effect. Indeed, the committees of the Commons and of the Lords expressed their indignation at the practice of the persons involved referring to the Pretender as 'the King' or their 'royal master'.

Four examinations of Christopher Layer are printed in the Report of the House of Commons Committee, one undated, the second on 19 September, the third on 21 September and the fourth on 1 October 1722.[1] At his first examination, taken before a Committee of the Council on 21 September 1722 and signed by him, Layer said that Lord Orrery had told him the nation was ruined and that nothing could save it but a restoration. He added that Lord Orrery had told him that Lord North and Grey, Lord Strafford and Sir Henry Goring 'were going to do a rash Thing in favour of the Pretender' which could hinder the success for another time. Layer admitted that Lord Orrery questioned him about the character and behaviour of the Pretender. All the world knew, Layer added, that Lord North and Grey was a Jacobite. Lord

---

* Except where otherwise stated, this chapter is based on the account of Christopher Layer's trial published in London, 1723.

North had told him that Lord Orrery was 'a timorous fellow'. Layer said he believed there was a design this summer to bring in the Pretender and that these lords had such an intention. He added that 'Lord Orrery thought nothing could be done but in a parliamentary way' and that Lord Cowper had told Orrery there were 'two hundred Tories and ninety angry Whigs who would make their utmost efforts'. Layer owned that Plunkett travelled with him to Italy and that General Dillon's code name was Digby. In a second unsigned examination on 1 October before the Lords of the Council, Layer took the whole responsibility for the conspiracy upon himself: 'the whole Projection was entirely his own'. 'The whole Nation', Layer added, was for James 'except those who had Places or Money due to them from the Government.' Lord North had said that Ormonde was 'the soldiers Darling', and that the duke, not he, should be the general. Layer owned the christening of his child with the 'Pretender' as godfather, which was granted him as 'a token', and that it was done by Aaron Thompson, whom he identified at his trial as chaplain to the Duchess of Ormonde. Thompson was Lord Burlington chaplain, as Layer well knew, but he probably did not wish to implicate Burlington. What Layer admitted was mostly what the government already knew. He was more forthcoming in what he said about Sir William Ellis and Francis Kennedy, who were in Rome and out of British jurisdiction. It was noticeable that when he spoke about the other prisoners in the Tower, he showed 'great shyness and reserve'. Lord Orrery, Layer said, had called the raising money on receipts sent by the Pretender an 'Idle project' and that neither he nor Lord North would be concerned in it (which was untrue). He mentioned Stephen Lynch going to see Lord North in Essex and that Lynch (who had been arrested and turned evidence) had agreed to seize General Cadogan. Lord North had said the 'business' might be done 'by the People of England' without foreign forces and that Lord North was to engage the officers. Layer added that he did 'not care to say any thing in prejudice of other people'. In view of the strong-arm tactics employed on prisoners by Walpole and Townshend we can only speculate on how some of the statements in his examinations were obtained. There was no mention of Atterbury, the government's real target, then or subsequently.[2]

The trial of Layer

The trial of Christopher Layer for high treason, which began in the Court of King's Bench at Westminster on 31 October 1722, was the talk of the town and a 'prodigious number of people' attended it.[3] Lord Lansdowne commented that Layer 'is marked down as the first sacrifice' and that his trial 'will open a great deal of what may be expected in other cases'.[4] James thought it showed the government's determination 'to break everybody with the utmost rigour'.[5]

What seems surprising is that the indictment of high treason for 'compassing and imagining the death of the King' was found by the grand jury of Essex to be precise for levying war against the king by force of arms *at Leytonstone in Essex* on 25 August 1722. A puzzling accusation, as virtually all of Layer's activities had taken place in London.[6] Layer's counsel throughout the trial repeatedly drew attention to this incongruity. Many people thought that the whole thing was stage-managed by the government, that the Essex jurors had been hand-picked by the government and that bribes had been given to the two 'scandalous' witnesses against Layer. The explanation seems to be that with two Tory sheriffs and a Tory lord mayor of London, as well as many sympathisers in the Common Council and Common Hall, the Whig government would have faced verdicts of ignoramus from juries of the type Charles II suffered during the Exclusion Crisis, when the 1st Earl of Shaftesbury and the Whigs dominated the popular part of the City of London and were immune from prosecution.

Layer was generally agreed to have defended himself with pride and determination.[7] His first statement to Lord Chief Justice Pratt at the King's Bench was:

> My Lord, I am brought here in Chains, in Fetters and Chains. My Lord I have been used more like an Algerine Captive than a Freeborn Englishman. I have been dragged thro' the Streets at the hands of gaolers, and have been made a shew and a Spectacle of.

He was said to have been placed in irons after he refused to give evidence against Atterbury.[8]

Layer asked for a 'candid and fair Tryal, and not to be made

> a Sacrifice to the Rage and Fury of any Party, or the necessity of the Times ... I have been insulted since I came into the Hall: A Gentleman came and told me, Either I must die, or the Plot must die. My Lord, This is usage insufferable in a Christian Nation, and I think I can lay my Hand upon my Heart and say, I have done nothing against my conscience.

It was unprecedented in the eighteenth century for a prisoner to appear in court in chains or indeed to be kept shackled in the Tower. This was done at the insistence of George I himself. Lord Carlisle, the Governor of the Tower of London, objected to Layer being kept in chains and criticised the arbitrary punishment of prisoners of state without going through due process of law. As a result, Carlisle was dismissed from his office.[9] The two counsels for Layer were John Hungerford, a prominent Tory MP and a skilful speaker, who had supported Sunderland in the South Sea affair. The other counsel was Abel Ketelby MP a successful Tory lawyer who had defended the Jacobite prisoners at Carlisle in 1716 and who was Landgrave (proprietor) of South Carolina.[10] Hungerford said that the chains would allow Layer to sleep only on his back in the Tower, that no prisoner had been shackled in the Tower before, and that he could not stand in the dock unless his jailor held up his shackles for him. Ketelby argued that Layer was entitled to have his chains taken off before he pleaded. The Lord Chief Justice commented that Layer and his counsel were appealing to public sympathy, but had the chains taken off while he was in court. Hungerford and Ketelby argued that Latin names had been misspelt in the indictment and that Layer's name was misspelt, yet the Attorney-General and Solicitor-General replied that since the Treason Act of 1696 (7 & 8 Wm. III cap. 3), misspelling or improper Latin were no longer grounds for quashing an indictment. All objections were overruled by the Lord Chief Justice. Layer pleaded not guilty of high treason and the court adjourned.

On 3 November Layer, again shackled, was brought back to the King's Bench. Hungerford objected that being kept in chains prevented Layer from writing to prepare his defence. He said he had been shackled since his fourth or fifth examination and that his wife and his sister had not been allowed to visit him in the Tower. Subsequently, his wife, but not his sister, was able to visit him provided she was searched by the gaoler first. The prosecution objected that the chains were necessary as Layer had already escaped once, but his keeper testified he had made no attempt to escape since. Layer was told he could challenge 35 of the Essex jurors, no more, and he challenged the maximum number. The trial was fixed on Wednesday 21 November. The charge was that Layer had sought at Leytonstone in Essex on 22 August 1722 to subvert the government of the kingdom, depose his present majesty and to advance to the crown and government 'the Person in the Life of the late King James the Second pretending to be Prince of Wales', who had taken the title of 'James the Third'. Sergeant Pengelly for the

Crown pointed out that Layer had abjured 'an attainted and abjured Pretender', yet had sought to raise a rebellion, to seize the sacred person of the king, had published a seditious declaration, incited the king's subjects to take up arms and to 'debauch the Army' at the breaking of the camp in Hyde Park, in order to bring in the Pretender. He then proceeded to give details of preparations at the 'place of execution', London, which was to be the prelude to a general rising in the counties. It was accurate enough, but it did not take place in Essex. The details were taken from the Scheme written in Layer's hand (see above), which he had hidden with other papers the day before his arrest at Mrs Mason's, the brothel-keeper, either because he did not have time to destroy his papers, or as he assumed the government would not look for them there.

Stephen Lynch

Layer was the only accused against whom the government brought two witnesses and was the only one brought to court. The first witness was Sergeant Stephen Lynch, a man of Irish origin born in Flanders who had taken part in the Fifteen rebellion and escaped abroad. He was 'suspected to be a rogue' by the Jacobites, but the Duke of Perth, who had known him in Flanders, had vouched for him.[11] Lynch then went to the Canaries, where he commanded a Spanish privateer.[12] He had returned to England in April 1722. According to Lynch's testimony, Dr Murphy, a physician who had also been a rebel in 1715, introduced Lynch to Layer and they met several times at the Griffin tavern and at Layer's own house in Old Southampton Buildings, London. Lynch deposed that Layer told him they were to be assisted by a great many officers and common soldiers as well as many of the nobility and gentry. He testified that his part was to seize General Cadogan, Marlborough's successor as commander of the army, at his London house. In addition, Lynch alleged that he was entrusted with the task of seizing Lord Townshend, Carteret and Walpole. This is not confirmed by other evidence. Hungerford objected that the 'overt acts' of treason given in this evidence had taken place in Middlesex and that this was not relevant to an indictment in Essex, but this objection was ignored. Layer was said to have given money to Lynch and to have sent him more through Dr Murphy. Layer asked if Lynch had taken a reward for swearing against him, but the Lord Chief Justice ruled he could not ask that question. When questioned, Lynch denied that he had received a pardon from the government. Going on with his evidence, Lynch stated that Layer always called the Pretender the King, and that he had been at Layer's house on the day the Bishop of Rochester was arrested. They went on to have a meal at the Green Man Inn in Essex and then to visit Lord North and Grey in Epping.

Layer and his two counsels concentrated on trying to discredit the evidence given of events in Essex and to argue there was only one witness, Lynch, as to events there, and not two, as required by law. In pleading that he was innocent, Layer followed the example of Algernon Sidney and Lord William Russell who, when accused in the Rye House Plot in 1683, argued that they were innocent because there were not two witnesses to every charge against them.[13] Ketelby tried to get Lynch to describe the layout of Lord North's house and Layer questioned him about the persons he claimed to have seen there, but he received evasive answers. Hungerford argued there was no evidence that Layer's and Lynch's horses were put up at the Green Man and pointed out that Lynch had testified that Cadogan had been taken into custody (by the Jacobites), which was false. Lynch alleged Layer had taken the Pretender's Declaration out of his pocket at the Green Man. Layer's defence said if it was the Declaration recently burnt by the common hangman (see above), it was a mere libel, and not a document written by Layer.

Among the witnesses for Layer was Mackworth, the landlord of the Green Man who said 'I don't know that Mr. Lynch was ever at my house' on 20 August and that he had never seen Layer 'in my life before'. Mackworth testified further that the Duke of Grafton and Lord Halifax (two leading Whigs) had been at his house and told him 'you and your friend Layer are to be hang'd', to which he replied he knew nothing of Layer and had never heard of the Declaration. John Paulfreeman, a servant of Mackworth, said he remembered nothing of Layer being at the inn on 20 August.

Layer had called Lord Orrery and Lord North as witnesses. L'Hermitage, the Dutch envoy, thought it was to give them an opportunity to clear themselves.[14] Lord Orrery, whose health was poor, was now seriously ill through his confinement in the Tower, so that he did not appear. Lord North came, testifying that:

> I little thought that my having seen him [Lynch] twice at my House, should be the occasion of my coming here in such a manner. The Gentleman was wholly a stranger to me, and I have not seen him since. I know nothing of him personally. It is a little hard for a Man of Honour to betray a Conversation, that passed over a Bottle of Wine in Discourse, but since Your Lordship requires it, I must submit.

He was represented to me as a Stranger newly come to England, and had a mind to see my House and Gardens. He was introduced, and brought there by Mr. Layer and I receiv'd him civilly. In process of time he told me the History of his life thus: That he was not a Spanish, but an Irishman, and, my Lord, I think educated in the Camp under an uncle of his. He told me, that when he was a young Man, he had taken a great many Liberties.

There, Lord North was interrupted by Sergeant Pengelly for the Crown who said no character of Lynch had been asked for. Hungerford interjected that Lord North was merely repeating the account Lynch had given of himself, adding 'if my Brief be true the whole ten Commandments [were] broken by him'. Ketelby then asked 'what character in general would he give of Lynch?' Lord North replied:

I don't know how to answer it, as to his giving a general character of himself. Thus much I must say, I saw him twice. The first time he was brought down by the Gentleman at the Bar; the second time he came he was ill receiv'd; and I order'd it should be told him, that in case he design'd to stay there, that I had no room or any Lodging for him. As to particular things, I don't care to speak of them. I should be very sorry to say it in my Company and under my Roof.

Lord North was then allowed to return to the Tower, where he too was a prisoner. It had been said that the toast North and Layer had drunk at Epping was 'The King, the Queen, the Prince', the Jacobite toast at that time.

John Talbot, another witness called by Layer said he had met Lynch in the Canaries, where he had 'a very bad character', was extravagant and 'kept very bad company'. Another witness, Winchman, said he had known Lynch for 14 years, that he did not believe anything Lynch said, and that Lynch was thrown out by one Wilson, an Irish gentleman, in the Canaries because of his bad character. At this point, Hungerford complained that the passage of Layer's witnesses was being obstructed. When access was cleared, another, John Blake, testified that Lynch was a bigamist and 'wanted money'. According to Blake, Lynch told him Lord Townshend was 'of a Morose Temper, but my Lord Carteret was of a better temper'. Blake went on to say Lynch visited two or three times a week a lady who was the mistress or daughter of one of the chief ministers of England, but he was stopped by the Lord Chief Justice before he could give her name. Many other witnesses attested to the bad character of Lynch, including a Mr Keating who said Lynch 'was a drunken idle Fellow, always kept company with other Women'. The Solicitor-General intervened when Layer said Lynch had been promised '£500 a year' by the government for his evidence.

The Crown brought fewer witnesses as to Lynch's character. A Mr Vernon, who kept a tavern named the Sun and Runner, said he had seen Lynch and Layer together there and that Lynch paid 'honestly'. Hungerford observed that Lynch paid his debts only since he was in custody. A Captain Malthus said Lynch behaved well when he was a merchant in the Canaries. Other witnesses called were non-committal.

Matthew Plunkett

The other witness against Layer was Sergeant Matthew Plunkett, currently serving in a company of Invalids in George I's army. Plunkett testified that he came over from Ireland 'when the Army was broke' (presumably in 1713). He then went over to Spain, serving in a Jacobite regiment in Spanish service in the Canaries, where Lynch also lived. He knew Layer five years before 1722 and renewed their acquaintance through a Major Barnewell, a Yorkshireman who became a debtor in the Marshalsea, until Layer paid his debt. Barnewell was said to have recruited a couple of men in the Grenadier Guards for Layer. Layer, Plunkett said, had given him half a crown to eject bailiffs, who had 'wrongfully' tried to seize some of Layer's goods. Layer and Plunkett had arranged to meet at the Italian Coffee House in Russell Court, could not do so, and came together again in Lincolns Inn Fields in June 1722. Plunkett testified that he had said to Layer that the Pretender was a papist, to which Layer replied 'there was no difference between a Papist and a Lutheran King'. Thereupon, Plunkett volunteered the information that he knew 20 of 29 sergeants (25 of whom had been dismissed from the army) and that he could enrol them for the Pretender and give Layer a list of their names and places of abode. Along with others, Plunkett was taken to hear Dr Sacheverell preach in St Andrew's, Holborn. According to Plunkett, Layer named the Earl of Strafford, General Primrose, 'a Fine general', and General Webb as being involved in the conspiracy. Layer asked Plunkett if he had borrowed money from him, which the sergeant denied. Ketelby elicited an admission from Plunkett that he could not read and, if this was the case, how did he know 'what was in letters' he gave testimony about? In any case, Hungerford pointed out that all this took place in Middlesex, not Essex, and was irrelevant.

Ketelby then called character witnesses against Plunkett. Thomas Brown, who had known Plunkett for ten years, said that he could not be believed. Another witness, Keating, deposed that Plunkett was 'a drunken idle Fellow', who 'always kept company' with women other than his wife. Sir Daniel O'Carroll, with whom Plunkett had a dispute about the purchase of a horse in the Canaries, testified that Plunkett had 'a mighty bad character'. He was Plunkett's former colonel and it was Plunkett, who had caused him 'to be brought to Town to be examined' (as we have seen). O'Caroll thought Plunkett's evidence would not 'hang a dog'. Hungerford pointed out that Plunkett was trying to hang not a dog but 'a Protestant'. Furthermore, Hungerford protested that Sir Daniel O'Carroll had been 'tumbled about' on his way in and that other witnesses for the defence had been forcibly prevented from coming in. Major Barnewell' described as 'a soldier, a Man of Honour' said Plunkett had made 'so many mistakes' in what he had said about his own life, that 'by God, I would not take his word for a halfpenny'. Patrick Malone deposed he had known Plunkett for a great many years and that he was 'a great Lyar, and not to be believed'. A neighbour of Plunkett's said he had told her 'he was going to get a settlement for life ... for what he said of Mr. Layer'. Another, Alice Dunn, said Plunkett 'lived with another man's wife', had a bad character and could not be believed.

For the Crown, there were few witnesses for Plunkett's good character. One of them, Colonel Manning, said Plunkett was 'an honest man'. Another, Major Hamel deposed that Matthew Plunkett 'was a drummer in the Regiment, and always did his Duty well; I never heard him complained of; he always had a good character'.

Mrs. Mason

Mrs Mason was the brothel-house keeper with whom Layer deposited the papers produced at his trial the day before his arrest. She had come forward hoping to get a reward from the government, so that these papers were exhibited in evidence against Layer. Mrs Mason could not read or write, though her testimony was used to identify the different bundles of papers Layer had left with her. There were many witnesses, who testified that Mrs Mason had a bad character. She was described as 'a Bawd', also known as Mrs Buda, Mrs Herbert or Mrs Bevan, who made a living 'by deluding young Women, and carrying them about for Money'. One witness, Mrs Clayton, said Mason had told her 'she was to be paid [for her evidence], or else she would not do it'. The Lord Chief Justice stopped other witnesses from going into details, saying only a general character was needed. Mrs Wilkinson, another witness, said Mason was 'a vile woman'. For the Crown, Sergeant Pengelly asked of Mrs Peirce, one of the witnesses, if she had seen Layer at Mrs Mason's and she agreed she had. A Mr Dyer testified that Mason had lived at his house 13 or 14 years, that she had robbed his shop and had been sent to Bridewell, so that she was not to be credited. Major Barnewell said Mason had tried to cheat him of £1500, while Mr Lebatt testified that Mason 'would take any Body's Life away for the value of a Farthing'. There were *no* witnesses as to the good character of Mrs Mason.

For Layer's defence, Hungerford argued that Layer was being tried for overt acts of treason for agreeing to raise a rebellion (under 25 Elizabeth I cap. 3) and not under the Act of Parliament of the last year of William III's reign to attaint the Pretender and make corresponding with him and his adherents an offence (13 & 14 Wm. III cap 6), therefore Layer's going to Rome and corresponding with the Pretender (if he did so) was irrelevant. Being in Rome was not 'a fact of High Treason'. He made light of Plunkett's evidence and said that two 'very great men' such as the Earl of Strafford and General Primrose were 'too well known to be blemished by such an incredible evidence'. He derided what he described as a 'chimerical plan' for seizing the general of the army, the Tower, the Exchange and the Bank of England and enlisting Plunkett in this undertaking by giving him half a crown. Moreover, he tried to discredit the evidence of Layer's papers by pouring ridicule on the idea that Layer 'with the assistance of only a Bundle of Papers, and of Mr. Lynch and Mr. Plunkett [would attempt to] overturn and enslave the whole kingdom'. The arms found in Layer's house were no more than what was required to defend a gentleman's house. He maintained that 'The Scheme' was not written in Layer's handwriting and a Mr Bennet had testified he had written it for Layer, together with the lists of the army. In any case, Hungerford argued that Layer being in Rome, listing soldiers for the Pretender's service' was 'nothing', unless it were an overt act done in Essex.

In his own defence, Layer declared:

> If a Man's Life is to be taken away by such scandalous Evidence as hath appear'd against me, there is an end of all your Liberties, your wives may be taken from you, your Children made Slaves, and all that is valuable to you, your Lives and Estates will be but very precarious.

The two counsels for the defence, however, were cut short, while the Lord Chief Justice spoke for two hours in his summing up to the jury, which included all the evidence objected to by Hungerford, as well as many references to a popish Pretender, arbitrary power and slavery. Deliberating for half an hour only, the Essex jury found Christopher Layer guilty. The trial had lasted from 9.a.m. on the 26th until 4 a.m. the next day, the 27th, with no intermissions.[15]

During the day on 27 November 1722 Layer, still in chains, was brought back to the King's Bench. His chains were taken off for him to be sentenced. First Layer made a short statement:

> I have nothing more to say now because my Counsel has given it up. But after Your Lordship hath passed Sentence upon me, I hope and desire, for the sake of other People more than myself, those that I have had very great Dealings and Correspondence with, particularly my Lord Londonderry, and several others, that I would do justice to; that your Lordship would give me reasonable time to make up their Accounts; and when that is done, I hope your Lordship will give me still a further time to make up that great Account which I have in another Place: When this is done, if his Majesty doth not think fit graciously to continue me in this world, I will dare to dye like a Gentleman and a Christian, not doubting but that I shall meet with a double Portion of Mercy and Justice in the next World, though 'tis denied me in this.

The dreadful sentence for high treason was then passed:

> to be led to the Place from whence you came, and from thence you are to be drawn to the Place of Execution, and there you are to be hang'd by the Neck, but not till you are to be dead, but you are to be cut down alive, and your Bowels be taken out, and burnt before your face; your Head is to be sever'd from your Body, and your Body to be divided into four quarters; and that your Head and quarters be deposed of where His Majesty shall think fit.

Walpole and Townshend could not believe that, Layer knowing the type of death he was facing, would not turn king's evidence. Time and again Layer was reprieved by the government in the belief that he would co-operate. Layer's friend, James Hamilton, described him at that time as:

> a man of virtue and entire honour, the unprecedented severitys of E[lector]. Hannover's agents towards him is a strong vindication

of his probity and steadiness. I fear he will fall a sacrifice to their malice for ... they are fully acquainted with the particulars of the christening of his child.[16]

Pressure was put on Layer's wife and daughter to get him to accuse Atterbury. When Mrs Layer presented requests for mercy, Lord Townshend told her Layer 'could save himself and become rich' if he would turn king's evidence. She replied she would sooner see him die than have him play such a rôle.[17]

Lord Lansdowne reported that the government had sent an emissary to see Layer's 13-year-old daughter in France, to try and get her to persuade her father to 'make a frank confession of all he knew' when:

The young creature offended at such a thought, instantly replied that as well as the Lord she loved her father tenderly ... [but] she had rather wish her own eyes to be a witness at his death, than hear he had saved himself by betraying the cause or any man that had trusted him. Is there among the Romans an instance of a braver spirit?[18]

The fate of Orrery and Lord North, as well as that of Atterbury depended on Layer's silence. James III grieved at Layer's plight with all his heart, but remained convinced he would 'never do a base thing to save his life'.[19] Layer was covered in sores through being in irons for so long. He was freed from his chains only to testify before the committees of the House of Commons and the House of Lords in February 1723. He was reprieved six times in the hope he would give evidence to save himself. Lord Lansdowne described this process as 'a sort of torturing the soul, keeping poor men betwixt life and death, between hope and despair, sometimes with threats, sometimes with promises'.[20]

On 17 May 1723, using irregular proceedings to the end, Christopher Layer was not taken to Tower Hill, the usual place of execution for prisoners in the Tower, in which case he would have been handed over to the two Jacobite Sheriffs of London (Humphry Parsons and Francis Child), who might have let him escape. Instead, he was taken out of the Tower by the east wharf gate (which was technically in Middlesex) in the care of the Sheriff of Middlesex.[21] He had asked for Aaron Thompson to attend him to the scaffold, but this was refused by the court of King's Bench on the grounds that Thompson was in custody himself. Layer was attended by Dr Hawkins, chaplain to the Tower, instead.[22] Layer was hanged, drawn and quartered at Tyburn, dying with calmness and resignation. In his dying speech he declared:

> I come here to suffer an ignominious death, not for an ignominious crime, but for following the dictates of my conscience, and endeavouring to do my duty. As I die for so doing, I doubt not but I shall soon be happy. But am certain this nation can never be so, nor even easy, until their lawful King is placed upon the throne.[23]

This was what has been called the theatre of death at its most powerful.[24] Mrs Layer fainted as she saw him die.[25] There had been public discontent at the irregularities in Layer's trial and his bravery had made him a public hero. Mrs Layer asked Lord Townshend for Layer to have a normal funeral with hearse, pall and bearers, but Townshend replied if she persisted in this 'indecency' he would not allow him to be buried, but would leave his quarters exposed. In the end, the undertaker agreed to have him buried quietly in the country. Layer's head was set on Temple Bar. When it fell off, Bishop Rawlinson of Oxford, a nonjuror, had it brought to him, kept Layer's skull on his desk during his life and deemed that he should be buried holding Layer's skull in his right hand.[26] Mrs Layer fell on hard times subsequently. In June 1724 she was 'so impudent' as to visit Orrery at his house, which alarmed him. It had the desired effect, however, as he secured a pension of £100 a year for her for life from James III.[27]

8

The Trials of John Plunkett and George Kelly

The legal procedure

Walpole was unable (and in the case of Plunkett apparently unwilling) to have John Plunkett and George Kelly tried for high treason as Layer had been, because of the lack of witnesses and legal evidence in a common law court. As in the case of Sir John Fenwick, who was attainted in Parliament in 1696, the government disregarded the safeguards of the statute passed by Parliament itself earlier that year: the Treason Trials Act of 1696, which required the testimony of two lawful witnesses and gave the accused the right to know what the charges against him were, in order to prepare his defence. Plunkett and Kelly were not tried by bills of attainder, which carried the death penalty, but by bills of pains and penalties brought against them before the House of Commons and the House of Lords, with the outcome decided in divisions along party lines, carried by the Whig majority. It was another case of what has been called 'Parliament's right to do wrong' and was regarded as setting dangerous precedents.[1]

Since the Revolution of 1689, the Jacobites had survived by becoming past masters at remaining within the letter of the law, leaving nothing which could be pinned down to them as treasonable for the government to find. It was generally known that letters could be opened by the Post Office and their contents revealed to ministers.[2] Atterbury and his associates (Arran, Strafford, North and Grey and Goring) did not use the Post Office for correspondence with the Stuart Court. Instead, as we have seen, James Hamilton and Anne Oglethorpe took letters, memorials etc., personally to Rotterdam and brought back letters through the same port.[3] Other Jacobites, sending less important letters by post, used ciphers. Walpole had skilful code-breakers, Edward

Willes particularly, but letters in code did not constitute legal evidence. Once again, Walpole and Townshend circumvented this by breaching the laws to suit their political purposes.

The trial of John Plunkett

Plunkett had been arrested on 8 October 1722. Perhaps because of his contacts in the diplomatic world, he was not sent to the Tower, but he remained in the custody of a messenger. Two things made him a special target for the ministry. First, he was believed to have served as an amanuensis to Atterbury.[4] Secondly, he had taken part in writing the pamphlet *The Advantages that have accrued to England by the succession in the illustrious House of Hanover*, which had so outraged George I.[5]

Walpole secured an all-Whig secret committee to enquire into the conspiracy, albeit one elected by secret ballot. William Pulteney (who was still an ally of Walpole) was its chairman. Walpole was in total control of the evidence put before the committee and he sent the Speaker a trunkful of documents on which Pulteney's report and its many appendices were based. The committee proceeded to examine Plunkett on 23 January 1723. Lord Anglesey, a Tory, then moved that consideration of the whole affair should be moved to the Lords as the supreme tribunal, but lost the division by 50 votes to 30.[6]

In his examination before the Committee of the House of Commons on 25 January 1723 Plunkett spoke with a good deal of irony and gave answers which were not likely to win favour with the ministers.[7] He declared 'he knew no more of the conspiracy than the Child unborn'. He knew nothing of Layer's transactions and never spoke to anyone in his life about an insurrection, indeed Layer had warned others not to trust him as he was regarded as devoted to the interest of the present government. He had met Layer in a coffee house and agreed to travel with him to Italy 'as he might do with other Gentlemen', the more readily as Layer offered to bear his expenses. Venice, he thought, was their destination because of a lawsuit relating to a sister of Lady Yarmouth (Lord Yarmouth was one of Layer's clients). Layer, he said, did ask him to find out by the means of Monsieur Chammorel whether the Regent would be disposed to come into Tory measures. He denied he was ever employed by the Pretender or his agents.

The Committee repeatedly asked him about a list, of which the government had no copy, considered so important it was merely referred to as 'the List', which Layer carried (the 1721 list, Appendix B), but Plunkett replied he knew nothing of it. As to his stay in Antwerp, he agreed he did go there with Layer but he denied that he received there a letter from Digby (Dillon) telling him how to proceed in order to introduce Layer to the Pretender. Digby was a man he met two years ago, who was tutor to the Duke of Berwick's children. In Rome he said he met Francis Kennedy in a coffee house and had no private discourse with him. He saw the Pretender in a garden (the usual way for British people to see him safely) in the company of 20 others and did not meet Colonel Hay. Asked about the Burford Club, he said he had heard it was a Loyal Club either 'Loyal to their Country, or to King George, for ought he knows'. As to Monsieur Chammorel, he saw him now and then about legal procurations, but he did not discuss state affairs with him or with Monsieur Destouches. He knew Kelly, alias Johnson, as a coffee house acquaintance only. As to Simon Swordfeger and Aaron Thompson, he knew them through selling them some wine and saw them in Layer's house once in company of seven others, who were strangers to him. He admitted, however, that he was introduced to the late King James's queen, ten or eleven years ago.

Asked if he was willing to leave his case with the Committee 'thus weakly defended by Answers, which can be proved false from the Evidence now before them', Plunkett replied he was willing to have everything reported 'just as he has answered'. At the end, however, alluding to the Burford Club, he declared he knew 'his Innocency, and Affirms with Imprecations, that he never would be concerned with the *Tories* in his Life'. The Secret Committee of the Commons reported on 1 March 1723 that there was a plot to bring foreign troops into the kingdom, to capture the Tower and the City of London and to seize the persons of the king and of the Prince of Wales and voted that Plunkett was one of the principal agents and instruments of the conspiracy.[8]

The evidence produced against Plunkett in the Report of the Secret Committee of the House of Commons was the basis of Plunkett's trial. There were 14 letters seized in his papers, which were written between 1713 to 1716 from Plunkett to the Duke of Berwick. They gave an account of events in England and of European affairs, fairly general in content, but showing his commitment to Mary of Modena and her son, James III. All the letters were in code, with false names for persons and the subject hidden under the language of merchants and lawyers, as was usual in Jacobite letters. The three ciphers found at Plunkett's lodgings at Richard Coleman's, tailor, in St Martin-in-the-Fields, did not decode either the letters or the documents available to the Committee. There were five letters from Sir William Ellis, James's treasurer, which showed Plunkett knew him well, as he also knew James's secretary, Francis Kennedy. Sergeant Matthew Plunkett (no relation of John), one of the two witnesses against Christopher Layer, testified against Plunkett (whom he called James Plunkett). He spoke of Plunkett's contacts with great persons such as Lord North and Generals Webb and Primrose who, according to Sergeant Plunkett, were said by Layer to be in favour of a rising, and involved in attempts to recruit soldiers in London.[9] Knatchbull, a reliable source, noted that there were two witnesses against John Plunkett.[10] This meant he could have been tried in a common law court. We do not know the identity of the second witness. Perhaps a trial involving the death penalty against John Plunkett would have caused diplomatic difficulties and this is why he was tried by a bill of pains and penalties in the same way as Kelly and Atterbury, who had no witnesses against them.

Other documents produced at Plunkett's trial were letters from him (as James Rogers) to and from General Dillon (Digby) intercepted and copied at the Post Office, which were among the most interesting correspondence printed in the Commons Report. Letters from General Dillon to Plunkett were directed to Mr Arthur, Banker in King Street, London. He belonged to the great Irish banking dynasty founded by Sir Daniel Arthur in Paris. Letters from Plunkett to Dillon were directed to George Waters, banker in Paris.[11] Not decoded by the government decipherers, the main interest of these letters are the references to Burford's (Lord Orrery's) Club. On 21 May 1722 Plunkett reported that Burford and his club seemed to think Mr Joseph (a cant name used for James III in some Jacobite correspondence) was 'their only refuge' (the motto used in the Unica Salus medal) and 'would have a finger in the Pye if they can'. On 31 May Plunkett wrote on 'how to make Burford Club' exert themselves, although because of the attitude of Steel (the Regent) he thought they would 'hardly come into any Thing this season'. This tallies with Lord Orrery's reluctance to act without support from the Regent. On 5 July Plunkett reported a long conference 'with Mr. Steel's agent' (probably Chammorel rather than Destouches), who 'had no great opinion of Burford and the Club', adding that if the Club had 'a true Concert' the Regent 'would come in with them'. The most damning document was the letter signed by James in Rome to Plunkett about how he and his companion (Layer) were to come privately to see him at night. This was found by the King's Messengers in a chest of drawers at the lodgings in Wardour Street, Soho, of Mrs Isabella Creagh, with whom he had formerly lodged. He had sent it to her in a packet and she testified she did not know what was in it. Presumably

Plunkett could not bear to destroy a letter written in the hand of his king and had thought it would be safe at Mrs Creagh's. Unlike Mrs Mason in Layer's case, Mrs Creagh did not betray Plunkett, as the information seems to have come from her servant, one Mary Fagan.[12]

On 19 March Sir Robert Raymond, the Attorney-General, a Tory 'rat' who had gone over to the Whigs in order to obtain office, presented in the House of Commons a bill of pains and penalties against John Plunkett. Two days later, Lords Scarsdale, Strafford, Cowper, Craven, Gower, Bathurst and Bingley complained that the printed Commons Report on the Conspiracy contained a statement that Plunkett told Layer that they belonged to a Club of persons well affected to the Pretender's service, called Burford's Club, chaired by Lord Orrery, which met monthly, and consisted of seven Lords and six commoners which they declared to be false and groundless. Earl Cowper declared he wished to defend the rights and privileges of the peerage and the fundamental laws of England, confirmed by Magna Carta. He went on to say that he had shown his attachment to the Church of England and his majesty's person and was offended to see his name bandied about in a list of a 'Chimerical' club. Lord Cowper and Archibald Hutcheson published declarations protesting that the evidence was hearsay. Cowper called for all the evidence to be laid before the House of Lords and was strongly supported by Tory Lords, who demanded that Plunkett be summoned to the Bar of the House of Lords to be questioned about his deposition and made to swear if the matters mentioned in his papers were true. Lord Townshend declared that 'upon a trivial circumstance, Lord Cowper should not ridicule as a fiction, a horrid and execrable conspiracy'. Lord Bathurst, supported by Lord Craven and Lord Kinnoul 'insinuated as if the main drift of the Plot was a base contrivance of their enemies'. At this stage Lord Cadogan (who was named but not accused) said he had been mentioned in the report and did not trouble himself about it. Lord Strafford spoke with even greater warmth, declaring 'he had the honour to have more ancient noble blood running in his veins than others, so, he hoped, to be allowed to express a more than ordinary resentment against the insults offered to the Peerage'. The motion to summon Plunkett before the House of Lords was defeated, however, by 81 votes to 26.[13]

On 28 March the bill against Plunkett reached its second reading in the Commons and orders were given that the Speaker's chamber and the lobby should be cleared of all persons except counsel, solicitors and witnesses (in other words excluding the public). The Attorney-General, Raymond, opened the case against Plunkett arguing that there was a necessity of using the legislative power when the courts below could not reach people that were grown so artful in plots as to do everything that was really treason but not within the strict rules of law.

The opposition side pointed out the dangers of such precedents. John Plunkett, presumably well knowing the sort of justice a Catholic was likely to receive, made no defence before the Commons by himself or by counsel. Edmund Miller, a Whig MP moved for the death penalty against Plunkett (as there were two witnesses against him) and was supported by several other Whigs. This was opposed by Robert Walpole and his brother, Horatio Walpole, who insisted on a bill of pains and penalties, which did not 'reach life'. William Shippen and a few Tories opposed the bill of pains and penalties 'in great heat' saying 'how slender the evidence was and that people without doors might say it [the evidence] was extorted, suborned and bought', but they were stopped by the Speaker. Raymond proposed imprisonment for life during the king's pleasure. Any attempt to escape would be treated as a felony without the benefit of clergy. On its third reading, the bill passed by 280 votes to 91 and was taken up to the Lords.[14]

On 26 April Plunkett was brought to the Bar of the House of Lords to defend himself against the bill. He objected that he had never been heard by the House of Commons, but the Lord Chancellor overruled him. Then Plunkett declared:

That if this bill affected none but himself, he would be unconcerned about it, and give their lordships no trouble, well knowing he was too inconsiderable to merit the attention of so noble an assembly, and being besides advanced in years, he little cared whether he was able to pass the remainder of his days in the wide world, or in a prison; but that he opposed this bill for the good of the whole nation, whose liberties and properties would become precarious, if such an unprecedented bill, unsupported by any legal proof should pass into a law: and as the peers of the realm were no less concerned than the commoners in this extraordinary proceeding, he doubted not but their lordships would, with their usual wisdom and equity, maturely weigh the ill consequences of it; and in the first place he begged their lordships to consider, whether extracts of intercepted letters, some of them anonymous and by unknown persons, should be admitted as evidence.

Lord Townshend justified the Commons' proceedings and said that 'the conspirators had used all sort of art and industry to conceal the true names of the persons concerned, in order to avoid the danger of legal conviction'. He was opposed by Lords Cowper, Strafford, Bingley, Trevor and Lechmere, but the Lords continued to proceed with the bill of pains and penalties, although 23 peers, all Tories, registered a protest. Counsel for the bill went on to read Neynoe's examinations and confessions before the committee of the Privy Council, which named George Kelly but not Plunkett. Plunkett objected that these were examinations of a dead man, neither sworn nor signed by him and therefore could not be read as evidence. Lord Cowper asked whether Neynoe's examinations were signed and taken on oath. Townshend admitted they were not, as Neynoe, fearful of being sent to Newgate, had escaped and was drowned before signing them. After a long debate the Lords voted to admit Neynoe's examinations as evidence, with 19 Tory Lords objecting. On 27 April Plunkett produced several witnesses, principally to discredit the evidence of Sergeant Matthew Plunkett whose depositions 'bore hardest against him'. However, the bill of pains and penalties against Plunkett passed on 29 April by 87 votes to 34, whereupon 33 Lords, including Cowper and Oxford signed a protest.[15] At this stage, Plunkett was sent to the Tower on the orders of the House of Lords. He was placed in irons there, probably on the order of George I.[16]

The trial of George Kelly

A large section of the Report of the Secret Committee of the House of Commons concerned George Kelly. It began with his examination on 21 May 1723, after his first arrest, when he testified that he called himself Johnson because he was in debt (and therefore feared arrest) and that his journeys to France had been solely occasioned by his speculation in Mississippi stock. Kelly said he did not know anyone by the names of T. Jones or T. Illington (the code names for Atterbury). He gave a little dog he brought over from France, who had a broken leg, to Mrs Barnes, as it was meant for her. Unfortunately for him, Mrs Barnes had testified, inadvertently, to the Lords of the Council on 23 May 1722 that Harlequin, the little dog with a broken leg she was looking after, was 'designed for the Bishop of Rochester'.[17]

The most serious charges against Kelly were contained in Neynoe's examinations; they had not been taken under oath or signed, and, as as we have seen, Neynoe was dead. Neynoe had said Kelly had been a frequent visitor at the Bishop of Rochester's and Sir Henry Goring's. Most damning was Neynoe's statement that Kelly had told him that Atterbury corresponded with the Pretender and his agents and that Kelly was employed by the bishop in writing and carrying on this correspondence. Neynoe added he had seen several ciphers in Kelly's hand, which Kelly had told him were for corresponding with the Pretender. All this was true, of course. Yet, In order to give himself a more important rôle and be worth more as an informer, Neynoe had invented stories of his having been employed in writing memorials for the Regent of France, asking for armed assistance in restoring the Pretender, which he had drafted from notes given to him by Kelly. Even more implausibly, Neynoe claimed that the Earl Marischal (who was serving in Spain under Ormonde at the time) had been involved in giving him material for such memorials. Neynoe revealed that Kelly had followed James to Avignon in 1716, in the train of Ormonde, which was true.[18]

Walpole had no real proof against George Kelly. Yet there are voluminous appendices supposedly relating to his case in the Report of the Committee of the House of Commons designed to give the impression that he had been collecting treasonable letters from Will's Coffee House in Covent Garden and Burton's Coffee House in King Street. The clerks at the Post Office testified that they had copied these letters and forwarded them on. In his examination taken on 21 May 1722 Kelly stated that he had called at coffee houses to collect letters for James Talbot 'who was under a Cloud having several Bargains on his Hands' and who had gone over to France (and was out of Walpole's reach). James Talbot was described as 'a tall black [dark] man', whose London address was the Cocoa Tree in Pall Mall, the Tory Club. It turned out that James Talbot, a friend of Kelly's', had taken part in the Battle of Preston in 1715, escaped, and went into Spanish service.[19] The letters said to have been intercepted, copied and forwarded by the Post Office,[20] however, were either giving the news of the day in England or France or were, as was the Jacobite custom, couched in the language of merchants and lawyers with the names of persons in a code the clerks of the Post Office did not decipher. These letters could not be ascribed directly to or from Kelly. The exceptions however, were the three letters of 20 April 1722 to General Dillon, Lord Mar and 'the Pretender', said to have been in Kelly's handwriting and dictated to him by Atterbury, and two letters said to be from Mar to Kelly of 5 May and of Kelly to Mar of 7 May 1722. It was these five letters which secured Atterbury's conviction and it is our view that they were forgeries (see Chapter 9). At any rate, the staff of the coffee houses reported to have been frequented by Kelly denied the allegations and did not give evidence against him. The only witness produced to testify that Kelly had collected a treasonable letter from Burton's, John Collet, could not recognise Kelly at his trial (see below) and was presumably bribed by Walpole.

Kelly was examined by the Committee of the House of Commons on 2 February 1723 and urged to make 'a candid and ingenuous confession of all he knew relating to the conspiracy' to secure his own life and gain the intercession of the Committee, adding that what he said would not be used against him but could be used against others. In other words, he was invited to turn king's evidence. Replying that he understood their meaning 'very well', he said he was an 'entire stranger' to any conspiracy or design for an insurrection. He denied that any of the letters produced by the Committee were his. Asked about his journeys to France between 1721 and 1722, he said these were on 'private affairs' relating to his investments in the Mississippi Company and that he had used fictitious names for the persons involved as they had been 'undone' by the crash of that company. He was asked if he ever conferred in France with General Dillon, Lord Mar, Christopher Glastock, Colin Campbell of Glendarule or Alexander Gordon of Boulogne. He replied that he had carried an Act of Parliament relating to General Dillon's family estate to France, that he did not know Lord Mar, that he did see Captain Glastock, who was a captain in Dillon's regiment, and that had seen Colin Campbell in a coffee house but had never spoken to him. As to having set up a channel of communication by boats to and from Boulogne, he said he knew nothing of that. He said he knew of no bills of exchange sent from London to Paris via Calais, nor of sums of money to buy arms for the Pretender and that, as he was a stranger in England, it was improbable that anyone would make him privy to such matters. Asked if he had any ciphers or fictitious names in his custody, he replied no. Admitting that James Talbot was his 'intimate friend', he said he knew nothing of Talbot's dealings and did not send a package of letters to Alexander Gordon at Boulogne to be delivered to Talbot. He agreed that he brought a little dog over from France, which he delivered to Mrs Barnes, as it was meant for her. He owned he had seen John Plunkett, but only at coffee houses 'as a newsmonger' and never had any dealings with him. As to Neynoe, he had not seen him from November 1721 to April 1722 and never employed anyone to draw up memorials to the Regent. In view of Kelly's unco-operative attitude, the

Committee did not put the rest of their written questions to him.[21] James III was 'very pleased' with Kelly, adding 'I could not read his examination without laughing'.[22]

George Kelly was voted to have been centrally involved in the plot on 11 March by 280 votes to 111.[23] On 11 March, on the report of the Secret Committee on Layer and others, the Commons had resolved:

> that George Kelly, alias Johnson, had been a principal Agent and Instrument in the said horrid and detestable Conspiracy; and had carried on several treasonable Correspondences to raise Insurrections and a Rebellion at home; and to procure a foreign Force to invade those kingdoms from abroad.

The motion to bring in a bill of pains and penalties against George Kelly was carried by 280 votes to 111, with Robert Walpole and Bubb Doddington acting as tellers for the Yeas and two Jacobites, Dixie Windsor and Sir Christopher Musgrave, acting as tellers for the Noes.[24] The Solicitor-General, Sir Philip Yorke (later Earl of Hardwicke) presented the bill of pains and penalties against George Kelly, alias Johnson, on 19 March. On 23 March George Kelly petitioned to be heard by himself and by counsel against the bill. He was allowed to defend himself at the Bar of the House and asked to have Atterbury's friend, Sir Constantine Phipps, and Nicholas Fazakerley, a prominent Tory MP as counsel and Dennis Kelly as his solicitor, but Dennis Kelly was objected to by the prosecution. Fazakerley would not act, so that he was represented by Phipps and Nott.[25] Hungerford presented a petition on the 27th to postpone the second reading because of Kelly's need to get affidavits from witnesses in France: Michael Birmingham, surgeon, and Messrs Bask and Burgonio, merchants in Paris, and Mr Gordon, banker in Boulogne, who were material witnesses. This was rejected on the grounds that affidavits could not be read in the House. Sir Edward Knatchbull wrote in his diary that this was a move to postpone Kelly's trial until after Atterbury's 'which would have benefited both of them'.[26] Kelly was ordered to appear on Monday next. Jane Barnes, Edward Bingley (who lived in the same house as Kelly), John Malone (a servant dismissed by Mrs Barnes) and William Wood were summoned to appear as witnesses.

On 1 April Kelly appeared before the House of Commons, when 'as in Sir John Fenwick's case the mace stood by the prisoner at the Bar so that no member could ask any question'. Objection was made to Neynoe's examinations as not taken on oath or signed and as the dead

Neynoe could not 'be cross examined and confronted by the prisoner', which was a new and dangerous way of introducing evidence, but it was carried on a division to allow this evidence. The next day, extracts of 'copies' of three treasonable letters of 20 April 1722, said to be in Kelly's handwriting and to have been dictated to him by Bishop Atterbury (the letters used to convict Atterbury) were produced. Counsel for the bill endeavoured to authenticate Kelly's handwriting by a letter of 20 August 1722, which was proved to be his. Kelly denied this letter was in his handwriting and asked why his handwriting was not identified, instead, by the letters he had written to Lord Townshend since he had been in custody? Several members, who had seen Nicholas Paxton, the solicitor to the Treasury, slip the 'proved' letter of 20 August into his pocket and substitute it for another 'fell into great heat and shewed a just indignation at such an imposition and then the letter was produced.'.

Another extraordinary incident that day concerned the only witness the Crown had been able to find to testify that George Kelly had collected a treasonable letter from a coffee house. The episode was reminiscent of Titus Oates in the Popish Plot. This concerned John Collet, a Frenchman, and a wine cooper in St James's, who had claimed to know Kelly 'very well'. Collet testified that he went to Burton's Coffee House at the corner of King Street, St James, and saw a treasonable letter addressed to 'James Baker' (one of the names in letters said to have been intercepted by the Post Office) delivered there. Collett read it and put it back in the same place. A quarter of an hour later, he saw Kelly, alias Johnson, collect this letter, read it and put it in his pocket. Asked to identify Kelly, Collett 'looked round about him and full in Kelly's face 4 or 5 times and did not know him', pointing instead to Nott, Kelly's counsel. It was not until Paxton pointed Kelly out to Collet that Collet identified Kelly at last.

In his defence Kelly 'spoke short but in a decent manner'. He drew attention to 'Neynoe his accuser's poverty when he knew him, and how of a sudden he was lush of money and to a profligate affluence when the plot began to break out'. Kelly protested that he had never written any letters by the direction of the Bishop of Rochester, 'had never had any treasonable correspondence on his account' and had seen the bishop only twice in three years. Notwithstanding, next day the bill was committed by 246 votes to 100.[27]

The bill against Kelly was heard in the Lords on 30 April 1723, when he was brought from the Tower to the Bar of the House. Kelly's counsel 'strenuously opposed the reading of Neynoe's examination' as not taken on oath nor signed by him, but was overruled. Then the information of Neynoe (much of it overlapping the 'evidence' given to the Commons) was read. It stated that George Kelly, who also went by the name of Johnson, frequently told him that the Bishop of Rochester held correspondence with the Pretender and his agents; that Kelly was employed by the bishop in carrying on his correspondence and that the Pretender relied more on the advice of the Bishop of Rochester than on any other person; that the bishop went sometimes by the name of Jones and sometimes by the name of Illington; that he had seen several ciphers in Kelly's hands. According to Neynoe's deposition, Kelly said he had notice that the Bishop of Rochester was going to be arrested from one of the Lords of the Council and that Kelly warned the bishop.

Counsel for the bill brought as evidence the three letters of 20 April 1722 said to have been enclosed in a packet from Kelly to Gordon junior, banker in Boulogne. The letters were said to have been dictated by Atterbury to Kelly and to have been in Kelly's handwriting. They were supposed to have been intercepted and copied at the Post Office and then forwarded, so that the originals were never produced. The clerks of the Post Office claimed to have been able to memorise the handwriting of George Kelly in the three letters and to have identified it from the letter of George Kelly of 20 August, four months later. The packet supposedly contained a letter to Chivers (General Dillon) signed T. Jones, another to Musgrave (Lord Mar) signed T. Illington and a third signed in a numerical code to Jackson, whom the decipherers identified as the Pretender. In the cipher in which Chivers was General Dillon and Musgrave was Lord Mar, however, Jackson was Lord Lansdowne. The identification was changed, presumably because writing to James III was high treason, whereas writing to Lansdowne was not. In any case, the method for correspondence between Lord Mar and Atterbury arranged by Kelly earlier was by special boats called 'bye boats', and *not* through the Post Office. It will be argued in the next chapter that all three letters were forgeries. Kelly took strong objection to this 'evidence'. Lord Bingley examined the decipherers Willes and Corbiere as to the rules and reliability of their art, and they owned there could be variations. A debate ensued as to whether letters intercepted at the Post Office and deciphered (inadmissible in a court of law), could be used as evidence in Parliament, but they were voted admissible on a division.

The case resumed on 1 May. For the defence, Sir Constantine Phipps showed the dangers of proceeding without legal proofs in cases where lives, liberties and properties were at stake. Edward Bingley, a witness for the defence, said Neynoe had told him that in order to humour those in power he told them of a pretended conspiracy and obtained £300–£400 in return. He also alleged that Walpole suggested to Neynoe that he should plant a list of names of persons concerned in the conspiracy in one of Kelly's drawers for Walpole to find. The next day, 2 May, Walpole himself appeared before the Lords as a witness. Walpole admitted he gave Neynoe £200 and three sums of £150 to 'encourage' him, but alleged that this was before Kelly's first arrest in May (instead of after Neynoe's own arrest). A motion for admitting the evidence of witnesses that certain letters were not dictated to Kelly by the Bishop of Rochester was lost on a division. A protest that these proceedings were 'highly dishonourable' to the House of Lords was signed by 41 peers, including Cowper, Wharton and, the Bishop of Sarum (Richard Willis).

Kelly then spoke in his own defence at the Bar of the House on 2 May. He said he was never acquainted with the Earl Marischal and that he never employed Neynoe in this or any other affair. He hardly knew Neynoe and would not have confided such 'gross and notorious falsehoods' to him. He went on:

> I do solemnly declare to your lordships upon the faith of a Christian, That I never wrote or received a letter of any kind for the bishop of Rochester, or was privy to any correspondence of his at home or abroad: that I never shewed him any letter that ever I wrote to France, or ever sent one by his privity or direction: that I am little known to his lordship, went very rarely to wait on him ... I have not seen him above three or four times these two years past, and not above eight or ten times in my whole life.

He declared the little dog was given to him by a surgeon at Paris and that it was designed for the person he gave it to (Mrs Barnes). Kelly added that the Bishop of Rochester had no intercourse with Lord Mar or with any other disaffected persons. He went on to ridicule the whole reports of the conspiracy: how could six to eight battalions of Irish troops come over from Spain, when Britain and Spain were on terms of such strict friendship? How could £200,000 have been raised by the disaffected? How could 800 men be raised in London without discovery? These were 'idle, inconsistent tales', the hearsay of infamous men. 'I believe', he continued, 'no man in England can be sure of his life and liberty an hour since two people may talk him into high treason whenever they please.'

Kelly particularly objected to the charge of writing three treasonable letters for the Bishop of Rochester supposed to be to the Pretender, the Lord Mar and General Dillon, sent by him to Mr Gordon at Boulogne and collected there by James Talbot. How could the Post Office clerks identify his handwriting in the three letters of 20 April they had seen but once and compared it to a letter of 20 August, when they saw hundreds of letters in between? He objected to two of the witnesses against him, who had been dismissed from employment at his request or by him, and therefore had a grudge. An affidavit from Gordon of Boulogne was produced stating he never received any such letters from Kelly, nor ever corresponded with or had any acquaintance with him. Kelly complained also that some witnesses on his side had been sent to Newgate to stop them from testifying for him, while witnesses of the 'meanest rank' were plucked out of Newgate to testify against him. The evidence produced was unreliable, as James Talbot could be proved to have been in London on the very day the letters said to have been written by Kelly were alleged to have been collected by him in Boulogne. Kelly went on:

> This minister [Walpole] had declared a personal prejudice, upon some private account, against the bishop of Rochester; was resolved to pull down the pride of that haughty prelate, and to squeeze me (as I think the expressions were) to that purpose.

Persons in the coffee houses where Kelly was said to have collected and left treasonable papers testified that nothing of the kind was done by Kelly. He denounced Mrs Mason, one of the chief witnesses against him as 'a vile infamous creature all her life'. When he had declared himself a stranger to the conspiracy, he was sorry to find that a noble lord (Townshend) had 'so base an opinion of me, he seemed to wonder, that I would neglect so good an occasion of serving myself, especially when I might have any thing I pleased to ask for'. He expressed his gratitude to the previous governor of the Tower (Lord Carlisle) for promising him an allowance from the government for his upkeep, which the present governor (Lord Lincoln) had been good enough to pay, but complained that this allowance was now diverted for the use of the staff of the Tower (presumably Williamson and his friends). In conclusion, he reminded the Lords that the great characteristic which distinguished England from neighbouring states was 'the excellency of her laws, of which your lordships are the great guardians' and that they should not be broken so as 'to render life and liberty precarious'.

George Kelly had spoken with spirit and wit in a speech which ended at 12 o'clock at night. On the third reading of the bill against him the next day, 3 May, Lord Bathurst proposed that Kelly should be allowed to go into exile and never return without the consent of the king or his successor, but it was defeated on a division by 83 votes to 38. The bill of pains and penalties passed by 79 votes to 41. A Lords protest was drawn up saying that Kelly should have been tried in one of the courts of justice, and that copies of letters taken by the clerks of the Post Office should not be used in evidence against persons accused of high treason when the originals were no longer available to compare them with, so that mistakes and falsifications could not be detected. The protest was signed by 38 lords, including Wharton.[28]

Plunkett and Kelly had lied to and misled ministers working for a German king, as well as to the Commons and the Lords, not in order to save themselves, but for the good of their cause and to protect their fellow conspirators. They were much in the same position as members of the Resistance in Europe in the years 1940–44 who were questioned by the Germans. They showed great courage by sacrificing themselves and resisting pressure to turn king's evidence and offers of financial inducements if they did so. The Committee of the House of Lords when they had examined Layer, Plunkett and Kelly concluded that they

cannot reflect, without Pity and Compassion, on the misguided Zeal, and wretched Infatuation of those men, who rather chuse to expose themselves to the greatest Dangers, than to discover the Authors or Accomplices of their Treasons; thereby declaring to the World, that their Leagues and Confederacies of private Villany are dearer and more sacred to them than the strongest Tyes and Obligations of Society.[29]

9

The Trial of Bishop Atterbury

Atterbury's harsh treatment in the Tower

The chief persecutor of Bishop Atterbury during his long imprisonment in the Tower of London was Lieutenant General Adam Williamson, who was appointed deputy lieutenant (in fact resident governor) of the Tower in October 1722. A supporter of the 'Old Cause', Williamson described himself as a 'Christian Deist', whatever that could mean, who condemned 'the doctrine of a nonsensical Trinity' as 'not founded on the Gospel of Christ'. He regarded Charles I as being 'deservedly treated' at his execution in 1649 and described Charles II as 'a mere Viceroy to France'. Williamson was protégé of Lord Cadogan, who was regarded by Atterbury as 'a bold, bad, blundering, blustering, bloody, booby'. Cadogan had employed Williamson on gathering intelligence on the movements of James III in 1715 and sent him to the Dutch Netherlands in 1717 to 'take care' of Baron Göertz during his confinement there during the Swedish Plot. Everything about Williamson was anathema to Atterbury. On his side, Williamson wrote of 'the wicked Bishop of Rochester' 'who had with others Layd a dangerous Scheme for bringing in a Popish bigotted Pretender, and for which he was more than justly banished for life'.[1]

Samuel Wesley the Younger, a protégé of the bishop, likened Williamson to a kite, the cruel gaoler of a blackbird, who represents Atterbury:

> So, every day and every hour,
> He shows his caution and his power;
> Each water-drop he close inspects
> And every single seed dissects;
> Nay, swears with a suspicious rage,

> He'll shut the air out of the cage.
> The Blackbird with a look replies,
> That flashed majestic from his eyes;
> Not sprung from Eagle-blood, the Kite
> Falls prostrate, grovelling, at the sight.[2]

All provisions, bottles of drink and other articles brought in for the bishop were extensively searched prompting, perhaps, Atterbury's friend, Alexander Pope, to write:

> even pigeon pies and hogs puddings are thought dangerous by our governours, for those that have been sent to the Bishop of Rochester are opened and profanely pried into at the Tower. It is the first time dead pigeons have been suspected of carrying intelligence.[3]

Williamson would not allow Atterbury the sacrament when the bishop was ill of the gout, nor to see his own doctor. The sub-dean and chapter clerk of Westminster were allowed to see their Dean about the affairs of the chapter only in Williamson's presence. Atterbury's son and daughter were not given permission to visit him, so that he had to try to look out of 'a two pair of stairs window' to talk to them while they stood in the open air below. This was soon stopped by Williamson, who also prevented Atterbury from talking to his solicitor and son-in-law, William Morice 'at a low window'. When Atterbury complained to Lord Harcourt and others of Williamson's 'rashness & violence & absurd insolence' and the 'many indignities' he had been subjected to, Lord Cadogan jokingly suggested Atterbury should be thrown to the lions in the Tower menagerie.[4] However, Atterbury held his own in a scuffle with Williamson, who complained that the bishop had 'collared him, struck him and threw him down', upon which Dr Stratford, Atterbury's former opponent, commented that Williamson's was 'a pretty odd affidavit for a great officer to make – that he was beaten by a gouty bishop'. Atterbury's version of the incident was that Williamson entangled his foot in a chair and 'was thrown down flat on his back'.[5] It is not surprising, therefore, that subsequently Atterbury complained to the House of Lords of Williamson's conduct towards him.[6]

The bill of pains and penalties against Bishop Atterbury

Destouches thought that the trials of Plunkett and Kelly had destroyed the outer works protecting Atterbury, thus allowing for a central attack on the bishop, whose trial before the Commons and the Lords was the real test of Walpole's and Townshend's power. These gone, the government could proceed to a full frontal attack against Atterbury, their chief target, in the House of Commons and the House of Lords. Atterbury had been the most severe critic of the present government. The ministers believed he had been the receiver of all the money collected for the Pretender. The bishop had been too skilful to have left any legal proof for the government to find, and no witness had been cajoled, bribed or coerced to give evidence against him, so that he could not be prosecuted in a common law court. Instead, Walpole sought to humiliate Atterbury and, by using arbitrary measures, to drive him out of the country, so as to put it out of his power to embarrass the ministry.[7] The Report of the Secret Committee of the House of Commons on 1 March 1723 stated that Atterbury was principally involved in the conspiracy by 'aiding and employing the said Kelly in the prosecution of his treasonable designs'.[8] Sir Edward Knatchbull, a neutral observer, regarded the evidence presented to Parliament against Atterbury as 'very weak'.[9] The Deanery of Westminster and Atterbury's house in Bromley were torn apart in search of evidence, but the result was meagre. The government did not even have a specimen of Atterbury's handwriting because Atterbury would not allow even 'a bit of paper' in his handwriting to be taken out of his houses.[10] The evidence against Atterbury, such as it was, was printed in the appendices of the Secret Committee's report. It consisted of Neynoe's unsigned examinations previously produced at Kelly's trial, which testified that the Bishop of Rochester, Lord Orrery, Lord North and Grey and Sir Henry Goring were 'the principal leaders of the conspiracy'. A later document was the deposition of one Andrew Pancier, formerly a lieutenant and acting captain in Lord Cobham's Dragoons, who had had to sell his commission as a result of his losses in the South Sea and had thought of going into the King of Spain's service, had it not been that he did not want to leave his wife behind. He said he had confided his plight to one Skeene, a relation of Lord Mar, probably Major Andrew Skeene of the Earl of Portmore's regiment (2nd Dragoons), who left the regiment in May 1715 as a result of the purge of Tory officers. Skeene fought in the Jacobite army in the Fifteen as adjutant to Brigadier Mackintosh, was taken prisoner at the Battle of Preston, escaped, and went on to take part in the 1719 expedition to Scotland. Pancier alleged that Skeene offered him good prospects in the Pretender's service. The crucial part of Pancier's deposition, as far as Atterbury was concerned, was the statement that Skeene had told Pancier that the raising of £200,000 was 'put into the Management of the Bishop of Rochester who with Lord North and Grey were the leading men among them and that Lord Strafford and Lord Kinnoul knew of the Thing'. As Skeene refused to give evidence, Pancier's testimony was hearsay. Nevertheless, it was used at the trial. William Pulteney, however, excused Lord Strafford and Lord Kinnoul from testifying.[11]

A Margaret Kilburne of Little Ryder Street, where Mrs Barnes and George Kelly lived, testified that a servant was sent by the Bishop of Rochester to enquire after Johnson (Kelly), who was ill, and that Neynoe had frequently visited Johnson. This was presumably to show that Kelly was the Johnson in the cipher and that he was in contact with Atterbury and Neynoe.[12] Two brief notes established that Captain Halstead (who was to bring Ormonde home from Spain) had paid two visits to Atterbury beforehand.[13]

Thomas Moore, the bishop's chaplain refused to give any evidence at all. William Wood, coachman to Atterbury, gave details of the bishop's movements between Bromley in Kent and Westminster in the spring and summer of 1722. A baker testified that Atterbury's most frequent visitors to Bromley last summer were Lord North and Grey, Lord Bathurst, Sir Constantine Phipps, 'Mr. Aldridge, a clergyman' (Henry Aldrich, Dean of Christ Church) and Mr Wynn, counsellor at law (who was the bishop's counsel at his trial).[14] None of this incidental evidence would have been admissible in common law, yet it was now accepted in support of a bill of pains and penalties by Parliament.

The documents which secured Atterbury's conviction, however, were not the above, but four letters in cipher said to have been written or dictated by Atterbury and two further letters also in cipher (see Appendix E), the first said to be written by Lord Mar and the second by George Kelly. The first letter, 'to Mr. Dubois, 16 December', had little to say beyond securing to establish that George Kelly, commonly known as Johnson, wrote Atterbury's letters for him. It was said to have been seized in a close stool at the Deanery of Westminster at the time of the bishop's arrest, when he protested that it had been planted there. It was 'proved' to be in Atterbury's handwriting and sealed with his seal (a Tully's head) after comparison with the letter and seals seized on Atterbury's servants in the Tower. The other three letters, all dated 20 April 1722, the day after Sunderland's death, to General Dillon, Lord Mar and 'the Pretender' were the most crucial. They were said to have been dictated to George Kelly by Atterbury and sent together as a packet by Kelly through the Post Office, copied there, their seal replaced or mended and sent on to the addressees, so that no originals were ever produced. As it happens no originals are to be found in the Stuart Papers. Thomas Hearne, the Jacobite antiquary in Oxford, wrote that the government 'forged three letters in his name in cipher, which Wills [Edward Willes] the decipherer hath interpreted'. As the trial proceeded satires were published pouring ridicule on the 'proofs' (the three letters) against Atterbury and the part played by a dog at the heart of the conspiracy.[15] Some of the code names in the cipher, however, were real code names. They were those used in Atterbury's correspondence with James III, presumably given to Colonel Churchill or Sir Luke Schaub by Lord Mar in May 1722. This must have come as a shock to the bishop. We know now that the bishop did not send letters through the Post Office and that his Jacobite correspondence was taken to and from Rotterdam by James Hamilton, the Jacobite agent in London.[16] These alleged letters are long-winded and lack the clarity and incisiveness of Atterbury's prose and serve little purpose beyond identifying Atterbury and Kelly. The bishop enjoined that nothing should be sent to the Post Office, yet Kelly, allegedly, sent the whole packet through the Post Office. The third letter signed R [offen] was to 'Jackson', a name which stood for Lord Lansdowne in this cipher, but it was now identified as written to the Pretender, which made it treasonable. The two other letters were from Lord Mar to George Kelly of 5 May and from Kelly to Mar of 7 May 1722. The last two letters allude to Mar's agreement with 'Hacket', Lord Oxford, who was not identified in the Commons Report or during Atterbury's trial, and to the gift of 'Harlequin' the dog to Mrs Atterbury. We know, however, that Atterbury sent Kelly, to Paris to reach a verbal agreement with Lord Mar precisely because he did not want written correspondence about it, let alone in letters sent through the Post Office. Moreover, the postscript to the second letter shows it is not genuine: Mrs Atterbury is said to be 'in great Tribulation' about Harlequin's injury eleven days after she had died! One is therefore confronted by two opposing hypotheses. First, that Kelly against the strictest and most well-understood instructions, used the Post Office. Secondly, that, as Hearne thought, the letters were forged. Since Kelly had no motive in disobeying Atterbury, while Walpole had every motive to produce 'evidence' we think these letters were forged at the Post Office before being sent to the Secret Committee of the House of Commons. The letters from and to Lord Mar would have been written drawing on genuine information given by him, but the people writing them made mistakes about the circumstances of the events they were describing. The Duke of Ormonde suspected a 'false friend' in our midst[17] and Atterbury did not take long to conclude that it was Lord Mar.

The report of the Secret Committee on 1 March 1723 declared that Atterbury had held 'treasonable correspondence' with the Pretender and had employed George Kelly 'in the prosecution of his treasonable designs'.

On 8 March Walpole placed before the House of Commons a letter of 26 February, the first specimen of Atterbury's handwriting the government had. It had been forcibly seized out of the pocket of one of the bishop's servants in the Tower on the order of Lord Townshend. Knatchbull summarised it as 'containing an account of what he apprehended was coming upon him, and instructions to his friends how to behave and taking care of his deanery'. Atterbury expected to be impeached, even if an attempt to do so 'with *confessedly* no living Evidence whatsoever against him, will be barbarous, especially after waiting *six* months to get some such evidence'. He thought what they had on Neynoe, Sample and Layer did not affect his case, but he did not draw much comfort from it:

> For whose Liberty is safe, if the H[ouse] of C[ommons] may accuse any one, even when they *own* they have no *Legal Proof* against him? They are the Grand Inquest of the Nation, and should find their Bills, as the Grand Jurys do, upon some positive Evidence; they cannot, they ought not, to proceed solely upon Conjectures and Probabilities.

He asked that part of the letter be shown and the opinion sought of Mr Br–y. This was William Bromley, a prominent Jacobite Tory MP, who had been Atterbury's ally in bringing in the bills against Occasional Conformity in Queen Anne's reign. He urged that the absent Tory peers be whipped in, as well as all the bishops, adding that Lord Anglesey could bring in Lord Abingdon, who had been absent from the Lords for all the session.[18] In Atterbury's trial, this letter was used to authenticate the bishop's handwriting in the supposed letter to Dubois.[19] The trials and convictions of Plunkett and Kelly had blocked several lines of defence for Atterbury and he needed all the support he could in the Upper House.[20] Lord Oxford, whose health had improved, came up to town to do whatever he could on Atterbury's behalf. James III expressed his satisfaction at Oxford's conduct, though he could not write to him directly in present circumstances.[21] Lord Bathurst, on his side, wrote to Lord Gower to ask all Tories to attend Parliament during Atterbury's trial.[22] After long months of waiting, during which Atterbury was confined in the Tower, uncertain of his fate, of what charges would be brought against him, or how to defend himself, his case finally arrived before the Commons on 11 March 1723. William Yonge, Walpole's alter ego, spoke of

> how deeply Dr. Francis Atterbury, bishop of Rochester, had been concerned in this detestable Conspiracy; aggravating his crime from his holy function and high station in the church of England, a church ever conspicuous for its loyalty; from the solemn oaths he had, on so many occasions, taken to the government, and by which he had abjured the Pretender; when at the same time he was traitorously conspiring to bring him in, upon the ruin of his country and all that was dear and valuable to us as freemen and Christians.

After which he moved

> that Francis, Lord Bishop of Rochester was principally concerned in forming, directing and carrying on, the said wicked and detestable conspiracy for invading these Kingdoms with a foreign Force; and for raising Insurrections, and a Rebellion, at home, in order to subvert our present happy Establishment in Church and State, by placing a Popish Pretender upon the Throne.

This was opposed by Sir William Wyndham, William Bromley, Shippen, Archibald Hutcheson and Dr Freind on the grounds that there was 'little or indeed no evidence besides conjectures and hearsays' for bringing in such a bill. The motion, however, was carried by 285 votes to 152 with Lord Stanhope (later Earl of Chesterfield) and Sir John Rushout, a friend of William Pulteney's, as tellers for the Yeas, and Lord Morpeth, Lord Carlisle's son, and Sir John Bland, a Jacobite, as tellers for the Noes. A bill of pains and penalties was brought in against Atterbury by a committee consisting entirely of Whig government supporters, including the Attorney-General and the Solicitor-General, who steered the bill, while Yonge took the chair. Two days later, Walpole informed the Commons of the arrest of Dr Freind for high treason, refusing to give any details. Shippen suggested this was because of Freind's warm defence of Atterbury earlier and that such an arrest put an end 'to the liberty of speech which every member of that House had a right to', which threw Walpole in a passion wondering 'how any gentleman could think any ministry capable of so base a thing'? Pulteney thought that Freind speaking in defence of the bishop had been a question of one traitor endeavouring to excuse another. On

22 March Yonge presented the bill of pains and penalties, which had its first reading. It was resolved to send a copy of the bill to the bishop and to allow him the use of pen and paper for the first time, as well as counsel and solicitors. This was a political trial, as Plunkett's and Kelly's had been, and just as Sir John Fenwick's trial in 1696 had been. Even the order of the Commons to send the bishop a copy of the bill, so that he could defend himself, was flouted by sending him only the preamble.[23]

On 29 March Lord Bathurst presented a petition from Atterbury to the House of Lords saying he was innocent of the 'supposed crimes' he was accused of and that under a standing order of the House of Lords of 29 January 1673 'no lord may appear by council before the House of Commons, in answer to any accusation there'. A motion was put 'That the bishop of Rochester being a Lord of Parliament, ought not to answer or make his defence by council or otherwise in the House of Commons, to any bill or accusations there depending'. This was strongly supported by Lord Lechmere, Earls Cowper and Strafford and Lords Trevor and Bathurst. But it was opposed by Lords Macclesfield, Carteret and Townshend, the Dukes of Wharton and Argyll and the Earls of Peterborough and Coningsby and the motion was lost by 78 votes to 31.[24]

Lord Lechmere, who had made a stinging attack on the conduct of the ministers, particularly that of Carteret, in the debate, followed Carteret out of the House and challenged him to a duel, but Carteret slipped away. Lord Cadogan, who watched, took the side of Carteret, which turned Lechmere's fury upon him. Getting into his coach, Lechmere whipped his horses to try and run over Cadogan, who beat Lechmere's coachman with a cane and called Lechmere a rascally lawyer. Lechmere demanded satisfaction and they met next day in St James's Park. Lechmere drew his sword and made a few thrusts at Cadogan. Cadogan, a skilled swordsman, used only a hunting knife to parry the blows, disarmed his opponent and went off laughing. The incident was the talk of London for some days.[25]

On 4 April the Speaker read a letter from the Bishop of Rochester stating that he would make no defence before the House of Commons, but would instead defend himself 'before another House of which he had the Honour to be Member'. The same day Colonel Williamson and four warders of the Tower of London burst in on Atterbury while he was having dinner, searched him without producing a warrant and seized his instructions to his counsel and his list of witnesses, though he had been allowed them to make his defence by order of the House of Commons. Atterbury wrote them down again the next day, and when there was another attempt to get hold of them, the bishop kept Williamson at arm's length, while he destroyed his notes by eating them. However, three seals were seized 'one whereof was supposed to be the Tully's head with which the letter to Dubois was sealed'. This seal, together with the letter in Atterbury's handwriting produced earlier by Walpole, was used to 'prove' that the letter to Dubois was in his handwriting and bore his seal.[26] A petition was presented to the House of Lords from Atterbury, complaining of the violence used in searching him in the Tower and the seizure of a letter to his solicitor about the management of his case while he was 'under the protection of Parliament'. Atterbury sought 'relief and protection' from the Upper House against 'such unprecedented illegal and insolent usage'. Lord Cowper and Lord Strafford moved to summon Williamson and the warders at the Bar of the House of Lords to answer for their conduct, but it was opposed by the Court and defeated by 56 votes to 24. A strong Protest ensued led by Strafford, Cowper and Bathurst.[27]

The House of Commons was cleared of all members of the public while the bill of pains and penalties against Atterbury was heard in committee of the whole House on 6 April. The court party proposed that Atterbury

> should be deprived of his office and benefice, banished the kingdom, be guilty of felony if he returned, and that it should not be in the King's power to pardon him without the consent of Parliament; but without forfeiture of goods and chattels.

Gilfrid Lawson, a moderate Tory, objected that as the evidence against the bishop was 'either hearsay, or conjecture' he should have no punishment at all. James Edward Oglethorpe, Anne Oglethorpe's brother, cleverly declared that:

> It was plain the Pretender had none but a company of silly fellows about him; and it was to be feared, that if the bishop, who was allowed to be a man of great parts, should be banished ... [he would] do more mischief by his advice, than if he was suffered to stay in England, under the watchful eye of those in power.

But the question was carried without a division and the bill was read for a third time and sent up to the Lords on 9 April.[28]

Atterbury at the Bar of the House of Lords

6 May 1723

Atterbury was escorted out of the Tower to Westminster on 6 May, when, at the door of Westminster Hall, he was transferred to a sedan chair and carried through to the House of Lords. A special chair had been made for him, so that he would not have to stand at the Bar. He was flanked on one side by the King's counsel (the Attorney-General and the Solicitor-General), and on the other by the bishops, who sat 'in boxes made for the purpose'. He had been provided with a complete copy of the bill of pains and penalties against him by the House of Lords. William Morice was said to have been able to smuggle into the Tower a summary of the chief accusations against the bishop, 'leaked by someone in the ministry's confidence'.[29] This was most probably Wharton, who remained on the court side until he could find out from Walpole himself details of the accusations against Atterbury, after which he kept the promises he had made to Sir Henry Goring and Sir John Bland by returning to the Jacobite fold when most needed (see below). The proceedings were opened with the reading of extracts of letters received from abroad by the government, including the letter from Sir Luke Schaub from Paris to Lord Carteret in April 1722, revealing the existence of a conspiracy. Sir Constantine Phipps and Serjeant Wynn, counsel for Atterbury, objected to the reading of letters without producing the originals and demanded to know the source of the advice in Schaub's letter (Cardinal Dubois), but they were overruled on a division.

Then counsel for the bill produced 'copies of letters intercepted at the Post Office, part of them written in cypher and afterwards decyphered'. This was strenuously opposed by the bishop and his counsel, who questioned the Rev. Edward Willes, one of the decipherers, 'to give an account of his decyphering several letters, by what rules it was he judged that these cyphers meant what he pretended'. Willes refused to answer that question as 'disserviceable to the Government' and helpful to its enemies.

Atterbury then exclaimed: 'In the name of God, what are these decypherers? They are a sort of officers unknown to the English nation. Are they the necessary implements and instruments of ministers of state?' He demanded that 'this blind art' should be explained to the House 'that he might have an opportunity perhaps of unravelling it'. He desired to have 'the key itself which they had discovered as belonging to these letters and from which they made out these several words that are pretended' to be laid before the Lords, but this was rejected by a great majority. His demand that Willes should produce the key of the cipher was defeated by 80 votes to 43.[30]

7 May

Next day counsel for the bill proceeded to read Philip Neynoe's examinations and confessions, which was strongly opposed by the bishop and his counsel, but Lord Townshend affirmed and Robert Walpole attested their authenticity and it was voted by 85 votes to 41 to admit them as evidence. Then counsel for the bill offered to read several letters intercepted at the Post Office. Atterbury insisted that the clerks of the Post Office be examined as to '1. Whether they had sufficient warrant and authority to stop and open the said letters, and from whom they had such authority? 2. Whether the clerks of the post-office who copied the letters, whose originals had been forwarded, had intercepted the said letters themselves, or received them from somebody else?' (in other words that they were a plant by Walpole). This was voted to be 'inconsistent with public safety'. A strong protest was made against the illegality of this, as cross-examining witnesses was necessary for the defence of the prisoner in detecting 'fraudulent evidence' against him. The Protest was signed by the Duke of Wharton, who in accordance with his covert strategy, had now publicly switched sides and became one the bishop's chief defenders.

On that day, three MPs were given leave of the House of Commons to appear at the Bar of the House of Lords as witnesses for the bishop's defence. They were Archibald Hutcheson, John Walter, a very rich West Indian merchant who was knight of the shire for Surrey, and Thomas Chapman, who had been brought in for Amersham by Montagu Garrard Drake, a friend of Atterbury's.[31]

8 May

The three letters of 20 April 1722 were read, when Atterbury

> desired that he might have copies of them with the cyphers as they were in the original, that he might have an opportunity of examining into the justness of the decyphering that was pretended on the side of the King. He thought this could not be denied him since so much depended upon it.

This was opposed by king's counsel, but Lord Townshend (who managed the Lords for the court) agreed to let the bishop have 'a copy of the letters and cyphers together with the words as decyphered.'

Then William Wood, the bishop's former coachman was produced as evidence of the times the bishop was at Bromley or went to London and 'the time of the death of the bishop's wife, and his having the gout' which 'answered exactly to the Bishop of the Jones-Illington letters'. Thereupon, Atterbury asked Wood 'what reward he had received, or been promised, to depose against his master?'

The king's counsel then told the story of Harlequin and produced the examination of Mrs Barnes, when she admitted the dog brought over from France by Kelly was for the Bishop of Rochester. They went on to prove that Atterbury was well acquainted with George Kelly from the evidence of two chairmen, who carried Kelly to see the bishop four years previously and that of a porter who took a letter from the bishop to Kelly.

Then the persons who had seized the bishop's papers were examined, when Atterbury denied the letter to Dubois was in his handwriting. Two engravers were brought in to prove that the seal on this letter (a Tully's head) matched the seal on the letters seized on the bishop's servants in the Tower. Counsel for Atterbury objected that seals might be counterfeited. Lord Strafford put this to the test by producing two impressions of a seal in wax he had on paper. When one of the engravers judged them to be from an original seal, Lord Strafford showed them both to be copies of his own seal, thus demonstrating how easy it was to counterfeit a seal. Atterbury wanted further demonstrations, but this was opposed by Lord Townshend as 'going too far into the secrets of state', so that the matter dropped. The letter to Dubois was then admitted as evidence.[32]

It was on this day that Alexander Pope gave evidence as a character witness on behalf of Atterbury. All writers at the time, it is safe to say, were spell-bound by the extraordinary proceedings, whatever their political sympathies, but only Pope was actually involved in the trial. For this reason the episode is worthy of a brief discussion here.

Atterbury had written to Pope on 10 April 1723 that the outcome of his 'Case' was 'already determined'. Yet he wrote: 'I know not but I may call upon you at my Hearing, to say some what about my way of Spending my Time at the Deanery, which did not seem calculated [note the careful language] towards managing Plots and Conspiracys.'[33] Pope, as we have seen, probably had a shrewd idea of what had been going on, and had intimated to Atterbury that he wished to keep clear.[34] Pope, whose skill in trimming as a Catholic in the penal period was highly developed, nevertheless agreed to appear for Atterbury. His decision was the more significant in that he was probably already under the suspicion and disfavour of Walpole. First, his close relatives, the Rackett family, had been discovered involved in Jacobite Blacking; secondly, Pope had overseen the publication of the Duke of Buckingham's *Works* (1723) which in a few pieces derided the 1689 settlement, and which Walpole had called in and had expurgated; and finally, he was known to be close to the Caryll family, well-known Jacobites, one of whose members, Philip Caryll, had been arrested and gave evidence (possibly having been threatened with torture, possibly after torture) against the conspirators, including Atterbury himself.

Pope expected to be interrogated as to his Catholicism, and in a most interesting letter to Simon, Lord Harcourt, he attempted to rehearse honest yet politically acceptable answers.[35] When it came to the moment, however (according to his own account on 1 September 1735 to his Whiggish friend Spence), and ' I was to appear for the Bishop of Rochester in his trial, though I had but ten words to say, and that on a plain easy point ... I made two or three blunders in it, and that notwithstanding the first row of Lords (which was all I could see) were mostly of my acquaintance.'[36]

Pope's letters to Atterbury in April and May 1723 reveal how he felt about the trial of the bishop. Despite the suspicions, even possibly inside knowledge, he is likely to have had, he strongly stresses Atterbury's 'Innocence'. He sees Atterbury in a heroic light and compares him with Cicero, Bacon and Clarendon, all, he thinks, at their greatest at the time of their public disgrace. These are exceptionally emotional and eloquent letters from a man whose normal epistolary style was easy and informal. Even though Pope knew himself to be in jeopardy, he agreed to 'appear for the Bishop' in a case in which the bishop did not expect to prevail. We suggest that this was because both men knew that the trial was a show-trial (as the trial of Sacheverell had been designed to be).

At this trial Atterbury wanted Pope as a witness so that posterity would record that the man whom the bishop esteemed to be the greatest poet of that time had been on his side against the government. Pope, we suggest, in his letters to Atterbury in which he writes of 'my Protest to your Innocence', was motivated by two considerations, one ideological, one legal. The ideological consideration was that neither Pope nor Atterbury thought in his heart that it was treason to correspond with James III. Each appreciated that it was considered treason under the Hanoverian régime. Then, secondly, each man did not expect that Walpole could come up with genuine evidence against Atterbury, but feared that Walpole was capable of having the evidence forged. Pope's last loyal letter to Atterbury, which he went as far as to include in his published *Letters* (1737), is evasively dated: 'May 1723'. It begins: 'Once more I write to you as I promis'd, and this once I fear will be the last!' It was forbidden to correspond with the bishop after 25 June. This letter takes for granted Atterbury's exile. To conclude our account of this episode, Pope's motives for appearing as a witness for Atterbury were complex. This was certainly the moment in his life when he was in the greatest political danger. Something carried Pope over into the intention to support the bishop at his show-trial, whatever the outcome (he would speak speculatively of his own possible exile in his letter to Atterbury), but, when he might have been eloquent in public, he made only blunders. It is not out of the question that he intentionally made blunders in order to seem an inconsiderable threat to Walpole.

At the end of the day (8 May) Atterbury raised the matter of the 'tumults and noise' as well as 'insolent language' which took place on his return from Westminster Hall to the Tower at night. In scenes reminiscent of the riots accompanying the trial of Dr Sacheverell in 1710, rival Whig and Tory mobs fought in Charing Cross, one side crying out 'No king-killing bishop' and the other 'God Bless the bishop and High Church'.[37]

9 May

On 9 May Sir Constantine Phipps spoke for an hour for the defence. Sergeant William Wynn spoke for three-quarters of an hour when, Dudley Ryder reported that 'he said a great many good things, but 'imprudent on account of the harshness of this to the ministry'. The substance of it was that the 'plot' was 'a forged design of Walpole's'. They called three witnesses to discredit Neynoe's evidence: Edward Bingley, Mr Skeene and Mr Stewart, who had been taken into the custody of a messenger when Neynoe was arrested. The personal animosity between Atterbury and Walpole became blatant, when Atterbury asked that Walpole, who was to be a witness against him, should not hear what other witnesses said, whereupon Walpole was asked to withdraw.

Edward Bingley, who had lodged in the same house as George Kelly and had studied at Trinity College, Dublin with Kelly and Neynoe, said Neynoe knew 'nothing of moment of the plot at all, nor that there was any, but was forced to tell something about one to gratify Walpole, but he knew of two other plots, one of Walpole's against the protesting Peers, and another of his own to get £20,000 from Walpole'. Neynoe,

Bingley continued, had been arrested for publishing several scurrilous libels against the government in the *Freeholders Journal* and he was alternatively threatened with the utmost severity of the law and tempted with large rewards if he would accuse the Bishop of Rochester, Lord Orrery and others of having formed a conspiracy. Lord Townshend, Bingley added, had his own score to settle against Atterbury and was determined 'to pull down the pride of that haughty prelate'. Walpole briefed Neynoe on what to say in his examination before the Lords of the Council and gave him several great sums of money as a reward. Neynoe secured Walpole's consent to go to France to get further intelligence of the conspiracy by observing Lord Mar and Lord Lansdowne. But Walpole grew suspicious and had Neynoe arrested at Deal before he could get to France. Bingley had gone with Neynoe to keep an eye on him, and he was also arrested at Deal, when Walpole offered him £300 if he would testify against the Bishop of Rochester. This he refused to do. Lord Townshend interrupted Bingley, saying 'no regard ought to be had to the evidence of a notorious and tedious Jacobite, who had been convicted, whipt, pilloried and imprisoned at Dublin, upon two indictments, one for publishing a treasonable Book called "Nero", the other for speaking treasonable words, and this after having taken the oaths to the government' which made him 'a less credible witness'.

Skeene confirmed Bingley's testimony, and said that Neynoe had told him 'he had rather be torn in pieces by wild horses, than be an evidence and confirm by oath, before a court of judicature, what he had been obliged to say before the lords of the council'. He then went on to discredit Pancier's testimony by stating he had never given Pancier any information. Stewart confirmed Bingley and Skeene's depositions, adding that Neynoe had tried to get him to give evidence against Lord Orrery, whom he had met but once getting some books for him. Corbet Kynaston, who had represented Shrewsbury, was devoted to Ormonde and was a friend of Thomas Carte, confirmed everything Bingley, Skeene and Stewart had testified.

On that day Atterbury cross-examined Walpole, on his dealings with Neynoe particularly, and did so so severely that he wrote to the Duchess of Buckingham afterwards that his examination of the minister before the House of Lords 'can never be forgotten and will scarce be forgiven by him and much less he forgive me the injuries he has done me'.

Counsel for the bishop then endeavoured to clear him from the most material evidence against him: the three letters of 20 April 1722 which he was said to have dictated to George Kelly, by pleading that

Atterbury had been indisposed at the time, that he had several servants about him, who had testified that no stranger came that day and that Kelly was not the bishop's secretary. An affidavit from Mr Gordon, banker at Boulogne, was produced, stating that he had never received any packets from George Kelly and that he had never had dealings or correspondence with Kelly. These proceedings lasted until 11 o'clock at night, when the House adjourned.[38]

10 May

At this stage, in order to discredit the Dubois letter and the three letters of 20 April, Atterbury called Erasmus Lewis, a former Tory MP attached to Oxford, who was chief clerk in the secretary of state's office until he was dismissed after the Hanoverian succession. The bishop asked Lewis if he knew one Broquett, formerly employed by the Post Office to open letters and copy them in a hand so like the original and seal them again with a seal so like the original seal and to forward the copies and keep the original without being discovered by the correspondent. Lord Townshend interposed to stop Broquett from being questioned, saying it would discover secrets of state. He was supported by Lord Chancellor Macclesfield, who said Broquett 'must say or discover nothing that came to his knowledge by the means of his being concerned in the Post Office'. Next, to show his seal on the letter to Dubois was counterfeited, the bishop called several witnesses to demonstrate how a seal could be copied or be broken and then repaired without any sign of a visible break. Witnesses for the Crown were brought in to deny this could be done.

11 May

The bishop's speech at the Bar of the House of Lords seemed to those who heard him, even his opponents, worthy of Demosthenes or Cicero. Something of its impact can be judged by the reaction of Dudley Ryder, a staunch whig who described Atterbury's speech in his own defence as 'full of the best and finest oratory that ever I heard or I think read'. It was printed and distributed in advance, which made a great impact on public opinion. As in the case of the orations of the elder Pitt, who could keep Parliament entranced for hours at a time, it is difficult to convey the magic of this speech from the reports which have come down to us. The best accounts of Atterbury's defence are the notes taken by his son-in-law, William Morice, and those taken by Dudley Ryder. Pope thought, and said in 1735 that it was roughly twice as long as the versions at the time printed.[39]

Atterbury began by complaining of the way he had been treated during his long confinement by Williamson which had impaired his health and the use of his limbs. The charges against him were 'unsupported by any *living* witness whatsoever', there was no legal evidence and his trial 'constituted the most extraordinary proceedings that ever were heard of'. Yet, on their basis, he was threatened

to be deprived of all his preferments, to suffer *perpetual* exile, to be rendered *incapable* of any *office* or *employment*, or even of any *pardon* from the crown.

He spoke of the nature of the evidence produced against him, making seven specific complaints:

1. That only parts and extracts of foreign letters without name without knowing from whence they came, were read against him without giving him leave to have any other parts read, to explain or clear up the right.
2. Another hardship was that he was not allowed to examine the decypherers concerning the rules by which they discovered the pretended meaning of the letters.
3. That he was not allowed to examine the persons of the Post Office as to matters which were necessary to his defence, for fear of discovering the secrets of that office.
4. That he was not allowed to examine one that had been ten years ago in the Secretary's office [Brockett] in relation to matters that he knew by being in that office.
5. That examinations without oath, inconsistent in themselves and not signed [Neynoe's] were read against him.
6. That he had been denied upon his petition to have copies of the letters with the cyphers charged upon him till his trial, when his own decypherers could not have time to consider of this.
7. That he had not the liberty of reading any of the papers laid upon the table in order [to prepare] his defence but such as were read to him. (D. R.)

Atterbury next went on to rebut the charges of having had consultations with other persons to foment an insurrection within this kingdom, to procure a foreign force to depose his majesty and to place the Pretender on his throne, and to have corresponded with the Pretender. The bishop tried to expose the three letters of 20 April 1722, said to have been dictated by him to George Kelly, alias Johnson, the letter to Dubois and the letters of 5 and 7 May 1722 attributed to and from Lord Mar, as bearing 'all the marks of fraud and contrivance'. On 20 April, when he was said to have dictated the letters to Kelly in private, his wife was approaching death, while he was so incapacitated by the gout that he was confined to bed, attended night and day by his servants, who had testified no one came near him at that time. In addition, visitors were coming in relating to the Westminster dormitory affair, so that he was under constant observation. 'Can anything be more absurd than to imagine such correspondence carried on by the general post [which] was plainly designed to be intercepted?' Why should he have kept in the Deanery the only specimen of his handwriting found in his papers, sealed with his seal, sent to someone under the feigned name of Dubois, which mentioned Johnson, the name Kelly went by, a letter which could be of no use to him, but could cause him much hurt? As to the letter of 5 May from Mar, supposedly intercepted at the Post Office, he asked was it 'likely he should correspond with Earl of Mar in a treasonable way at a time when it was well known to all the world he [Mar] had left the Court of the Pretender and was supported by a pension from this Crown?' Would this be a good reason 'for me to enter into confidence with him about restoring the Pretender?' Would he have done this, not by messages, but in letters containing accounts of his circumstances at that time, sent, not by expresses, but by the common post, ready to be intercepted? Would he write that he was resolved to send nothing by the post and then send this very letter through the Post Office? He went on:

> the letter from Motfield [Mar] to Illington [Atterbury] of 11/22 May, cannot reasonably be thought to have been written with any other view than that of being intercepted, and of fixing to me the letter of April 20 to Musgrave [Mar], the receipt of which is there owned; and something is further added, to point out my function and circumstances, and prevent mistakes. This letter is committed to the common post, and sent upon its errand! One may doubt *who* wrote it: but one cannot doubt with what design it was written. (*Epist. Corresp.* ii 131)

Harlequin, the little dog sent by Lord Mar as a present to Mrs Atterbury, became lame and was looked after by Mrs Barnes until he recovered. This episode was used to identify Atterbury in the 'intercepted' letter of 7 May when 'Mrs. Illington' (Mrs Atterbury) was said to have been 'in great tribulation for poor Harlequin', five days after she had been buried. *'One intercepted dog'*, the bishop argued, 'might be as useful to this purpose as *ten intercepted letters.'* (*Epist. Corresp.* ii 136).

The evidence against him, Atterbury continued, was in all circumstantial, none of the charges had been made good, and he laboured 'under the difficulty of proving a *negative'*.

Neynoe's and Pancier's informations that he had met Lords Orrery, North, Strafford, Kinnoul and Sir Henry Goring who were 'concerned in the management of this affair' was hearsay. It had been denied by Kelly, who was supposed to have said this to Neynoe, while Skeene denied he had ever said anything of the kind to Pancier. The bishop owned he had met these lords at different times but never three of them together. He had dined once with Lord Strafford, but never with Lord North, for whom he had 'great honour', but who had appeared against him in the Westminster dormitory case. He had not seen Lord Kinnoul even once in the last two years. He had met Lord Orrery on the business of Parliament, but never at any club of which Orrery was said to be chairman (the Burford Club); the existence of such a club Atterbury denied. The charge that he was raising a military chest of £200,000 for the use of the conspirators rested on Pancier's deposition of what Skeene was supposed to have told him, which Mr Skeene 'a sensible man' denied. The only money which had passed through his hands was £1200 for the use of the Westminster dormitory. Sir Harry Goring had come to see him in connection with placing his sons in Westminster School.

Atterbury admitted that he knew, although he was in no way intimate with, George Kelly. In a passage cancelled in Attesbury's draft he owned he had procured the living of Hinckley from the chapter of Westminster for John Carte, but had seen John's brother, Thomas Carte the nonjuror, 'very rarely'. In his speech he went on to pour scorn on Neynoe's evidence as hearsay and unsigned. He ridiculed Neynoe's testimony about having shared a bed with the Earl Marischal (who was in Spain) and having received 'heads' from him to write three memorials to the Regent. Neynoe would

> doubtless have *known who* my correspondent *Dubois* was, had the scheme of my writing that letter myself been then thought of. He would have found out a reason for my corresponding with the Cardinal of that name; and £500 would have made him affirm, that he carried the letter *himself*; though, perhaps afterwards he would not have stood to his word! (*Epist. Corresp.* ii 146)

He was particularly ironic about the evidence taken down by the Chancellor of the Exchequer (Walpole):

> A right honourable person hears *Neynoe* say, that he had heard *Kelly* say, what he must have heard persons of greater figure say, that they had heard the Pretender say, concerning the Bishop of Rochester. And by this chain of hearsays, thus deduced, am *I proved* to be a sort of *first Minister* to the Pretender. (*Epist. Corresp.* ii 147)

He had sat in chapters, in convocations, in parliaments, but never in a council of war, much less at the head of it. What would his motives have been in doing to be given to persons in order to make them confess, would it not be contrary to our constitution mild and gentle?[40]

Atterbury compared the bill of pains and penalties against him to that for banishing the Earl of Clarendon:

> The Great Man ... carried a great *fortune* with him into a foreign country: he had *languages*, and was well acquainted abroad, and spent the best part of his years in *exile*, and was therefore every way qualified to support it. The reverse of all this is my fate. (*Epist. Corresp.* ii 166)

During the course of his defence Atterbury invoked another figure. This was 'Father Paul', Paolo Sarpi (1552–1622), provincial of the order of Servites of Venice. His dying words were supposed to have been 'Esto perpetua', a prayer for the state of Venice. 'I for my part', said Atterbury,

> will voluntarily and chearfully go into perpetual exile, and please myself with the thought that I have in some measure preserved the constitution by quitting my country: and I will live, wherever I am, praying for its prosperity, and die with the words of Father Paul in my mouth, which he used of the Republic of Venice, 'Esto perpetua!' The way to perpetuate it is, not to depart from it. Let *me* depart; but let *that* continue fixed on the unmovable foundations of law and justice, and stand for ever.[41]

Atterbury's allusion to Sarpi, like his comparison of himself with Clarendon, was in part a reflection on the significance of the exile which he regarded as certain. It was also a protest against the irregularity of Walpole's proceedings, as the bishop saw them. There was, however, more to the allusion. Sarpi had been a Venetian patriot at the time when the Republic of Venice had been under papal interdict. Always a Catholic, Sarpi opposed some of the temporal claims of the papacy. Further, as Atterbury knew, Sarpi had maintained an irenic attitude to members of the Church of England.[42] Pope's letter to Lord Harcourt on the political implications of being a Catholic might have been inspired by the record of Sarpi. The significance of Atterbury's allusion is, in the circumstances, quite clear. For a staunchly Protestant early eighteenth-century bishop, who looked to a Roman Catholic dynast to save his church, Sarpi's example seemed to embody the independence of the state against papal claims, and a tradition of Catholicism kindly disposed to the Church of England.

Dudley Ryder and others noted that in Atterbury's defence 'there was 'nothing of his loyalty or affection to King George or present establishment'.

Should the House of Lords be induced to pass this bill in any shape

> I shall dispose myself quietly and patiently to submit to what is determined. *God's will be done! Naked came I out of my mother's womb, and naked shall I return thither; the Lord gave, and the Lord hath taken away; and* (whether in giving or taking) *blessed be the name of the Lord!* (*Epist. Corresp.* ii 180)

13 May

On 13 May Atterbury was brought to the Bar of the House of Lords for the last time. Counsel for the bill replied to Atterbury's speech and attempted to discredit his witnesses, concluding by quoting Ecclesiastes, x. 20:

> Curse not the King, no not in thy thought, and curse not the rich in thy bed-chamber: For a bird of the air shall carry the voice, and that which has wings shall tell the matter.

Then the Bishop of St Asaph (John Wynne) told the Lords that at the very time when the Bishop of Rochester had said he was disabled in his chamber, too ill to attend to correspondence, he had received a letter in the bishop's handwriting. Atterbury rather fired with indignation, than daunted by so unexpected a charge, absolutely denied the fact, boldly challenged his accuser to prove it, and offered to put the whole trial upon that single point.

St Asaph, however, was unable to produce this letter, whereupon Atterbury animadverted on the crime of 'endeavouring to fix perjury upon a man of his holy function'.

15 May

The third reading of the bill of pains and penalties against Atterbury was on 15 August. The skill of Atterbury's defence in arguing that to condemn him would be 'flying in the face of all legal procedures and laws of the kingdom' had brought ten peers over to his side, who had been against the bishop at first and it took all the 'money, influence and threats' of the Court to bring them back to the fold.[43]

Earl Poulett spoke first in the committee stage of the debate, saying that the trial, 'swerving from the fixed rules of evidence, and consequently from justice, must inevitably be attended with the most fatal consequences to our excellent constitution'.

For the bill, Richard Willis, Bishop of Salisbury (1664–1724) declared it was not at all extraordinary to deprive a bishop of all his preferments and to prohibit him from the use and exercise of his function during his life. Fisher, Bishop of Rochester, was so deprived in the reign of Henry VIII. Nearly all the bishops were deprived at the beginning of Elizabeth's I's reign. A large number of 'Presbyters' were removed after the Restoration of 1660 and several bishops were deprived after the Revolution of 1688. Atterbury was accused of treason, a crime of a civil nature, which was no concern of any ecclesiastical authority. He thought that Captain Halstead spending over an hour with Atterbury before going to Spain to fetch Ormonde was a particularly damning fact. According to Willis, the Jacobites had to bear responsibility for keeping up popular disaffection and thus had forced the king to impose heavier taxes in order to increase the army.

The Bishop of Chester, Dr Gastrell, thought that as the conspiracy had been discovered, extraordinary measures had become unnecessary, but Dr Gibson, the Bishop of London, a protégé of Walpole's, retorted that had Atterbury's design taken effect, the Pretender would be on the throne already.

Next to Atterbury's, the Duke of Wharton's speech had the greatest impact on public opinion. George Lockhart described Wharton's behaviour in the House of Lords on this occasion as 'truely great'. According to Walpole's son, Horace, Wharton, while still outwardly a court supporter before the trial began, found out from Walpole the details of the case against Atterbury, then left the government side in order to defend the bishop. His detailed analysis and demolition of the charges and evidence against Atterbury was devastating. First of all he reminded the Lords that

persons without doors would be apt to cast different reflections on the particular behaviour of every lord this day; That those who were for the passing of this bill, would be accused of malice and partiality, and those who were of contrary sentiments, would be branded with disaffection to the present happy establishment.

He went on to urge the Lords to cast such thoughts aside, but to proceed on the evidence and the rules of justice only. The best way of showing zeal to the king and the present government 'is to act in all cases both in our judicial and legislative capacities, with the honour'd impartiality, as ought to flourish in this great council of the nation'. If the power of the legislature

is abused, if ever it is employed to destroy innocent persons, it is evident that the lives, liberties and fortunes of every subject in Britain are in the utmost danger and liable to be sacrificed to the fury of a party. ... the proper consideration now before us, is, whether the evidence offered against the unfortunate prelate is sufficient to induce your lordships to believe him guilty of the heavy crimes of which he stands accused?

Was it possible, Wharton continued,

for a bishop of the Protestant church, who had signalised himself in defence of the Reformation, and the only one of that bench where he had lately the honour of sitting that ever wrote in defence of Martin Luther, to engage in a conspiracy for introducing Popery and arbitrary power amongst us?

He turned to the lack of proof as there was 'not one living witness that could charge the Bishop with anything, nor even so much as a letter under his own hand'. The House had not desired.

to see copies of the whole letters produced, nor of the originals and even admitted an anonymous letter as evidence, even so the Bishop of Rochester was not named in this correspondence and it is difficult to see why so much time was taken reading papers with no bearing on this case.

As for Captain Halstead, mentioned by Bishop Burnet, he was a tenant under the bishopric of Rochester and had other reasons for seeing Atterbury. He made a direct attack on Edward Willes and the other government decipherers and repudiated their evidence. Hearsay and the uncertain art of decipherers, he continued, should not sway their judgements. With great skill he exposed the inconsistencies in and unreliability of the evidence produced and pointed out that the only part of Neynoe's testimony given upon oath was that 'there were two plots; one of Mr. Walpole's, against the protesting lords, and one of his, to bite Mr. Walpole of money'. He cited Sir Heneage Finch in the case of the Earl of Clarendon: 'We have an accusation upon hearsay, and if it is not made good, the blackest scandal hell can invent, lies at our doors.' In conclusion, citing the case of Thomas Cromwell in Henry VIII's reign, he reminded his fellow peers that such bills 'like Sisyphus's stone, have frequently rolled back upon those that were the chief promoters of them'.

Lord Bathurst reflected that he

> could hardly account for the inveterate hatred and malice, some persons bore the learned and ingenious bishop of Rochester, unless it was that they were intoxicated with the infatuation of some of the Wild Indians, who fondly believe they inherit not only the spoils, but even the abilities of any great enemy they kill.

He was supported by Lords Strafford, Gower, Lechmere and Trevor, who defended Atterbury. The Duke of Argyll, on the other side, said the bishop 'had debased his holy function and character', and was supported by Lord Harcourt (Simon Harcourt, Atterbury's ally during the Sacheverell trial, and a Tory 'rat' who had gone over to the Whigs).

Next to Wharton's, the best speech in defence of Atterbury was delivered by Lord Cowper, who said this bill had sullied 'the honour and dignity of the crown, the dignity and authority of this House, and the credit and reputation of the House of Commons'. The Commons had voted the bishop guilty of high treason before hearing any evidence against him. The consequence of that vote should have been impeachment before Parliament or a prosecution before a court of law. The method adopted by the Commons was to make themselves both judge and jury. 'They found themselves obliged to hear him, and yet they could not acquit him, because they had already prejudged him.' This bill, Cowper argued infringed the privileges of the House of Lords by making the House of Commons 'equal judges with themselves' in a legal case. Passing a bill against a bishop of the Church of England may 'give a handle to the clamorous, to raise an odium against his Majesty's administration'. If the Bishop of Rochester is indeed guilty of high treason, he should be punished accordingly. In conclusion, Cowper declared:

> Upon the whole matter, I take this Bill to be derogatory to the dignity of Parliament in general, to the dignity of this House in particular: I take the Pains and Penalties in it to be much greater, or much less than the bishop deserves; I take every individual branch of the charge against him to be unsupported by any evidence whatsoever. I think there are no grounds in my private opinion of the bishop's guilt, but what arises from private prejudice only; I think private prejudice has nothing to do with judicial proceedings, I am therefore for throwing out this bill.

The Archbishop of York (William Dawes, a Hanoverian Tory) had been absent throughout and very few of the bishops who had attended the trial voted for the bill. The bill, however, passed along party lines by 83 votes to 43. Thirty-nine peers, including Oxford signed the protest against it.[43]

Atterbury's friends

To help Atterbury in exile, there had been collections of money for him in which Dr Sacheverell was very active. They amounted to £15,000, plus £880 raised by the Deanery of Westminster. The sale of the bishop's furniture amounted to £4000. On 18 June 1723 Williamson escorted Atterbury out of the Tower for the last time to put him on board the *Aldborough* (a name associated with the Duke of York and the Battle of Sole Bay), a man of war, to send him into exile. The Duke of Wharton went on board with the bishop and stayed until midnight to show his affection and concern. The duke, who had taken Thomas Moore as his own chaplain, presented the bishop with a fine sword inscribed on one side with the words 'Draw me not without Reason' and on the other 'Put me not down without Honour'. As the *Aldborough* sailed, the banks of the Thames were lined with crowds of well-wishers, while a flotilla of small boats accompanied Atterbury on his way down the river. True to form, Williamson, who stayed on board part of the way, recorded in his diary that he and Atterbury 'parted as ill friends as an honest Whig and a Jacobite tory should'.[44]

10
The Aftermath

Atterbury in exile

It was a characteristic of Jacobitism, at least until the failure of the French design of 1759,[1] that it would not lie down and die. This has been attributed by many commentators in the broad Whig historical tradition to a propensity for mad schemes and crazy optimism – the other side of the coin, perhaps, from another Whiggish discovery, the politics of Jacobite paranoia.[2] Of course there is something in each charge, but a different note would shortly be struck by a man destined to be important in the life of the now exiled Atterbury. John Hay, a Scottish Protestant who had already performed signal service to King James, and was in due course to become Earl of Inverness in the Jacobite peerage, wrote on 27 February 1725 to Lewis Innes, that he was not unaware of his own defects, but that since the king had commanded him he must do his best, and beware of dangers. 'Jealousies', he says, 'cannot be helped ...' 'A King on a throne must do something not advisable for one not in possession. As for subjects of a deprived king, they should follow his cause more faithfully' and 'consult their own interests less'.[3] Hay's comments partly allude to James's discreet treatment of the Earl of Mar whose double-dealing between Jacobite and Hanover had by this date been pretty well established, and partly to his own imminent elevation to be James's secretary of state at Rome, a position which Atterbury had declined. Such developments might have been expected to generate wild optimism, or self-defeating paranoia. Hay's letter is, on the contrary, sane, balanced and faithful.

This has been to anticipate. Once Atterbury commenced his exile, in Brussels, he collapsed into an entirely understandable bout of physical illness and depression. James III at once wrote him a frank and generous letter, praising him as 'the Chief support for the good Cause at that time', most earnestly requesting his attendance at Rome, and assuring him that he, James, would lay down his own life for the happiness of his country.[4] James followed this up with another letter, on 31 August, by which time he seems to have learned something of the Bishop's illness, and now wrote chiefly to establish a special cipher for correspondence.[5] As Christmas approached, James charged John Hay to travel in secrecy to Brussels to talk with the bishop. On 23 December Atterbury dated a letter to James III to say that he was still too ill to undertake any labour. He was not any longer well informed about the state of affairs in England. He was gloomy, not very respectful, discoursed a good deal on providence, but was not entirely without hope.[6] He had talked to John Hay.

Paranoia is not the only term (though, anachronistic as it is, it tells us something) which we need to describe how the post-Atterbury Plot Jacobites began to think about the Earl of Mar. Mar had received very little of his pension from the Westminster government which James had, retrospectively, allowed him to accept, having regard to Mar's record in the Fifteen, his current loss of his estates, and the hope that he could be kept within the Jacobite fold. Given that the famous dog, Harlequin, which Mar had sent for Atterbury's sick wife, at a time when Mar was a leading participant in the Plot, and that allusions to this dog had, it was claimed, helped to break the Jacobite code and shown that Atterbury was 'Illington', thus constituting the flimsy grounds for Atterbury's condemnation by Parliament, it is no surprise that Atterbury was already very suspicious of him. That Hay and Murray in Rome had also grown suspicious of Mar is the more interesting since each might earlier have been considered a client of Mar, or at least of his faction. The contrary was the case. Hay's secret winter mission to Atterbury had a double purpose. As stated above, James wanted Atterbury at his elbow as his secretary of state at Rome. The Protestant Atterbury did not want to go to Rome, but was willing to serve his king in France. Hay wanted to nail the case against Mar, which would have important consequences for the other members of the Jacobite Triumvirate in Paris: the credulous but loyal Dillon and the unpredictable and impecunious Lansdowne. As King James's envoy to the French court, Atterbury was willing to try to clear up all these allegations. Meanwhile Hay seems to have agreed to serve, in conjunction with Atterbury in Paris, as *de facto* secretary of state in Rome. Later, as we have seen above, Hay's position would be formalised.[7]

One of the great questions, then, in the aftermath of the Atterbury Plot is: what did Atterbury discover about the conduct of Mar? Atterbury had full authority from James to demand Mar's papers and correspondence. Mar, still wishing to keep on terms with the Stuart king, handed over to Atterbury a portfolio of documents. The two recent historians of this episode consider that this was Mar's fatal mistake.[8] It was now inevitable that Atterbury would prove Mar's double-dealing. It beggars belief, however, that Mar would have handed over anything incriminating which he did not think he could explain. Murray, who went through the papers with Atterbury, confirms this, 'I find ... there are several letters wanting and particularly of Martels [Mar] to Lord Stair', the influential Hanoverian politician and ambassador to Paris. Murray reported this to James on 10 June 1724.[9] In the same letter Murray wrote: 'I wish Mr. Hay had informed him [Atterbury] of your having approved of his [Mar's] pension as it now appears to him [Atterbury].' What Atterbury found in the papers, then, was evidence of Mar's pension. The bishop himself, writing to James on 19 June 1724, used the words: 'the Discoveries I have made'.[10] But what seemed a discovery to Atterbury, or at least strong new evidence for what previous circumstances had seemed to point to, was well known to Hay, perhaps to Murray, and of course to James. Mar kept the evidence in the portfolio because he knew he could cite the Stuart king's permission, and perhaps because he knew James would come out of the affair badly. For the rest, Murray's long letter to James about Mar recited the full story of how Mar collaborated with London to incriminate the bishop, but did not claim that proofs of *this* were found in Mar's papers.[11] By comparison with Murray's letter, itself a retrospective source for Atterbury's trial, Atterbury's letter of 19 June to James is more cautious and general. He claims to have made 'Discoveries' but does not say what they are. He says they confirm what he suspected or knew in Brussels or indeed England. That he has in mind chiefly the pension is clear from the emphasis he places on James's 'subsequent Approbation' for what Mar has done: his defence of his conduct is weak because in almost every instance it depends on subsequent approval. The evidence which Mar thinks will save him, Atterbury sees 'in a very different Light'.[12]

If the case of Mar's papers is thus less clear than previously claimed, the consequences were plain enough. Atterbury, not recognised but not expelled by the French Court, supplanted the Triumvirate at Paris. Hay and Murray were in the saddle at Rome. Atterbury and James agreed on damage limitation in a discreet treatment of the discredited

Mar.[13] Hay's correspondence, for example with the Abbé Southcott,[14] confesses that he and others had been deceived by both Mar and Ramsay. His final judgement on Mar occurs in a letter to Lord Orrery of 24 January 1725: 'His later projects have chiefly consulted his own interests. His idea was to become useful to England and change only if the King's restoration looked probable.'[15]

Meanwhile, the man the Abbé Southcott considered to be an even greater Christian genius than Archbishop Fénelon, now appointed tutor to the young Prince Charles Edward, was discreetly dismissed under the suspicion of being one of Mar's protégés. Mar, it was thought, hoped that Ramsay, once at the Stuart Court, would find it easy to rise to be James's secretary of state. Charles Edward thus lost the guidance of probably the most brilliant intellectual in the Jacobite diaspora. This looks like guilt by association only, but no doubt James and his advisers felt that they could not now be too careful. James Murray became governor of the prince, and was ennobled as Earl of Dunbar.[16]

Atterbury remained in France. Protestant as he was, he probably hated the idea of living in Rome and working for the king daily at the Palazzo Muti. It was different, he may have felt, for Protestant laymen such as Hay and Murray. Nevertheless he continued loyal to James and, not only active on his behalf in unmasking Mar, was eager to exploit the changing diplomatic alliances of the European powers in order to promote the interests of the Jacobite cause. In 1725 Bourbon Spain and the Hapsburg Empire suddenly drew together in the first Treaty of Vienna. The alliance was rightly seen as favourable to James III, or at least ready to play the Jacobite card. Atterbury and Hay moved heaven and earth to secure the adhesion of Russia to the new coalition, a northern power being needed for an effective move against Hanover (not necessarily direct), and perhaps a new invasion of Britain. Atterbury's broad European approach to a new project for a restoration was in part, no doubt, a reaction against the recent conspiracy which had been forced back onto a main reliance on a native rising. Readiness of the Jacobites at home to rise was, of course, as important as ever. Here the project failed, and even the Highland chieftains in exile (Seaforth, Clanranald, Lochiel and Sir Hector MacLean) were indisposed, at least at present, to risk more for the cause of King James. Equally the new triple alliance was in the end reluctant to enter upon a new military *démarche*. For the time being – and for the remaining life of the elderly Atterbury – the game was suspended.

Atterbury's retirement

Atterbury's letters to James III were never fulsome. His own reputation for being a difficult man was acknowledged, at least once, by James himself.[17] James decided, with a characteristic blend of delicacy and concealment, to appoint a new envoy to the French Court, but certainly not publicly to dismiss Atterbury. The new envoy, Daniel O'Brien, was appointed without Atterbury being told. Atterbury himself now decided to retire from Paris to Montpellier, in the south. As Alexander Pope had praised him as a second Clarendon at the time of his trial and exile from England, so now he liked to compare himself with Clarendon who had also spent his last days in exile in Montpellier. Literary interests and friends back in England flowed once again into his mind. His son-in-law, Morice, had been bringing him greetings from Pope since he arrived in France;[18] more satisfying to him, however, must have been something to be found in Part III, Chapter 6, of his friend Jonathan Swift's *Gulliver's Travels* (1726).

Gulliver, visiting the misruled land of Balnibarbi, offers a few suggestions as to how the rulers and cognoscenti might improve their projects. In 'the kingdom of Tribnia [Britain], by the natives called Langden [England]', says Gulliver,

> the Bulk of the People consist in a manner wholly of Discoverers, Witnesses, Informers, Accusers, Prosecutors, Evidences, Swearers, ... The Plots in that Kingdom are usually the Workmanship of those Persons who wish to raise their own Characters of profound Politicians ... to stifle or divert general Discontents ... . It is first agreed and settled among them, what suspected Persons shall be accused of a Plot: then effectual Care is taken to secure all their Letters and other Papers, and put the Owners in Chains. These Papers are delivered to a Set of Artists, very dexterous in finding out the mysterious Meanings of Words, Syllables and Letters. For Instance, they can decypher a Close-stool to signify a Privy-Council; a Flock of Geese, a Senate; a lame Dog, an Invader; the Plague, a standing Army; a Buzzard, a prime Minister; the Gout, a High Priest; a Gibbett, a Secretary of State; a Chamberpot, a Committee of Grandees; a Sieve, a Court lady; a Broom, a Revolution; a Mousetrap, an Employment; a bottomless Pit, the Treasury; a Sink, a C-t ... and so on.[19]

Gulliver's Travels, first published anonymously, makes clear allusion here to Atterbury's trial. The 1760 edition of Swift's *Works*, published for Charles Bathurst, annotated the reference to the lame dog: 'See the proceedings against Dr. ATTERBURY; bishop of Rochester.'[20] By this time Atterbury, Swift and Walpole were all dead. To the contemporary reader of 1726, Swift's allusion would have been obvious, and of course it is not the 'lame dog' alone. The choice of a victim BEFORE evidence was procured, the putting of 'criminals' in chains (Layer and Plunkett), the connection of the gout with an 'high Priest' all point to the Atterbury Plot and would, if taken literarlly, disclose a suspicion if not a conviction on Swift's part that Walpole had forged evidence against Atterbury for his own ends. But of course Swift's satire is comically cryptic, and thus somewhat evasive, while it is obvious that it is also of general implication.

Two literary labours occupied Atterbury's final years. One was a vindication of Aldrich, Smalridge and himself against the charge brought against them by John Oldmixon in his *History of England* that when, long ago, Christ Church had helped to bring out Clarendon's great *History*, they had politically tampered with the text.[21] Atterbury's *Vindication* was dated 26 October 1731, from Paris. The other project, probably written during the period at Montpellier, was a Virgilian investigation, attempting to identify the physician Antonius Musa with Iapis in *Aeneid*, XII. This was *Antonius Musa's Character, represented by Virgil, in the person of Iapis* (1741).[22]

There is something poignant and significant about Atterbury's brief last labour of love in belle-lettres. Of course, an elderly and sick man may have good reason to be grateful to a good physician. An old devout man, such as Atterbury, may well have mingled human skill and divine providence, according to Virgil's narrative, in thinking about any physical cure achieved. But of course the story of the *Aeneid* had been invoked by the Lord Maitland and John Dryden, and many later writers, as a myth for the project of the restoration of the Stuarts.[23] As a result of Iapis's divinely sustained cure, Aeneas was enabled to renew his combat with Turnus and, ultimately, to re-establish the Trojans in a new land. Atterbury may have been wrong to argue that Iapis was modelled on Antonius Musa, the physician supposed to have cured the Emperor Augustus from his sickness, but the myth, not the scholarship, was what attracted him to the episode. It was first published in 1741.[24] Atterbury's brief final work, a minor labour of love, reminds us not only of his continuing interest in literature, but of the ways in which literature and the public world met in his mind.

Final fidelities

Two late letters by Atterbury and a short poem by Pope, seem to complete the human record. The first letter, dated 12 November 1731, was to James III. Commenting on his vindication of himself in regard to Clarendon's *History*, Atterbury pursued the parallel between Clarendon and himself. He notes that Clarendon was sent into exile by Act of Parliament, and that Charles II's later advisers turned out to be less loyal than Clarendon himself. This may have borne a few implications for James to reflect on in view of his own sidelining of Atterbury. The bishop, however, carries steadily on:

> I can indeed dye in Exile asserting y^r Royal Cause, as He did: but I see not, what other way is now left me of contributing to the support of it.
> May wisdome govern, and Success attend all your Counsels!
> I am
> S^r
>
> > Your Majestys
> > Most Dutifull & Faithful
> > Subject & Servant
> > Fra. Roffen[25]

There has been speculation that, at the end of his life, Atterbury wanted to recant his Jacobitism and return to England.[26] This letter teaches us that personal exhaustion is one thing, repudiation of a cause quite another.

Very different from the dignified signing off of Atterbury's letter to James is his long, angry and openly injured letter to John Hay, written on 3 March 1732, the last day of his life. Hay, now dismissed from his post at James's Court owing to pressure from Queen Clementina but still high in the king's esteem, had converted to the Catholic Church without consulting Atterbury. Hay seems to have been quite sincere. Atterbury was aghast, and his anger and grief show how highly he had regarded Hay. They also show that, even after living so long in Catholic France, Atterbury remained fiercely loyal to the end to the Protestant Church of England.[27] The bishop died in the small hours of 4 March 1732.

This was the moment for the other great man of letters within his circle of friends to pay tribute to him. If Swift had excoriated the discoverers of plots in the early 1720s, Pope was struck by the tragic moment when Atterbury's daughter, having endured the long journey by sea and land to meet her father in Toulouse, died in his arms, Atterbury supposing himself then not far from death. Pope's remarkable verse epitaph on the two chooses the difficult and rare form of a dialogue of the dying. Emotional yet marmoreal, the short epitaph is in fact full of echoes of Atterbury's and Pope's shared literary interests, in Horace, Virgil, Shakespeare – and in Paolo Sarpi whom Atterbury had quoted in his own defence in his speech at his trial in the House of Lords, and whom he had quoted in his last letter to Pope on 23 November 1731.[28] In the context of this letter it is clear that Pope's final line is a rendering of Sarpi's wish for his native Venice: '*Esto Perpetua.*'

EPITAPH
For Dr. FRANCIS ATTERBURY,
Bishop of Rochester,
Who died in Exile at Paris, in 1732.
[His only Daughter having expired in his arms, immediately after she arrived in France to see him.]

DIALOGUE.

SHE. Yes, we have liv'd—one pang, and then we part!
May Heav'n, dear Father! now, have *all* thy Heart.
Yet ah! how once we lov'd, remember still,
Till you are dust like me.

HE.

Dear Shade! I will:
Then mix this Dust with thine—O Spotless Ghost!
O more than Fortune, Friends, or Country lost!
Is there on earth one Care, one wish beside?
Yes—*Save my Country, Heav'n,*
—He said, and dy'd.[29]

Atterbury has been rightly designated, by his most recent biographer, 'a tragic figure',[30] but not, perhaps, for the particular reasons alleged. His extraordinary talent, energy and fidelity to principle are not in question but, it has been argued, these were devoted to 'a return to the past' and a doomed cause. These phrases have all the confidence of retrospective history. Atterbury fought for the doctrines and institutions in which he believed because, like all his contemporaries including men such as Addison and Walpole, he had no sense of a probable future development save what his own efforts and those of others might serve to bring about. He was not tragic because he did not foresee the partial success of a Whig historical project: nobody did, though some longed for it and some feared it. Atterbury was probably tragic in his own eyes. This is likely to have been partly because of the series of signal successes and reverses which marked his career. There is, however, almost certainly something more, and this is likely to reside in his quotation to Pope of the closing lines of *Paradise Lost*, on the eve of his going into exile:

. . . I shall not part with you now, till I have clos'd this Letter, with three Lines of Milton, which you will know, readily, and not without some degree of concern apply to/your ever affectionate Friend/and faithful Servant/Fra, Roffen.

> Some natural Tears he dropt, but wip'd them soon:
> The World was all before him, where to choose
> His place of rest; and Providence his Guide.[31]

The application of these lines to himself is partly in acknowledgement that he, like Adam (Milton had 'they' but Atterbury's wife was dead), was now cast from Eden into a wider and stranger world, but it must surely also impute guilt to himself. Guilt for what? For becoming a Jacobite? That can hardly be since Atterbury consented to become King James's minister so early in his exile. Rather the guilt he was conscious of is likely to have been his ambition to lead what he hoped to be the triumphant royal party in a new restoration, with all which that might have meant for him thereafter, and perhaps also his error of judgement in pressing on with the Plot after it had ceased to have a fighting chance of success. Atterbury could have felt himself in a truce with George I; instead he did what was for a man of his age the more difficult thing and threw in his lot with James III.

Once done, however, whatever his personal feelings, he never changed his principle. He is in the end of the line of the great tragic churchmen of England: Beckett, More, Cranmer, Laud and Sancroft. In different degrees, though in each case memorably, each confronted the state, and each fell victim to it.

John Law

The various phases of the Atterbury Plot, and Walpole's brutal repression which followed, profoundly changed the lives of most of the people involved, as well as the influence of the Tory party in Parliament and in the country at large. John Law, the man best placed to put an end to the Anglo-French alliance which was the best guarantee of the Hanoverian succession, had to leave France, with a passport from the Regent, after his enemies, Dubois in the lead, had brought about the collapse of his System. Before he left, he wrote to the Regent on 19 December 1720, saying he was accused of assisting the Pretender and having links with Spain. What he had done, he wrote, was to help unfortunate people who wanted bread (the Jacobites), some of whom had helped him in the past. The 'Duc d'O' [Ormonde], in particular, had saved his life. His aim had been to establish ties of friendship and trade with Spain and every step he had taken had been approved by the Regent.[32] Law was honest, his accounts were in perfect order, all he had was in France, and he had not salted away a vast fortune elsewhere as Dubois and Destouches seemed to believe.[33] All he took with him was about £600 and, indeed, a magnificent collection of paintings including works by Michelangelo, Raphael, Rubens, Tintoreto, Titian and Van Dyck.[34] His wife and daughter, who remained in France, were given a pension of 12,000 *livres* a year by the Regent.[35] William Law, Law's brother, was imprisoned for a time but he weathered the storm and his descendants played a prominent part in French society.

Arriving in Brussels, Law received an invitation from the Tsar, Peter the Great, whom he had met in Paris in 1717, to take charge of Russian finances, but he declined, perhaps because he did not know Russia, or because he still hoped that the Regent would recall him. Instead, Law proceeded to Italy and was expected in Rome where he was considered for the post of James's secretary of state. This appointment did not happen and James wrote to Lord Orrery in May 1721:

> His circumstances are so much altered, as things now stand the supposition of his being employed about me can no more be put. After that, he was certainly a true friend to me and as such I cannot but wish him well.[36]

In December 1721, to general surprise, Law arrived in London, carried over on Admiral Norris's flagship, with the permission of the

British government. Lord Peterborough was believed to have arranged this. In December the judgment against him for murder was reversed in King's Bench, where he went in triumph accompanied by the Duke of Argyll and Lords Islay, Londonderry, Orkney and Selkirk.[37] This enabled him to travel more freely in Europe. He spoke respectfully of the Regent, but in private he remarked that the French had not been intelligent enough to understand how his System worked. True enough, the return to the old, corrupt, inefficient financial system led to the bankruptcy of the state, which was eventually one of the chief causes of the French Revolution. He was received by George I, to whom he sold some of his paintings, including a Canaletto.[38] Many thought he had changed sides, but Destouches still regarded him as devoted to James. His position was made untenable by attacks on him in Parliament as a renegade Protestant, who had embraced popery, and as a friend to the Pretender.[39]

Law then returned to Italy and lived in Venice, where he was said in 1727 to have had two meetings with James III, who visited the city incognito. He died there in 1729 and was buried in an obscure grave. A century later, Law's brother's great-nephew, James Law, comte de Lauriston, Napoleon's governor of Venice (and subsequently a marshal of France in the reign of Louis XVIII), had his body reburied in a splendid tomb in San Moise, a rococo church near St Mark's.[40]

Dubois and the Regent

Dubois, so long a thorn in the flesh of James III and the Jacobites, died in August 1723 as a result of an infection contracted after a bladder operation. He had lost so much weight before his death that he looked like a skeleton. On becoming a cardinal he had become a priest. As he was dying he specified that he would receive Extreme Unction only from the hands of another cardinal, probably a delaying tactic, so that he died without the last sacraments. He wanted all his papers to be destroyed and the Regent had this done. There was a violent storm on the day of Dubois's funeral and as the funeral cortège passed through the streets, some people said they saw sparks coming out of the coffin. The Regent, Philippe Duke of Orléans, the person on whom so many Jacobite hopes had centred, did not long survive his tutor. His health ruined by a life of debauchery, he died suddenly of an apoplectic fit in December 1723. A contemporary lampoon depicted the Regent's descent into Hell, where he was greeted by Dubois, who complained there was no money to be got down there.[41]

Exile, loyalty and the Stuart cause

After his release from the Tower, Lord North and Grey in 1724 went into Spanish service under Ormonde, who was Captain-General of all the Armies of Spain. By 1728 North was a lieutenant general in the Spanish army and governor of the coasts in and around Barcelona. He became a Catholic, much to the disgust of his friends in England and, presumably, Ormonde's disapproval. Judging from the terms of his will, however, his conversion was real, not a political move. He died in Madrid on 31 October 1734, leaving an illegitimate son, William Grayson, to whom he left £4000 and £1500 a year. His estates were encumbered with mortgages amounting to £15,000, his wife's jointure of £10,000 and £1922 worth of debts in Spain. The sale of Epping House for £31,000 more than covered his debts, with a life interest for his wife, who had stayed in England and by whom he had no issue. Catlidge, near Newmarket, and his other estates were left to his cousin Francis, 3rd Earl of Guildford, provided he assumed the name of North. They then devolved to Lord Guildford's son, Lord North, George III's prime minister.[42]

After the death of Lord Cowper, Orrery took over the organisation of the Protests in the House of Lords. Over the years he had gained James's trust and esteem. Orrery's opposition to a political conversion to Protestantism on James III's part would have been appreciated in Rome.[43] Orrery succeeded Atterbury as James's representative in England, with a pension from the Stuart Court. Walpole, while discussing the connections of several politicians with the Pretender, told Sir Dudley Ryder in February 1743 that Orrery had a pension from *'that government'*, which he 'well earned'.[44] In November 1724 the Scottish Highlanders were armed and about 10,000 of them were said to be ready to rise if General Dillon and James III would go to Scotland and 'the people of England would give general assistance'. Orrery's answer, however, was that 'the scheme, as things now are, was by no means to be ventured upon'. He believed that 'four in five of the whole nation' wished well to James, but that

> people of reflexion and fortunes will hardly venture their lives and estates unless they have some tolerable chance to succeed, and soldiers will hardly desert unless there is a body of soldiers to desert to;

those that govern at present are generally despised and abhorred, but their power is too great not to be feared.

In Parliament the Tories had been brought to heel, staying away in order

to give no provocation where there is no prospect of success to people who have the command of great forces and vast sums of public money, and who act with no other rules but their own arbitrary and cruel wills.[45]

For the rest of his life he did his utmost to obtain foreign assistance for a restoration. An opportunity presented itself as a result of British interference with the trade of the Ostend Company, which led Austria to conclude the Treaty of Vienna with Spain in November 1725.[46] As a result, Lord Orrery, Lord North and the Duke of Wharton met in Brussels in 1726 to concert measures before Wharton proceeded to Vienna. Wharton, it seems, did not consult Atterbury about his mission to the Imperial Court. In his work, Orrery relied increasingly on the assistance of his friend Colonel William Cecil, who eventually succeeded him in charge of James's affairs in England. In 1730, he planned to go to Paris to support the plans of Lord Cornbury for a Stuart restoration, but was too ill to make the journey and died on 28 August 1731.[47] He was buried in Westminster Abbey.

John Plunkett remained in the Tower for sixteen years. He was granted an allowance of 5s. a day to live on, but we know little about his life there or the petty persecutions Williamson, no doubt, inflicted on him. He died on 14 August 1738, after being cut for the stone, a fate later shared by his great enemy, Sir Robert Walpole.[48]

For the first two years of his imprisonment, George Kelly was strictly confined to a small airless room in Beauchamp's Tower, which affected his health. The Rev. John Creyke (or Creake), a nonjuror who had resigned his Fellowship of St John's College, Cambridge in 1715, and became chaplain to the Duchess of Ormonde, was allowed to attend him for divine service. In 1725 he was transferred to a more pleasant apartment in the Tower and allowed to walk outside. He was allowed 5s. a day for his keep, but complained that warders appropriated part of his allowance. However, Watkyn Williams Wynn, the wealthy Tory magnate, provided for him while he was in the Tower, so that he was able to live in some style and dine with the best company in the Coffee House there. His easy manners and charm made him generally popular, especially with ladies. By 1730 he was allowed to take the air within 10 miles of London accompanied by a gentleman gaoler, who brought him back to the Tower every night. At length in 1736 he escaped to Broadstairs. He was brought to Calais with the assistance of two fishermen, who regretted later that they had not known his identity as there was a reward of £200 on his head.

Kelly then made his way to Avignon, where he became chaplain to the Duke of Ormonde, who was living there like a prince. He joined Prince Charles Edward at Dunkirk to take part in the abortive 1744 French expedition. Next year he was one of the seven Men of Moidart, who landed in Scotland with the prince, who liked and esteemed him. This led to jealousy on the part of some of the prince's Scottish followers, who demonised him, describing Kelly's qualities as 'trick, falsehood, deceit, and imposition'. Andrew Lang's portrait of Kelly as 'learned, discreet, witty, brave and a general favourite with men and women' is more accurate. Speaker Onslow went as far as to describe Kelly as 'a man of far more temper, discretion and real art' than Bishop Atterbury. After the Forty-five Kelly became the secretary and trusted intimate of Prince Charles Edward and a close friend of Henry Goring (Sir Henry's son), who was the prince's equerry. Kelly argued that Britain could not be regained by the back door, that is by a landing in Scotland, but only by a descent on England. This was opposed by the Scottish Jacobites, who insisted on a landing in Scotland, thus replicating the situation in 1721–2. The Earl Marischal, who was called to Paris by the prince as his personal adviser, secured the dismissal of Kelly in 1749. George Kelly had been excepted from the Act of Indemnity of 1747 and died in exile in 1762.[49]

Conclusion

The Atterbury Plot has in the past been generally considered a hopeless muddle and absurd daydream on the part of the Jacobites. When it has received attention it has usually been as an episode in a longer narrative or wider survey with a different focus. This study has drawn on a large body of new evidence, and of evidence known of but not previously deployed, to offer the first full-scale account of the Plot. It is revealed to have been, not a comprehensive muddle or set of illusions, but a serious and intelligent project which adapted itself thrice to the rapidly changing situation of an England in extreme crisis. It is clear that the great economist, John Law, was a serious Jacobite. During the success of his System, when he was high in the favour of the Regent, the Duke of Orleans, and effectively first minister of France, he sought to effect a *rapprochement* between France and Spain, so that the Jacobite regiments in the service of these two kingdoms could be used to effect a restoration of the Stuart line. Law would have welcomed such an outcome.

Then, after the collapse of the Mississippi scheme and the bursting of England's South Sea Bubble, in which monarch, mistresses and ministers appear to have received unpaid-for stock, there opened up a crisis of government comparable to that of 1659–60, if not even more grave. This was rightly perceived as an extraordinary opportunity for a restoration. The military tactics were largely devised by the militarily experienced Lord North and Grey, assisted by the committed and intelligent Christopher Layer. Layer travelled to Rome to present to James III a list of probable supporters of a rising in English and Welsh counties, probably drawn up by Lord North and Grey and his associates. It is, in a way, amusing that earlier historiography from J. H. Plumb to G. V. Bennett has dismissed Layer's part in the Plot as that of a more or less isolated fantasist. This is, of course, because they based their conclusions on the case for the defence at Layer's trial. But at that trial Layer and his counsel naturally attempted to minimise his part, and, more important, were resolved, by his only confessing what they knew the government knew, to save the greater conspirators in the Plot, Lord North and Grey, Strafford and Atterbury.

Recent work, now drawn on for a more continuous narrative of the Plot, has shown the crucial role of the Earl of Sunderland. James III and the 4th Earl of Orrery were, as we have seen, rightly suspicious of Sunderland, but there was a period when, in the deadly rivalry between Sunderland on the one hand and Walpole and Townshend on the other, in the aftermath of the South Sea crisis, Sunderland had to turn to the Tories to save himself from impeachment.

Further, Sunderland's longer-term fear was the early death of George I, after which he would suffer the consequences of the unconcealed hostility of the Hanoverian Prince of Wales. The Tories wanted a free Parliament brought about by elections free from government pressure. They were confident they could win such a general election, after which a more or less peaceful Stuart restoration seemed a probability. In France the Regent and his minister, Dubois, withheld from the British government what they knew of Jacobite military preparations. Only the unexpected death of Sunderland transformed the scene. Dubois, who was generally believed to have had a pension from the English government, now disclosed what he knew to London and the Jacobite regiments were recalled from the French and Spanish coasts.

James III rightly observed that the scheme had been conducted in England on too narrow a base, so that insufficient money to buy arms had been collected. There was now a serious attempt to associate the Earl of Oxford with Atterbury in the leadership of the Plot. Most leading Tories in Parliament were involved in or sympathised with the Plot, out of loyalty to the Stuarts and/or to seek to reverse the proscription of their party. Large sums of money, estimated at £200,000, were collected to buy arms and pay for ships under the direction of Lord Orrery and in collaboration with Atterbury. What emerged in the last phase of the Plot was the strong Jacobite popular support in the City of London, where their position was as strong as that of the Whigs during the Exclusion Crisis of 1679–81. This probably led Walpole to bring in the City Elections Act of 1725, which curbed the powers of the Common Council by reimposing the veto of the Whig-dominated Court of Aldermen over its decisions and disenfranchised over 7000

London voters. In 1722 numerous soldiers and seamen in George I's army and navy readily enlisted in James III's service, as did the London watermen. Popular support came too from people marginalised in Hanoverian society, such as the Waltham Blacks and the hordes of poor debtors, many of whom had been ruined as a result of the South Sea Bubble, who sought sanctuary around the Mint. A new feature of strategy here was the design to seize the capital first, with a well thought-out plan directed by Lord North, assisted by Christopher Layer. A landing of arms and officers from the Jacobite regiments in Spain would provide support for the provincial risings which would follow.

Almost all was now up to the intelligent and ruthless Walpole, who was back as prime minister on the basis of his not very convincing plan to restore public credit after the South Sea crash, and who used the exposing of the Jacobite plotters to reunite the Whigs and consolidate his own power. To do him justice, he was not simply cynical. He feared the Jacobite threat and did what he thought was politically right. Walpole, at first, found very little real evidence of the Plot. He knew whom he suspected: Arran, Strafford, Orrery, North and Grey, Sir Henry Goring and Atterbury. With little or no legal evidence to go on, in the summer of 1722 Walpole stopped the Plot by the preventative illegal arrests of the chief suspects. They were held in prison without bail or being brought to trial though the Habeas Corpus Act was not suspended by Parliament until October, thus putting Walpole in breach of common law. If Walpole could achieve a successful anti-Jacobite prosecution, it would be the making of his career.

The trial of Layer, the only suspect against whom there was legal evidence, was rigged to be an Essex rather than a London trial, as a dry run to see how things would go. Layer was, with difficulty, found guilty. After that it was clear that Walpole could not rely on ordinary court procedure, even for minor players such as Plunkett and Kelly. In any case, Walpole was not interested in the small fry: he wanted to target a major figure and make an unforgettable example. He might have targeted Lord North and Grey. Given his lack of hard evidence at the outset Walpole had ample room and verge enough to choose his adversary, as well as the arena for conflict. Clearly, Walpole considered Atterbury, the turbulent and eloquent churchman-politician, the more dangerous man. How to try him? Here again one notes a ruthless balance in Walpole's mind. He might have gone all out for Atterbury's impeachment and execution. Instead, no doubt aware of the less than overwhelming evidence he could hope to amass against Atterbury, he decided on a bill of pains and penalties which, if passed, could at least send Atterbury into exile, remove him from the English public scene, and make an example to the disaffected. A fresh look at the evidence on which Atterbury was condemned to exile is not altogether reassuring. The three letters allegedly written for Atterbury by Kelly and sent through the ordinary post exist only in the Report and Appendices of the Secret Committee on the Plot, despite the fact that the common practice of the Post Office's examination of correspondence was to open a letter, decipher (if possible), re-seal it and send it on its way. Atterbury was well-known for his absolute refusal to use the ordinary post for confidential or dangerous letters, whether or not they were in cipher. Knowing as we do of the real danger of the project in which Atterbury and Kelly were involved, it is incredible that such letters would not have been dispatched secretly via their normal safe channels to the continent. Walpole's intelligence, together with the bribed evidence of Neynoe, gave him the general picture. He knew of the Jacobite cipher with James III. His difficulty was nailing names in the cipher to particular suspected individuals. It is clear from the prosecution of Atterbury that the government had only an approximate understanding of the cipher. Atterbury in his own defence, basing himself on what the government revealed, pointed out the many inconsistencies in the government's interpretation. The name 'Jackson' in Atterbury's cipher signified 'Lansdowne' but it was, it seems, deliberately changed to identify Jackson as 'the Pretender', because a letter dictated by Atterbury to Lord Lansdowne would not be treasonable, whereas a letter to James III was. This served to substantiate the accusation that Atterbury corresponded with the Pretender. We have here suggested that Walpole, in his quandary, probably commissioned the forging of the three letters which were to prove fatal to Atterbury (see Chapter 9). It is a serious hypothesis, and one more plausible, it may be thought, than that Atterbury and Kelly sent Jacobite letters, which had little to say beyond identifying them in the cipher, through the ordinary post. What is clear, however, is that Walpole knew that the three letters required an additional patina of reality. This was where the Earl of Mar and his British pension entered the picture. Colonel Churchill's confidential visit to Mar in Paris produced a real letter from Mar to Atterbury which, by allusion to various circumstances in Atterbury's current life, linked the bishop to his names in the cipher. Even then, the case against Atterbury might have been thought rather precarious, but for Walpole's mastery of the House of Commons and

Townshend's management of the House of Lords. All they needed was a majority in both Houses and the outcome proved them right.

The story of the Atterbury Plot displays, among other things, the precariousness of George I's government especially in the early 1720s. The Whig project, with its roots in the Exclusion Crisis, the invasion of the Prince of Orange, and the prosecution of a continental war against France, was itself a remarkable and risky démarche. Its chief enemies were the exiled royal line, the high-church Anglicans at home, and the Tories out of place. It has been often claimed that Walpole exaggerated the Jacobite threat to aggrandise his own power but, towards the end of his career when he had no motive in swaying public opinion, his conversations with Sir Dudley Ryder (decoded only in the twentieth century) show that he always took Jacobitism as a serious danger. For the Whig project to have survived, some major change of policy had to be made. This was (following the example of Cromwell) the policy of an alliance with France, which had the additional advantage for the Whigs of driving James III further away from the shores of the British kingdoms. In Atterbury Walpole saw joined together all that he most opposed: a talented, turbulent and independent high churchman, a Tory and a Jacobite.

Perhaps we must credit the Whig politicians of the earlier eighteenth century with the invention of the show-trial. Henry Sacheverell's trial had been a full-scale impeachment, and had Parliament been able to agree on more severe penalties after having found him guilty, it would have looked very different. Even so Sacheverell's crime was not any concrete act of treason, but of preaching a series of sermons, and that on 'False Brethren' in particular, which seemed to imply that the expulsion of James II in 1688 had been illegitimate and out of accordance with seventeenth-century Church of England doctrine. The Whigs would seem to have arraigned him, nevertheless, to attempt to check an increasing current of traditional opinion. The term 'show-trial' has thus still some applicability to what happened to Sacheverell. Walpole and the later Whigs learned from this experience. With Atterbury himself they took on a far more formidable religious and political figure. Whatever those who circulated the image of the imprisoned Atterbury holding an engraving of Archbishop Laud may have expected, Walpole is likely to have understood that he would only defeat himself by trying to go too far. Atterbury was arraigned only on a bill of pains and penalties. Exile always seemed the most likely penalty, but this time the managers of the trial made sure they had Parliament under stronger control. In his allusion to Paolo Sarpi, in his final speech in his own defence, Atterbury may have hinted that he would go voluntarily into exile, rather than see English law tainted by a trial apparently resting on corrupt proceedings and rigged evidence. If so, Walpole would have none of it. Not only did he want to remove a formidable and dangerous adversary from the political scene; he wanted to create an unforgettable public example, which would alter the current of political and religious thought.

Appendix A: 'Considerations on the Nature of Oaths at present'

When Lord North and Grey was arrested on 29 September 1722 the government found in his papers, in his study at Catlidge, a very interesting document written by him (*A Report from the Lords Committees to whom the Report and Original Papers Delivered by the House of Commons at several Conferences were referred*, London 1723, pp. 2–3). It was entitled 'Considerations on the Nature of Oaths at present' and is an analysis virtually unique in explaining the thoughts of a Jacobite who took the oaths in order to sit in Parliament. It deserves, therefore, to be quoted in full:

At a Time when nothing is so common as Reproaches, and when Words are slung about by People who know not their Meaning, and one calls the other Perjured and Traytor, being Ignorant of the true Meaning of either of those Terms, it will be not unuseful, however not unacceptable, to say a little on the former Word, and explain what is Perjury: for the latter there are so many able Expositions of the Law ready to Interpret Traytor in the favourable Sense (I mean to the Government) that I my self, who will endeavour to keep as clear of the *forum humanum* as possible, do not know but that a Code of Conscience may be construed within the Stat. of 15 of *Edward III* and I to shew my Parts against Mr. Attorney and the King's Council. I'll conceal my self therefore, and, if I can help it, will stand no Tryal but in my own Country, a Place where Justice is practised, a great way off hence. But before I come to the Design of this little Tract, which is to explain what Oaths are obligatory, and consequently the Breach of what Oaths is Perjury, I cannot forbear observing how ridiculous the Reproach of Perjury comes out of the Mouth of my *Britain* that can remember 30 Years. They that thought the Revolution no breach of the Oaths of Allegiance, can they reproach any one with a Breach of these? But there are some People anti-Casuists, that think an Oath only obliges in unlawful Matters, that like a very Lewd Fellow that used to assert every Falsity with an Oath, saying a Truth could shift without it. But thus much, and perhaps too much, by way of Preface. Now to the Point. The Ingenious and Pious *Dr. Sanderson* defines an Oath to be a Religious Act by which God is called as a Witness to confirm a doubtful Matter; He likewise lays down five Hypothesis, of which I shall mention but the 3.4. and 5. they being only to our Purpose. 3. No Oaths takes away a Prior Obligation*. 4. What is impossible cannot oblige; now what you cannot lawfully do is look'd upon as impossible, *id tantum Possumus; quod jure Possumus*. 5. We cannot oblige our selves to do what is unlawful, for if it is an unlawful Thing which you were to do, the Perjury is in Swearing, not in breaking that Oath.* An Oath has an Obligatory Force with it, but not Destructive, but Constructive only; that is to say, it may bring a new Obligation where there was none before, or to confirm one that preceded it, but it cannot remove any Obligation that it finds already entered into, or superimpose other repugnant to it. He gives some Instances the mutual Obligation between Man and Wife, Father and Son, Master and Servant, King and Subject. Thus far out of that great Casuist; which is enough to determine what Force the Oaths of Allegiance and Abjuration under the Present Powers can possibly have. I shall only therefore apply them to that Purpose. *First*, As to the Oath of Allegiance if there was no Obligation in the People of *England* neither by natural Duty to any other Prince, nor Antecedent Oaths to him and his Successors before the time of this Revolution, then the Oaths to King *William* etc., are certainly valid; but if the contrary were true, then according to the 3d Hypothesis the first Obligation remains in full Force notwithstanding the Oath. Again, if there are no Powers in the People to make a King, and if there be any Acts of Parliament unrepealed which declare the Subject to have no coercive Power o'er the King; nor even both Houses of Parliament; then tho' you Swear to such a Person as King, it neither makes him such, nor obliges to any Allegiance, but comes within 4th Hypothesis. Whether the 5th Hypothesis is concerned in this Question will appear to any one who will examine the Law of Nations, particularly our own, and Declarations of Acts of Parliament of the King's Rights (I mean a lawful Assembly of Kings, Lords and Commons) and if there he finds that Kings are subject to none but God, particularly the King of *England*; that the Monarchy is Hereditary, not Elective, and that either of both Houses of Parliament have no coercive Power over the King, why then to transfer Allegiance whilst the Rightful Monarch is in Being is unlawful; an Oath to that Purpose is consequently Invalid, has no manner of Force whatsoever against our natural Duty. But before I leave this Point, I must take notice how *Dr. Sanderson* answers an Objection here made, and shall Answer otherwise than he does; The Objection is, But not fulfil what you promise, is Perjury? Yes, (says my Author) but if the thing was unlawful which you swore, you were perjured when you took that Oath, not when you broke it. With all the Respect due to so great a Man, I think this Expression too Rhetorical for a Casuist, for there is need of both Tropes and Figures to make the taking of any Promisary Oath Perjury; I cannot agree with him therefore in this, that the Breach of such an Oath is Perjury; it is certainly a Sin and a very grievous one. God forgive them that shall take such; but I think cannot be called by that Name, for that which never carried any Obligation with it, the Breach of it cannot be Perjury; as in Marriage (a most Holy Vow) there is no setting aside the Contract (except for Cause of Fornication) without declaring it null and void from the Beginning, so in Promisary Oaths, except the Person sworn to so releases you and *ut Supra*, nothing can set them aside except they be null and void from the Beginning, as Prior Obligations, Impossibilities and Injustice makes them.

The Committee of the House of Lords commented that it contained 'several very extraordinary Reasonings on the Nature of Oaths; tending to prove that Oaths to the present Government are not obligatory but unlawful & a grievous sin if inconsistent with prior oaths and obligations'.

Appendix B: 'A State of England' (RASP 65/16)

Cornwall
Strong in Tinners and Fishermen a bold, hardy and well affected people
Lord Lansdowne chief
Sir John St Aubyn of Clowance
Sir Richard Vivian of Trelowren
Alex. Pendarvis of Roscrow
Mr. Williams of Truthern
Mr. Basset of Redruth
Mr. Tonkin of Treuanance
Mr. Polekinham of Helston
Mr. Hawes of Kellew
Mr. Collins near Truro
Mr. Paint near St. Columb
Sr. Wm. Pendarves
Mr. Macworth of Trevethan
Mr. Killigrew of Falmouth
Mr. Kemp of Kosteage
Mr. Kemp of Carclew
Majr. E. Salte of Penrice
Mr. Rashleigh of Menebilly
Mr. Goodall of Foway
Mr. Grills
Mr. Glyn
Mr. Anstis near Leskard
Captn. Gilbert
Majr Nance
Sr. William Carew near Saltash
Sr. John Coriton
Capn. Piper
Mr. Phillips
Coll. Whaddon

[Dubious]

Mr. Trevanion of Carhays	Henry Scobel
Mr. Nicolas Vincent	Mr. Buller
Mr. Trelawny	Mr. Mannaton old
Francis Scobel	

[Whiggs]

Mr. Boscawen	Mr. Williams of Trauaray
Mr. Moile of St. Germin	Mr. Gregore near Tregony

Devonshire
Numerous in Cloathiers and Manufacturers most idle at present and discontented

Sr. William Courtenay
Sr. Coplestone Bampfylde
Sr. Nicolas Morris
Sr. Jn. Chichester
Sr. Thomas Bury of Exeter
Mr. George Courtenay
Mr. Basset of Heaton Court
Mr. Northmer
Mr. Carew of Corelly
Captn. Stafford

Mr. Day
Mr. Goold
Mr. Elford
Mr. Prescot
Mr. Wolcombe
Mr. Tothill
Mr. Quick
Mr. Champernoon
Mr. Fownes
Mr. Northleigh
Lord Clifford

[Dubious]

E. Radnor
Sr. Thomas Pitt
Sr. William Pole

Mr. Role of Ackueston
Mr. Bulteel

[Whiggs]

Sr. Francis Drake
Mr. Edgecumbe
Mr. Treby

Sr. George Chudleigh
Sr. Walter Yonge

Somersetshire
A trading populous county wherein the number of honest people is by much
Superior as in Bristol, Bath and Wells.

E. Pawlett
Sr. Wm. Windham
E. Castlehaven
Lord Storton
Colonel Pratter of Frome
Captn. Lansdown
Mr. Horner of Mellis
Mr. John Horner his brother
Sr. Jon Trevilian
Sr. Phillip Sydenham
Lord Lansdown's credit is great here

Mr. Bamfield of Hetercomb
Mr. Fownes of South Poorton
Mr. Phillipps of Montacute
Mr. Palmer of Fairfield
Mr. Poo of Bridgewater
Mr. Farwell
Captn. Farwell of Horsington
Mr. Newman of Northeadbury
Capn. Fox of Bristol
Mr. Pye of Bristol

[Dubious]

Mr. Brewer

[Whiggs]

Cap. Pigot
Mr. Spike of Lakinton

Mr. Bubb alias Doddington
the magistrates of Bristol

Glocester Shire
Numerous in discontented cloathiers and manufacturers

Lord Bathurst chief
Lord Conway
Lord Tracy
Mr. Jon Howe
Mr. Chamberlin of Mesbury
Mr. Masters of Cirencester

Capn. Burghe steward to the
Duke of Beaufort
Mr. Jon. Barkley
Coll. Pool
Mr. Aylesse
Mr. Chester near Bristol

Mr. Catelman of Cubberly

Mr. Snell of Glocester
Mr. Hyall of Glocester

[Whigg]

Lord Barkley
All the towns in this Shire are in right way

Wiltshire
Inhabited by cloathiers and manufacturers at Bradford, Tunbridge, Warminster, Westbury and Hindon

Lord Bruce first chief
3 Pophams
Mr. Ernel of Brinsted
Mr. Talbot of Layerick
Mr. Seef of Maxham
Mr. Nicolas
Mr. Halls of Ketless
Mr. Ernell of Whetham
Sr. James Long
Mr. Rolt
General Webb 2nd chief
Sr. Richard Howe
Mr. Hyde
Colonel Lambert
Mr. Franton

Mr Wainwright
Mr. Jones of Ramsbury
Mr. Whitlock of Chilton

[Whiggs]

The Trenchards
Pitts

Dorset Shire
Lord Digby of Sherburn chief
Mr Strangways and family
Mr Harvy of Clifton

Sr. Nathaniel Nappier
Mr. Chaffix

Hampshire & Sussex
Sr. Hary Goring chief
Sr. William Oglander
Coll. Holmes
Coll. Stephens

Sr. Peter Mews
Mr. Lewis
Mr. Flemming
Sr. Symon Stuart

[Whiggs]

D. Bolton

D. Somerset

Surrey And Kent
Lord Winchelsea chief
Sr. Hewit Archer
Sr. Wm. Hardress
Major Hardress
Col. Broadnax

Sr. Richard Head
Sr. Philip Boteler
Mr. Scot
Mr. Percival Stuart

The Onslows

[Whiggs]

Middlesex
No other particular of this shire but that the Tory party was commonlye strongest for the election in the countrey when even that of the Whiggs was prevalent in London the genius of this people is at present pretty obvious.

Essex
Observation is made of this shire that five years ago during the suspension of the habeas corpus act about 20 of the Gentlemen here were confined on suspicion of dissatisfaction.

Suffolk

E. of Dysert	Mr. Firebrace
Sr. Robert Davers	Mr. Cowance
Sr. Jon. Rouse	Mr. Bridgeman
Sr. Robert Kemp	Major Alston
Sr. Edward Turner	Mr. Waring
Mr. Croft	
Mr. Barnardiston	

Norfolk
Walpole and Townsend have great intrest in this Shire, however state may be made on the fishermen about Yarmouth and manufactutors of Norwich.

[Whiggs]

In the three following shires
Ld Manchester   Lord Orford

Cambridge, Huntingdon & Bedford
Lord North and Grey chief   Sr. John Chester
the Cottons in their several branches   Mr Harvey
Sr. Vincent Charnock

Heartford
A shire filled with honest men and able horses.
E. Salisbury   Mr Cesar
Sr. Thomas Seabright   Mr. Robbinson of Knebworth

Buckshire
Influenced by two great families of D. Wharton and Bridgewater
Lord Fermanagh   Cap. Chapman
Mr. Drake   Mr. Lownds of Winslow
Mr. Fleetwood   Mr. Woodner
Mr. Warren

Berkshire

Lord Craven chief
Lord Stawell
Sr. John Stonehouse ˙

Mr. Packer
Mr. Blagrave
Mr. Bennet

Oxfordshire

Lord Abingdon chief
Sr. Robert Jenkinson
Sr. Jonathan Cope
Sr. Wm. Glyn

Mr. Shephard of Ruebright
Mr. Rowney the University

Northampton

The shire most inhabited by noblemen yet the people have more confidence in the following gentlemen

Lord Strafford chief
Sr. Justinian Isham
Mr. Isham
Mr. Washborne
Mr. Stradford of Overston

Mr. Robinson
Mr. Gore of Northampton
Mr. Alicock of Loddington
Sr. Robert Clarke

Leicestershire

Very well stored with good horses and honest gentlemen who carried the elections against the D. of Rutland

Sr. Geo Beaumont
Sr. Woolston Dixey
Mr. Morice of Dodington
Sr. Richd Halford

Sr. Clobery Noel
Mr. Boothby of Tooley
Mr. Philips of Garendon
Mr. Bracebridge of Lindley

Warwickshire

This shire has hardly a whigg in it. Ld Denbigh and Lord Brooke have lost much of their credit. Lord Leigh leads a private life and Lord Digby is old tho' well affected.

Lord Craven first chief
Sr. Wm. Kite
Mr. Mordant
Mr. Prescot
Mr. Peyto
Sr. Jon. Shuckbury
Mr. Harvey of Hocton
Sr. Ed. Boreghten
Sr. Fuller Skipwith
Mr. Gregory
Mr. John Craven
Mr. Green near Coventry
Mr. Bracebridge
Mr. Reppinton
Mr. Inge

Mr Bracebridge

Mr. Alderby of Hams
Mr. Jessen of Langley
Mr. Holden of Erdington
Mr. Jennings and Doctor Davis both nonjurors, have 12000 men and armes
Sr. Jon. Packinton 2nd chief
Mr. Lane
Mr. Hoo of Bar
Sr. Jon. Wrottesly .
these four are men of spirit, undoubted principle and great interest amongst the
ironworkers.

Worcestershire
This shire is adjacent to Warwickshire in the same principle and interest especially
by them.

E. of Plimouth chief	Mr. Savage of Hamby Castle
Sr. Jon. Packinton	Mr. Hickford
Sr. Hen. Parker	Mr. Ellison
Mr. Harkley Green of Coleridge	

Staffordshire
Noted for perpetuated loyalty and influenced by

Lord Gower chief	Mr. Sneyd
Mr. Crampton of Stonepark	Mr. Charles Adderley
Mr. Mainwaring of Whitmore	The Bagots
Mr. Whiler	

Shropshire

Lord Gower	Mr. Cresset
Mr. Corbit of Kinaston	Mr. Clayton
Mr. Cotes of Woodcot	Mr. Waring of Oldbury
Mr. Owens of Portington	Mr. Cotton of Bellaport
Sr. Jn. Astley	
Mr. Baldwin	

[Whiggs]

the Lord Bradford
the Whitmores
some Corbets

Herefordshire
Is governed by Duke Chandos and Lord Oxford since the death of Lord Scudamore
and Sir Thomas Morgan the gentlemen are well affected but have no chief

Monmouthshire
Composed of honest people on Duke of Beaufort and Morgan of Tredegars vast
estates as well as Lord Windsors who is a striving man would be fit to be chief.
Sir Charles Keymish
Capn. Bourgh steward to Duke of Beaufort   Mr. Ray

Mr. Coghran agent to the Dutchess
Mr. Jones

Mr. Gregory
Mr. Hughes
Mr. Price

Glamorganshire
Lord Mansels son chief of one party
Sir Charles Keymish of another
Sir Edward Stradling
Mr. Lewis
Mr. Jones
Mr. Powell

Breconshire
Mr Vaughan of Treberriard   Mr Penry Williams
These two govern all the Shire

Carmarthenshire
Is mostly infected by the Marquis of Winchesters interest the Tory party having
no Chief of repute

Pembrockeshire
Most inhabited by honest people and gentlemen very well disposed.
Mr. Barlow of Galby is become cautious since he married Lord Harcourt's
daughter was very forward & fit to be tried.
Mr. Barlow his Uncle is right.
Sr. George Barlow   Mr. Campbell of Stackpole Court
Mr. Phillips of St Brides
Mr. Wogan of Weston   Mr. Lloyd of Kilbruch
Doctor Powell of Pembrock   Mr. Skrim
Mr. Langhorne of Pontuchan   Mr. Knolles
                                             Mr. Parry

Cardigan
Since the death of the most worthy patriot
Lewis Price of Gogerthan who ruled all this shire the principals are
Mr. Parry of Noyad   Mr. Williams of Lambaden
Mr. Lloyd of Coitmore
Mr. Abertinan   Mr. Powell of Nanteos
Mr. Hedman

Radnorshire
Thinly inhabited of no great use and most under the jurisdiction of Lord Oxford

Montgomery
Under the jurisdiction of Lord Hereford and Mr Piegh of Natharem both worthy
men and firm to be relyed on

Anglesey Caernarvon & Merioneth

Lord Bulkeley

Mr. Brynkyr

Mr. Coitmore

Mr. Holland

Mr. Thomas

Mr. Davies

Flintshire And Denbigh

Very usefull shires by the neighbourhood of Chester abundant in coal and lead mines wherein numbers are imployed

Sr. Richard Grosvener

Sr. George Warburton

Mr. Mostyn

Mr. Robinson of Guersyt

Mr. Shaekerley

Mr. Egerton

Mr. Eaton of Leasewood

Mr Lloyd of Guernhalagh

Mr. Robert of Haywood

Mr. Watkin Williams and all the rest of the gentlemen

[Whiggs]

Lord Cholmley

Warrington

Cheshire

Lord Gower chief

Mr. Leigh of Lyme

Mr. Thomas Ashton

Sr. William Meredith

Mr. Willbraham of Nantwich

Mr. Chomeley of Valleroyal

Mr. Massey of Cottington

Captn. Hueston of Newton

Captn. Warburton

Alderman Bourroughs and Edward Fowkes in Chester

Note that before the case of Preston Lord Chomley tendered the oath to the militia of Cheshire who all unanimously refused to take them

Lancashire

A county well known for Spirit and Principle the citty of Manchester can furnish 15000 fighting men.

Mr. Ratcliff of Foxdenton

Mr. Holland Egerton of Eaton

Sr. Ralph Middleton

Mr James Warren of Hoppert etc.

Darbyshire

Lord Scarsdale chief

Mr Bayliss in Derby town

Coll. Beresford

the generality of the gentlemen

Yorkshire

Lord Strafford chief and Lord Caermarthen

Lord Downe
Sir John Blande
Captn. Beaumont of Whitley
Mr Stapleton
The generality of the gentlemen even the whiggs whom Aislaby drew into the
S.S Scheme and ruined.

Nottingham

Lord Middleton	Mr. Borlase Warren
Lord Lexington	Mr. Lewis of Hanford
Mr. Lewings	Mr. Digby of Mansfield

[Whiggs]

D. Newcastle	D. Kingston

Lincolnshire
Well situated by the sea for service and most of the gentlemen and people well
affected

Durham

The Bishop	Mr. Stedworth
Sir John Eden	Mr. Baker

Cumberland Westmorland and Northumberland
Plentiful in Colliers and Workmen

Mr. Shippen	Mr. Wrightson

Appendix C: 'Loyal Gentlemen in the County of Norfolk' (RASP 65/10)

A list of some few of the loyal gentlemen in the county of Norfolk and their estates viz.

Sr. Ralph Hare of Stow Bardolph £3000
Sr. John Wodehouse of Kimberly £5000
Sr. Thomas Robinson of Dearham Grange besides an annunity of £1200 per. ann. for life £500
Sr. Edmund Bacon of Garboldesham first Bart. in England £1500
Sr. Edmond Bacon of Gillingham £1600
Sr. Horatio Pettus of Rack heath £1000
Sr. Basingborough Gawdy of Harling £600
Sr. Nicholas L'Estrange of Basham N.j. £2500
Christopher Layer of Booton N.j. £800
Thomas Coke of Holkham £12000
Roger North of Rougham £3000
Thornhaugh Gurdon of Letton £1000
John Berny of Westwick £800
Richard Dashwood of Cockley Cley £1200
Roger Pratt of Ryston £1000
Beaupre Bell of Outwell £1100
Samuel Taylor of Watlington £1000
Henry Heron of Ketteringham £2000
Samuel Burkin of Watlington £500
Hewer Oxburgh of Outwell £400
Erasmus Earle of Heydon £1400
Erasmus his son £500
William Kemp of Antingham £600
Benjamin Dethwick of Wereham £600
Thomas Swift of Mewell £600
Thomas Lake of Wisbitch, merchant, £400
Henry Safrey of Downham merchant, £300
John Davis of Watlington £700
Dr. Massey of Wisbith £200
Thomas Wright of East Harling £1200
Thomas Hoogan of Dunham £800
John Ropps of Matlask £600
Peter Elwin of Tullington £1200
Thomas Chute of Pickenham £900
Thurlow Stafford of Below £400
James Large of Swafham £200
Joseph Elden of Aylsham £300
Robert Curtis of the same £200
Doctor Boys of the same N.j. 000

Robert Burrows of Diss £500
Roger Downe of Waxham £300
Thomas Stone of Beddingham £500
Robert Knights of Winterton £600
Charles Bladwell of Swannington £300
Robert Donne of Creak £200
John Welch of Ludham £200
Andrew Chambers of Homing £400
Henry Smith of Colishall attorney at law £200
John Green of North Walsham ditto £200
Robert Davy of Dishingham counsell at law £800
Robert Suckling of Wooten £900
Stroud Bedingfeld of Ditchingham £1300
Henry L. Warner of Walsingham £3000
Mr. Tasburgh of Flixton £1000
William Gilbert of Moulton £400
Neave of Loddon £200
Wogan of Reddinghall £1000
John Sayer of Eye £300
Christopher Beddingfeld of Wighton £700
Walgrave Britiffe of the same £300
Thomas Palgrave of Pulham £400
William Palgrave of the same £300
Robert Disipline of Stanhow £400
Augustine Hall of Twyford £300
John Curties of Wells £1500
Thomas Harris of Burnham £800
Roger Manser of Walsingham £400
Richard Godfrey of Hindringham, now one of the masters in Chancery, £500
Richard Ferrier of Yarmouth £600
Captn. Clarke of Clippesby £300
John Clarke of Bale £200
Thomas Seaman of Heigham £1000
William Gibbon of Thursford £700
Edward Lomb of Melton £2000
Leonard Mapes of Rollsby £400
Sr. Richard Palgrave of Barningham £700
Thomas Halcott of Castleacre £200
Henry Negus of Hoveton £600
Thomas Blofeld of the same £500
Edmund Blackburne of Wymondham £400
Thomas Rant of Yelverton £800
Thomas Damant of Lamas £400
Phillip Vincent of Marlingford £300
Edward Osborne of Sedon £900
William Newman of Baconsthorpe £700
Mr. Freeston of Mendham £1200
Cleere Garnish of Heddenham £1000
In the City of Norwich

Richard Berny councellr at law £500
Alderman Vere £600
Doctor Amyas £400
Alderman Beny £1000
Alderman Newton £400
Alderman Nall £300
Alderman Harwood £500
Thomas Seaman Merchant £800
Robert Seaman his brother £300
Mr. Russell £1000
William Rolfe attorney at law £400
Thomas Risebrow attorney at law £500

Persons of the Church of England that have temporal estates in the County of Norfolk and the City of Norwich viz.

John Beddingfield of Ditchingham £800
Thomas Arrow Smith of Storston £300
John Solly of Long Stratton £200
Robert Monsey of Booton N.j. £500
James Verdon of East Dearham N.j. £100
John Robinson of Keepham £150
James Norris of Marsham £150
Mr. Thorneton of Saxlingham £100
Mr. Lake late of Spartham N.j. £250
James Hunt of the same £50
Lawrence Womack of Buxton £200

Note. Appendix B was printed to include only Members of Parliament in *HC* (Sedgwick i. 109–13). The lists in Appendix B and C printed in Fritz, pp. 143–55 contain many errors and omissions which have been corrected here.

Appendix D: Rep. BY 18

A list of wealthy Londoners found in Layer's papers probably includes those approached to give money, but who did not necessarily do so. They were:

Mr. Mead, Canary Merchant, worth 100,0001. Mr. Cook knows where he lives
John Cooke at the Fleece
Mr. Cleares, worth 60,0001
Mr. Emerson at the Angle in Cheapside China-man
Qr. Mr. Ram the Gold-Smith, worth 100,0001
Mr. Shales, the Gold-Smith high Tory, the best Banker in England
qr. Mr. Martin Gold-Smith, and his Three Brothers, very rich
Mr. Cambridge Merchant at Epsom 100,0001
Mr. Blashford Refiner, near Goldsmith Hall
Mr. Appleby, the Brasier, worth 60,0001
Mr. John Ward in Stock's Market
Mr. Lockwood and the other 4 return'd Members for the City
Mr. Hickman, an Attorney next to the Golden-Lyon, in Fetter Lane, Qr. between Whig and Tory
Mr. Mead the Goldsmith
Qr. The Dry-Salter in Thames-street the Lord L. [?Lansdowne] knows
Joseph Mott late living at the Vulture
Mr. Makins at the Popes-Head-Tavern
Mr. Foxhall late Secondary of the Counter, 100,0001
Mr. Strain the Bookseller
Mr. Eccleston a Quaker in Gracious-street
Mr. Pendarris a Director of the East India-Company
Mr. Cooper the Broker, late at Cooper's-Coffee-House
qr. Mr. Norris, Brother to James Norris
Mr. Warkhause, the Attorney
qr. Mr. Shepherd, a Distiller
Deputy Parke, if a Live very Rich
Mr. Tryon, a Merchant
qr. Young Mr. Perry, that marry'd Mrs. Cox's Daughter of Epsom
qr. Mr. Colebrooke, the Banker

Note. For Blachford see Peter Lole, 'A Digest of Jacobite Clubs' sub. Benn, *Royal Stuart Paper* LV (1999). The other MPs for London were Francis Child, Peter Godfrey, a Tory, and John Barnard, an independent Whig.

Appendix E: The 'Intercepted' Letters

The 'intercepted' letters which convicted Atterbury, believed to be forged
1. Rep. D 6 'A Letter superscribed to Mr. du Bois, December 16'. The letter ran:

> Forgive my Silence: You can easily conceive the Difficulties I am under in that Regard. I write this only to assure you of my sincerest and unalterable Respect, and refer you to the Bearer for News, and for every Thing, which otherwise I should have found some Way or other of writing to you myself. I have heard nothing from you for every Thing, which otherwise I should have found some Way or other of writing to you myself. I have heard nothing from you since the Letter I had about two months ago by Mr. *Johnson*, to which I immediately, in his Hand, returned my Answer: A Rumour has reached me of your having written hither since, but I can find no Body that owns he has seen your Letters.

2. Rep. D 10 T. Jones [Atterbury] to Mr. Chivers [General Dillon], 20 April 1722:

> I Ought to acknowledge in Form the several Papers i have successively received from you, if I were capable at present of doing any thing regularly; but indeed I am not, as *Hatfield* well knows, and why I am not; some Time must pass before I am any way capable of Business; In the mean time you are in the right to press the Gentlemen concern'd by all Manners of Ways you can think of, to furnish what by being hitherto not supplied, has rendered the Thing impracticable. They were desirous of having that Matter entirely in their own Management, and I not unwilling that they should have it, being always diffident of Success on my Part upon Interpositions of that kind, and therefore it gave me no Concern to be so freely excused from any Share (as I was for a great while) in that Trouble; at last indeed, when the Point was Found upon Trial to be more difficult than expected, I was pressed to undertake the Matter; but so late, that I did not think it reasonable for me to interpose, nor can I yet undertake any thing of that kind, it being what (since some former Mismanagements wherein I was deeply concern'd) I have constantly declined, hoping that I might not be altogether unuseful to the Service if I went on to promote it in my own, that is, in another way. I still hope so, and that a little Time, which must be employed in doing nothing but soliciting supplies, will give me room for entering into Measures that may be somewhat more significant than those formerly taken; this I shall endeavour, being at present perfectly tired by the distracting Measures which have been taken from several Quarters by Persons no ways equal to the Work, and at the same time not agreeing among themselves. This is all I can say at present, but that I am with the same entire Respect and Fidelity I ever was, I have communicated the Copies of Mr. *Mansfield* and *Jacob's* Letters,

which (besides the G—whereof they had a Copy) were the only ones of those transmitted that I was directed or indeed thought proper so to do; tho' I have for some time thought that nothing of Importance should be trusted to the Post, and am resolv'd my self not to send that way, yet the Death of Lord *Sunderland* makes such a Caution more indispensably necessary, for you may depend upon't, that those in Power here will now enter into Measures of more Severity and Strictness, and employ all their Diligence as well as Power on such Occasions.

3. Rep. D11 T. Illington [Atterbury] to Mr. Musgrave {Lord Mar] 20 April 1722 'Under a cover to Mr Gordon the Son Banker at Boulogne':

I received from Mr. *Hatfield* (after long Intermission of such Favours) a Letter which was very welcome to me; I have also considered very carefully what he had to offer to me in particular, and entirely agree with what is proposed; but my present bad Circumstances (of which he has already informed you) will not suffer me to be active soon, or even to set forward the Affairs entrusted with me in so speedy a manner as I could wish. The best is, that I cannot act openly, so neither is there, I think, any immediate Need of it, some Time being requisite towards ripening Matters, in order to fix the C—'d, which if hastily begun, may be attended with Suspicions and other Inconveniencies; but you may depend upon it, that the—s committed to my Care, shall be forwarded in Time to the Persons concerned, as also all such other—s as I judge (and at the Time I judge) they will best promote the Service. What is to be wished for, is, that the Person whom I am to act with would come to Town, and his doing so may be facilitated better from your Side, than by any Thing that can be done here. By that Time he comes I hope I shall be able to take my Part with him. I add no more now (being very unfit to say even thus much) but that I am with entire Respect and Confidence. *Sir, etc.*

4. Rep. D 12 R[offen] to 'Mr. Jackson' 'the Pretender' [Lansdowne in that cipher]:

I am Sorry to find by yours which *Hatfield* brought, that you know our Circumstances on this Side so well, because that Knowledge does not, I apprehend, give you any advantageous Opinion of us: However, let that be as it will, it is not fit you should be deceived, and rely on more than will be made good to you: if you guessed at my right Mind, I dare say it was agreeable to your own, and that you could not see through the Forwardness of all those unsupported pretending People. Notwithstanding this Opportunity is elapsed, I agree with you another may offer before the end of the Year, though not perhaps every Way so favourable; however, it became me to speak strongly on that Head, especially at the Time when the—was drawn, which was long before it was transmitted; for it was kept back a great while, in Hopes that Deeds might have accompanied Words, and sent at last rather to justify the Writer in Respect to that Part he had undertaken, than to push on any Design—in so unprovided a Condition. I find I was not mistaken, and am glad I was not so, though every Word of that—passed the View and Approbation of the Persons concerned, but they were to be, and shall always be by me treated tenderly, though nothing shall engage me to enter deep with them for the future. I had taken this resolution before *Hatfield's* Return, and am pleased to find that you concur with me in Opinion; as soon as God restores me to my Health, and some other melancholy Circumstances are blown over, which will be as soon as there is any Occasion for me, I will not be Idle; in the mean Time give me leave to withdraw my self seemingly from any Engagement of this Kind; I shall return to it, I doubt not, with more Ability to promote the Work; not that I will decline any proper Occasions that may offer themselves, to converse freely with the Men, and in the manner I have been used to do; for it is fit upon all Accounts I should do so, but by little and little that Confidence will cool, and make room, I hope, for somewhat of a more solid and important nature. I dictate this in great Pain, and for that Reason, and because I am not at present in any Readiness to go further, shall add only my faithful Assurances, of an entire and unalterable Respect for you.

5. *Rep. D 13* M. [Mar] to Mr. Hatfield [Kelly], 24 April/5 May 1722:

I had yours of the 16th of *April* by last Post, and nothing has pleased me so much a long while as to what you tell me of Mr. *Illington's* Willingness and good Intentions to make up Matters with Mr. *Hacket, thinking* it both their Interests, as well as for that of Mr. *Farmer*, and it will be a particular Satisfaction to me, to see these two Gentlemen well together. And I do not at all doubt but Mr. *Hacket* will receive the Proposal in the Way he might, and meet him half way, and come to town immediately upon it if he be in good Health.

I agree perfectly with Mr. *Illington*, that their making up and being in Concert together, should be kept a secret for some time, of which *Illington* is the best Judge. It has and shall be so for me, except to Mr. *Cane* and Mr. *Farmer*, who I understand *Illington* agrees should know it, and I have not so much as spoke of it to Mr. *Jodrell* [Lansdowne], only as wishing such a Thing would happen. Mr. *Illington* will soon see how great a Desire Mr. *Farmer* has for its being so, by a Letter *Jodrell* is to write to him, I believe, by this Post, and that *Jodrell* also thinks it ought to be, and wishes it much. By the Time you have this, Mr. *Illington* will, I suppose, have had an Answer from Mr. *Hacket*, and he will know best what is fittest to be said in Answer to Jodrell, and also when Mr. *Mansfield* should be acquainted with it, which Mr. *Cane* and I are resolved to let him be the Doer of himself.

Pray my Compliments to Mrs. *Illington* in the kindest manner, and I hope he has got the letter I sent you from him the 28th.

The little Dog was sent ten Days ago and ordered to be delivered to you. The Lady and the little one would certainly return the Compliments was sent them, had they known I was to write; but I thought it was better that should not be done than to tell them of my doing so.

I'll be very glad to hear from you sometimes, and I can assure you there is no body who has a juster Esteem of you, nor more your Friend and Servant than I. Adieu.

Will not the loss of so able a Minister as Lord *Sunderland* be of bad Consequence to the King, and all of us who wish well to the present happy Establishment? I believe' twill not be easy tho' to find one to replace him.

I am very glad Mr. *Illington* will be so good to do for the Boy I recommended [Mar's son was going to Westminster school].

6. *Rep. D 20* Extract from a letter from G. Hatfield to Musgrave of 7 May 1722:

I had the Favour of yours, which I communicated to Mr. *Jones*, who is come to town only for a Day; he desired me this Morning to make his Compliments to you, and let you know, that he has not yet been able to take any Measures as to Mr. *Hacket*, and believes that a Line from you or *Farmer* will bring him much sooner to Town than any Thing that he (*Jones*) can say, without which it will be impracticable for them to do Business together. His old Partners never visit him now, which he is very much rejoiced at, especially at this Juncture. He tells me he finds *Armstrong* and his Company very loth to be any Way concerned, having no Opinion of the present Hands, and believes you are by this Time pretty much of that Sentiment too; however, that it is still necessary to make the most of them.

Mrs. *Illington* is in great Tribulation for poor *Harlequin*, who is in a bad Way, having slipped his Leg again, before it was thoroughly well, however his Obligations to the Lady are as great as if he had come safe, which he desires to let her know.

Note: Only the names of the correspondents were identified in the Secret Committee's report. The names in code in the text of the letters were left undeciphered. In this cipher Mansfield stood for Ormonde. Hacket was Oxford. Farmer was James III. Jodrell was Lansdowne (as well as Jackson RASP 57/117 and 57/140, though it suited Walpole to identify Jackson as 'the Pretender'). Some of the other code names in these letters do not appear in the Stuart Papers at this time.

Notes and References

Note on dates

Letters and documents written in England are in the old style, the British calendar at this time. Those written in continental Europe are in the new style, eleven days ahead of Britain.

Abbreviations

Add. Mss.	Additional Manuscripts in the British Library
App.	Appendix
AECP Ang.	Archives étrangères, Correspondance Politique, Angleterre
BL	British Library
CJ	*Commons Journals*
Cobbett	William Cobbett, *The Parliamentary History of England* (36 vols; 1806–20)
ECS	*Eighteenth Century Studies*
EHR	*English Historical Review*
HC (Sedgwick)	*History of Parliament, The House of Commons 1715–54*, ed. Romney Sedgwick (2 vols, London 1970)
HC (Cruickshanks, Handley, Hayton)	*The House of Commons 1690–1715* ed. Eveline Cruickshank Stuart Handley and D.W. Hayton (5 vols. Cambridge 2002)
HJ	*Historical Journal*
HMC	Historical Manuscripts Commission
Pope, *Correspondence*	*The Correspondence of Alexander Pope*, ed. George Sherburn (5 vols, Oxford 1956)
Rep.	Report of the Secret Committee of the House of Commons 1723
RASP	Royal Archives Stuart Papers
LJ	*Lords Journals*
PRO	Public Record Office
SP Dom.	State Papers Domestic in the Public Record Office
CSP Dom.	*Calendar of State Papers Domestic*

References

Introduction: Continuous Conspiracy

1. Conrad Russell, *The Fall of the British Monarchies 1637–42* (Oxford 1991) ch. 1 and conclusion.
2. *The Restoration 1660–1688*, ed. Paul Seaward (Basingstoke 1991), Introduction.
3. *The Anglo-Dutch Moment. Essays on the Glorious Revolution and its Impact*, ed. Jonathan Israel (Cambridge 1991), pp. 1–2. *The World of William and Mary.*

Anglo-Dutch Perspectives on the Revolution of 1688–89, eds Dale Hoak and Mordechai Feingold (Stamford CT 1996), pp. 17–18.

4. Howard Erskine-Hill, 'John Caryll, First Lord Caryll of Durford and the Caryll Papers', in Eveline Cruickshanks and Edward Corp eds, *The Stuart Court in Exile and the Jacobites* (London 1995), pp. 78–81.

5. *The Epigrams of Sir John Harington*, ed. Norman Egbert McClure (Philadelphia 1926), p. 164.

6. See Eveline Cruickshanks, *The Glorious Revolution* (Basingstoke 2000). J. R. Jones, *The Revolution of 1688 in England* (London 1972). F. C. Turner, *James II* (London 1948).

7. *Memoirs of Thomas, earl of Ailesbury written by himself*, ed. W. E. Buckley (2 vols, Roxburgh Club 1890), ii. pp. 229–30, 232–3.

8. See App. A

9. G. E. Cokayne, *The Complete Peerage*. North and Grey matriculated at Magdalene College, Cambridge, in 1691 but, as was common with noblemen, did not graduate. As a member of the House of Lords, he must have taken the oaths to William III when he first took his seat in 1699, to Queen Anne in 1702 and to George I in 1715.

10. The works which made Robert Sanderson an authority on oaths and connected matters of conscience were: *De Obligatione Conscientiae*, written in 1647 (London 1660); *De Juramenti Obligatione*, which appeared as *Seven Lectures Concerning the Obligation of Promissary Oathes … Translated into English by His Majesties speciall Command* (London 1655); and *Five Cases of Conscience …* (London 1667), which was posthumously published. One of these cases concerned the vocation of the soldier, and may have attracted the attention of North and Grey to Sanderson as an authority.

11. Eveline Cruickshanks, 'Attempts to restore the Stuarts 1689–1696' in *The Stuart Court in Exile and the Jacobites* (London 1995) p. 4.

12. The words are those of Alexander Pope in 'Dialogue II' of his 'Epilogue to the Satires'; i. 75; *Imitations of Horace*, ed. John Butt (London 1939, rev. 1961), p. 317. For the role of Shrewsbury, see Daniel Szechi, *Jacobitism and Tory Politics, 1710–1714* (Edinburgh 1984), p. 182, and 'The Duke of Shrewsbury's contacts with the Jacobites in 1713' in *Bulletin of the Institute of Historical Research*, LVI (1983), 229–32.

13. Bruce Lenman, *The Jacobite Risings in Britain 1689–1746* (London 1980), pp. 126–8. Edward Gregg, 'The Jacobite Career of John, Earl of Mar', in Eveline Cruickshanks ed. *Ideology and Conspiracy: Aspects of Jacobitism, 1689–1759* (Edinburgh 1982), pp. 181–2.

14. Eveline Cruickshanks, *Political Untouchables: The Tories and the '45* (London 1979), p. 4.

15. See *HMC Stuart* i. Introduction, and Leo Gooch, *The Desperate Faction? The Jacobites of North-East England 1688–1745* (Hull 1995), chs. 3–5.

16. *HMC Stuart* ii. 477, iii. 8–14, 27, 375, 436, 479–85, iv. 75–7, 146–7. C. Nordmann, *La Crise du Nord au début du XVIIIe Siècle* (Paris 1962), pp. 80–152.

17. Lenman, op. cit., pp. 190–3. L. B. Smith, *Spain and Britain 1715–1718: The Jacobite Issue* (London 1967). William K. Dickson, *The Jacobite Attempt of 1719* (Scottish History Society 1895). Niall MacKenzie, *Charles XII of Sweden and the Jacobites* (Royal Stuart Paper LXII 2002)

18. Howard Erskine-Hill, 'The Satirical Game at Cards in Pope and Wordsworth', in *English Satire and the Satiric Tradition*, ed. Claude Rawson and Jenny Mezciems (Oxford 1984), pp. 183–92.

19. Commemorative medals were, at the Restoration, struck in honour of King Charles I, in which he was presented as the shepherd known to his sheep.

20. Noel Woolf, *The Medallic Record of the Jacobite Movement* (London 1988). As the whole range of the Hanoverian and Stuart medals illustrated by Woolf shows, each dynasty sought to keep the images of its kings before the public eye. The Stuarts, however, had an obviously stronger reason for doing so and, at this stage, clearly patronised better artists, engravers and medallists. See too Richard Sharp, *The Engraved Record of the Jacobite Movement* (Aldershot 1996).

21. Gernot Gürtler's essay on the escape of Princess Clementina from Innsbruck, *Deceptis Custodibus, or Liberty Lost – Liberty Regained* (Royal Stuart Paper XXXVI) is probably the last word on the subtleties of this crisis. The emperor, or his advisers, were not entirely averse to conniving at letting Clementina out of captivity in order to marry James III. The letter published by Maurizio Ascari, *James III in Bologna: An Illustrated Story* (Royal Stuart Paper LIX), as from George I, beseeching him to prevent the marriage at all costs, could, it has recently been suggested by Niall MacKenzie to have been Jacobite propaganda.

22. Howard Erskine-Hill, *The Social Milieu of Alexander Pope* (New Haven and London 1975), pp. 193–5. This book was in debt to John Carswell, *The South Sea Bubble* (London 1960), the revised edition of which (1993), while providing more fascinating information, has not changed the facts of this particular point.

23. See the discussion of the conduct of Sunderland in Chapter 2.

24. Daniel Defoe, *Colonel Jack*, ed. Samuel Holt Monk (Oxford 1970), p. 222.

25. On the ancient constitution, see J. G. A. Pocock's classic study, *The Ancient Constitution and the Feudal Law* (Cambridge 1957); also J.P. Kenyon, *Revolution Principles: The Politics of Party, 1689–1720* (Cambridge 1977). A. M. Ramsay's *Life of Fénelon*, translated into English by Nathaniel Hooke, and published in 1723, recounts the conversations in 1709 between the Archbishop of Cambrai and (in the less explicit English version) 'a young prince' (actually James III). Fénelon gave him a large amount of advice on religion likely to be welcome to the English, and subsequently went on record in expressing his good opinion of the 'young prince'.

26. RASP 212/8.

27. See Jane Clark, 'The Stuart presence at the Opera in Rome' in *The Stuart Court in Rome*, ed. Edward Corp (Edinburgh 2003), pp. 85–94.

28. See D. K. Money, *The English Horace: Anthony Alsop and the Tradition of British Latin Verse* (Oxford 1998), pp. 100–5.

29. G. Thorne Drury ed., *The Poems of Edmund Waller* (London 1893) I, pp. xix, xxi.

30. Pope, *Corresp.* ii. 129.

31. Bennett, p. 41.

32. Sir Harold Williams, ed., *The Correspondence of Jonathan Swift* (5 vols, Oxford 1956) i. 378. Pope, *Corresp.* i. 378.

33. See Mark Goldie, 'The Nonjurors, Episcopacy and the Origins of the Convocation Controversy' in *Ideology and Conspiracy*, op. cit., pp. 15–35.
34. Geoffrey Holmes, *The Trial of Doctor Sacheverell* (London 1973).
35. *The Tryall of Dr. Henry Sacheverell* ... (London 1710), pp. 34–5, 91.
36. Boyer, *Political State* IX (1715), pp. 15–23 and RASP 63/108 James Hamilton to James, Rotterdam 4 Dec. 1723. Dr Charlton (see below) was probably Arthur Charlton of Trinity College, Dublin.

1 John Law and the First Phase of the Atterbury Plot

1. Eveline Cruickshanks, 'Attempts to Restore the Stuarts, 1689–96' in *The Stuart Court in Exile and the Jacobites*, ed. Eveline Cruickshanks and Edward Corp (London 1995), pp. 1–15.
2. Bruno Neveu, 'A Contribution to an Inventory of Jacobite Sources' in *Ideology and Conspiracy*, ed. Eveline Cruickshanks (Edinburgh 1982), pp. 144–5, 152–6.
3. Daniel Szechi, *Jacobitism and Tory Politics 1710–1714* (Edinburgh 1984), chapters 4 and 5.
4. *HMC Stuart i.* pp. xlviii et seq. *Mémoires du Maréchal de Berwick* (Collection des Mémoires Relatifs à l'histoire de France, 2nd ser., LXVI (1828), ed. Petitot et Monmerqué, pp. 221–3.
5. *HMC Stuart i.* pp. xlviii et seq. Eveline Cruickshanks, 'The Tories and the succession to the Crown in the 1714 Parliament, *Bulletin of the Institute of Historical Research*, 1973, 176–85.
6. E. Gregg, 'Marlborough in exile 1712–1714', *HJ* XV (1972), 599.
7. E. Gregg, *Queen Anne* (1980), p. 122.
8. *HMC Stuart* i. 312, 317, 358–63.
9. *The Dukes of Ormonde, 1610–1745*, ed. Toby Barnard and Jane Fenlon (Woodbridge 2000), Introduction and chapters 6–10. Toby Barnard, 'The Viceregal Court in later Seventeenth Century Ireland' in *The Stuart Courts*, ed. Eveline Cruickshanks (Stroud 2000), pp. 258–60.
10. *HMC Egmont Diary* i. 400–1.
11. Lord Mahon, *History of England from the Peace of Utrecht* (7 vols, London 1858) i. 279.
12. P. E. Lemontey, *Histoire de la Régence* (2 vols, Paris 1832) i. 89.
13. *HMC Townshend*, p. 162. Ormonde's secretary was not Sir John Maclean of Duart, as stated in the report on the Townshend manuscripts, but has been identified recently as Lachlan Maclean (see Nicholas Maclean-Bristol, 'Which Maclean Betrayed the Jacobites in '15?', *West Highland Notes & Queries*, 3rd series, No. 2 (February 2001).
14. *HMC Stuart* ii. 466, 469–70.
15. *HMC Stuart* vii. 393.
16. Louis Wiesener, *Le Régent, l'Abbé Dubois et les Anglais* (3 vols, Paris 1891) i. pp. ix–xii.
17. Duc de Saint-Simon, *Mémoires completes*, ed. A. de Boislisle (41 vols, Paris 1923–30) xxvi 284, xxx. 4. *Journal du Marquis de Dangeau*, eds Soulié et Dussieux (19 vols, Paris 1854–60) xviii. 203.
18. *Correspondance*, Recueil Prunet ii. 4, 282–3.
19. St Simon, xxvi. 264, xxx.4. Dangeau, xviii. 203.
20. Wiesener, i. pp. ix–xii, 95.

21. M. de Vissac, *Mylord Duc d'Ormond et les derniers Stuart* (Paris 1914), p. 16
22. AECP Ang. 75 f. 176, quoted in G. H. Jones, *The Main Stream of Jacobitism* (Harvard, Cambridge 1954), p. 125.
23. *Recueil des Instructions aux ambassadeurs et ministres de France, Angleterre,* III. 1698–1791, ed. Paul Vaucher (Paris 1965), pp. 182, 199–200, 211–30.
24. Wiesener, i. 9.
25. ibid.
26. St Simon, xxiv. 302, 374. Dangeau, xx. 373. *Mémoires du Marquis d'Argenson,* ed. E. J. B. Rathéry (9 vols, Paris 1859–67) ii. 345.
27. RASP 48/69 and 52/70.
28. *Annals and Correspondence of the First and Second Earls of Stair* (2 vols, Edinburgh 1875) [*Stair Annals*] ii. 33. BL Stowe Ms. 250 ff. 85–6.
29. Eveline Cruickshanks, '101 Secret Agent', *History Today,* April 1969, 273–6.
30. HC 'Sedgwick' (London 1970) i. 63, 514. *HMC Stuart* ii. 446–7, iv. 453, v. 416. J. F. Chance 'The Swedish Plot of 1716–17' *EHR*, xviii (1903), 81–106. *The Journal of Mary Freman Caesar 1724–41,* ed. Dorothy B. T. Potter (Lampeter 2002), pp. 4–5, 20.
31. Henri Baudrillart, *Philippe V et la Cour de France* (5 vols, Paris 1890–1900) ii. 371–3, 384–5, 412, 419.
32. Ibid.
33. Niall Mackenzie, *Charles XII of Sweden and the Jacobites,* Royal Stuart Paper LXII (2002). See also Voltaire, *Histoire de Charles XII,* ed. von Proschwitz (Oxford 1996) and Claude Nordmann, *La Crise du Nord au début du XVIIIe siècle* (Paris 1962).
34. L. B. Smith, *Spain and Britain 1715–19* (London 1987), pp. 81–5.
35. William K. Dickson, *The Jacobite Attempt of 1719* (Scottish History Society 1895).
36. John Carswell, *The South Sea Bubble* (2nd edn, Stroud 1993), p. 6.
37. For Law's System, We are greatly indebted to comments and suggestions from Professor Larry Neal and Professor Patrick O'Brien
38. H. Montgomery Hyde, *John Law. History of an Honest Adventurer* (London 1996), p. 19
39. John Philip Wood, *Memoirs of John Law of Lauriston* (London 1825), pp. 1–5.
40. Antoin E. Murphy, *John Law; Economic Theorist and Policy-Maker* (Oxford 1997), chapter 4. Narcissus Luttrell, *A Brief Relation of State Affairs* (6 vols, Oxford 1857) iii. 241, 296–7, 299, 308, 395, 400. *Calendar of State Papers & Domestic.* 1695 p. 162
41. See W. Gray, *The Memoirs, Life and Character of the Great Mr. Law and his Brother at Paris* (London 1721).
42. Eveline Cruickshanks, *The Oglethorpes, a Jacobite Family,* Royal Stuart Paper XLV (1987). For the Oglethorpe sisters, see Patricia Kneas Hill, *The Oglethorpe Ladies and the Jacobite Conspiracies* (Atlanta 1977).
43. Murphy, chapter 6.
44. St. Simon, xxiv. 34.
45. Wood, p. 162, Carswell, p. 69.
46. St. Simon, xxxviii. 77.
47. Dangeau, xvii. 169–70, 225, 311.
48. Dangeau, xvii. 172, 256. St Simon, xxxiii. 1.

49. Wood, pp. 62–3, 73.
50. Dangeau, xvi. 115, 359, xvii. 204, 365. Carswell, pp. 69–70.
51. Carswell, p. 73.
52. Dangeau, xviii. 372, 374, 421, 488–9, 509. Wood, pp. 29–41.
53. Jean Buvat, *Journal de la Régence 1715–23*, ed. E. Campardon (2 vols, Paris 1865) ii. 14, 31, 82–3. Dangeau, xvii. 281.
54. Cruickshanks, *Oglethorpes*.
55. Wood, pp. 69, 73.
56. *Stair Annals* ii. 72n. Carswell, p. 68.
57. For Stair's network of Jacobite intelligence, see Paul Fritz, 'The Anti-Jacobite Intelligence System of the English Ministers 1715–1745' *HJ* XVI (1973), 279–81. For the attempt to assassinate James III see Lemontey, i. 126, ii. 373–83 (who publishes the judicial proceedings).
58. *Stair Annals* ii. 124–5, 389.
59. Buvat, iii. 249. Dangeau, vii. 39. St Simon, xxxvii. 16. Wood, pp. 159–60. *Journal de Mathieu Marais*, ed. de Lescure (4 vols, Paris 1863–8) i. 264–80.
60. *HMC Stuart* ii. 354–5, 499, vi. 129.
61. *HMC Stuart* vii. 219.
62. Martin Haile, *James Francis Edward, the Old Chevalier* (London 1917), p. 270. RASP 46 / 14. *Stair Annals* ii. 396.
63. 'A List of Gratifications given by Mr. Law', RASP 281 / 166.
64. Buvat, ii. 43.
65. RASP 46 / 47, 46 / 114.
66. Carswell, pp. 73–4, 78.
67. Wood, pp. 49–60.
68. St Simon, xxxvii. 206–7.
69. Carswell, p. 79.
70. Cruickshanks, *Oglethorpes*, and Kneas Hill.
71. William Coxe, *Memoirs of the life and administration of Sir Robert Walpole* (3 vols, London 1798) ii. 308–9.
72. National Library of Scotland JY III C 34 (unfoliated). Ramsey's *Collected Papers* ed. Burns, Martin and John Oliver (6 vols, Edinburgh Scottish Text Society 1945–74).
73. RASP 46 / 110.
74. RASP 48 / 77.
75. Aix-en-Provence, Bibliothèque Méjanes MS 614 (Law papers).
76. RASP 49 / 99.
77. Barnard ed., *Dukes of Ormonde*, pp. 246–8. Baudrillart, ii. 404–5. RASP 47 / 102.
78. RASP 47 / 33.
79. Dangeau, xviii. 258.
80. RASP 46 / 129, 48 / 120.
81. Buvat, ii. 43.
82. 46 / 33, 47 / 84. Except where otherwise stated this account of Lord Strafford's career is based on *The Wentworth Papers*, ed. J. J. Cartwright (London 1883).
83. Except where otherwise stated this account of Lord Orrery's life is based on Lawrence B. Smith 'Charles Boyle, 4th Earl of Orrery 1674–1731', University of Edinburgh PhD thesis 1994.

84. Bennett, pp. 38–43.
85. RASP 46 / 93 Orrery to James 1 May 1720. For the English Lords and Gentlemen of the Bedchamber not being allowed to enter George I's Bedchamber and his Turkish servants robing and disrobing him, see AECP Ang. 348 f. 130.
86. RASP 46 / 33.
87. Ibid.
88. RASP 46 / 61.
89. RASP 46 / 111.
90. RASP 46 / 122.
91. Jones, *Main Stream*, p. 149.
92. Carswell, p. 98
93. RASP 47 / 4.
94. RASP 47 / 4 and 47 / 143.
95. Murphy, pp. 246–50.
96. Marais, i. 271.
97. RASP 47 / 84.
98. RASP 47 / 102, 47 / 110, 48 / 19.
99. RASP 48 / 26.
100. RASP 48 / 55.
101. RASP 46 / 150.
102. Smith, p. 161.
103. RASP 47 / 132.
104. RASP 54 / 34. PRO SP78 / 91 f. 121 (quoted Smith, pp. 319–20). RASP 47 / 132. For Lord Lexington being an 'old friend' of James see RASP 54 / 145. James Francis Edward Oglethorpe, brother of the Oglethorpe sisters, lived in the same house in London as Colonel Cecil (Cruickshanks, *Oglethorpes*).
105. RASP 47 / 106.
106. RASP 48 / 32.
107. RASP 46 / 150 and Smith, p. 317.
108. RASP 48/21.
109. RASP 48/17, 48/21.
110. RASP 48/57, 49/12.
111. RASP 49/28.
112. RASP 48/70, 48/109.
113. RASP 49/69.
114. RASP 48/71.
115. RASP 48/107.
116. RASP 49/78.
117. Murphy, chapters 18 and 19.
118. Buvat, ii. 43–4.
119. Murphy, pp. 286–98.

2 A Jacobite Opportunity

1. P. G. M. Dickson, *The Financial Revolution in England* (Oxford 1967). Carswell, op. cit.
2. Daniel Defoe, *The Anatomy of Exchange Alley: or a System of Stock-Jobbing* (London 1719) pp. 37–8, 39–40, 62–3. Pope, *Corresp.* ii 54.

3. George Berkeley, Bishop of Cloyne, *Works*, ed. A. A. Luce and J. E. Jessop (London 1948–57) vi. pp. 69, 80–1.
4. RASP 52/137.
5. Philip Woodfine, *Britannia's Glories: The Walpole Ministry and the 1739 War with Spain* (Woodbridge, Suffolk, for the Royal Historical Society, 1998), pp. 166–8.
6. Except where otherwise stated, this account is based on John Carswell, *The South Sea Bubble* (rev. edn, Stroud 1993).
7. Howard Erskine-Hill, *The Social Milieu of Alexander Pope* (London 1975), pp. 166–97.
8. *HC*. Sedgwick i. 434–5.
9. *HMC 14th. Rep. IX*, pp. 499, 511.
10. Cobbett, vii. 712.
11. BL Add. Ms. 47076 ff. 111, 132. For Gibbon see RASP 249/113 and *HC*. Sedgwick ii. 62.
12. BL Add. Ms. 47076 f. 129. For Chester, see Carswell, p. 247.
13. For the debate see Cobbett, vii. 646–7.
14. AECP Ang. 336 f. 16. For a discussion of George I's South Sea 'investments' and proof that they were not 'genuine' (i.e. paid for) see Carswell, App. B.
15. Woodfine, op. cit.
16. Coxe, *Walpole*, iii. 190–1.
17. *HMC 14th Rep. App. IX*, 504.
18. *HMC Moray* 198.
19. RASP 49/45. The Declaration is printed in *HMC Various* v. 242–3.
20. RASP 51/76.
21. RASP 49/78 Atterbury to General Dillon, 22 October 1720.
22. Cobbett, vii. 692, 697.
23. HC (Sedgwick), ii. 436.
24. Carteret was in contact with the family of his relation Sir Charles Carteret MP, Black Rod at the Court of James II in St Germain and asked for commissions in the French army for Sir Charles's sons. He was in touch too with his first cousin, Sir Thomas Higgons, a Jacobite exile in the service of James III. Nevertheless, Destouches regarded Carteret as more hostile to France as Britain's natural enemy than Stanhope had been. AECP Ang. 335 ff. 43, 91, 217 and 339 f. 139.
25. *HMC Portland* vii. 295.
26. *Recueil des Instructions ... Angleterre* iii. pp. 106–7. Balteau, *Dictionnaire de Biographie francaise*.
27. Cobbett, vii. 746.
28. AECP Ang. 335 ff. 99–100.
29. ex. inf. Carswell.
30. AECP Ang. 336 f. 192.
31. *CJ* XIX 425–32.
32. Cobbett, vii. 746.
33. RASP 52/137.
34. AECP Ang. 337 f. 122. Harrowby Mss. (Lincoln's Inn) Doc. R 21. This was not a piece of political propaganda on the part of Walpole to keep the Tories out of office, but private conversations with Ryder locked in a shorthand not decoded until the 1960s.

35. John, Lord Hervey, *Some Materials towards Memoirs of the Reign of George II*, ed. Romney Sedgwick (3 vols, London 1931), p. 849. Coxe, op. cit. i. 300. *HC*. (Sedgwick) i. 32 Note XXXIX 108–9 ii. 434

36. Clyve Jones, 'Jacobites under the Bed', *British Library Journal* (1999), pp. 35–53. Susanna Smith 'The Westminster Dormitory, in *Lord Burlington: The Man and his politics. Questions of Loyalty*, ed. Edward Corp (Lampeter 1998), pp. 51–70.

37. *HMC Portland* vii. 293.

38. RASP 52/70.

39. BL Add. Ms. 61496 ff. 54–5.

40. AECP Ang. 336 ff. 48–50, 62–3.

41. AECP Ang. 336 ff. 96–8. *HMC 14th Rep. App 9*, pp. 506–9.

42. RASP 52/70, 53/78, 53/87.

43. RASP 52/70 and 55/111.

44. RASP 52/105.

45. RASP 52/100.

46. *HC* (Sedgwick) ii. 490. Rebecca Wills, *The Jacobites and Russia 1715–1750* (East Linton 2002), pp. 43–50, 73 and n. 75.

47. RASP 52/105.

48. *CJ XIX* 482.

49. RASP 53/13 and 15.

50. *Lockhart Papers* (2 vols, London 1817) ii. 68–71.

51. AECP Ang. 336 f. 46.

52. RASP 53/13 and 15.

53. RASP 53/42.

54. RASP 53/43, 53/150.

55. RASP 53/43 and 49.

56. See *Albion* XXIII (1992) 681–96 and XXVI (1994) 27–40 and *HJ* XXXVI (1993) 309–29.

57. Harrowby Mss. Doc. 21 op. cit.

58. *The Journal of Mary Freman Caesar*, ed. Dorothy B.T. Potter (Lampeter 2002), p. 30.

59. AECP Ang. 338 ff. 232–3. Destouches was presumably using the word Caballe in the French sense: a claque organised to bring down a play or an opera (*La Grande Encyclopedie*) rather than the Cabal of ministers in Charles II's reign.

60. SP Dom. 35/23/179, quoted in Bennett, *Tory Crisis*, p.226.

61. J. Clavering to Lady Cowper 7 June 1716, quoted in Lewis Melville, *Philip, Duke of Wharton* (London 1913), p. 28.

62. *HMC Stuart* ii. 470–2, iii. 37–8.

63. *HMC Portland* vii. 279.

64. RASP 57/5. *Letters of George Lockhart of Carnwarth*, ed. Daniel Szechi (Edinburgh 1989) p. 212. For Bland see *HC* (Sedgwick) i. 468.

65. *HJ* XXXVI (1993) 309–29. Atterbury's canvassing list is in SP Dom. 35/40/423–4.

66. For the Lords' Protests see Cobbett, vii. 599–978; for their speeches cited ibid. 552–3, 938, 942–4, 976, 978–9. BL Add. 47076 ff. 246, 340. For the dutiful efforts of the clergy to get Convocation to sit see Paul Langford, 'Convocation and the Tory Clergy, 1717–61, in *The Jacobite Challenge*, ed. Eveline Cruickshanks and Jeremy Black, pp. 107–22.

67. Rep., App. B 8,9. SP Dom. 35/43/15 Pt. 2.
68. Mq. of Townshend Mss, Raynham Hall, 2nd Mq. of Townshend, Secretary of State Papers 1721-6.
69. Rep. C57, C61.
70. Rep. C56 and C61.
71. Howell's *State Trials*, xvi. 457-9. BL Add. 17677 KKK 5 ff. 531-2. Lord Cowper consulted the Jacobite Mary Caesar on the draft of his Declaration (*Journal*, pp. 26-7). When he was a prisoner in the Tower, Lord Orrery sent out a letter, plainly designed to be intercepted, dismissing the Burford Club as a 'downright fable', Add. 61830 ff. 48-50 15 Jan 1723, quoted by L. Smith, p. 37-50.
72. AECP Ang. 336 ff. 48-50, 63-4.
73. AECP Ang. 336 ff. 96-8.
74. AECP Ang. 336 ff. 71-108.
75. *LJ* XXI 582-3. *CJ* XIX 640. AECP Ang. 336 ff. 71-101.
76. RASP 52/100, 54/56, 54/67, 59/154.
77. RASP 55/116. AECP Ang. 338 ff. 42-3.
78. RASP 56/62, 56/136.
79. RASP 55/57.
80. RASP 55/67.
81. AECP Ang. 338 ff. 65-8.
82. RASP 57/113. Mrs Caesar's *Journal*, p. 24.
83. RASP 56/52, 57/107.
84. RASP 57/112.
85. RASP 56/78.
86. RASP 57/18.
87. RASP 58/38.
88. AECP Ang. 340 ff. 34-7.
89. RASP 55/67.
90. RASP 56/41.
91. Noel Woolf, *The Medallic Record of the Jacobite Movement* (London 1988), p. 83. We are most grateful to Neil Guthrie for allowing us to draw on his unpublished article, 'Unica Salus (1721): A Jacobite Medal and its Context' (2003).
92. RASP 55/152.
93. *A Letter from an English Traveller at Rome to his Father.* Daniel Szechi, 'The image of the court: idealism, politics and the evolution of the Stuart Court, 1689-1730' in *The Stuart Court in Rome*, ed. Edward Corp (Aldershot 2003), pp. 49-64.
94. AECP Ang. 336 ff. 132-6.
95. RASP 54/144.
96. AECP Ang. 336 ff. 248-53. It made such an impact that the Commons spent a whole session debating it before condemning it as an 'infamous libel' (Cobbett, viii. 908).
97. RASP 57/68. This suggests that Knight may have brought his Green Book to Rome as evidence.
98. AECP Ang. 340 ff. 70-3.
99. *Floridante* was performed in London throughout the Atterbury Plot period. See Emmett L. Avery *et al.*, (eds), *The London Stage, 1660-1800, Part 2:*

1700–1729 (Carbondale, Illinois; 1960), pp. 651–701. See too Stanley Sadie (ed.), *The New Grove Dictionary of Music* (1980), VIII. 91, 115. These two authorities disagree on the dates of certain performances of *Floridante*, but it would appear that the contemporary political relevance of the opera struck English and French observers alike in later December 1721, arising, perhaps, from report or direct experience of performances on 16–18 December of that year. While the political implications of English drama (often highly subtle) are now generally accepted in literary criticism, this kind of commentary is not yet widely accepted by musicologists. For a significant exception, however, see Ruth Smith, *Handel's Oratorios and Eighteenth-Century Thought* (Cambridge, 1995), pp. 211–15, and 404, where *Floridante* is mentioned, and other commentators acknowledged.

100. Howard Erskine-Hill, 'Alexander Pope: The Political Poet in his time', *Eighteenth-Century Studies*, XV, 2 (Winter 1981–2), 143–6.
101. RASP 63/108.
102. AECP Ang. 340 ff. 153–4, 221–3, 250–2. 341 ff. 14–6, 21–2. *HC* (Sedgwick) i. 285–6, 280–1, 339–40, 357. AECP Ang. 341 ff. 14–6, 21–2.

3   A Call to Arms

1. RASP 49/74.
2. RASP 51/38. F. McLynn, *Charles Edward Stuart* (Oxford 1988), pp. 7–9.
3. *HC* (Sedgwick) ii. 53. *Post Boy* 7–10 July 1722.
4. RASP 58/116.
5. RASP 51/44, 52, 53, 55, and 80.
6. RASP 53/1.
7. RASP 51/80.
8. RASP 51/86.
9. RASP 50/94.
10. RASP 51/52.
11. RASP 52/61.
12. *Jacobite Challenge*, pp. 92–3. Cobbett, vii. 61.
13. GEC *Complete Peerage*; DNB. *Hearne Collections* (11 vols, Oxford Historical Society, 1884–1918) v. 110–11.
14. RASP 63/108. Many documents for this period were bound out of place in the Stuart papers at Windsor, so that the references do not seem to follow.
15. Ruvigny, *Jacobite Peerage*, p. 233 (Ruvigny published the lists of appointments and warrants in the Stuart papers). For Lansdowne's career, see *New DNB* (forthcoming) and Elizabeth Handasyde, *Granville the Polite: The Life of George Granville, Lord Lansdowne 1666–1735* (Oxford 1933).
16. See *New DNB* (forthcoming) and *HC* (Cruickshanks, Handley, Hayton) iv. 79–83.
17. RASP 52/142.
18. Ruvigny; N. Genet Rouffiac in Cruickshanks and Corp, *The Stuart Court in exile and the Jacobites*, p. 16. Ó'Ciardha, op. cit. 134, 206–7, 259; AECP Ang. 339 ff. 143–4.
19. *Earl of Mar's legacies* (Scottish History Society, ser. 5 lxxvi 1896) 186–7. We are grateful for Daniel Szechi for this reference.
20. E. Gregg 'The Jacobite Career of John, Earl of Mar' in *Ideology and Conspiracy*, ed. Cruickshanks, pp.179–200, which provides a very useful

account of Mar's dealings with Lord Stair, but assumes wrongly that Mar was betraying the Jacobite cause during the whole of his exile. For Mar's efforts to promote the cause in Russia and the activities of the powerful Erskine clan there' see Rebecca Wills, *The Jacobites and Russia* (East Linton 2002), pp. 43–50. *HMC Mar and Kellie*, intro. *Lockhart Letters*, ed. Szechi, 76–7, 103–4. *Lockhart Papers* i. 114. Pittock, *Jacobitism*, p. 36.

21. Cruickshanks, 'The second Duke of Ormonde and the Atterbury Plot' in *The Dukes of Ormonde*, ed. Toby Barnard and Jane Fenlon (Woodbridge 2000), pp. 243–54. AECP Ang. 336 ff. 233–7. St Simon, *Mémoires*, ed. Boislisle xxxix 262, 313–14 (the quotation has been translated into English). *HMC Portland* v. 157. RASP 48/177, 51/157.
22. Rep. B 33 and C 41. RASP 48/81. *Jacobite Challenge*, pp. 93–4. Layer and Plunkett left England in the company of two other persons, landed in France, and made for Antwerp. Robert Knight and his son left London in secret on a private yacht on 22 January 1721, landed in France and proceeded to Antwerp. While working on Layer, I had found a piece of evidence (which I cannot now trace), suggesting they travelled together. In view of Knight's Jacobite contacts (see below) and the need of both parties to avoid interception by customs officers or government agents, this is not unlikely.
23. RASP 53/83.
24. Rep. C 69.
25. Rep. B 36.
26. *Jacobite Challenge*, p. 95.
27. RASP 61/35 Layer to James 24 July [1722].
28. Rep. B 35.
29. Cruickshanks. 'The Political Career of the Third Earl of Burlington' in *Lord Burlington: Architecture, Art and Life* eds Toby Barnard and Jane Clark (London 1995), pp. 201–17; Jane Clark, 'Lord Burlington is Here', ibid., pp. 251–310. Roger Turner, 'Proper Missionaries: Clergymen in the Household of Lord Burlington', in *Lord Burlington, the Man and his Politics*, ed. Edward Corp (Lampeter 1998), pp. 92–104 and ibid. Jane Clark, 'His Zeal is too furious': Lord Burlington's agents, pp. 182–92.
30. RASP 51/80.
31. RASP 51/2.
32. RASP 50/00, 51/38.
33. RASP 51/38.
34. AECP Ang. 339 ff. 99–100, 111–2, 116–7. RASP 50/112.
35. RASP 49/80, 50/112, 53/46, 55/137. AECP Ang. 339 f. 18.
36. RASP 56/57.
37. RASP 56/92, 95, 96, 121, 57/60, 68. Something similar happened in the Charitable Corporation affair in 1732 (see Cobbet, viii. 1164–6) when Thompson, the cashier to the Charitable Corporation, offered his books as evidence to James III in Rome. Belloni, James's banker in Rome, sent a letter to Sir Robert Sutton offering them to the Commons committee of inquiry. Belloni's letter was ordered to be burnt by the common hangman, but a major propaganda coup was scored by the Jacobites.
38. RASP 48/21, 49/99, 50/02, 91, 94.
39. RASP 51/52, 70.

40. RASP 46/3, 52/61.
41. RASP 52/72. AECP Ang. 338 ff. 254–5.
42. RASP 58/66, quoted in Eamonn O'Ciardha, *Ireland and the Jacobite Cause, 1685–1766* (Dublin 2002), p. 121 and n. 158.
43. RASP 49/99, 52/141, 53/171.
44. RASP 52/141.
45. RASP 53/48.
46. *HC* (Sedgwick) ii. 72–3.
47. RASP 52/171.
48. RASP 53/138.
49. RASP 54/7.
50. RASP 65/60.
51. RASP 63/108.
52. RASP 43/141, 53/83.
53. Ruvigny, p. 247. RASP 53/165, 54/2, 7 and 141, 58/48.
54. AECP Ang. 339 ff. 138–40.
55. RASP 52/105. AECP Ang. 338 ff. 254–5, 340 ff. 15–22.
56. RASP 54/45.
57. AECP Ang. 336 ff. 119–22, 132–6, 233–7, 268–70. RASP 52/71, 53/76 and 87.
58. AECP Ang. 336 ff. 132–6. RASP 53/31, 57/125.
59. RASP 52/105.
60. RASP 55/80, James to Ormonde 2 Nov. 1721.
61. *Jacobite Challenge*, p. 96. Rep. AA 7–14 and B38. After Walpole's discovery of a plot, the *Phineas* had to return to England.
62. RASP 65/143.
63. RASP 56/149.
64. RASP 57/1.
65. Ruvigny, p. 238.
66. RASP 57/2.
67. RASP 54/99.
68. RASP 57/6.
69. RASP 57/7.
70. Ruvigny, pp. 247–8.
71. RASP 52/2, 55/132, 57/110, 112.
72. RASP 57/6. The Duke of Montagu, a Whig, sent assurances of support to James through Goring at the same time.
73. RASP 57/4.
74. RASP 57/163. The letter, dated 12 Feb. 1722, signed with the initials R.W. was presumably written under Atterbury's direction. It is published in the Lords Committee report App. 6.
75. RASP 57/26, 34.
76. RASP 57/55.
77. RASP 58/116.
78. RASP 58/91.
79. RASP 58/113 and 135.
80. RASP 58/111.
81. RASP 56/124.
82. RASP 59/15, 65/33.

83. RASP 59/7 and 14. Philip Caryll's further examination on 23 March 1723 in Boyer, XXV 429.
84. RASP 59/5, 65/33, 65/35.
85. RASP 59/14. Kelly was acquainted with Mar since 1716 at least, when they were in Avignon in the train of James III (Bibliothèque Municipale d'Avignon Ms. 2827 f. 611).
86. RASP 58/140. This letter was to Ormonde not to James as Dr Bennett states (p. 240). Bennett combines this letter with the intercepted letter of 12 Feb, 1722, which was written in different circumstances, and was sent by the common post.
87. RASP 59/15.
88. RASP 59/143.

4   Walpole and the 'Horrid Conspiracy'

1. Transcript of a list of election results annotated by Sunderland at Blenheim. This document does not seem to have reached the British Library when they acquired the Blenheim archives.
2. AECP Ang. 340 ff. 26–7.
3. AECP Ang. 341 ff. 51–2.
4. BL Stowe ms. 150 f. 73. AECP Ang. 341 ff. 23–6, 103–4.
5. RASP 59/115 Strafford to James 18 May 1722. RASP 66/160 James to Lansdowne 11 April 1723.
6. AECP Ang. 340 ff. 60–75.
7. RASP 60/16.
8. RASP 60/88.
9. RASP 59/126.
10. RASP 53/105.
11. To Carteret, 1 June 1722, BL Add. 9129 ff. 49–50.
12. BL Add. 61443 f. 152. Quoted in *EHR*, CX III (1998) p. 66.
13. *Memoirs of Sir Robert Walpole*, i. 65, 220.
14. AECP Ang. 342 ff. 17–22.
15. RASP 60/23.
16. *Mrs. Caesar's Journal*, p. 62.
17. RASP 59/125.
18. *Epistolary Correspondence*, i. 120.
19. RASP 56/27.
20. RASP 88/27. Smith, p. 365. AECP Ang. 342 f. 241.
21. Herts RO, Panshanger papers.
22. RASP 59/126.
23. RASP 59/126.
24. RASP 59/125, 59/126.
25. Bennett, chapter 13. J.H. Plumb, *Sir Robert Walpole* (2 vols 1956–60) i 337.
26. RASP 59/125 and 126.
27. RASP 60/7.
28. RASP 60/26.
29. Greg, p. 191.
30. BL Add. 22522 (Carteret papers) ff. 229, 241. BL 22517 Carteret to Sir Luke Schaub 1 June 1722. Bennett, pp. 244–9.
31. Rep. D 24.

32. BL Add. 22517 f. 116. PRO SP 78/179 ff. 328–9, quoted Greg, pp. 190–1.
33. RASP 59/118.
34. AECP Ang. 341 ff. 64–5, 86–9.
35. AECP Ang. 341 ff. 40–2, 150–3 ff. 342 ff. 111–12.
36. AECP Ang. 341 ff. 90–2. RASP 59/118.
37. Boyer, *Political State* XXIII 228.
38. AECP Ang. 342 ff. 111–14. Add. 17677 KKK 5 f. 228.
39. Rep. E1. *Memoirs of Rev. G.K*[elly], pp. 3–4.
40. REp. E2 and E4.
41. AECP Ang. 341 ff. 101–2, 150–3. Rivington, *John Barber* (York 1989), p. 102.
42. AECP Ang. 342 ff. 15–6.

5 The Military and Naval Resources of the Jacobites

1. RASP 59/118 to James 18 May 1722, 59/71 James to Orrery 29 April 1722.
2. RASP 60/55 James to Orrery 19 June 1722.
3. RASP 60/73 to Orrery 13 June 1722.
4. RASP 60/11 James to Atterbury 8 June, 60/13 James to Dillon 8 June 1722.
5. RASP 60/54 James to Charles Caesar 19 June, 59/125 James Hamilton to F. Kennedy 19 May 1722.
6. RASP 59/116 James to Dillon 27 May 1722.
7. RASP 60/130.
8. RASP 61/16 James Hamilton to James 21 May 1722.
9. RASP 60/88 James to Lord Lansdowne 25 June 1722, 60/54.
10. RASP 60/63 Lord Falkland to James 21 June, 60/150 James to Lord Strafford 12 July 1722.
11. RASP 59/143 James Hamilton to James 21 June, 63/108 same to same 20 October, 60/52 same to same 19 June, 63/103 James to Dr Charlton 20 October 1722.
12. RASP 62/103.
13. Rep. A6 and Cholmondeley Houghton ms. 69/1.
14. RASP 60/144 James Hamilton to F. Kennedy 10 July 1722. Similar expressions were used in 1660 about the aldermen who supported the Restoration.
15. See *HC* (Cruickshanks, Handley, Hayton) v. 290. *HC* (Sedgwick) ii. 336–7, i. 549, 593, ii. 141–2. 222–3.
16. Rep. BY 18.
17. This list may be based on data given to Layer in Rome (see *Parliamentary History* XXI (2002) 253. Godfrey,was a Tory, and John Barnard, an independent Whig
18. RASP 60/160 James Hamilton to James 13 July 1722.
19. RASP 60/91 and Rep. C71
20. RASP 61/71 James to Dillon 2 August 1722.
21. RAS, p 61/71. Rep. BY 31. See *Jacobite Challenge*, pp. 96–7.
22. Rivington, p. 101.
23. RASP 49/4 Orrery to James 17 September 1722.
24. RASP 60/55 James to Orrery 19 June 1722.
25. Rep. BY 36. For Tory control of the common council and Whig efforts to fight the influence of 'disaffected persons' in the City, see 'Minutes of a Whig Club, *London Politics 1713–1717*, ed. H. Horwitz (London Record Society 1981), pp. 55, 61, 64.

26. RASP 60/115 James to Lansdowne 4 July 1722.
27. RASP 60/128 5 July 1722.
28. RASP 49/4 to James 17 September 1722 Smith, p. 365.
29. RASP 47/135 and 49/3 Orrery to James 17 September 1722.
30. RASP 60/130.
31. Rep. BY 7.
32. AECP Ang. 341 ff; 92–3, 176. *Jacobite Challenge*, pp. 96–7.
33. RASP 61/35 Christopher Layer to James 24 July [1722]. Smith, p. 370.
34. RASP 61/35.
35. *HMC Stuart* ii. 69–70.
36. *The Trial of Christopher Layer* (1723) p. 57.
37. Rep A 4. BL Stowe 250 ff. 75–6.
38. AECP Ang. 342 ff. 175–8.
39. Rep. BY 5.
40. *Jacobite Challenge*, p. 97.
41. Rep. BY 26.
42. Rep. BY 27.
43. Rep. BY 21 and 23.
44. Rep. BY 28.
45. Rep. BY 29.
46. Rep. BY 32.
47. *Jacobite Challenge*, p. 97
48. *The Trial of Christopher Layer* (1723), pp. 77–9 and Rep. We are grateful to Professor Jeremy Black for his opinion, as a military historian, as to the feasibility of Layer's scheme: 'his scheme was reasonable given his resources, but all is risk'.
49. Rep. BB2.
50. *Jacobite Challenge*, pp. 97–9.
51. Cobbett, viii. 66–95.
52. Cruickshanks and Erskine-Hill, 'The Waltham Black Act and Jacobitism, *Journal of British Studies*, XXIV (1985), 358–65. For the legal argument about the Act, see Sir Leon Radinowicz, *A History of English Criminal Law* (1948), i. 77 and Thompson, *Whigs and Hunters* (1975), pp. 22–3.
53. Rep. A 9. *Memoirs of the Life, Travels and Transactions of the Rev. G[eorge] K[elly]* (London 1736), p. 19. There was a substantial Jacobite colony in Boulogne, as the local cemetery attests
54. Rep. A 9 and A 10. BL Add. 27980 ff. 1–3.
55. Rep. A 30.
56. For Morgan see *Dukes of Ormonde*, p. 247.
57. RASP 63/171.
58. AECP Ang. 343 ff. 8–10. Rep. A 26.
59. Rep. A 35.
60. Rep. A 38.
61. Ó'Ciardha, pp. 220, 295.
62. Rep. A 31. BL 27980 ff. 3–4.
63. Rep. A 27.
64. Rep. A 21, 28 and 30.
65. Rep. A 34.
66. Rep. A 20 and 42.

67. RASP 60/88 copy of a letter from King of Sweden to General Dillon 25 June 1722.
68. RASP 61/120 Camocke to James, Madrid 20 July 1722. For Camocke see *Dukes of Ormonde*, pp. 247, 251.
69. Rep. A 43 and 45. For Charles XII as a Jacobite hero, see Niall MacKenzie, 'Charles XII of Sweden and the Jacobites', *Royal Stuart Paper* LXII (2002).
70. Rep. A 45. BL Stowe Ms. 250 f. 51. James III had sent 'blank powers' in advance to the King of Sweden and the tsar to act on his behalf (RASP 59/77). For the Swedish handing over of the *Revolution* to Jacobite naval officers see RASP 59/144.
71. Rep. A 33. For James in Bologna, see Maurizio Ascari, 'James III in Bologna', *Royal Stuart Paper* LIX (2000).
72. Rep. A 36 and 37.
73. H. of L. Rep. 24 April 1723.

6 The Arrests

1. RASP 61/75.
2. AECP Ang. 342 ff. 283–8.
3. AECP Ang. 343 ff. 10–13.
4. RASP 61/159 James to Dillon 1 Sept. 1722.
5. Add. 27980 ff. 2–3.
6. Boyer, XXIV 96.
7. AECP Ang. 342 ff. 175–6, 180–1.
8. *Flying Post*, 20 April 1723.
9. Rep. E 70.
10. RASP 61/75. *Williamson Diary*, p. 173.
11. Rep. E 65, E 66. *HMC Townshend*, p. 93. Fritz, p.5.
12. Boyer, XXIV 187.
13. Boyer, XXIV 185–6.
14. CUL Ch. H. 69/7 and E 67.
15. Rep. E 69.
16. H. of L. Rep. 1 March 1723. Williamson, p. 43
17. H. of L. Rep. L, L18, Rep. E 70.
18. Rep. E 7. *HC* (Sedgwick) i. 340. Cobbett, vii. 086. Fritz, p. 89.
19. RASP 53/88 and 64/58.
20. *HC* (Sedgwick) ii. 423, 39.
21. O'Ciardha, pp. 176–8, 677. Bingley is also called Edward in the papers relating to the plot.
22. *Jacobite Challenge*, pp. 100–1.
23. Fritz, pp. 90–1.
24. Rep. E 68, G 2, G 9
25. SP 35/63 ff. 313–4. Herts RO, Panshanger Ms. D/EPF/86. A Mrs Elizabeth Brown claimed a reward of £40 plus a pension for denouncing Sample (Fritz, p. 87).
26. Cobbett, vii. 985–6. RASP61/126, 64/58.
27. RASP 62/98.
28. Rep. D 45.
29. AECP Ang. 342 ff. 254–5.
30. RASP 40/4.

31. AECP Ang. 343 ff. 10–13. For Atterbury as Cicero see DNB sub. George Kelly and *Memoirs of Rev. G. K.*
32. AECP Ang. 342 ff. 243–4.
33. RASP 49/4.
34. Fritz, p. 93. We are obliged to Roger Turner for legal advice on the working of the Habeas Corpus Act.
35. AECP Ang. 342 ff, 27–57.
36. Cobbett, vii. 967–8. RASP 62/38.
37. AECP Ang. 343 ff. 14–15.
38. Cobbett, vii. 986. RASP 62/15.
39. SP Dom 35/41 f. 29.
40. AECP Ang. 343 ff. 19–22. Dalton's *Army Lists*, vi. 261–2. O'Ciardha, pp. 266–7.
41. AECP Ang. 342 ff. 254–5.
42. AECP Ang. 342 ff. 10–13. Boyer, XXIV 312.
43. *Jacobite Challenge*, p. 101.
44. AECP Ang. 342 ff. 311–12.
45. AECP Ang. 343 ff. 10–13, 30–2.
46. Boyer, XXIV 312, 314.
47. SP Dom 35.41 f. 29. AECP Ang. 343 ff. 33–4.
48. RASP 343 ff. 16–18.
49. *Jacobite Challenge*, p. 101.
50. AECP Ang. 343 ff. 19–22.
51. Boyer, XXIV 314.
52. AECP Ang. 343 ff. 19–22.
53. *Jacobite Challenge*, p. 103.
54. RASP 62/102, 62/107.
55. RASP 63/33, 63/7.
56. AECP Ang. 343 ff. 30–2.
57. SP Dom. 35/34 f. 27.
58. RASP 62/102, 62/103, 62/147.
59. AECP Ang. 343 ff. 49–52, 65–9.
60. AECP Ang. 343 ff. 35–7.
61. AECP Ang. 343 ff. 49–52.
62. RASP 63/7.
63. Cobbett, viii. 48–51. AECP Ang. 343 ff. 63–9.
64. RASP 63/33.
65. AECP Ang. 343 ff. 81–6.
66. Williamson, p. 177.
67. Cobbett, viii. 44–6.
68. RASP 63/20.
69. Cobbett, viii. 47–50, 358–61.
70. AECP Ang. 343 ff. 114–16, 127–8. RASP 63/129.
71. AECP Ang. 343 ff. 199–20.
72. RASP 62/157.
73. RASP 63/103.
74. SP Dom 35/34 f. 61. For Jacobite riots and commemorations in Norwich, see Monod, pp. 177, 182–3, 210–11.

75. RASP 63/20.
76. Rep. E 80.
77. 'The Waltham Black Act and Jacobitism', op. cit.
78. Williamson, p. 174
79. *HC* (Sedgwick) ii. 53–4.
80. Rep. A 44.
81. H. of L. Rep. pp. 47–8.
82. Copy in RASP 63/138.
83. Williamson, pp. 38, 42, 43, 186.
84. SP Dom 32/14 f. 257.
85. *HC* (Sedgwick) ii. 114.

7   The Case of Christopher Layer

1. Rep. B 8, 9, 10 and 11. BL Add. 27980 ff. 23–4.
2. AECP Ang. 343 ff. 30–2.
3. AECP Ang. 343 ff. 211–21.
4. RASP 60/20.
5. RASP 63/110.
6. AECP Ang. 344 ff. 28–31.
7. AECP Ang. 343 ff. 211–21.
8. AECP Ang. 343 ff. 20–2.
9. SP Dom 35/41/17 and 35/41/29. Williamson, p. 160. AECP Ang. 344 ff. 106–8.
10. *HC* (Sedgwick) ii. 161–2, 189.
11. RASP 64/129. Lynch's examinations are printed in Rep. B 1, 2, 3 and 4.
12. RASP 62/57 James Hamilton to Francis Kennedy 5 Nov. 1722.
13. Paul Hopkins, 'William Penn and James II' in *Ideas, Aesthetics and Inquiries in the Early Modern Era*, ed. Kevin L. Cope (vol. 8, New York 2003), p. 191.
14. BL Add. 17677 KKK 5 ff. 389, 401, 405.
15. AECP Ang. 343 ff. 225–6.
16. RASP 63/33 to James 20 Nov. 1722.
17. AECP Ang. 343 ff. 238–41.
18. RASP 64/56 to James 21 Dec. 1722.
19. RASP 64/52 to Sir Henry Goring. G. V. Bennett's statement (p. 260) that before long Layer 'was blabbing all he knew' is wide of the mark.
20. RASP 66/36 to James 6 Feb. 1723.
21. Williamson, p. 42. Parsons and Child were elected sheriffs in the summer of 1722 to serve until the summer of 1723 (*Post Boy*, 5–7 July 1722).
22. Roger Turner, op. cit. p. 101. Williamson, p. 34.
23. SP Dom 35/43 f. 34. Although Layer gave a copy of his dying speech to a friend as well as to the Sheriff of Middlesex, the government managed to prevent its publication because of the 'gross reflections' it contained (BL Add. 27,980 ff. 53–4).
24. Daniel Szechi, 'The Jacobite Theatre of Death', in *Jacobite Challenge*, pp. 74–91.
25. AECP Ang. 344 ff. 100–4.
26. *Jacobite Challenge*, p. 103.
27. RASP 78/128.

8 The Trials of John Plunkett and George Kelly

1. Knatchbull, p. 15. Robert J. Frankle, 'Parliament's Right to do Wrong. The Parliamentary Attainder against Sir John Fenwick, 1696', *Parliamentary History* IV (1985), 71–85.
2. See K. Ellis, *The Post Office in the Eighteenth Century* (London 1958).
3. See Chapter 9, n. 16.
4. AECP Ang. 343 ff. 33–5.
5. SP Dom. 35/42/26.
6. AECP Ang. 344 ff. 52–5.
7. Rep. C 73.
8. The report of the Secret Committee of the House of Commons, with its voluminous Appendices was printed in 1723. It is reprinted in Cobbett, without Appendices (viii. 95–195).
9. Rep. C 42, 43, 44 50, 51 and 52.
10. Knatchbull, p. 15
11. Rep. C 57–61. For Sir Daniel Arthur, see Nathalie Genet Rouffiac, 'Jacobites in Paris and Saint-Germain-en-Laye' in *The Stuart Court in Exile and the Jacobites*, ed. Eveline Cruickshanks and Edward Corp (London 1995), pp. 31–3.
12. Rep. C 56, 57 and 61.
13. Cobbett, viii. 203–7.
14. Knatchbull, p. 18.
15. Cobbett, viii. 234–7.
16. Williamson, pp. 40, 41, 175.
17. Rep. E1 and E4.
18. Rep. E 7. 8, 9 and 10.
19. Rep. E 25, 36, 40, 50 and 55.
20. Rep. E 26–35, 38–49, 52–76.
21. Rep. E 81.
22. RASP 62/114.
23. Knatchbull, p. 15.
24. *CJ* xx 165.
25. Williamson, p. 40.
26. Knatchbull, pp. 18–19.
27. Knatchbull, pp. 19–20.
28. Cobbett, viii. 239–53.
29. Lords Report p. 16.

9 The Trial of Bishop Atterbury

The four chief primary sources for the trial of Atterbury are: 1 Atterbury's MS. of his speech in his own defence which (with some cancelled passages) was given to his son-in-law, William Morice, and first printed by John Nichols in his *Epistolary Correspondence of Francis Atterbury* (2 vols. London 1783), ii. 105–80; the second account of the trial is the diary of Dudley Ryder only decoded in the twentieth century (Harrowby MSS. at Sandon Hall); 3 Cobbett's *Parliamentary History* viii. 261–347; and 4. the proceedings in the House of Commons in *The Parliamentary Diary of Sir Edward Knatchbull* (Royal Historical Society, Camden, third series, vol. xciv, 1963). Morice and Ryder sometimes need to be balanced against one another, Morice showing what Atterbury planned to say, Ryder reporting on the debates themselves. Long quotations from Atterbury's final speech in his defence in the Lords are drawn from Morice (with page references to Nichols at the end of each). A long quotation from Ryder is marked 'D.R.' at the end.

1. Williamson, pp. 5–16, 25.
2. Samuel Wesley's poem is printed in Williamson, p. 152.
3. Quoted in Williamson, p. 142.
4. Williamson, pp. 30, 34, 142–3, 146–8, 152–4.
5. *HMC Portland* vii. 344.
6. Nicholls, *Epistolary Correspondence* ii. 105.
7. AECP Ang. 344 ff. 103–4, 156–8, 345 ff. 39–41.
8. Cobbett, viii. 143.
9. Knatchbull, p. 20.
10. Rep. D 1–32. Cobbett, viii. 144.
11. Rep. D 12. BL Add 17677 KKK 5 f. 531. Dalton, *George I's Army*, i. 107, 218.
12. Rep. D 3. Knatchbull, p. 15. A genuine intercepted letter of 12 Feb. 1722 (Lords Rep. App. 6) was written 'to be intercepted' (RASP 58/91), that is as disinformation. There is no indication that it was written by Atterbury himself.
13. Rep. D 8 and 9.
14. Rep. D 50, 48 and 47.
15. Hearne, viii. 75. BL Add. 17677 KKK 5 ff. 331–2.
16. For the Rotterdam route for Jacobite letters and James Hamilton delivering them personally to recipients in England see RASP 59/125 and 126, 62/157, 63/108, 66/173, 69/47, 70/90 and 197, 84/21.
17. RASP 63/143 Ormonde to James, 10 December 1722.
18. Rep. D 52. Williamson, pp. 37–8. Knatchbull, p. 15.
19. Knatchbull, p. 20
20. See n. 7.
21. RASP 63/7.
22. Linda Colley, *In Defiance of Oligarchy* (Cambridge 1982), p. 200.
23. Cobbett, viii. 197–8, 207–8. *CJ* XX 165, 176.
24. Cobbett, viii. 209–12.
25. AECP Ang. 344 ff. 195–201. BL Add. 17677 KKK 5 f. 573.
26. Knatchbull, p. 21.
27. Cobbett, viii. 213–16.
28. Cobbett, viii. 216, Ryder diary, Doc. 29 Pt. 2.
29. Bennett, p. 266.
30. Cobbett, viii. 260–1, Ryder diary. Doc 29 Pt 2 (Sandon Hall).
31. Ryder diary Doc. 29 Pt 2 (Sandon Hall). Cobbett, viii. 263–7. Knatchbull, p. 23 *HC* (Sedgwick) ii. 517, i. 542. Montagu Garrard Drake gave an annuity to Atterbury during his banishment, ibid.
32. Ryder diary Doc. 29 Pt 2 (Sandon Hall).
33. *The Correspondence of Alexander Pope*, ed. George Sherburn (5 vols, Oxford 1956) ii. 165.
34. Pope to Atterbury, 19 March 1722, *Correspondence* ii. 109.
35. Pope to Lord Harcourt, 6 May 1723, *Correspondence* ii. 171–2.

36. Joseph Spence, *Observations, Anecdotes, and Characters of Books and Men* ed. J. M. Osborn (2 vols, Oxford 1966) item 234; i. 102. (letters to Atterbury of 20 April, and of May [no other date] 1723
37. BL Add. 27980 ff. 39–40
38. B.L. Add. 34714 ff. 55–6 (Lord Chancellor Macclesfield's notes at the trial). Bennett p. 268 misdates it as 14 May. Ryder diary Doc 29 Pt 2 (Sandon Hall). Knatchbull p. 23. Cobbett viii. 263–7. For Corbet Kynaston, see HC (Sedgwick) ii. 194–5
39. Dudley Ryder diary. Doc 29 Pt 2 (Sandon Hall).
40. AECP Aug. 345 ff. 78–80. Dudley Ryder diary. Doc 29 Pt 2 (Sandon Hall). *Epistolary Correspondence* ii. 105–80. Cobbett viii. 268–90. B.L. Add. 27980 ff. 45–6. Spence, *Anecdotes* item 233; i 102
41. *Epistolary Correspondence* ii. 176–7
42. *Epistolary Correspondence* i. 297
43. Ryder diary Doc 29 Pt 2 (Sandon Hall). AECP Ang. 345 ff. 73–77. Someone called Henry took down reports of parliamentary debates for the French embassy (AECP Aug 344 ff. 169–70).
43. Cobbett viii. 293–353. AECP. Ang. 345 ff. 72–7. B.L. Add. 27980 ff. 45–6. *Lockhart Letters* ed Szechi p. 212. Horace Walpole, *Royal and Noble Authors,* ed. Thomas Paske (5 vols. 1806) iv. 123
44. B.L. Add. 27980 ff. 59–60. Hearne, viii. 90. B.L. Add, 17577 KKK 5 ff. 571, 582. Williamson pp. 157–8

10   The Aftermath

1. Claude Nordmann, 'Choiseul and the last Jacobite Attempt of 1759', in E. Cruickshanks, ed. *Ideology and Conspiracy* (Edinburgh 1982), pp. 201–17.
2. Edward Gregg, 'The Politics of Paranoia' in *Jacobite Challenge*, pp. 42–56.
3. RASP 80/101.
4. RASP 68/63.
5. RASP 68/124.
6. RASP 71/93.
7. The agreement is set forth in Bennett, pp. 278–9.
8. Bennett, p. 280. Edward Gregg, 'The Jacobite Career of John, Earl of Mar' op. cit. p. 192, Their broad-brush treatment seems to oversimplify the evidence.
9. RASP 74/130.
10. RASP 75/6.
11. RASP 74/130.
12. RASP 75/16.
13. James to Atterbury, 19 August 1724, Atterbury to James 2 October 1724, RASP 76/42.
14. RASP 77/97, 77/132. 78/57.
15. RASP 79/91, see also Gregg, p. 187.
16. RASP 7/97, 77/132 and 77/136.
17. James to Hay Sept. 1728 RASP 120/67.
18. These messages were, when written, sent by Morice through the general post, and copied for Walpole. See Howard Erskine-Hill, 'Alexander Pope: The Political Poet in his Time' in *Eighteenth-Century Studies*, XV, No. 2 (Winter 1981–2), 134–5.

19. *Gulliver's Travels*, ed. Paul Turner (Oxford 1986) pp. 191–2.
20. Howell's *State Trials* VI. Jonathan Swift, *Works* (London 1760) i. 182.
21. See Pope's *Correspondence* iii. 245–6.
22. 'ANTONIUS MUSA'S CHARACTER, represented by VIRGIL, in the person of IAPIS. In a Letter to Dr. JOHN FREIND'. *Epistolary Correspondence* (1788), i. 329–76.
23. Murray Pittock, *Poetry and Jacobite Politics in Eighteenth Century Britain and Ireland* (Cambridge 1994), pp. 38–43; Howard Erskine-Hill, 'Poetry at the Exiled Court' in Edward Corp ed., *A Court in Exile. The Stuarts in France, 1688–1718* (Cambridge 2003).
24. *Epistolary Correspondence* (1788) i. 329.
25. RASP 150/15.
26. Bennett, pp. 301–5.
27. RASP 151/185.
28. Pope, *Correspondence* iii. 220–9, 248. A full account of the literary origins of Pope's Epitaph will be found in Howard Erskine-Hill, 'Life into Letters, Death into Art: Pope's Epitaph on Francis Atterbury' in Claude Rawson and Jenny Mezciems eds, *The Yearbook of English Studies*, Vol. 18: *Pope, Swift and their World*, Special Number (1988) Modern Humanities Research Association, pp. 200–20.
29. *The Twickenham Editions of the Poems of Alexander Pope*, eds John Butt et al. (11 vols, London 1939–69) vi. 343–45.
30. Bennett, pp. 309–10.
31. Pope, *Correspondence* ii. 165.
32. Aix-en-Provence, Bibliothèque Méjanes Ms. 614.
33. AECP Ang. 238 ff. 10–11, 210–11.
34. Wood, p. 172. Murphy, pp. 327–8.
35. RASP 51/138 and 51/131.
36. RASP 53/145.
37. AECP Ang. 436 ff. 28, 47–54, 216–18.
38. Murphy, pp. 327–8.
39. AECP Ang. 340 ff. 85; 338 f. 156.
40. Wood, p. 188, Hyde, p. 15.
41. Buvat, ii. 452, 463–4. Peter Campbell, *Power and Politics in Old Regime France 1720–1745* (London 1996), pp. 57, 64–5.
42. *Jacobite Challenge*, p. 104. HMC Portland v. 450. Bodleian Lib. North mss. c. 10 f. 139, a. 7 ff/ 119–23, 341–2, b. 3 ff. 3–7. b. 16 ff. 9–12, b. 28 ff. 80–90.
43. Smith thesis, p. 312.
44. Harrowby mss. 21 (L. Inn). This corrects the assumption in *HC* (Sedgwick) i. 67 that Orrery's pension was from the British government through Walpole. On reflection, Walpole's expression that Orrery had a pension from 'that government', which he 'well earned' cannot mean Walpole's government nor is there any evidence that Orrery ever gave intelligence to Walpole.
45. RASP 70/46, 70/158.
46. See Jeremy Black, *British Foreign Policy in the Age of Walpole* (Edinburgh 1985), pp. 138–59. Bennett, p. 287.
47. Atterbury, *Epistolary correspondence* v. (1798) 331. Smith thesis, pp. 445–6. Bennett, p. 287.
48. Williamson, pp. 174–6.

49. Williamson, pp. 69, 166–72. *HC* (Sedgwick) ii. 543. *Memoirs of the Life of ... G. K.*, pp. 618, 682. *Hearne Colls.* vi. 55. *Memorials of John Murray of Broughton*, ed. R. F. Bell (Scottish History Society xxvii 1848) 371–2. Andrew Lang, *Pickle the Spy* (London 1897), pp. 48, 61, 90 and *The Companions of Pickle* (London 1898), pp. 19, 23, 41, 121. See Doron Zimmermann, *The Jacobite Movement in Scotland and in Exile, 1746–1759* (Basingstoke 2003), pp. 51, 58, 66.

Notes on Sources

Principal manuscript sources

Stuart Papers in the Royal Archives, Windsor Castle: vols 46–74.
Despatches and documents in the archives of the Ministère des affaires étrangères, Correspondance politique Angleterre in the Quai d'Orsay, Paris: vols 331–48.
Transcripts of the Dutch Despatches in BL Add. 17677 KKK 5.
Harrowby mss at Sandon Hall and in Lincoln's Inn (Dudley Ryder diaries).
State Papers Domestic George I, in the Public Record Office.
Cambridge University Library, Walpole papers in the Cholmondeley Houghton collection, vol. 69 Jacobite papers.
Bodleian Library, Oxford, North c Lord North and Grey's papers.
BL Stowe ms 250 (Jacobite papers).
BL Add. 34714 Lord Chancellor Macclesfield's notes at Bishop Atterbury's trial.
BL Add. 27980 (newsletters).
BL Add. 22522 Carteret papers.
BL Add. 35837 Sir Luke Schaub papers.

Principal primary sources

Francis Atterbury, *The Epistolary Correspondence of the Right Reverend Francis Atterbury*, ed. J. Nichols (4 vols, 1783–90. For works attributed to Atterbury see G. V. Bennett, *The Tory Crisis in Church and State 1688–1730: The Career of Francis Atterbury, Bishop of Rochester* (Oxford 1975), pp. 315–24.
Abel Boyer, *The Political State of Great Britain* (60 vols, London 1711–1740).
Jean Buvat, *Journal de la Régence*, ed. E. Campardon (2 vols, Paris 1965).
The Journal of Mary Freman Caesar, ed. Dorothy B. T. Potter (Lampeter 2002).
William Cobbett, *The Parliamentary History of England* (36 vols, London 1806–20).
William Coxe, *Memoirs of the Life and Administration of Sir Robert Walpole* (3 vols, London 1798).
Journal du Marquis de Dangeau, eds Soulié et Dussieux (19 vols, Paris 1854–60).
Collections of Thomas Hearne, ed. C. E. Doble (11 vols, Oxford Historical Society, 1884–1918).
HMC Stuart Papers, vols i–vii.
Memoirs of the Rev. G[eorge] K[elly], London 1736.
The Parliamentary Diary of Sir Edward Knatchbull 1722–1730, ed. A. N. Newman (Royal Historical Society, Camden Society 3rd series XCIV 1963).
The Lockhart Papers, ed. Anthony Aufrere (2 vols, London 1817).
Letters of Lockhart of Carnwarth 1698–1732, ed. Daniel Szechi (Scottish History Society, Edinburgh 1989).
J. G. Nichols ed., *The Letters of Pope to Atterbury when in the Tower of London* (Royal Historical Society, Camden Miscellany IV 1859).

The Correspondence of Alexander Pope, ed. George Sherburn (5 vols, Oxford 1956).

Alexander Pope, Selected Letters, ed. Howard Erskine-Hill (Oxford 2000).

The Whole Proceedings upon the Arraignment, Tryal, Conviction and Attainder of Christopher Layer, esq. for High Treason (London 1723) from a collection of legal papers relating to the Atterbury Plot (including the following three Reports) purchased from the Birmingham Law Library by Eveline Cruickshanks and Howard Erskine-Hill.

A Report from the Lords Committees to whom the Report and original Papers delivered by the House of Commons ... [to] the House of Lords, with Appendices 1–48 (London 1723).

A Report from the Committee Appointed by Order of the House of Commons to examine Christopher Layer and Others [with] ... several Papers and Examinations laid before the House, relating to the Conspiracy (London 1722) with Appendices. This report is reprinted in *Sessional Papers of the Eighteenth Century*, ed. Sheila Lambert, vol. 3 George I, the Atterbury Plot (Wilmington, Delaware 1975).

A Report from the Lords Committees to whom the Report and Original Papers Delivered by the House of Commons ... [to] the House of Lords to examine Christopher Layer and ... other Persons (London 1723).

Duc de Saint Simon, *Mémoires complètes*, ed. A. de Boislisle (41 vols, Paris 1923–39).

Annals and Correspondence of the First and Second Earls of Stair (2 vols, Edinburgh 1875).

The Official Diary of Lieutenant-General Williamson, Deputy Lieutenant of the Tower of London 1722–1747, ed. Charles Fox (Royal Historical Society, Camden Society 3rd series XXII 1912).

Joseph Spence, *Observations, Anecdotes and Characters of Books and Men*, ed. J. M. Osborn (2 vols, Oxford 1966).

Select secondary sources

Toby Barnard and Jane Fenlon eds, *The Dukes of Ormonde, 1610–1745* (Woodbridge 2000).

Henri Baudrillart, *Philippe V et la Cour de France* (5 vols, Paris 1890–1900).

J. V. Bennett, *The Tory Crisis in Church and State 1688–1730: The Career of Francis Atterbury, Bishop of Rochester* (Oxford 1975).

J. V. Bennett and J. D. Walsh eds, *Essays in Modern Church History* (Oxford 1966).

Jeremy Black, *British Foreign Policy in the Age of Walpole* (Edinburgh 1985).

Jeremy Black, *Walpole in Power* (Stroud 2001).

Jeremy Black ed., *Britain in the Age of Walpole* (London 1984).

John Brewer, *The Sinews of Power, War, Money and the English State 1688–1783* (London 1989).

John Carswell, *The South Sea Bubble* (London 1960, rev. edn, Stroud 1993).

Linda Colley, *In Defiance of Oligarchy: The Tory Party 1714–60* (Cambridge 1982).

Edward Corp, *The Stuart Court in Rome* (Edinburgh 2003).

Edward Corp ed., *The Stuart Court in Exile. The Stuarts in France 1699–1718* (Cambridge 2003).

Eveline Cruickshanks, *Political Untouchables: The Tories and the '45* (London 1979).

Eveline Cruickshanks, *The Stuart Courts* (Stroud 2000).

Eveline Cruickshanks, *The Glorious Revolution* (Basingstoke 2000).

Eveline Cruickshanks ed., *Ideology and Conspiracy: Aspects of Jacobitism 1689–1759* (Edinburgh 1982).

Eveline Cruickshanks and Jeremy Black eds, *The Jacobite Challenge* (Edinburgh 1988).

Eveline Cruickshanks and Edward Corp eds, *The Stuart Court in Exile and the Jacobites* (London 1995).

H. T. Dickinson, *Bolingbroke* (London 1970).

H. T. Dickinson, *Walpole and the Whig Supremacy* (London 1973).

H. T. Dickinson, *Liberty and Property: Political Ideology in Eighteenth Century Britain* (London 1977).

H. T. Dickinson ed., *A Companion to Eighteenth Century Britain* (Oxford 2002).

P. G. M. Dickson, *The Financial Revolution in England* (Oxford 1967).

William Dickson, *The Jacobite Attempt of 1719* (Scottish History Society 1895).

K. Ellis, *The Post Office in the Eighteenth Century* (London 1958).

Archibald Foord, *His Majesty's Opposition 1714–1830* (Oxford 1964).

Paul Fritz, *The English Ministers and Jacobitism between the Rebellions of 1715 and 1745* (Toronto 1975).

Leo Gooch, *The Desperate Faction? The Jacobites in North-East England 1688–1745* (Hull 1995).

Elizabeth Handasyde, *Granville the Polite: The Life of George Granville, Lord Lansdowne 1666–1735* (Oxford 1933).

M. R. Harris, *London Newspapers in the Age of Walpole* (London 1987).

Ragnhild Hatton, *George I: Elector and King* (London 1978, 2nd edn, New Haven 2001).

J. D. Henderson, *The Chevalier Ramsay* (London 1952).

Howard Erskine-Hill, *The Social Milieu of Alexander Pope* (New Haven and London 1975).

Howard Erskine-Hill, *Poetry of Opposition and Revolution: Dryden to Wordsworth* (Oxford 1995).

Howard Erskine-Hill, *The Augustan Idea in English Literature* (London 1983).

Patricia Kneas Hill, *The Oglethorpe Ladies and the Jacobite Conspiracies* (Atlanta 1977).

W. S. Holdsworth, *A History of English Law* (3rd edn, 17 vols, London 1903–1972).

Geoffrey Holmes, *The Trial of Dr. Sacheverell* (London 1973).

Geoffrey Holmes, *Politics, Religion and Society in England, 1679–1742* (London 1986).

Geoffrey Holmes, *British Politics in the Age of Anne* (London 1967, 2nd edn London 1987).

Julian Hoppit, *A land of liberty? England 1689–1727* (Oxford 2000)

H. Montgomery Hyde, *John Law: History of an Honest Adventurer* (London 1925).

Clyve Jones ed., *Britain in the First Age of Party 1680–2750: Essays Presented to Geoffrey Holmes* (London 1987).

Clyve Jones and David L. Jones eds, *Peers, Politics, and Power: The House of Lords, 1603–1911* (London 1988).

J. P. Kenyon, *Revolution Principles: The Politics of Party, 1689–1720* (Cambridge 1977).

Gary S. De Krey, *A Fractured Society: The Politics of London in the First Age of Party 1688–1715* (London 1985).

Paul Langford, *The Eighteenth Century 1688–1815* (Oxford 2002).

Bruce Lenman, *The Jacobite Risings in Britain 1689–1746* (London 1980).

Frank McLynn, *Charles Edward Stuart: a Tragedy in many Acts* (London 1988).

Lewis Melville, *The Life and Writings of Philip, Duke of Wharton* (London 1913).

D. K. Money, *The English Horace: Anthony Alsop and the Tradition of British Latin Verse* (Oxford 1998).

Paul Monod, *Jacobitism and the English People 1688–1788* (Cambridge 1989).

Antoin E. Murphy, *John Law, Economic Theorist and Policy-Maker* (Oxford 1997).

Éamonn Ó'Ciardha, *Ireland and the Jacobite Cause 1685–1766* (Dublin 2002).

Frank O'Gorman, *The Long Eighteenth Century: British Political & Social History 1688–1837* (London 1997).

Mark Blackett-Ord, *Hell-Fire Duke: The Life of the Duke of Wharton* (Windsor 1982).

Murray G. H. Pittock, *Jacobitism* (Basingstoke 1998).

Murray G. H. Pittock, *Poetry and Jacobite Politics in Eighteenth Century Britain and Ireland* (Cambridge 1994).

J. H. Plumb, *Robert Walpole* (2 vols, London 1956–60).

J. G. A, Pocock, *The Ancient Constitution and the Feudal Law* (Cambridge 1957).

Sir Leon Radzinowicz, *A History of English Criminal Law and its Administration from 1750* (1948).

C. B. Realey, *The Early Opposition to Sir Robert Walpole 1720–1727* (Philadelphia 1931).

John Roberts, *The Jacobite Wars: Scotland and the Military Campaigns of 1715 and 1745* (Edinburgh 2002).

Richard Sharp, *The Engraved Record of the Jacobite Movement* (Aldershot 1996).

L. B. Smith, *Spain and Britain 1715–1718: The Jacobite Issue* (London 1967).

Lisa Staffen, *Defining a British State: Treason and Political Identity, 1608–1820* (Basingstoke 2001).

Daniel Szechi, *Jacobitism and Tory Politics 1710–1714* (Edinburgh 1982).

Daniel Szechi, *The Jacobites: Britain and Europe 1699–1788* (Manchester 1994).

E. P. Thompson, *Whigs and Hunters: The Origins of the Black Act* (London 1975, 2nd edn Harmonsworth 1977).

Louis Wiesener, *Le Régent, l'Abbé Dubois et les Anglais* (3 vols, Paris 1891).

E. N. Williams, *The Eighteenth Century Constitution: Documents and Commentary* (Cambridge 1960).

Philip Wood, *Memoirs of John Law of Lauriston* (London 1825).

Noel Woolf, *The Medallic Record of the Jacobite Movement* (London 1988).

Doron Zimmermann, *The Jacobite Movement in Scotland and in Exile 1746–1759* (Basingstoke 2003).

Select articles and single essays

Susannah Abbott, 'Clerical Responses to the Jacobite Rebellion in 1715', *Historical Research*, LXXVI (2002), 332–46.

Maurizio Ascari, *James III in Bologna: An Illustrated Story* (Royal Stuart Paper LIX 2001).

J. C. D. Clark, 'The Politics of the Excluded: Tories, Jacobites and Whig Patriots 1715–60, *Parliamentary History*, II (1963), 209–22.

Eveline Cruickshanks, *The Oglethorpes: a Jacobite Family* (Royal Stuart Paper XLV 1987).

Eveline Cruickshanks, 'Lord Cowper, Lord Orrery, the Duke of Wharton and Jacobitism', *Albion* (1994), 27–40.

Eveline Cruickshanks, 'Charles Spencer, Third Earl of Sunderland and Jacobitism', *EHR*, CXIII (1998), 65–76.

Eveline Cruickshanks, 'Jacobites, Tories and James III', *Parliamentary History*, XXI (2002), 247–54.

Eveline Cruickshanks and Howard Erskine-Hill, 'The Waltham Black Act and Jacobitism', *Journal of British Studies* (1985), 358–65.

Paul Fritz, 'The Anti-Jacobite Intelligence System of the English Ministers 1715–1745', *HJ* (1973), 265–89.

Gernot Gürtler, *Deceptis Custodibus or Liberty Lost – Liberty Regained* (Royal Stuart Paper LXXVI).

Andrew Hanham, 'So Few Facts', *Parliamentary History*, XIX (2000), 233–58.

Howard Erskine-Hill, 'Alexander Pope: The Political Poet in his Time', *ECS*, XV (1981–2), 123–6.

Howard Erskine-Hill, 'Under which Caesar? Pope and the Journal of Mrs. Charles Caesar 1724–1741', *Review of English Studies*, XCIII (1982), 436–44.

Howard Erskine-Hill, 'Life into Letters, Death into Art: Pope's Epitaph on Francis Atterbury' in Claude Rawson and Jenny Mezciems eds, *The Yearbook of English Studies*, XIX (Modern Humanities Research Association 1988), pp. 200–20.

Clyve Jones, 'The Impeachment of the Earl of Oxford and the Whig Schism of 1717', *Bulletin of the Institute of Historical Research*, LV (1982), 66–87.

Clyve Jones, 'Jacobitism and the Historian: The Case of William, 1st Earl Cowper', *Albion*, XXIII (1992), 681–96 and '1720–1723 and All That: a reply to Eveline Cruickshanks', ibid. XXVI (1994), 41–53.

Clyve Jones, 'The new Opposition in the House of Lords 1720–23, *H J*, XXX (1994), 309–29.

Clyve Jones, 'Whigs, Jacobites and Charles Spencer, Third Earl of Sunderland', *EHR*, CIX (1994), 52–73 and 'Evidence, Interpretation and Definitions in Jacobite Historiography: A Reply to Eveline Cruickshanks', ibid. CXIII (1998), 66–77.

Clyve Jones, 'Jacobites under the Bed', *British Library Journal* (1999), 35–53.

Niall MacKenzie, *Charles XII of Sweden and the Jacobites* (Royal Stuart Paper LXII 2002).

Theses

Paul Chapman, 'Jacobite Political Argument in England 1714–1766' (University of Cambridge PhD thesis 1983).

J. C. Findon, 'The Nonjurors and the Church of England, 1689–1716' (University of Oxford DPhil thesis 1978).

Mark Goldie, 'Tory Political Thought, 1689–1714' (University of Cambridge PhD thesis 1977).

Paul Hopkins, 'Aspects of Jacobite Conspiracy in England in the Reign of William III' (Cambridge University PhD thesis 1981).

Nathalie Genet Rouffiac, 'Un épisode de la présence Britannique en France: Les Jacobites à Paris et à Saint-Germain-en-Laye 1689–1715' (École des Chartres thesis 1991).

Nathalie Genet Rouffiac, 'La première génération de l'exil Jacobite à Paris et Saint-Germain-en-Laye 1688–1715' (Doctorat, École practique des Hautes études 1995).

Lawrence Smith, 'Charles Boyle, 4th Earl of Orrery 1674–1731' (University of Edinburgh thesis 1994).

G. M. Towend, 'The Political Career of Charles Spencer, 3rd Earl of Sunderland 1685–1723' (University of Edinburgh thesis 1985).

Index

Note: those marked 'MP' are biographed in *The House of Commons 1660–1690*, ed. B. D. Henning (3 vols, London 1983), or in HC (Cruickshanks, Handley, Hayton), or in HC (Sedgwick)
[I] = an Irish title, [J] = a Jacobite title, [S] = a Scottish title

Earle, Erasmus 255
Earle, Erasmus the younger 255
Earle, Erasmus ensign 141
Eaton, Mr. 253
East India Company 36
Eccleston, Mr. Quaker 258
Eden, Sir John, 2nd Bt, MP 254
Edgcumbe, Richard MP 247
Edmonds, Brigadier 140–1
Edinburgh 32, 37
Egerton, Mr. 253
Egerton, Holland 253
Elden, Joseph 255
Elford, Jonathan MP 247
Elizabeth I, Queen 4, 180, 220
Ellis, Sir William 96, 105 107, 172,
    186
Ellison, Mr. 251
Elwin, Peter 103, 255
Emerson, Mr. 258
Emperor, the, (Charles VI) 12, 51, 91,
    101, 167
Ernel, Mr. 248
Ernell, Mr. 248
Erskine, Dr. Robert 100
Essay towards Preventing the Ruin of
    Great Britain 56
Exeter 24
Eugene, Prince, of Savoy 102

Fagan, Mary 188
Fairfax, Barnaby 106
Falkland, Lucius Henry Cary, 6th Vis.,
    Earl of Falkland [J] 134
'Farmer', code name for James III 261
Farnese, Elizabeth, Queen of Philip V
    116
Farringdon Within 139
Farwell, Mr. 247
Farwell, Capt. 247
Fazakerley, Nicholas MP 193
Fénelon, François de Salignac de la
    Mothe, Archbishop of Cambrai
    14, 85, 86, 185, 265 n.25
Fenwick, Sir John MP, 169, 184, 193,
    206
Fermanagh, Lord, Ralph Verney, 2nd
    Vis. [I] MP 249
Ferrier, Richard 256

Fifteen, the 10, 11 14, 27, 29, 38, 47,
    49, 85, 100, 103, 113, 139, 149,
    151, 156, 175, 201, 225
Finch, Sir Heneage 222
Firebrace, Cordell later 3rd Bt. MP 249
Fisher, John, Bishop of Rochester 220
Fleetwood, ?Henry MP 157
Fleetwood, John MP 249
Flemming, Richard MP 248
Floridante (Handel), 85, 272–3 n.99
Foley, Thomas, 2nd Bt., 71
Forbes, Sir Francis 138, 152
Fordyce, Major 169
Fortescue, Lady 82
Fortune, the ship 152
Fowey 96
Fowkes, Edward 253
Fownes, Mr. 247
Fownes John MP 247
Fox, Capt. 247
Foxhall, Mr. 258
Franklin, Robert, second mate 169
Franton, Mr. 248
Frederichstadt 9, 151
Freeston, Mr. 256
Freeholder, The 71, 157–8
Freeholders Journal 213
Freind, Dr. John MP 92, 120, 121,
    125, 128, 168, 170, 205, 285 n.22
Fortune, the, ship 152

Gallas, Count, Imperial Envoy, 105
Galloway, James Stewart, 5th Earl of
    [S] 161, 169
Gardiner, Capt. Andrew (Galloway)
    152, 169
Garnish, Cleer 256
Garrard, Sir Samuel, 4th Bt. MP 138
Gastrell, Francis, Bishop of Chester
    220
Gawdy, Sir Basingborough 255
Genoa 101, 151, 152, 169
George I, Georg Ludwig, Duke of
    Brunswick Lüneberg, Elector of
    Hanover, King 5–8, 11–13, 14, 16,
    23–5, 28–9, 31, 41, 44, 47, 56–8,
    61, 64–6, 71, 74, 76–7, 79, 83–7,
    89, 95, 97, 99, 100–2, 110, 116–7,
    123–4, 126–7, 129, 131–2, 139,